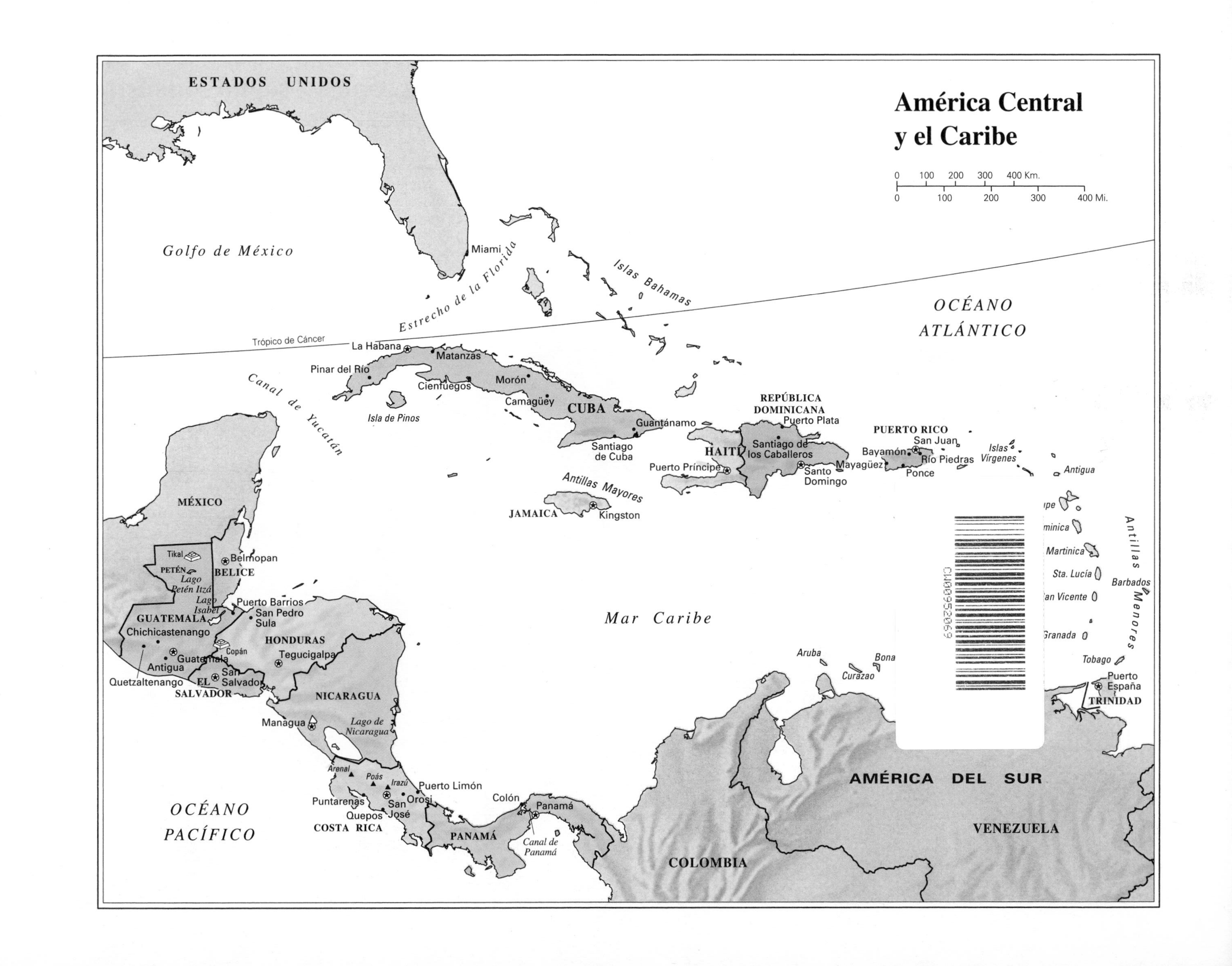
América Central
y el Caribe
0 100 200 300 400 Km.
0 100 200 300 400 Mi.
ESTADOS UNIDOS
Golfo de México
Miami
Estrecho de la Florida
Islas Bahamas
OCÉANO
ATLÁNTICO
Trópico de Cáncer
La Habana
Matanzas
Pinar del Río
Cienfuegos
Morón
Camagüey
CUBA
Isla de Pinos
Canal de Yucatán
Guantánamo
Santiago
de Cuba
REPÚBLICA
DOMINICANA
Puerto Plata
Santiago de
los Caballeros
HAITÍ
Puerto Príncipe
Santo
Domingo
PUERTO RICO
San Juan
Bayamón
Río Piedras
Mayagüez
Ponce
Islas
Vírgenes
Antigua
Antillas Mayores
JAMAICA
Kingston
Martinica
Sta. Lucía
Granada
Antillas Menores
Barbados
Tobago
Puerto
España
TRINIDAD
Aruba
Curazao
Bona
Mar Caribe
MÉXICO
Tikal
PETÉN
Lago
Petén Itzá
Belmopan
BELICE
Lago
Isabel
Puerto Barrios
San Pedro
Sula
GUATEMALA
Chichicastenango
Guatemala
Antigua
Quetzaltenango
Copán
HONDURAS
Tegucigalpa
EL
SALVADOR
San
Salvador
NICARAGUA
Managua
Lago de
Nicaragua
Arenal
Poás
Irazú
Puerto Limón
Puntarenas
San
José
Orosi
Quepos
COSTA RICA
Colón
Panamá
PANAMÁ
Canal de
Panamá
OCÉANO
PACÍFICO
COLOMBIA
AMÉRICA DEL SUR
VENEZUELA
CW00952069

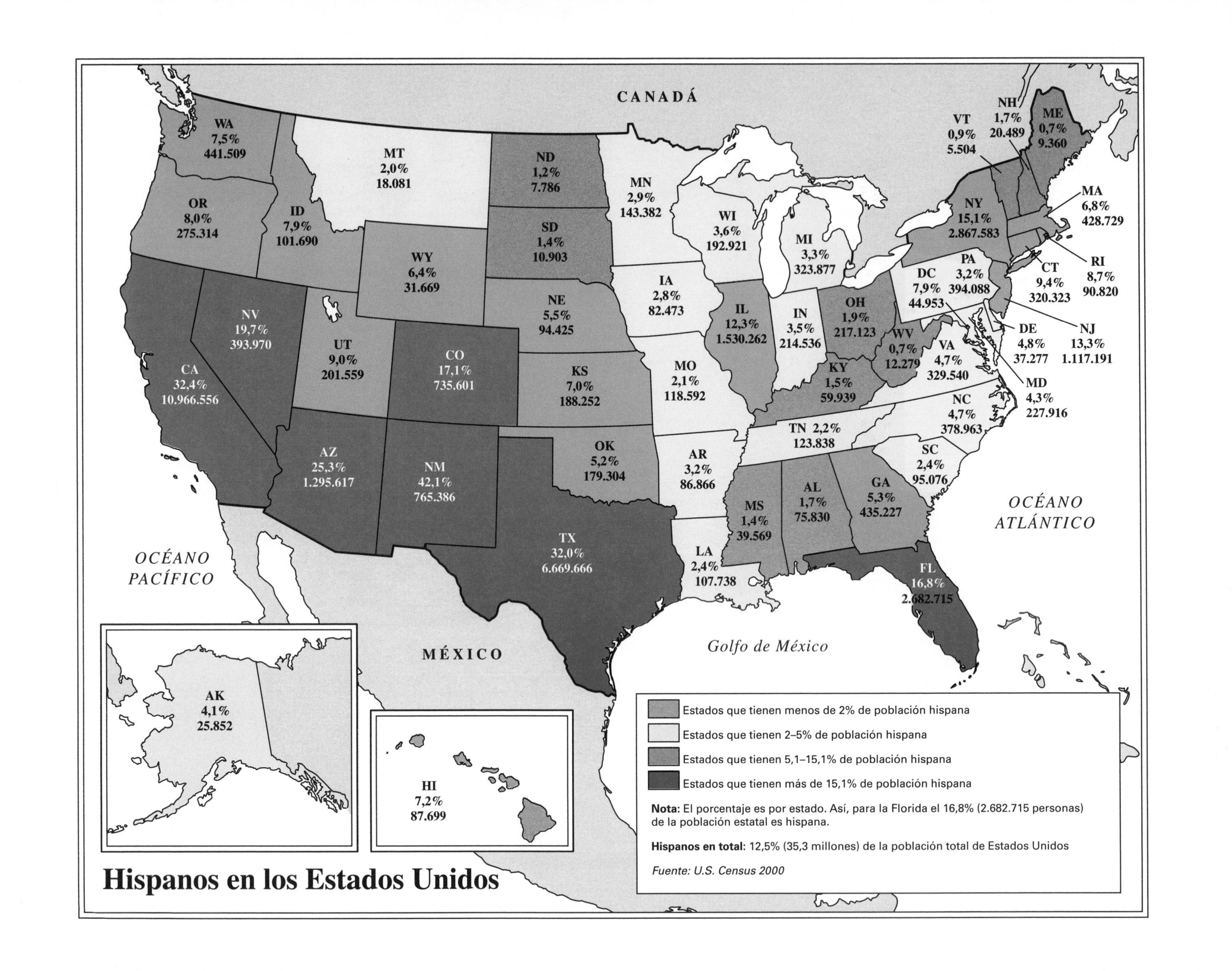
CANADÁ
MÉXICO
OCÉANO PACÍFICO
OCÉANO ATLÁNTICO
Golfo de México
WA 7,5% 441.509
OR 8,0% 275.314
CA 32,4% 10.966.556
NV 19,7% 393.970
ID 7,9% 101.690
MT 2,0% 18.081
WY 6,4% 31.669
UT 9,0% 201.559
CO 17,1% 735.601
AZ 25,3% 1.295.617
NM 42,1% 765.386
ND 1,2% 7.786
SD 1,4% 10.903
NE 5,5% 94.425
KS 7,0% 188.252
OK 5,2% 179.304
TX 32,0% 6.669.666
MN 2,9% 143.382
IA 2,8% 82.473
MO 2,1% 118.592
AR 3,2% 86.866
LA 2,4% 107.738
WI 3,6% 192.921
IL 12,3% 1.530.262
MI 3,3% 323.877
IN 3,5% 214.536
OH 1,9% 217.123
KY 1,5% 59.939
TN 2,2% 123.838
MS 1,4% 39.569
AL 1,7% 75.830
GA 5,3% 435.227
FL 16,8% 2.682.715
SC 2,4% 95.076
NC 4,7% 378.963
VA 4,7% 329.540
WV 0,7% 12.279
PA 3,2% 394.088
DC 7,9% 44.953
MD 4,3% 227.916
DE 4,8% 37.277
NJ 13,3% 1.117.191
NY 15,1% 2.867.583
CT 9,4% 320.323
RI 8,7% 90.820
MA 6,8% 428.729
VT 0,9% 5.504
NH 1,7% 20.489
ME 0,7% 9.360
AK 4,1% 25.852
HI 7,2% 87.699
Estados que tienen menos de 2% de población hispana
Estados que tienen 2–5% de población hispana
Estados que tienen 5,1–15,1% de población hispana
Estados que tienen más de 15,1% de población hispana
Nota: El porcentaje es por estado. Así, para la Florida el 16,8% (2.682.715 personas) de la población estatal es hispana.
Hispanos en total: 12,5% (35,3 millones) de la población total de Estados Unidos
Fuente: U.S. Census 2000
Hispanos en los Estados Unidos

THE BASIC SPANISH SERIES

BASIC SPANISH FOR MEDICAL PERSONNEL

ANA C. JARVIS
Chandler-Gilbert Community College

RAQUEL LEBREDO
California Baptist University

HOUGHTON MIFFLIN COMPANY
Boston New York

Publisher: *Rolando Hernández*
Sponsoring Editor: *Van Strength*
Development Editor: *Judith Bach*
Senior Project Editor: *Tracy Patruno*
Manufacturing Manager: *Karen Banks*
Executive Marketing Director: *Eileen Bernadette Moran*
Associate Marketing Manager: *Claudia Martínez*

Cover image: Street in Red, © Ruby Aranguiz. Reprinted by arrangement with Mill Pond Press, Inc., Venice, Florida 34285

Printed in the U.S.A.

Library of Congress Control Number: 2005924678

ISBN: 0-618-50577-6

123456789-HS-09 08 07 06 05

CONTENTS

Drawn from the successful *Basic Spanish Grammar,* Sixth Edition, and career manuals, ***The Basic Spanish Series*** offers a flexible, concise introduction to Spanish grammar and communication in an updated series to better address the needs of today's students, pre-professionals, and professionals needing a working knowledge of Spanish.

Basic Spanish for Medical Personnel

As a key component of *The Basic Spanish Series,* ***Basic Spanish for Medical Personnel*** is a communication manual designed to serve those in the medical professions who seek basic conversational skills in Spanish. Written for use in two-semester or three-quarter courses, it presents everyday situations that medical students, pre-professionals, and professionals may encounter at work settings such as hospitals, emergency rooms, doctors' offices, and clinics when dealing with Spanish-speaking patients and personnel in the United States.

Basic Spanish for Medical Personnel introduces essential medical vocabulary, practical reference information, and medical notes written from a cross-cultural perspective. It provides students with opportunities to apply, in a wide variety of practical contexts, the grammatical structures presented in the corresponding lessons of the ***Basic Spanish*** core text.

Organization of the text

Basic Spanish for Medical Personnel contains two preliminary lessons (*Lecciones preliminares*), twenty regular lessons, seven reading sections (*Lecturas*), and four review sections (*Repasos*). The lessons are preceded by five pages of detailed medical illustrations of the human body, including labels in Spanish and English: internal organs, the digestive system, reproductive organs, the head, and the skeleton and bones.

Each lesson contains the following sections:

- A **lesson opener** consists of the lesson objectives divided into two categories: *Structures* practiced from *Basic Spanish,* and *Communication.*
- A **Spanish dialogue** introduces and employs key vocabulary and grammatical structures in the context of the lesson theme. Divided into manageable segments, each dialogue features contexts specific to the medical professions. Audio recordings of the dialogues can be found on the In-text Audio CDs. Translations of the dialogues can be found on the Instructor's HM ClassPrep CD.
- The ***¡Escuchemos!*** activity, together with recordings on the In-text Audio CDs, encourage students to listen to the dialogue and check their comprehension with true/false questions.
- The ***Vocabulario*** section summarizes new, active words and expressions presented in the dialogue, and categorizes them according to their parts of speech. The vocabulary highlights the most important communication tools needed in a variety of professional situations. A special subsection of

cognates heads up the vocabulary list so students can readily identify these terms. The *Vocabulario adicional* subsection supplies supplementary vocabulary related to the lesson theme.

- ***Notas culturales*** give students up-to-date information that highlights Hispanic customs and traditions relevant to healthcare, as well as introduce contemporary health issues and medical concerns affecting Hispanics in the United States.
- ***Dígame...*** questions check students' comprehension of the dialogue.
- The ***Hablemos*** section provides personalized questions spun off from the lesson theme, where students are encouraged to work in pairs, asking and answering each of the questions presented.
- ***Vamos a practicar*** activities review grammar topics that students need to know before proceeding in the lesson.
- ***Conversaciones breves*** activities practice the lesson's vocabulary.
- The ***En estas situaciones*** section develops students' communication skills through role-playing in pairs or small groups and encourages more interactive speaking practice.
- The ***Casos*** activity establishes professional situations such as nurse/patient, dietician/patient, or doctor/patient. The entire class participates in open-ended role-playing that re-creates and expands on the situations introduced in the dialogue and the *En estas situaciones* section.
- The ***Un paso más*** section features activities that practice the supplementary words and expressions in the *Vocabulario adicional* section, some through realia.

  Pair and group icons indicate pair and group activities.

 Audio icons show what is available on the In-Text Audio CDs, including corresponding track numbers.

Web-search icons indicate activities related to the *Notas culturales* on the *Baisc Spanish for Medical Personnel* website.

Web-audio icons indicate vocabulary available in audio flashcards on the *Basic Spanish for Medical Personnel* website.

- **Five maps** of the Spanish-speaking world are included in the front and back of the text.
- For easy reference and to aid in lesson planning, the table of contents lists the **grammar structures** presented in the corresponding *Basic Spanish* text and practiced in *Basic Spanish for Medical Personnel,* plus the communication objective for each lesson.
- The text's grammatical sequence parallels the core text of the series, *Basic Spanish.*

Organization of the *Lecturas*

A reading section appears after lessons 3, 6, 9, 12, 15, 18, and 20.

- ***Lecturas*** deal with contemporary health issues, such as AIDS, drugs, and cancer.
- ***Conversaciones*** feature several brief conversations on the topic of the reading. These conversations are recorded on the In-text Audio CDs.
- ***Dígame...*** comprehension questions check students' comprehension of the *Lectura* and the *Conversaciones.*

Organization of the *Repasos*

After every five lessons, a review section contains the following materials:

- ***Práctica de vocabulario*** exercises check students' cumulative knowledge and use of active vocabulary in a variety of formats: selecting the appropriate word to complete a sentence, identifying related words, matching, true/false, and puzzles.
- A ***Práctica oral*** section features questions that review key vocabulary and structures presented in the preceding five lessons. To develop students' aural and oral skills, the questions are recorded on the *Basic Spanish for Medical Personnel* In-Text Audio CDs.

Appendixes

The appendixes of this book include the following information:

- **Appendix A, Introduction to Spanish Sounds and the Alphabet,** presents the alphabet and briefly explains vowel sounds, consonant sounds, linking, rhythm, intonation, syllable formation, and accentuation.
- **Appendix B, Verbs,** presents charts of the three regular conjugations and of the regular **-ar, -er,** and **-ir** verbs; stem-changing verbs; as well as lists of orthographic-changing verbs and some common irregular verbs.
- **Appendix C, Useful Classroom Expressions,** consists of a list of the most common expressions and directions used in the introductory Spanish language class.
- **Appendix D, Weights and Measures,** features conversion formulas for temperature and metric weights and measures, as well as Spanish terms for U.S. weights and measures.

End Vocabularies

Comprehensive Spanish-English and English-Spanish vocabularies contain all words and expressions from the *Vocabulario* section. Each term is followed by the lesson number where the active vocabulary is introduced. All passive vocabulary items found in the *Vocabulario adicional* sections, in marginal glosses to readings, and in glosses of direction lines or exercises are also included.

Components

For Students

Student In-Text Audio CDs

Packaged automatically with ***Basic Spanish for Medical Personnel,*** this two-CD set features recordings of the dialogues from the two preliminary lessons and all twenty regular lessons. The recordings of *Conversaciones* in the *Lecturas* and the *Práctica oral* section of the *Repasos* appear on the audio CDs in accordance with their order in ***Basic Spanish for Medical Personnel.***

Spanish Phrasebook

The ***Basic Spanish for Medical and Social Services Phrasebook*** contains vocabulary words and phrases arranged alphabetically, to provide professionals in the medical field with a handy reference for on-the-job situations.

Student CD-ROM (video)

This dual-platform CD-ROM contains video grammar presentations for 73 grammar topics presented in the ***Basic Spanish*** core textbook.

Student Website (www.college.hmco.com/students)

The student website contains the following:

- ACE practice tests for each grammar topic in the ***Basic Spanish*** core text
- ACE practice tests for the vocabulary in each chapter
- Web search activities related to the *Notas culturales* in each lesson and related to the seven *Lecturas*
- Audio flashcards organized by lesson for vocabulary and pronunciation practice
- A link to the SMARTHINKING™ website. SMARTHINKING™ offers a range of tutorial services including live online help, questions any time, and independent study resources.

For Instructors

Instructor's HM ClassPrep CD

This new CD-ROM contains:

- Testing program with Answer Key, available in PDF and Word Files; includes twenty quizzes, two midterms, and two final exams
- Answer keys for the worktext
- Audio scripts

- Transparency masters
- Translations of dialogs
- Lesson plans and syllabi
- Situation cards
- Script for oral test questions

Instructor's Website (www.college.hmco.com/instructors)

The instructor's website contains all the resources that exist on the Instructor's HM ClassPrep CD minus the testing program and the answer key, plus the answer keys for the worktext.

Instructor's Course Management Powered by Blackboard™ and WebCT

Both components provide materials in an online format for those instructors or institutions moving to online instruction. They include all the resources included on the Instructor's HM ClassPrep CD plus the Testing Program in Blackboard™ or WebCT format.

Feedback Welcome

We would like to hear your comments on and reactions to ***Basic Spanish for Medical Personnel*** and to ***The Basic Spanish Series*** in general. Reports on your experience using this program would be of great interest and value to us. Please write to us in care of:

Houghton Mifflin Company
College Division
222 Berkeley Street
Boston, MA 02116-3764

A Final Word

The many students who have used the previous editions of ***Basic Spanish for Medical Personnel*** have enjoyed learning and practicing a new language in realistic contexts. We hope that the new edition will prepare professionals in the medical field to communicate better with the Spanish-speaking people whom they encounter on their job on a day-to-day basis.

Acknowledgments

We wish to thank our colleagues who have used previous editions of ***Basic Spanish for Medical Personnel*** for their many constructive comments and suggestions:

Madelyn Alvariño, *Immaculata University*
Robert Adler, *University of North Alabama*
Debra Andrist, *University of St. Thomas, TX*
Dr. Harry J. Azadian, *Raytheon Health Services Department*
Cathy Briggs, *Northlake College, TX*
Steven Budge, *Mesa Community College*
Cristina Cabello C. de Martínez, *University of Texas at Austin*
Joan W. Delzangle, *Chaffey College*
Ozzie F. Díaz-Duque, *University of Iowa, Hospitals and Clinics*
Luz M. Escobar, *Southeastern Louisiana University*
Héctor Fernández L'Hoeste, *Georgia State University*
Angela Glaviano, *Middlesex Community College, CT*
Donald B. Gibbs, *Creighton University*
Martha H. Goldberg, *Cuesta College*
Elaine Graybill, *Tyler Junior College, TX*
Hope Hernández, *Community College of Southern Nevada*
Mónica Herrera, *Prince George's Community College*
Ann Hilberry, *Univeristy of Michigan*
Marie R. Jarrett, *Georgia Perimeter College*
Dr. Julio Machuca, *Dentist, Woodbridge, VA*
Violeta Mercado, *University of Wisconsin at Milwaukee*
Marisabel Novillo, *Utica College*
Fran Rakauskas, R.N., *Raytheon Health Services Department*
Elizabeth Rojas-Auda, *University of Texas at Arlington*
Perla Rozencvaig, *Columbia University*
Richard James Schneer, *Cedar Crest College*
Dr. Flavio Valdes, *Cardinal Cushing Center for the Spanish Speaking, Boston*

We especially would like to thank our two medical consultants: Luis Lebredo, M.D., F.A.C.S. affiliated with St. Luke's Medical Center, Sioux City, Iowa, and Shari Gold-Gómez, Manager of Interpretive Services at Beth Israel Deaconess Medical Center in Boston, Massachusetts. Their insights have helped bring more real-life perspectives to the variety of health situations that medical professionals face today and the common practices they use in their daily work.

Finally, we extend our sincere appreciation to the World Languages staff at Houghton Mifflin Company, College Division: Publisher, Rolando Hernández; Sponsoring Editor, Van Strength; Development Manager, Glenn Wilson; Development Editor, Judith Bach; Associate Marketing Manager, Claudia Martínez; and Executive Marketing Director, Eileen Bernadette Moran.

Ana C. Jarvis
Raquel Lebredo

The Human Body

The diagrams on these pages show the important parts of the human body. Study them carefully and refer to them when necessary as you progress through the text.

El cuerpo humano (The Human Body)
Vista anterior (Front View)
La mujer (Woman)

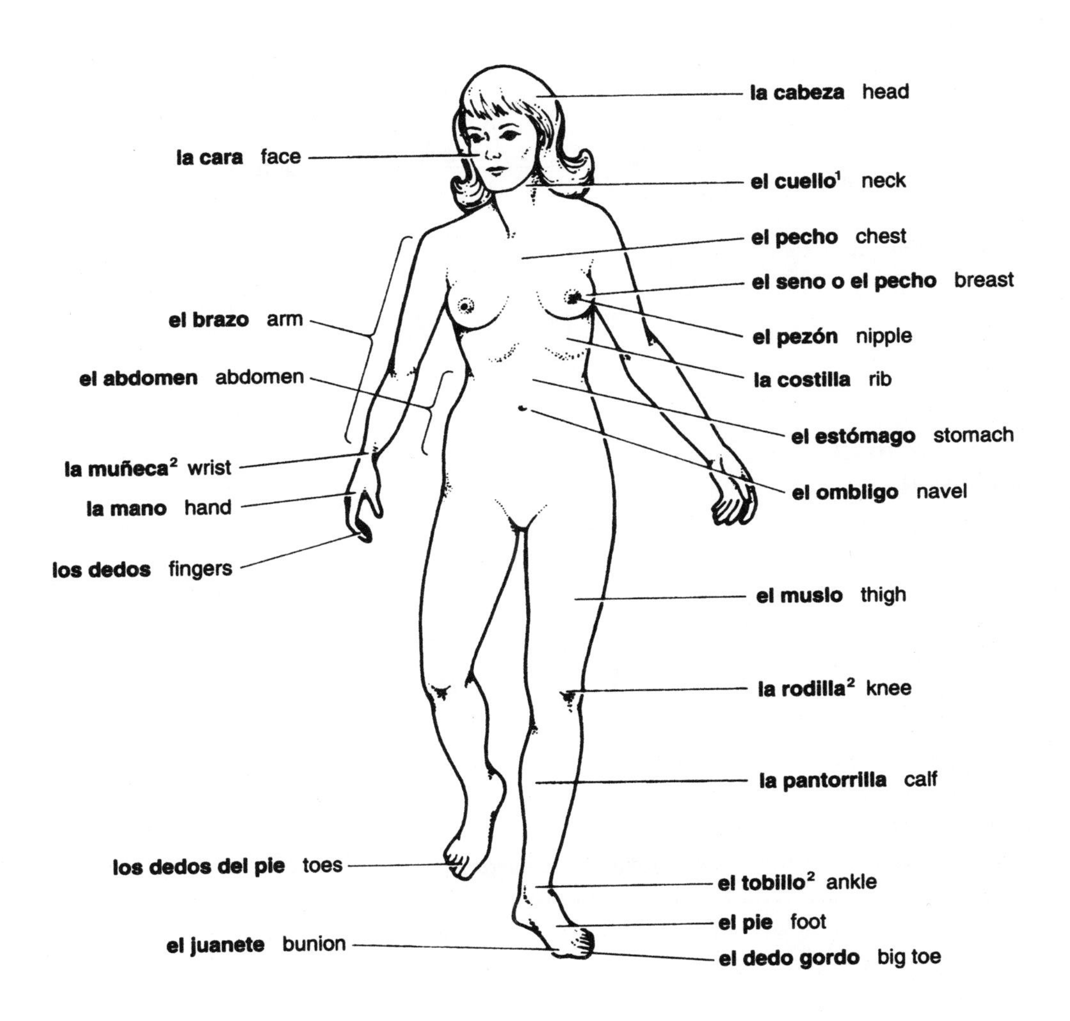

[1]Colloquialism: **el pescuezo.**
[2]**una articulación** (*joint*)

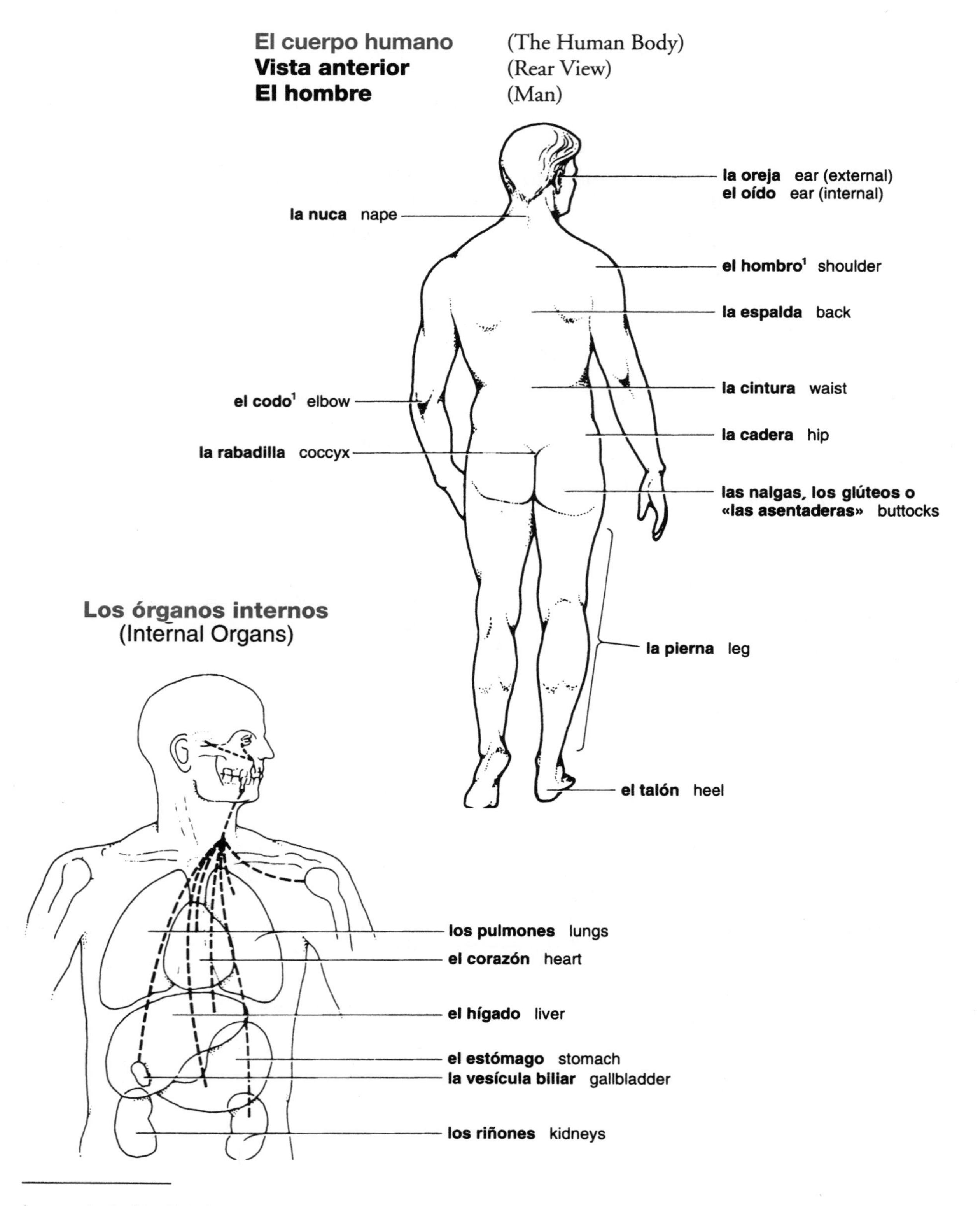

[1]**una articulación** (*joint*)

El aparto digestivo
(Digestive System)

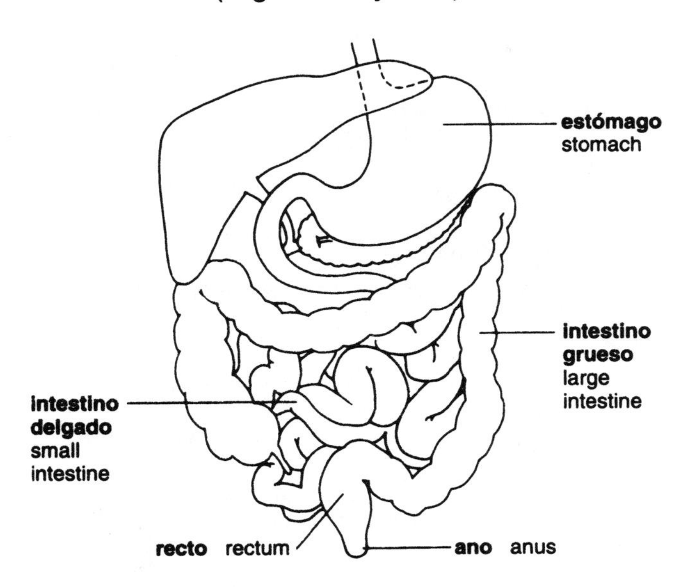

Los órganos reproductivos (Reproductive Organs)

La mujer (Woman) **El hombre** (Man)

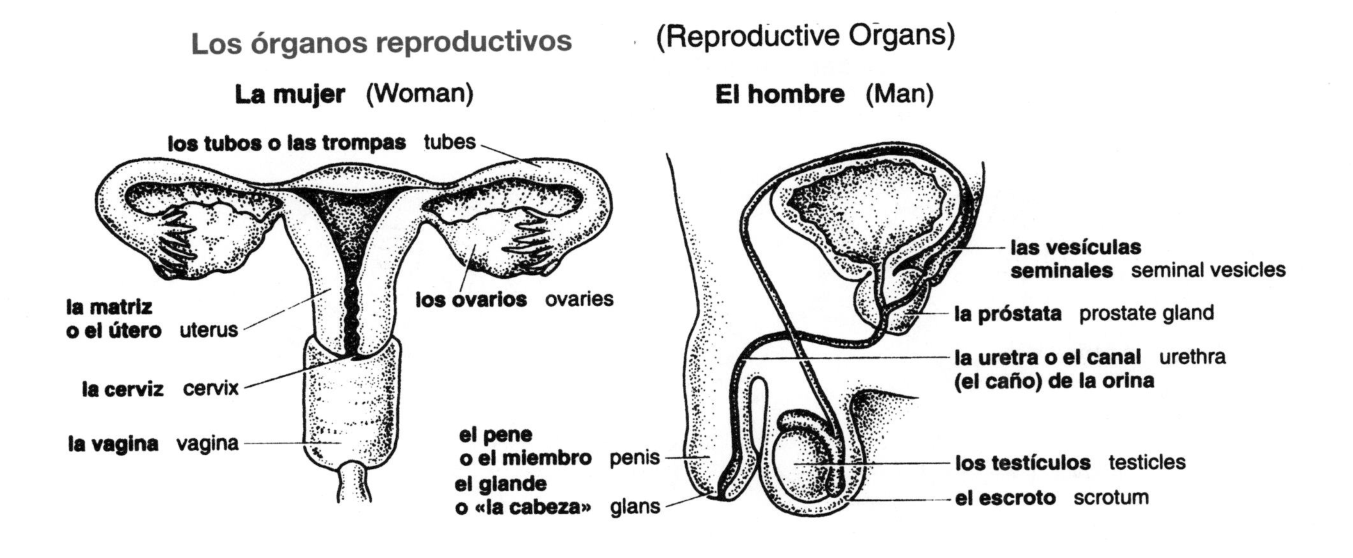

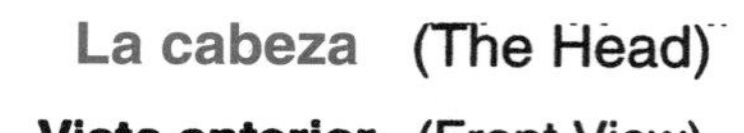

La cabeza (The Head)

Vista anterior (Front View)

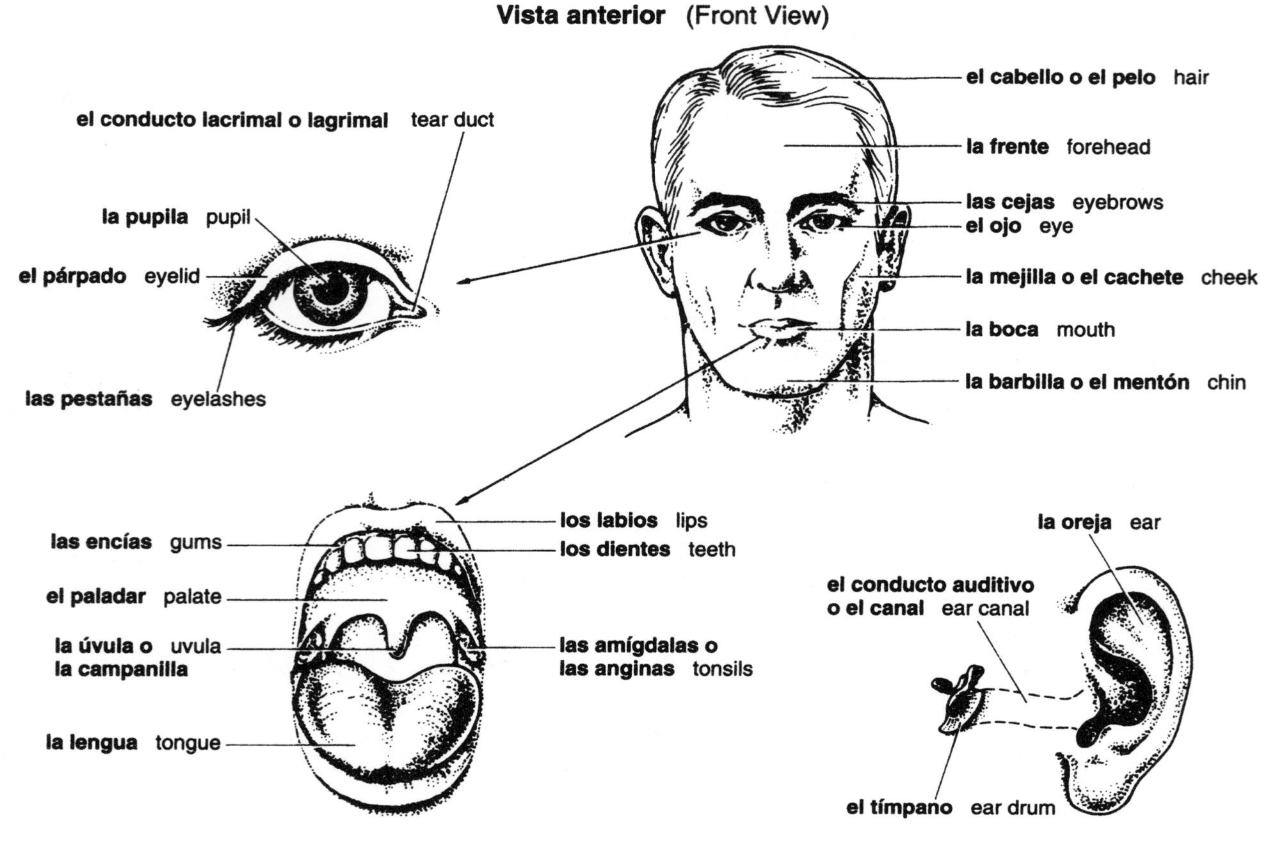

La cabeza ((The Head)

Vista de perfil (Side View)

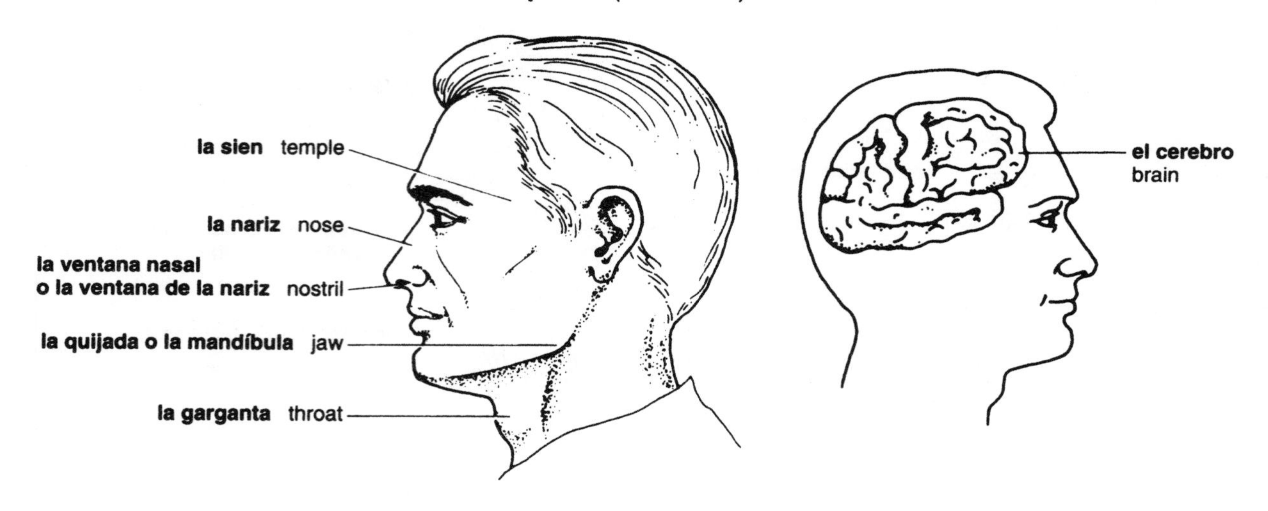

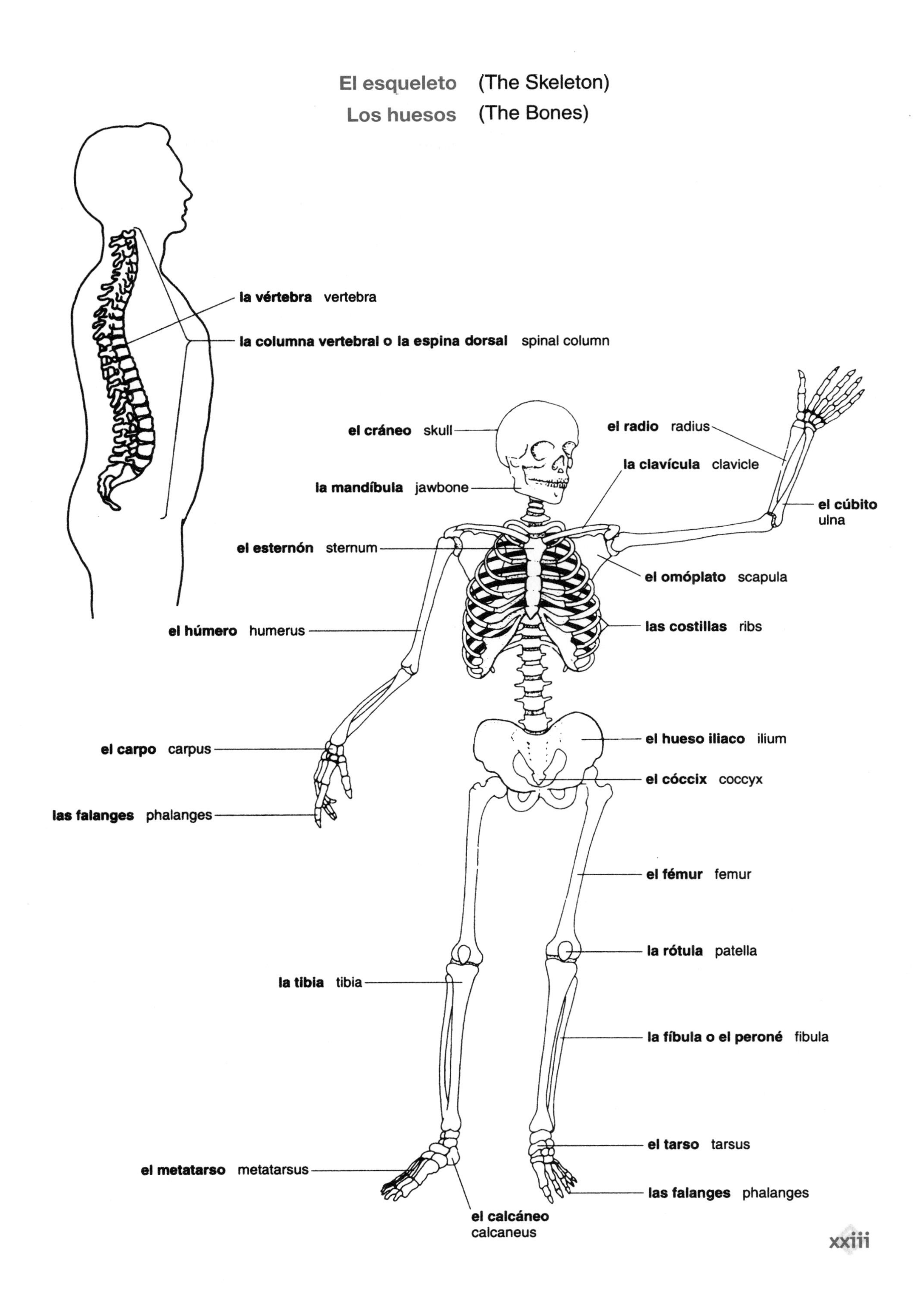
El esqueleto (The Skeleton)
Los huesos (The Bones)
la vértebra vertebra
la columna vertebral o la espina dorsal spinal column
el cráneo skull
el radio radius
la clavícula clavicle
la mandíbula jawbone
el cúbito
ulna
el esternón sternum
el omóplato scapula
el húmero humerus
las costillas ribs
el carpo carpus
el hueso iliaco ilium
el cóccix coccyx
las falanges phalanges
el fémur femur
la rótula patella
la tibia tibia
la fíbula o el peroné fibula
el tarso tarsus
el metatarso metatarsus
las falanges phalanges
el calcáneo
calcaneus

CONVERSACIONES BREVES (*BRIEF CONVERSATIONS*)

OBJECTIVES

Structures and Communication

- Greetings and farewells
- Cardinal numbers 0–9
- The alphabet
- Personal information
- Days of the week
- Months of the year
- Colors

CONVERSACIONES BREVES

1–2 **A.** —Buenos días, señorita Vega. ¿Cómo está usted?
—Muy bien, gracias, señor Pérez. ¿Y usted?
—Bien, gracias.
—Hasta luego.
—Adiós.

1–3 **B.** —Buenas noches, doctora Ramírez.
—Buenas noches, señora Soto. ¿En qué puedo servirle?
—Doctora, necesito hablar con usted.
—Bien. Tome asiento.

Nombre ______________________ Sección ______________ Fecha ______________

1-4 **C.** —Buenas tardes, señorita.
—Buenas tardes. Pase y tome asiento, por favor.
—Gracias.
—¿Nombre y apellido?
—José Luis Torres Fuentes.
—¿Dirección?
—Calle Juárez, número diez.
—¿Número de teléfono?
—Siete-tres-uno-treinta y nueve-veinticinco.
—¿Es usted casado o soltero, señor Torres?
—Soy divorciado.

VOCABULARIO (*VOCABULARY*)

SALUDOS Y DESPEDIDAS (*Greetings and farewells*)

Adiós. *Good-bye.*
Buenos días. *Good morning, good day.*
Buenas tardes. *Good afternoon.*
Buenas noches. *Good evening, good night.*
¿Cómo está usted?[1] *How are you?*
Hasta luego. *(I'll) see you later, so long.*
Bien. *Fine, well.*
Muy bien, gracias. *Very well, thank you.*

TÍTULOS (*Titles*)

doctor (Dr.), doctora (Dra.) *doctor*
señor (Sr.) *Mr., sir, gentleman*
señora (Sra.) *Mrs., lady, ma'am, madam*
señorita (Srta.) *Miss, young lady*

OTRAS PALABRAS Y EXPRESIONES (*Other words and expressions*)

el apellido *last name, surname*
la calle *street*

---

[1]**¿Cómo estás?** familiar form

Nombre ______________________ Sección ______________ Fecha ______________

casado(a) *married*
¿cómo? *how?*
con *with*
conversaciones breves *brief conversations*
la dirección, el domicilio *address*
divorciado(a) *divorced*
¿En qué puedo servirle? *How may I help you?*
¿Es[1] usted...? *Are you...?*
gracias *thank you*
Necesito hablar... *I need to speak...*
el nombre *name*
el número *number*
el número de teléfono *phone number*
o *or*
Pase. *Come in.*
por favor *please*
soltero(a) *single*
soy[1] *I am*
Tome asiento. *Have a seat.*
y *and*

VOCABULARIO ADICIONAL (*ADDITIONAL VOCABULARY*)

Hasta mañana. *See you tomorrow.*
Hola. *Hi, Hello.*
Muchas gracias. *Thank you very much.*
De nada. *You're welcome.*

COGNADOS (*COGNATES*)

Cognates (*cognados*) are words that are similar in spelling and meaning in two languages. Some Spanish cognates are identical to English words. In other instances, the words differ only in minor or predictable ways. There are many Spanish cognates related to the medical or health care professions, as illustrated in the following lists. Learning to recognize and use cognates will help you to acquire vocabulary more rapidly and to read and speak Spanish more fluently.

la anemia *anemia*
la bronquitis *bronchitis*
el cáncer *cancer*
la cirrosis *cirrhosis*
la deshidratación *dehydration*
la diabetes *diabetes*
la disentería *dysentery*
el enfisema *emphysema*
la epilepsia *epilepsy*
la hipertensión *hypertension*
el insomnio *insomnia*
la úlcera *ulcer*

continued

[1]From the verb **ser,** *to be*

Nombre ______________________ **Sección** __________ **Fecha** __________

la anestesiología *anesthesiology*
la cardiología *cardiology*
la ginecología *gynecology*
la oftalmología *ophthalmology*
la ortopedia *orthopedics*
la pediatría *pediatrics*
la urología *urology*

el (la) anestesiólogo(a) *anesthesiologist*
el (la) cardiólogo(a) *cardiologist*
el (la) ginecólogo(a) *gynecologist*
el (la) oftalmólogo(a) *ophthalmologist*
el (la) ortopedista, el (la) ortopeda *orthopedist*
el (la) pediatra *pediatrician*
el (la) urólogo(a) *urologist*

Actividades

Dígame... Write appropriate responses to the following.

1. Buenos días.

____

2. Buenas tardes. ¿Cómo está usted?

____

3. Muchas gracias.

____

4. Buenas noches.

____

5. Pase y tome asiento, por favor.

____

6. Nombre y apellido.

____

7. Hasta mañana.

____

Nombre ______________________ Sección ____________ Fecha ____________

Vamos a practicar (*Let's practice*)

A Write in Spanish the name of the place and the telephone number (in words) you would call in each of the following situations.[1] Since many of the words are cognates, guess at their meaning.

1. You need some medicine. ______________________
2. You have a toothache. ______________________
3. Your husband/wife is having a heart attack. ______________________
4. You have just witnessed a car accident. ______________________
5. You want to know when you can visit a friend who has just had a baby. ______________________

____

Hospital Municipal 257-1914
Ambulancia 235-3011
Dr. Manuel Montoya, dentista 265-1217
Policía 112
Farmacia "Marín" 241-3428

B You are responsible for making patients' appointments at a medical clinic. In order to verify that you have written the following names correctly in the appointment book, spell each one in Spanish.

1. Sandoval
2. Fuentes
3. Varela
4. Ugarte
5. Barrios
6. Zubizarreta

[1]Write the first three numbers individually and the rest in pairs: 2-5-7-19-14

Nombre ______________________ **Sección** ____________ **Fecha** ____________

En estas situaciones (*In these situations*) What would you say in the following situations? What might the other person say?

1. You greet your instructor in the evening and ask how he/she is.
2. You greet a patient, Miss Vega, in the morning.
3. Someone knocks on the door of your office.
4. You want to thank someone for a favor.
5. You are helping someone fill out a form. You ask for his/her first and last name, address, and phone number.
6. You ask someone whether he/she is married, single, or divorced.

CONVERSACIONES BREVES

OBJECTIVES

Structures and Communication

- Gender and number
- The definite and indefinite articles
- Subject pronouns
- The present indicative of **ser**
- Uses of **hay**
- Cardinal numbers 40–299

CONVERSACIONES BREVES

1-5 **A.** —Buenas noches, señor Rojas. Yo soy el doctor Díaz. ¿Cómo se siente?
—No muy bien, doctor.
—Lo siento...

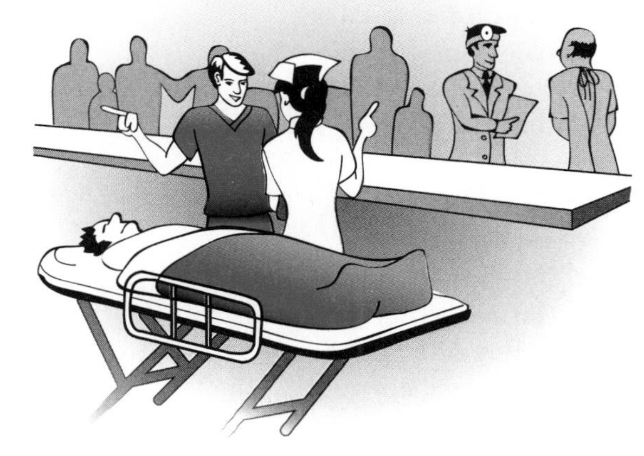

1-6 **B.** —¿Cuántos pacientes hay en la sala de emergencia?
—Hay nueve pacientes.
—¿Cuántos médicos hay?
—Hay solamente dos.

Nombre ______________________ Sección ______________ Fecha ______________

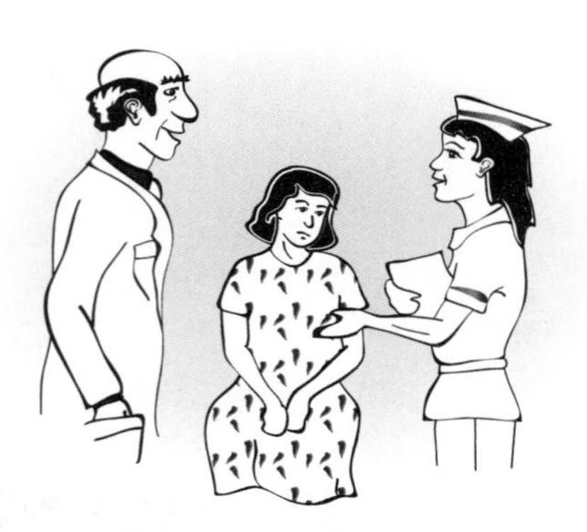

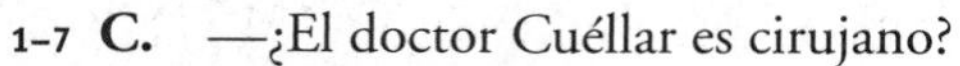

1-7 **C.** —¿El doctor Cuéllar es cirujano?
—No, él es cardiólogo.
—¿Y la doctora Peñarreal?
—Ella es pediatra.
—¿De dónde son ellos?
—Ella es de México y él es de Puerto Rico.

1-8 **D.** —¿Qué necesita la paciente?
—Unas radiografías y unos análisis.

VOCABULARIO

COGNADOS

el (la) cardiólogo(a)
la emergencia
el (la) paciente
el (la) pediatra

NOMBRES

el análisis *test*
el (la) cirujano(a) *surgeon*
el (la) médico(a) *doctor, M.D.*
la radiografía *X-ray*
la sala *room, ward*
la sala de emergencia, la sala de urgencia *emergency room*

VERBOS

ser *to be*

OTRAS PALABRAS Y EXPRESIONES

¿Cómo se siente? *How are you feeling?*
¿cuántos(-as)? *how many?*
de *from*
¿de dónde? *where from*
¿dónde? *where*
en *in, at*
hay *there is, there are*
Lo siento. *I'm sorry.*
¿Necesita ayuda? *Do you need help?*

Nombre ______________________ Sección ____________ Fecha ____________

Vocabulario adicional

Necesita
- **un electrocardiograma** *an electrocardiogram (E.K.G.)*
- **un examen físico, un chequeo** *a physical examination*
- **un mamograma** *a mammogram*
- **un papanicolau** *a pap smear*
- **una operación** *an operation, surgery*

Vamos a practicar

A Write the definite article before each noun and write the plural form.

1. ____________ apellido ______________________
2. ____________ dirección ______________________
3. ____________ doctora ______________________
4. ____________ señor ______________________
5. ____________ nombre ______________________
6. ____________ conversación ______________________
7. ____________ calle ______________________
8. ____________ número ______________________

B Write **un, una, unos,** or **unas** before each noun.

1. ____________ análisis (*pl.*)
2. ____________ radiografía
3. ____________ electrocardiograma
4. ____________ operación
5. ____________ mamograma
6. ____________ pacientes (*fem.*)
7. ____________ papanicolau
8. ____________ médicos

Nombre ______________________ **Sección** __________ **Fecha** __________

C Complete the following dialogue, using the present indicative of the verb **ser.**

—¿De dónde __________ ustedes?

—Nosotros __________ de México.

—¿De dónde __________ tú?

—Yo __________ de Cuba.

—¿Y el doctor Vargas?

—Él __________ de Venezuela.

D Write the following numbers in Spanish.

1. 298 ______________________
2. 151 ______________________
3. 275 ______________________
4. 197 ______________________
5. 263 ______________________

En estas situaciones

What would you say in the following situations?

1. You are talking to a patient and ask him/her how he/she is feeling.

   ____

2. You are telling a female patient that she needs a pap smear and a mammogram.

   ____

3. You ask the new doctor where he/she is from and tell him/her where you are from.

   ____

4. You tell a patient that he/she needs an E.K.G.

   ____

5. You ask someone how many doctors there are in the emergency room.

   ____

Objectives

Structures

- The present indicative of regular **-ar** verbs
- Interrogative and negative sentences
- Forms and position of adjectives
- Telling time
- Cardinal numbers 300–1,000

Communication

- Preliminary patient information

En el consultorio

1–9

La paciente entra y habla con la recepcionista.

Recepcionista —Buenos días, señora.
Paciente —Buenos días, señorita. Necesito hablar[1] con la doctora Gómez, por favor.
Recepcionista —Muy bien. ¿Nombre y apellido?
Paciente —Susana Vera Ruiz.
Recepcionista —¿Quién paga la cuenta, señora Vera? ¿Usted o el seguro?
Paciente —El seguro.
Recepcionista —La tarjeta de seguro médico, por favor. Necesito sacar una fotocopia.
Paciente —Aquí está.
Recepcionista —Ahora necesita llenar esta planilla.
Paciente —Muy bien. (*La paciente llena la planilla.*)

---

[1]When two verbs are used together, the second verb remains in the infinitive: **Necesito *hablar.***

Nombre ______________________ Sección ______________ Fecha ______________

La enfermera pesa a la paciente y luego la señora Vera habla con la doctora Gómez.

Médica —A ver... Usted pesa ciento cuarenta libras. ¿Cuánto mide?
Paciente —Cinco pies, seis pulgadas.
Médica —(*Mira la hoja clínica.*) Ajá... dolor de cabeza... dolor de estómago... y náusea...
Paciente —Sí, doctora. Vomito a menudo. Siempre después de las comidas.
Médica —¿Vomita sangre? ¿Hay sangre en el excremento?
Paciente —No, doctora.
Médica —Bueno, necesitamos radiografías y un análisis de materia fecal y de orina.
Paciente —Muy bien.

Con la recepcionista.

Paciente —¿Cuándo necesito regresar?
Recepcionista —Necesita regresar mañana a las ocho y media para los análisis.

1-9

¡Escuchemos! While listening to the dialogue, circle **V (verdadero)** if the statement is true or **F (falso)** if it is false.

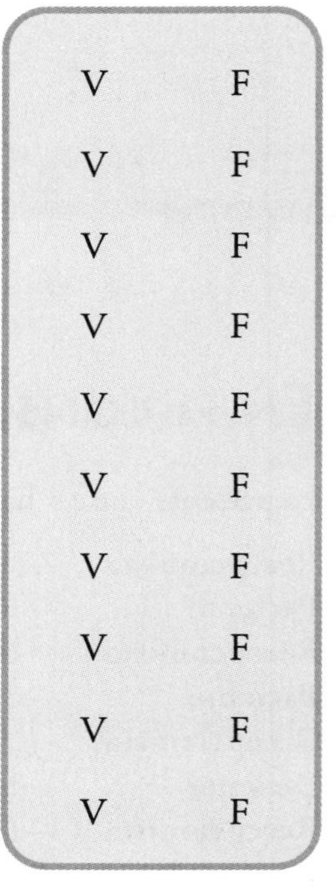

1. La paciente necesita hablar con la doctora. V F
2. La paciente paga la cuenta. V F
3. La recepcionista saca una fotocopia de la tarjeta de seguro médico. V F
4. La paciente pesa cien libras. V F
5. La paciente mide seis pies, seis pulgadas. V F
6. La paciente vomita después de las comidas. V F
7. No hay sangre en el excremento. V F
8. La médica necesita un análisis de materia fecal y de orina. V F
9. La paciente no regresa. V F
10. La recepcionista necesita regresar a las ocho y media. V F

Nombre ______________________ Sección ____________ Fecha ____________

INFORMACIÓN SOBRE EL PACIENTE (Llenar con letra de imprenta.)

Fecha: 3/10/2005

Sr.
Sra. (circled)
Srta. Vera Ruiz — Susana — Luisa
Apellido(s) — Nombre — Segundo nombre

Dirección: Magnolia 913 — Riverside — CA — 92314
Calle — Ciudad — Estado — Zona postal

Teléfono: (951) 686-9236

566-77-4832 — 4 de mayo de 1960 — 44 años
Número de seguro social — Fecha de nacimiento — Edad

Sexo: ____ Masculino
✓ Femenino

Ocupación: Secretaria

Lugar donde trabaja: Compañía Sandoval

Estado civil: ✓ Casado(a)
____ Soltero(a)
____ Divorciado(a)
____ Separado(a)
____ Viudo(a)

Nombre del esposo: Hugo Luis

Nombre de la esposa: ____________

En caso de emergencia, llamar a: Hugo Ruiz
Teléfono: (951) 686-9236
Nombre de la compañía de seguro: Blue Cross
Número de póliza: 792573
Firma: *Susana L. Vera Ruiz*

Nombre ____________________ Sección ____________ Fecha ____________

Vocabulario

COGNADOS

la compañía
divorciado(a)
la fotocopia
la información
la náusea
la ocupación
la póliza
el (la) recepcionista
el sexo
social

NOMBRES

la cabeza *head*
la comida *meal*
la compañía de seguro *insurance company*
el consultorio *doctor's office*
la cuenta *bill*
el dolor *pain, ache*
  el dolor de cabeza *headache*
  el dolor de estómago *stomachache*
la edad *age*
el (la) enfermero(a) (*male*) *nurse*
la esposa, la mujer *wife*
el esposo, el marido *husband*
el estado civil *marital status*
el estómago *stomach*
la fecha de nacimiento *date of birth*
la firma *signature*
la hoja clínica, la historia clínica *medical history*
la letra *letter, handwriting*
  la letra de imprenta, la letra de molde *print, printed letter*
la libra *pound*
la licencia para conducir *driver's license*
el lugar donde trabaja *place of employment*
la materia fecal, el excremento *stool, feces, excrement*
la orina *urine*
el pie *foot*
la planilla, la forma (*Méx.*) *form*
la pulgada *inch*
la sangre *blood*
el segundo nombre *middle name*
el seguro, la aseguranza (*Méx.*) *insurance*
el seguro social *Social Security*
la tarjeta *card*
  la tarjeta de seguro médico *medical insurance card*

VERBOS

entrar *to enter*
hablar *to speak*
llamar *to call*
llenar *to fill out*
mirar *to look at*
necesitar *to need*
pagar *to pay*
pesar *to weigh*
regresar *to return*
vomitar, arrojar *to throw up, to vomit*

ADJETIVOS

casado(a) *married*
clínico(a) *medical*
esta *this*
separado(a) *separated*
viudo(a) *widower, widow*

OTRAS PALABRAS Y EXPRESIONES

a la(s) + (time) *at* (+ *time*)
a menudo *often*
A ver... *Let's see...*
ahora *now*
ajá *aha*
aquí está *here it is*
bueno *okay, well*
¿cuándo? *when?*
¿cuánto? *how much?*
¿Cuánto mide usted? *How tall are you?*

Nombre ______________________ Sección ______________ Fecha ______________

después (de) *after*
en caso de *in case of*
luego, después *afterwards*
mañana *tomorrow*
para *for*
pesa a la paciente *weighs the patient*
¿quién? *who?*
sacar una fotocopia *to make a photocopy*
siempre *always*
sobre *about*

VOCABULARIO ADICIONAL (*ADDITIONAL VOCABULARY*)

Necesita una radiografía
- **de la cabeza** *head*
- **de la espalda** *back*
- **del pecho** *chest*
- **de la rodilla** *knee*
- **de la mano** *hand*
- **de la muñeca** *wrist*
- **de la pierna** *leg*

Necesita un análisis de
- **orina** *urine*
- **materia fecal** *stool, feces*
- **esputo** *sputum*

¿Dónde le duele? *Where does it hurt?*

Me duele
- **el cuello** *neck*
- **el estómago** *stomach*
- **el vientre** *abdomen*
- **el oído** *(inner) ear*
- **la garganta** *throat*
- **el hombro** *shoulder*
- **aquí** *here*

Me duelen[1]
- **los pies** *feet*
- **las piernas** *legs*
- **los brazos** *arms*
- **los dientes** *teeth*
- **los dedos** *fingers*

¡OJO! For additional anatomical terms, see the list on page 11.

[1]**Me duelen,** when referring to more than one part of the body.

Nombre ______________________ **Sección** ____________ **Fecha** ____________

NOTAS CULTURALES

Search

- In most Spanish-speaking countries, the day of the month is placed first. For example, 3/10/99 is equivalent to **el 3 de octubre de 1999,** or October 3, 1999. This is especially important not only for correct data on birth dates but also regarding correspondence related to future appointments. It is helpful to write the day of the week for follow-up appointments in addition to the date to avoid confusion.
- In Spanish-speaking countries, people generally have two surnames: the father's surname and the mother's maiden name. For example, the children of María **Rivas** and Juan **Pérez** would use the surnames **Pérez Rivas.** This custom may cause some confusion when completing forms, making appointments, or filing medical records. The proper order for alphabetizing Hispanic names is to list people according to the father's surname.

Peña Aguilar, Rosa
Peña Aguilar, Sara Luisa
Peña Gómez, Raúl
Quesada Álvarez, Javier
Quesada Benítez, Ana María

Actividades

Dígame... Answer the following questions, basing your answers on the dialogue on pages 1–2.

1. ¿Con quién necesita hablar la paciente?

   ____

2. ¿Quién paga la cuenta, la señora Vera o el seguro?

   ____

3. ¿Qué necesita sacar la recepcionista?

   ____

4. ¿Qué necesita llenar la paciente?

   ____

5. ¿Cuánto pesa y cuánto mide la Sra. Vera?

   ____

Nombre ______________________ Sección ____________ Fecha ____________

6. ¿Vomita la paciente a menudo? ¿Vomita después de las comidas?

____

7. ¿Vomita sangre? ¿Hay sangre en el excremento?

____

8. ¿Qué necesita la doctora Gómez?

____

9. ¿A qué hora necesita regresar mañana la paciente?

____

Hablemos (*Let's talk*) Interview a classmate, using the following questions. When you have finished, switch roles.

1. ¿Nombre y apellido?
2. ¿Estado civil?
3. ¿Fecha de nacimiento?
4. ¿Cuánto mide usted?
5. ¿Cuánto pesa usted?
6. ¿Necesita usted hablar con un médico?
7. ¿Usted necesita regresar mañana?

Vamos a practicar

A Complete the following exchanges, using the present indicative of the verbs given.

MODELO llenar

El paciente ____________ la planilla.
El paciente **llena** la planilla.

1. necesitar / hablar

—Nosotros ____________ hablar con la doctora Smith.

—¿La doctora ____________ español?

—Sí, ella y yo siempre ____________ español.

Nombre ______________________ **Sección** ____________ **Fecha** ____________

2. necesitar / pagar

—¿Ustedes __________ la tarjeta de seguro médico?

—No, nosotros __________ la hoja clínica.

—¿Usted __________ la cuenta?

—Sí, yo __________ la cuenta.

3. pesar

—¿Cuánto __________ tú?

—Yo __________ ciento cincuenta libras.

4. regresar

—¿A qué hora __________ ustedes?

—Yo __________ a las dos y la recepcionista __________ a las cinco.

—¿Y los pacientes?

—Ellos __________ a la una.

B Write the following numbers in Spanish.

MODELO 1.213
mil doscientos trece

1. 31.568 ______________________________

2. 22.738 ______________________________

3. 55.890 ______________________________

4. 470.915 ______________________________

C Write in Spanish what time the following people have scheduled appointments for today.

MODELO José Santos: 3:40 P.M.
a las cuatro menos veinte de la tarde

1. Ana María Santos: 9:15 A.M. ______________________________

2. Roberto Montes: 10:00 A.M. ______________________________

Nombre ______________________ Sección ____________ Fecha ____________

3. José Luis Vera Vierci: 10:45 A.M. ______________________

4. Dulce Peña: 11:30 A.M. ______________________

5. María Teresa Ruiz: 1:20 P.M. ______________________

6. Jorge Ibáñez: 2:50 P.M. ______________________

D Write appropriate adjectives to complete the following sentences.

MODELO El doctor Rivas es ____________.
El doctor Rivas es **viudo.**

1. El médico necesita las hojas ____________.

2. Es un seguro ____________.

3. La señora Vásquez es ____________ y el señor Valdivia es ____________.

4. La señorita Eva Cortés es ____________.

Conversaciones breves

Complete the following dialogues, using your imagination and the vocabulary from this lesson.

A La recepcionista y el paciente:

Paciente —______________________

Recepcionista —Buenos días. ¿Cómo se llama usted?

Paciente —______________________

Recepcionista —¿Lugar donde trabaja?

Paciente —______________________

Recepcionista —La tarjeta de seguro médico, por favor.

Paciente —______________________

Recepcionista —Ahora necesita llenar esta planilla.

Paciente —______________________

B El doctor Rivas y la paciente: *El doctor Rivas mira la hoja clínica.*

Doctor Rivas —______________________

Paciente —Sí, mucho dolor de estómago y dolor de cabeza.

Nombre ______________________ Sección ____________ Fecha ____________

Doctor Rivas —______________________________

Paciente —Sí, vomito a menudo. Siempre después de las comidas.

Doctor Rivas —______________________________

Paciente —Sí, a menudo vomito sangre.

Doctor Rivas —______________________________

Paciente —Muy bien, doctor.

En estas situaciones What would you say in the following situations? What might the other person say?

1. You are a receptionist and a patient comes into the office in the afternoon. You greet the person and ask if he/she needs to speak with the doctor (*f.*). You tell the person that he/she needs to fill out the form and ask if the insurance company is paying the bill.
2. You are a doctor. Greet your patient (it's morning), and ask how he/she is. Ask your patient how much he/she weighs and how tall he/she is. Then tell the person he/she needs X-rays and a blood test.

Un paso más (*A step further*)

A Review the **Vocabulario adicional** in this lesson and then look at the drawings on page 11. Write what part of the body hurts by matching the numbers in the activity to those in the drawings.

MODELO **3. Me duele el brazo.**

9. ______________________________

5. ______________________________

6. ______________________________

11. ______________________________

13. ______________________________

1. ______________________________

14. ______________________________

12. ______________________________

Nombre ______________________ Sección ____________ Fecha ____________

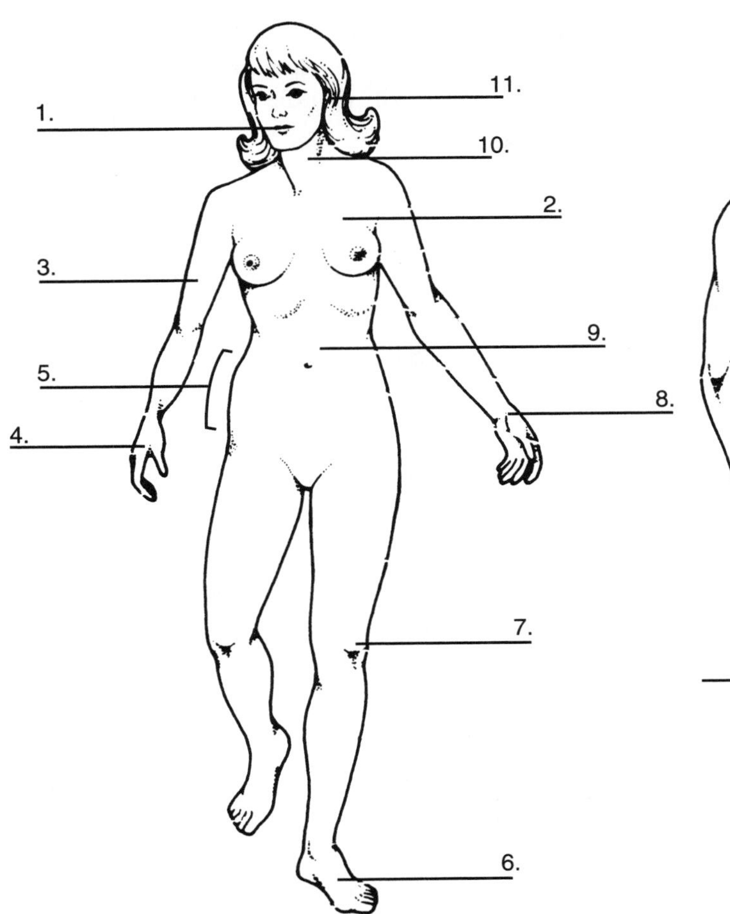

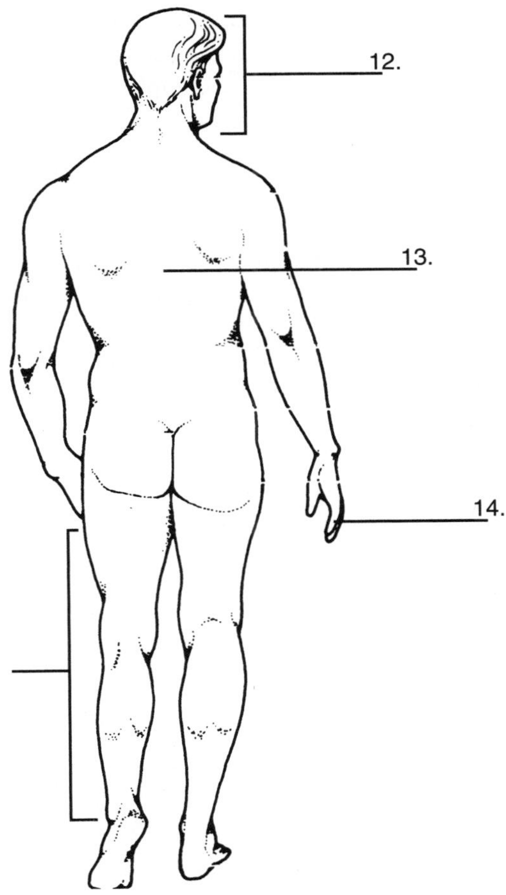

B Look at the drawings again and write what part of the body needs to be X-rayed.

Necesita una radiografía...

7. ______________________

8. ______________________

4. ______________________

5. ______________________

2. ______________________

Nombre ______________________ Sección ____________ Fecha ____________

C You work at the admitting desk in a hospital, and part of your job is to fill in the following form for each patient. Solicit the necessary information from a classmate by asking questions based on the form. After you have completed the form, ask your classmate to verify that the information you have written is correct and to sign the form.

INFORMACIÓN SOBRE EL PACIENTE (Llenar con letra de imprenta.)

Fecha: ____________

Sr.
Sra.
Srta. ____
Apellido(s) Nombre Segundo nombre

Dirección: ____
Calle Ciudad Estado Zona postal

Teléfono: ____________________

____
Número de seguro social Fecha de nacimiento Edad

Sexo: _____ Masculino
_____ Femenino

Ocupación: ______________

Número de la licencia para conducir: ______________________

Lugar donde trabaja: ______________________________

Estado civil: _____ Casado(a)
_____ Soltero(a)
_____ Divorciado(a)
_____ Separado(a)
_____ Viudo(a)

Nombre del esposo:
____
Nombre de la esposa:
____

En caso de emergencia, llamar a: ______________________
Teléfono: ________________________________
Nombre de la compañía de seguro: ______________________
Número de póliza: ______________________________
Firma: ________________________________

Lección 2 En el hospital (I)

Objectives

Structures

- Agreement of articles, nouns, and adjectives
- The present indicative of regular **-er** and **-ir** verbs
- Possession with **de**
- Possessive adjectives
- The personal **a**

Communication

- Checking into the hospital

En el hospital

1-10 La dietista habla con la Sra. López.

Dietista —¿Es Ud. la madre de Carlos López?
Sra. López —Sí, yo soy su mamá.
Dietista —¿Qué desea comer[1] el niño hoy?
Sra. López —Desea sopa, pollo y, de postre, fruta.
Dietista —¿Qué desea tomar?
Sra. López —Leche fría y agua.
Dietista —¿Y mañana, para el desayuno?
Sra. López —Jugo de naranja, cereal, pan tostado con mantequilla y chocolate caliente.
Dietista —¿Algo más?
Sra. López —No, gracias.

Con el Sr. Ramos:

Enfermera —¿Todavía tose mucho, Sr. Ramos?
Sr. Ramos —Sí, necesito un jarabe para la tos.
Enfermera —Cuando Ud. tose, ¿expectora sangre, Sr. Ramos?

---

[1]When two verbs are used together, the second verb is an infinitive: ¿Qué **desea comer?**

Sr. Ramos —No, señorita.
Enfermera —Ud. fuma mucho. No debe fumar tanto.
Sr. Ramos —Sólo fumo una cajetilla al día.
Enfermera —¡Ajá...! Bueno, necesitamos una radiografa de los pulmones y un análisis de sangre.
Sr. Ramos —Está bien. Ah, deseo una taza de café y necesito mis cigarrillos, por favor.
Enfermera —Lo siento, Sr. Ramos; está prohibido fumar en el hospital.

Con la Sra. Díaz:

Enfermera —Sra. Díaz, ¿usa Ud. dentadura postiza, anteojos o lentes de contacto?
Sra. Díaz —Uso lentes para leer.
Enfermera —¿Necesita Ud. algo?
Sra. Díaz —Sí, necesito otra almohada y una frazada, y también la pastilla para el dolor.
Enfermera —Muy bien. ¿Desea orinar ahora?
Sra. Díaz —Sí, por favor, necesito la chata.
Enfermera —No, Ud. debe ir al baño. ¿Necesita ayuda?
Sra. Díaz —Sí, y después hágame el favor de llamar a la Dra. Silva. Debo hablar con ella.

1-1 0

¡Escuchemos!

While listening to the dialogue, circle **V (verdadero)** if the statement is true or **F (falso)** if it is false.

1. La dietista habla con la mamá de Carlos López.
2. Carlos desea sopa, pollo y fruta.
3. Carlos no toma leche.
4. El niño desea tomar jugo de naranja y chocolate caliente.
5. El Sr. Ramos expectora sangre cuando tose.
6. La enfermera fuma una cajetilla al día.
7. Está prohibido fumar en el hospital.
8. La Sra. Díaz usa lentes para leer.
9. La Sra. Díaz necesita lentes de contacto.
10. La Sra. Díaz debe hablar con la Dra. Silva.

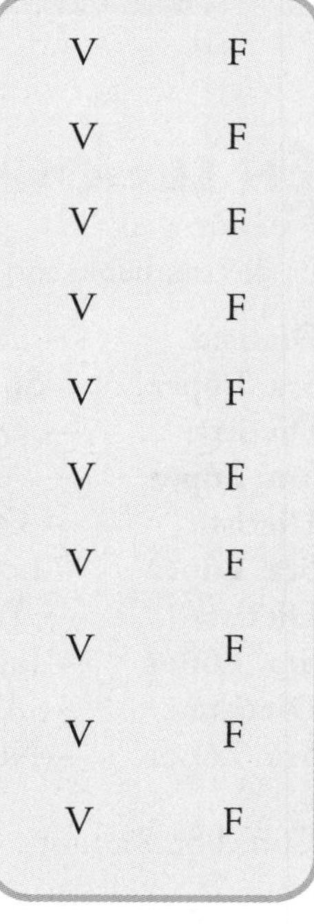

Nombre ______________________ Sección ____________ Fecha ____________

VOCABULARIO

COGNADOS

el cereal
el chocolate
la fruta
el hospital
los lentes de contacto
mucho

NOMBRES

el agua (*fem.*) *water*
la almohada *pillow*
los anteojos, los lentes, las gafas, los espejuelos(*Cuba*) *glasses*
la ayuda *help*
el baño, el escusado, el servicio *bathroom*
el café *coffee*
la cajetilla *pack of cigarettes*
la chata,[1] **la cuña** *bedpan*
el cigarrillo *cigarette*
la dentadura *teeth, set of teeth*
la dentadura postiza *dentures*
el desayuno *breakfast*
el (la) dietista *dietician*
la frazada, la manta, la cobija *blanket*
el jarabe para la tos *cough syrup*
el jugo *juice*
el jugo de naranja, el jugo de china (*Puerto Rico*) *orange juice*
la leche *milk*
la madre, la mamá *mother, mom*
la mantequilla *butter*
el (la) niño(a) *child, boy (girl)*
el pan *bread*
el pan tostado, la tostada *toast*
la pastilla *pill*
la pastilla para el dolor, el calmante[2] *pill for pain, painkiller*
el pollo *chicken*
el postre *dessert*
el pulmón *lung*
la sopa *soup*
la taza *cup*
la tos *cough*

VERBOS

comer *to eat*
deber *should, must*
desear *to want, to wish*
expectorar *to expectorate*
fumar *to smoke*
leer *to read*
orinar *to urinate*[3]
tomar, beber *to drink*
toser *to cough*
usar *to wear, to use*

ADJETIVOS

caliente *hot*
frío(a) *cool*
otro(a) *other, another*
postizo(a) *false*

OTRAS PALABRAS Y EXPRESIONES

al día *a day, per day*
algo *anything, something*
¿Algo más? *Anything else?*
Está bien. *Okay.*
Está prohibido *It's prohibited*
Hágame el favor de... (+ *inf*) *Please (+ command)*
ir al baño *to go to the bathroom*
hoy *today*
¿qué? *what?*
también *also*
tanto(a) *so much*
todavía *still, yet*

---

[1]A urinal for males is called **el pato.**
[2]The term **calmante** has two meanings: *painkiller* and *sedative.* **Calmante para el dolor** (*painkiller*) may be used to clarify the meaning.
[3]Colloquialisms: **hacer pipí, hacer pis. Hacer pipí** is frequently used by mothers when talking to small children.

Nombre ______________________ **Sección** ____________ **Fecha** ____________

VOCABULARIO ADICIONAL

Ud. debe
- **ir a la oficina de admisión** *go to the admissions office*
- **llenar la planilla de admisión** *fill out the admissions form*
- **firmar la autorización** *sign the authorization*
- **ingresar en el hospital** *be admitted to the hospital*

Deseo jugo[1] de
- **toronja** *grapefruit*
- **piña** *pineapple*
- **tomate** *tomato*
- **manzana** *apple*
- **uva** *grape*
- **pera** *pear*
- **durazno, melocotón** *peach*

Debe tomar
- **dos tabletas** *tablets*
- **dos cápsulas** *capsules*
- **la medicina** *medicine*
- **un sedativo, un calmante** *sedative*
- **un antidepresivo** *antidepressant*
- **un antidiarreico** *antidiarrheic*
- **un antiespasmódico** *antispasmodic*
- **un tranquilizante** *tranquilizer*

- As the U.S. population becomes increasingly diverse, it is important that the health professional develop multicultural competencies and skills. Several professional schools are now including course offerings on multiculturalism as part of their *curricula:* Harvard Medical School has dedicated a segment of its *Patient: Provider* course to interviewing limited-English speaking patients with the help of trained interpreters. They discuss cultural implications as part of the course.
- One of the 1998 issues of the journal *Family Medicine* was dedicated to issues on minority health. The School of Nursing of the University of California in San Francisco has published a manual on culture and nursing care. In addition to publications from specific organizations, there are many books on the subject. Three of the most recent ones are: *Cultures of Color in America: A Guide to Family, Religion, and Health* (1998); *Multicultural Clients: A Professional Handbook for Health Care Providers and Social Workers* (1996); and *Approaching Diversity: A Tool for Building Bridges* (1996).

---

[1]**zumo** (*España*)

Nombre ______________________ Sección ____________ Fecha ____________

- Many patients will remember the color or size of their pill more easily than the name of their pill. Therefore, one should encourage his/her patients to bring a list of their medications with them to their office visits. In addition, the health care provider may encounter a preference for injections over pills, since injections for many illnesses are more common in certain Spanish-speaking countries. It is also important to explain the reason for completing an entire course of medication, such as antibiotics, since if the patient feels better, it may not be understood that he/she still must complete the course of medicine.

Actividades

Dígame... Answer the following questions, basing your answers on the dialogues.

1. ¿Quién es la Sra. López?

   ____

2. ¿Qué desea comer el niño? ¿Qué desea de postre? ¿Qué desea tomar?

   ____

3. ¿Qué desea para el desayuno?

   ____

4. ¿Tose mucho el Sr. Ramos? ¿Expectora sangre cuando tose?

   ____

5. ¿Qué desea él tomar para la tos?

   ____

6. ¿Necesitan una radiografía de los pulmones o de la cabeza? ¿Qué más necesitan?

   ____

7. ¿Qué desea el Sr. Ramos?

   ____

8. ¿Qué está prohibido en el hospital?

   ____

9. ¿Usa lentes de contacto la Sra. Díaz?

____

10. ¿Qué necesita la Sra. Díaz?

____

11. ¿Necesita ayuda para ir al baño?

____

12. ¿A quién debe llamar la enfermera?

____

Hablemos Interview a classmate, using the following questions. When you have finished, switch roles.

1. ¿Qué desea comer Ud. hoy?
2. ¿Qué frutas come Ud.?
3. ¿Desea Ud. tomar leche fría, jugo de naranja, café o agua?
4. ¿Usa Ud. lentes de contacto?
5. ¿Necesita Ud. anteojos para leer?
6. ¿Usa Ud. dentadura postiza?
7. ¿Cuántas almohadas usa Ud.?
8. ¿Qué pastillas para el dolor toma Ud.?
9. ¿Fuma Ud.? ¿Cuántas cajetillas al día?
10. ¿Qué debo tomar para la tos?

Vamos a practicar

A Complete the following exchanges, using the present indicative of the verbs given.

Modelo comer

Él __________ frutas.
Él **come** frutas.

Nombre ______________________ **Sección** ____________ **Fecha** ____________

1. comer / beber

—¿Qué __________ Uds.?

—Nosotros __________ pollo. ¿Qué __________ tú?

—Yo __________ jugo de naranja o leche.

2. deber / leer

—¿Tú __________ usar anteojos para leer?

—Sí, cuando yo __________ necesito lentes.

3. toser

—¿Ud. __________ mucho, señora?

—Sí, (yo) __________ mucho.

B Complete the following sentences using possessive adjectives. Each adjective should agree with the subject.

MODELO Ella necesita __________ lentes.
Ella necesita **sus** lentes.

1. Yo necesito __________ almohada y él necesita __________ frazada.
2. Nosotros necesitamos __________ pastillas y tú necesitas __________ jarabe.
3. La enfermera necesita __________ anteojos y Uds. necesitan __________ cigarrillos.

C Give the Spanish equivalent of the words in parentheses.

1. Necesitamos llamar __________. (*the nurse*)
2. Mi hijo necesita __________. (*Jorge's phone number*)
3. El médico lee __________. (*Miss Vega's medical history*)

Conversaciones breves

Complete the following dialogues, using your imagination and the vocabulary from this lesson.

A La enfermera y el Sr. García:

Enfermera —______________________________

Sr. García —No uso dentadura postiza, pero *(but)* sí uso lentes de contacto.

Enfermera —______________________________

Sr. García —No, pero necesito otra frazada.

Nombre ______________________ **Sección** __________ **Fecha** __________

Enfermera —______________________________

Sr. García —Sí, señorita, toso mucho.

Enfermera —______________________________

Sr. García —No, yo no fumo mucho: sólo tres o cuatro cigarrillos al día.

Enfermera —______________________________

Sr. García —No, no deseo orinar ahora.

B La enfermera y la Srta. Ortiz:

Enfermera —______________________________

Srta. Ortiz —Deseo tomar leche fría.

Enfermera ______________________________

Srta. Ortiz —No, no deseo agua, gracias.

Enfermera —______________________________

Srta. Ortiz —Para el desayuno deseo jugo de manzana, cereal y una taza de café.

Enfermera —______________________________

Srta. Ortiz —No, no deseo tostadas con mantequilla.

Enfermera —______________________________

Srta. Ortiz —Para comer deseo pollo y sopa.

Enfermera —______________________________

Srta. Ortiz —No, no deseo postre.

C La enfermera y la Sra. Mora:

Enfermera —______________________________

Sra. Mora —Sí, necesito la chata.

Enfermera —No, debe ir al baño. ¿Necesita ayuda?

Sra. Mora —______________________________

Enfermera —¿Desea tomar la pastilla para el dolor?

Sra. Mora —______________________________

Enfermera —Aquí está. ¿Necesita agua?

Sra. Mora —______________________________

Nombre ______________________ Sección ____________ Fecha ____________

En estas situaciones

What would you say in the following situations? What might the other person say?

1. You are a nurse. Verify your patient's name and ask if he/she wears contact lenses or glasses. Then ask if he/she needs another pillow or a blanket.
2. You are a patient. Tell the dietician you want toast with butter and milk for breakfast and that today you want soup, salad, and chicken. Tell him/her you want to drink grape juice.
3. You are a doctor. Tell your patient that he/she needs an X-ray of the lungs and a blood test. Ask if he/she is still coughing a great deal, then tell the patient that he/she shouldn't smoke so much.
4. You are a nurse. Ask your female patient if she wants to go to the bathroom. Ask her if she needs help.
5. You tell someone that you need to call your mother.

Casos (*Cases*)

Act out the following scenarios with a partner.

1. A dietician and a patient discuss the menu for lunch and breakfast.
2. A nurse and a patient discuss the patient's needs.

Un paso más

Review the **Vocabulario adicional** in this lesson. Then give advice to the following people in these situations.

1. Your patient has a headache.

   ____

2. Your patient is very nervous.

   ____

3. The patient needs to give permission for surgery.

   ____

4. The person should be admitted to the hospital on Thursday.

   ____

5. Your patient wants some juice. Offer some choices.

   ____

EN EL CONSULTORIO DEL PEDIATRA (I)

OBJECTIVES

Structures

- The irregular verbs **ir, dar,** and **estar**
- **Ir a** + infinitive
- Uses of the verbs **ser** and **estar**
- Contractions

Communication

- In a pediatrician's office

EN EL CONSULTORIO DEL PEDIATRA (I)

1–11

La Sra. Leyva lleva a su hijo, que está muy enfermo, al consultorio del Dr. Méndez. Da su nombre y toma un número, y los dos van a la sala de espera. Al rato, la enfermera llama a Miguel Leyva. La Sra. Leyva y su hijo van a un cuarto y esperan al médico.

Con la enfermera:

Enfermera —¿Cuál es el problema de su hijo, Sra. Leyva?
Sra. Leyva —Está resfriado, y como él es asmático, sufre mucho, pobrecito.
Enfermera —A ver... Su temperatura es alta... ciento dos grados... ¿Qué tal el apetito?
Sra. Leyva —Come muy poco y siempre está cansado.
Enfermera —Está muy pálido... ¡Ah! Aquí está el doctor.

Con el Dr. Méndez:

Dr. Méndez —Miguel está muy delgado. Pesa sólo cuarenta libras. Muy poco para un niño de siete años.
Sra. Leyva —Mi hijo come muy poco, doctor. Y siempre está estreñido y aventado...
Dr. Méndez —Quizá está anémico. Necesitamos un análisis de sangre.
Sra. Leyva —¿Cree Ud. que es algo grave?
Dr. Méndez —No... necesita vitaminas y proteína.
Sra. Leyva —¿Y para el catarro y la fiebre? ¿Va a necesitar penicilina? Él es alérgico a la penicilina.
Dr. Méndez —No, su hijo no necesita penicilina.
Sra. Leyva —¿Va a necesitar alguna medicina?

Dr. Méndez —Sí, unas cápsulas y un jarabe. Debe tomar una cápsula después de cada comida y una antes de dormir.[1]
Sra. Leyva —¿Y el jarabe?
Dr. Méndez —Dos cucharaditas cada cuatro horas. Aquí está la receta.
Sra. Leyva —Muy bien. Ahora mismo vamos a ir a la farmacia para comprar la medicina. ¿Debe tomar aspirinas para la fiebre?
Dr. Méndez —No, Tylenol para niños, y debe tomar mucho líquido. Si la fiebre no baja, deben regresar mañana.
Sra. Leyva —Muchas gracias, doctor. ¡Ah! ¿Adónde llevo al niño para el análisis de sangre?
Dr. Méndez —Al laboratorio. Aquí está la orden.

1-11

¡Escuchemos! While listening to the dialogue, circle **V (verdadero)** if the statement is true or **F (falso)** if it is false.

1.	La Sra. Leyva está resfriada.	V	F
2.	El hijo de la Sra. Leyva come mucho.	V	F
3.	Miguel pesa ochenta libras.	V	F
4.	Miguel necesita vitaminas y proteína.	V	F
5.	Miguel es alérgico a la penicilina.	V	F
6.	Miguel no necesita medicinas.	V	F
7.	Miguel debe tomar una cápsula después de cada comida y una antes de dormir.	V	F
8.	La Sra. Leyva va a ir a la farmacia.	V	F
9.	Miguel va a tomar aspirinas para la fiebre.	V	F
10.	La Sra. Leyva debe llevar al niño al laboratorio.	V	F

[1]After prepositions, Spanish uses an infinitive: **antes de dormir:** *before sleeping.*

Audio

VOCABULARIO

COGNADOS

alérgico(a)
anémico(a)
el apetito
asmático(a)
la aspirina
la farmacia[1]
el laboratorio
el líquido
la medicina, el remedio
la oficina
la orden
la penicilina
el problema
la proteína
la temperatura
la vitamina

NOMBRES

el año *year*
el catarro, el resfrío, el resfriado *cold*
el cuarto *room*
la cucharadita *teaspoonful*
la fiebre, la calentura *fever*
el grado *degree*
el (la) hijo(a) *son, daughter*
la hora *hour*
el (la) pobrecito(a) *poor little thing*
la receta *prescription*
la sala de espera *waiting room*

VERBOS

bajar *to go down*
comprar *to buy*
creer *to think, to believe*
dar *to give*
esperar *to wait (for)*
estar *to be*
ir *to go*
llevar *to take (someone or something somewhere)*
sufrir *to suffer*
tomar *to take*

ADJETIVOS

alguno(a) *some, any*
alto(a) *high*
aventado(a), lleno(a) de gases *bloated*
cada *every, each*
cansado(a) *tired*
delgado(a) *thin*
enfermo(a) *sick*
estreñido(a), tapado(a), tupido(a) *constipated*
grave, serio(a) *serious*
pálido(a) *pale*

OTRAS PALABRAS Y EXPRESIONES

¿adónde? *where (to)?*
ahora mismo[2] *right now*
al rato *a while later*
antes de *before*
antes de dormir *before sleeping*
como *since*
¿cuál? *what?, which?*
estar resfriado(a), estar acatarrado(a), estar constipado(a) *to have a cold*
los (las) dos *the two of them, both*
para *in order to*
pero *but*
poco *little (quantity)*
que *that*
¿Qué tal... ? *How about...?, How is (are)...?*
quizá(s) *perhaps, maybe*
si *if*

---

[1] **la droguería** (in some Latin American countries)
[2] Colloquialism: **ahorita** (in some Latin American countries)

Nombre ______________________ Sección ____________ Fecha ____________

Vocabulario adicional

INSTRUCCIONES PARA TOMAR LAS MEDICINAS[1]

Tome (*Take*) / **Dele** (*Give him/her*) — **una cucharada** (*a tablespoon*) / **una cucharadita** (*a teaspoonful*) —

- **antes de cada comida** *before each meal*
- **cada... horas** *every... hours*
- **con las comidas** *with meals*
- **entre comidas** *between meals*
- **en ayunas** *before eating anything*
- **al acostarse** *at bedtime*
- **al levantarse** *first thing in the morning* (*when he/she gets up*)

LAS ALERGIAS (*Allergies*)

¿Es Ud. alérgico(a)

- **a algún antibiótico?** *any antibiotic*
- **a algún alimento?** *any food*
- **a la inyección contra el tétano (antitetánica)?** *the tetanus shot*
- **a la sulfa?** *sulfa*
- **a los analgésicos?** *analgesics*
- **a los barbitúricos?** *barbiturates*
- **a los descongestivos?** *decongestants*
- **a algún cosmético o perfume?** *any cosmetic or perfume*
- **al polen?** *pollen*

Notas culturales

- In many Spanish-speaking countries, people not only consult medical doctors about their health problems, but also their local pharmacists. In general, pharmacists in the Spanish-speaking world receive rigorous training and are up-to-date in pharmacology. They often give shots and recommend or prescribe medicines because many drugs such as antibiotics can be bought without a prescription.
- In some Latin American countries, especially in the Caribbean region, there are stores called **botánicas** where different kinds of herbs, roots, and powders can be bought. These products are used to cure headaches, backaches, and other similar problems. ***Uña de gato*** is one example of an herb commonly used among Latinos as a cure-all medicine.
- All Spanish-speaking countries use the metric system, which may cause some misunderstanding or confusion when discussing weights and measures with a Hispanic American patient. For example, the child in the dialogue weighs forty pounds or approximately eighteen kilograms. Also, temperatures are measured in degrees Celsius rather than degrees Fahrenheit. Thus, the child's temperature is 101°F or about 38°C. For more information, see the conversion charts in Appendix D.

---

[1]The **Instrucciones para tomar las medicinas** are not recorded on the audio program.

Nombre ______________________ Sección ____________ Fecha ____________

Actividades

Dígame... Answer the following questions, basing your answers on the dialogues.

1. ¿Adónde lleva la Sra. Leyva a su hijo?
____
2. ¿Cuál es el problema de Miguel?
____
3. ¿Cuánto pesa Miguel?
____
4. ¿Qué necesita el niño si es anémico? ¿Y para el catarro y la fiebre?
____
5. ¿Cuándo debe tomar las cápsulas? ¿Y el jarabe?
____
6. ¿Adónde van a ir la Sra. Leyva y su hijo ahora mismo?
____
7. ¿Qué debe tomar el niño para bajar la fiebre?
____
8. Si la fiebre no baja, ¿cuándo deben regresar?
____
9. ¿Adónde va a llevar la Sra. Leyva al niño?
____

Hablemos Interview a classmate, using the following questions. When you have finished, switch roles.

1. ¿Es Ud. anémico(a)? ¿Asmático(a)?
2. ¿Está Ud. cansado(a)?
3. ¿Qué tal el apetito? ¿Come Ud. bien?
4. ¿Necesita Ud. vitaminas? ¿Proteína?

5. ¿Está Ud. resfriado(a)?

6. ¿Qué toma Ud. cuando está resfriado(a)?

7. ¿Qué toma Ud. para el dolor de cabeza?

8. ¿Qué toma Ud. para la fiebre? ¿Para el resfrío?

9. ¿Es Ud. alérgico(a) a alguna medicina? ¿A cuál?

10. ¿Dónde compra Ud. las medicinas?

11. Estoy resfriado(a). ¿Debo tomar mucho o poco líquido?

12. ¿Yo estoy pálido(a)?

Vamos a practicar

A Complete the following exchanges, using the present indicative of **ir, dar,** or **estar.**

Modelo Ellos __________ a California.
Ellos **van** a California.

1. —¿__________ Uds. a la farmacia?
—Sí, __________ a la farmacia para comprar medicina. Yo __________ aventado y estreñido.
2. —La Dra. Soto no __________ su número de teléfono.
—Yo no __________ mi número de teléfono tampoco (*either*).
—Nosotros __________ el número de la oficina.
3. —¿Uds. __________ resfriados?
—Sí, __________ acatarrados y tosemos mucho.

B Complete the following exchanges, using the present indicative of **ser** or **estar.**

Modelo Ella __________ enferma.
Ella **está** enferma.

1. —¿__________ Ud. alérgico a alguna medicina?
—Sí, __________ alérgico a la penicilina.

Nombre ______________________ Sección ____________ Fecha ____________

2. —¿Dónde __________ el médico?

—__________ en el consultorio.

3. —¿Tú __________ el hijo de la Sra. Vega?

—No, __________ el hijo de la Sra. Morales.

4. —¿Cuál __________ el problema de su hijo, señora?

—__________ muy pálido últimamente (*lately*) y siempre __________ muy cansado. Además, __________ asmático. ¿Cree Ud. que __________ algo grave?

—No, no __________ grave.

C Write the following dialogues in Spanish.

1. "Where are you going to take your son, madam?"
"To the lab."

—______________________________

—______________________________

2. "Is Mr. Sosa's daughter very sick?"
"Yes, she needs to go to the hospital. He's going to call Dr. Paz."

—______________________________

—______________________________

____

Conversaciones breves

Complete the following dialogues, using your imagination and the vocabulary from this lesson.

A La doctora y el paciente:

Doctora —¿Cómo se siente?

Paciente —______________________________

Doctora —¿Come Ud. bien?

Paciente —______________________________

Doctora —¿Qué vitaminas toma Ud.?

Paciente —______________________________

Nombre ______________________ Sección ____________ Fecha ____________

B La enfermera y la madre (*mother*) de una paciente:

Enfermera —¿La fiebre de su hija es muy alta?

Sra. Calles —______________________________

Enfermera —La niña debe tomar Tylenol para niños.

Sra. Calles —¿Necesita otra medicina?

Enfermera —______________________________

Sra. Calles —Ahora mismo voy a la farmacia para comprar la medicina.

En estas situaciones

What would you say in the following situations? What might the other person say?

1. You are a doctor. Ask the patient's mother how she takes a temperature. Then tell the mother that her son/daughter must take Children's Tylenol every four hours and that they must return tomorrow if the fever doesn't go down.
2. You are a doctor. After giving a patient a prescription, tell him/her to take four capsules: one after each meal and one before sleeping. Also tell the patient that he/she must drink plenty of liquids.
3. You are the patient. Tell the doctor that you are constipated and bloated and that you don't eat very much. Ask the doctor if he/she thinks it is serious.
4. You are a doctor. Tell your patient that he/she may be anemic and that you need to do a blood test. Tell him/her that he/she must go to the lab.

Casos

Act out the following scenarios with a partner.

1. A parent discusses a child's health problems and symptoms with a doctor.
2. A doctor gives instructions to a patient who has a cold and a high fever.

Un paso más

A Review the **Vocabulario adicional** in this lesson. Then give your patients instructions about taking their medications that would approximately correspond to the times given.

1. a las seis de la mañana

____

2. a las siete de la mañana, a las doce y a las seis de la tarde

____

3. a las diez de la mañana y a las cuatro de la tarde

____

4. a las once de la noche

____

B You are a doctor. What would you say to the following people in these situations?

1. The patient has just visited a botanical garden and now has uncontrollable bouts of sniffling and sneezing.

____

2. The patient has hives and difficulty breathing.

____

3. The patient has developed a rash on her face and neck.

____

4. You are about to give a patient a tetanus shot.

____

5. You want to prescribe a drug containing sulfa for your patient.

____

6. The patient has a bronchial infection and you want to prescribe an antibiotic.

____

El asma

El asma es una enfermedad de los pulmones que dificulta la respiración.[1] Los síntomas son tos o dificultad para respirar.[2]

El asma es provocada por animales domésticos, polvo,[3] contaminación, ejercicio, moho,[4] cambios[5] en el clima, resfriado o gripe, polen, humo,[6] presión[7] o productos químicos.

Para controlar el asma, debe hacer lo siguiente:

1. Evitar[8] el humo de cigarrillos, pipa o cigarros o cualquier otro tipo de humo.
2. Controlar el polvo.
3. Usar almohadas de algodón[9] o de espuma.[10]
4. Cubrir las camas y almohadas con coberturas[11] de plástico.
5. Usar su inhalador y tomar las medicinas que receta su médico.
6. Usar un aparato para medir su respiración.

Debe llamar a su médico y obtener ayuda urgente si tiene uno de estos problemas:

1. La dificultad para respirar, la tos o la falta[12] de respiración aumenta después de tomar la medicina.
2. Es muy difícil respirar.
3. Es difícil caminar[13] o hablar.
4. El nivel[14] de respiración es bajo[15] o no mejora después de tomar la medicina o el nivel baja al 50 por ciento de su nivel normal.
5. Los labios[16] y las uñas[17] se ponen[18] grises o azules. Si esto pasa, debe ir a la sala de emergencia o llamar al 911 inmediatamente.

[1] *breathing*
[2] *to breathe*
[3] *dust*
[4] *mold*
[5] *changes*
[6] *smoke*
[7] *pressure*
[8] *Avoid*
[9] *cotton*
[10] *foam*
[11] *covers*
[12] *lack*
[13] *walk*
[14] *level*
[15] *low*
[16] *lips*
[17] *fingernails*
[18] *turn*

Nombre ______________________ Sección ______________ Fecha ______________

Conversaciones

1-12 —Doctor, mi hijo muchas veces tiene tos y dificultad para respirar. ¿Tiene asma?
—Es muy posible, señora.
—Tiene muchos problemas cuando está resfriado o tiene gripe o cuando hay cambios en el clima.
—Sí. También es necesario evitar el polvo, el humo y el moho.

1-13 —¿Qué debo hacer para controlar el asma?
—Es necesario evitar el humo, controlar el polvo y usar almohadas de algodón o de espuma.
—¿Necesito usar un inhalador?
—Sí, y también debe tomar esta medicina.

1-14 —¿Cuándo debo llevar a mi hijo a la sala de emergencia?
—Si los labios se ponen grises o azules.
—¿Es mejor llamar al 911?
—Sí, inmediatamente.

Dígame... Answer the following questions, basing your answers on the reading and the conversations.

1. ¿Qué es el asma?

____

2. ¿Cuáles son dos síntomas del asma?

____

3. ¿Qué debe controlar una persona que tiene asma?

____

4. ¿Qué tipo de almohadas debe usar?

____

5. ¿Con qué debe cubrir las camas y las almohadas?

____

6. Además de tomar la medicina, ¿qué debe usar?

____

7. ¿Qué debemos hacer si los labios y las uñas de una persona asmática se ponen grises o azules?

____

Con el ginecólogo

Objectives

Structures

- The irregular verbs **tener** and **venir**
- Expressions with **tener**
- Comparative forms
- Irregular comparative forms

Communication

- In a gynecologist's office

Con el ginecólogo

1–15

Estamos en el mes de marzo. La Sra. Soto no tiene menstruación desde enero y va al consultorio del Dr. Aranda. El Dr. Aranda es ginecólogo.

Con el Dr. Aranda:

Sra. Soto —Creo que estoy embarazada, doctor; no tengo la regla desde enero.
Dr. Aranda —Vamos a ver. ¿Tiene dolor en los senos? ¿Están duros o inflamados?
Sra. Soto —Sí, doctor, y están más grandes. También tengo los tobillos muy hinchados.
Dr. Aranda —¿Tiene mareos o náusea?
Sra. Soto —Sí, todas las mañanas, y siempre estoy cansada y tengo sueño. Estoy débil.
Dr. Aranda —Quizás tiene anemia. ¿Tiene dolores?
Sra. Soto —Sí, tengo mucho dolor de espalda, y también tengo dolor durante las relaciones sexuales.
Dr. Aranda —¿Orina con frecuencia?
Sra. Soto —Sí, con mucha frecuencia.
Dr. Aranda —¿Algún[1] malparto o aborto?
Sra. Soto —No, ninguno.

---

[1]The **o** in **alguno** or **ninguno** is dropped before a masculine singular noun.

El doctor examina a la paciente.

Dr. Aranda —Ud. tiene todos los síntomas de estar embarazada, pero necesitamos unos análisis para estar seguros.
Sra. Soto —Muy bien.
Dr. Aranda —Ahora Ud. tiene que comer bien, descansar y evitar los trabajos pesados. No debe fumar ni tomar bebidas alcohólicas.
Sra. Soto —Yo no bebo, pero fumo mucho.
Dr. Aranda —Tiene que dejar de fumar.
Sra. Soto —¿Por qué?
Dr. Aranda —Porque es malo para el bebé y para Ud. también.
Sra. Soto —Tiene razón, doctor. Debo dejar de fumar.

1–15

¡Escuchemos! While listening to the dialogue, circle **V (verdadero)** if the statement is true or **F (falso)** if it is false.

1. La Sra. Soto va al pediatra.
2. La Sra. Soto no tiene menstruación desde enero.
3. La Sra. Soto tiene dolor en los senos.
4. Los tobillos de la Sra. Soto están hinchados.
5. La Sra. Soto tiene dolor de cabeza.
6. La Sra. Soto orina con mucha frecuencia.
7. El Dr. Aranda tiene que evitar los trabajos pesados.
8. La Sra. Soto debe tomar muchas bebidas alcohólicas.
9. La Sra. Soto tiene que dejar de fumar.
10. La Sra. Soto cree que el Dr. Aranda tiene razón.

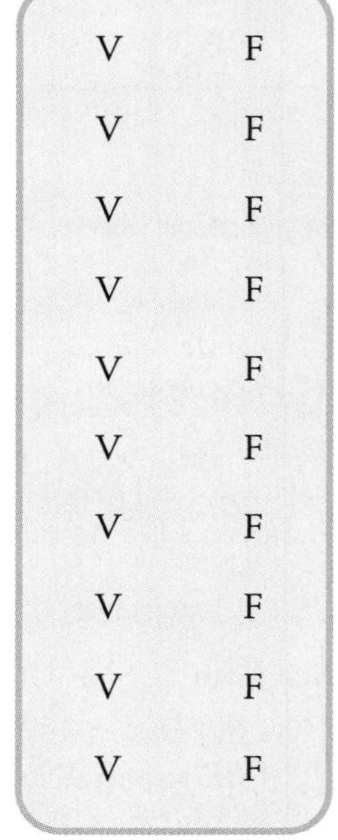

Audio

VOCABULARIO

COGNADOS

el aborto
el síntoma

NOMBRES

el bebé *baby*
la bebida alcohólica *alcoholic beverage*

Nombre ______________________ Sección ____________ Fecha ____________

el malparto, el aborto natural, el aborto espontáneo *miscarriage*
la mañana *morning*
el mareo *dizziness*
el mes *month*
la regla, la menstruación, el periodo *menstruation*
las relaciones sexuales[1] *sexual relations, sex*
los senos, los pechos *breasts*
el tobillo *ankle*
el trabajo *work*

VERBOS

descansar *to rest*
examinar, reconocer[2] *to examine*
tener *to have*

ADJETIVOS

débil *weak*
duro(a) *hard*
embarazada, encinta[3] *pregnant*
grande *big*
inflamado(a), hinchado(a) *swollen*
malo(a) *bad*
pesado(a) *heavy*
seguro(a) *sure*

OTRAS PALABRAS Y EXPRESIONES

con frecuencia *frequently*
dejar de *to stop (doing something)*
desde *since*
durante *during*
más *more*
ni *neither, nor*
ninguno(a) *not a one, none*
¿por qué? *why?*
porque *because*
tener dolor *to be in pain*
tener dolor de espalda *to have a backache*
tener que + ***infinitivo*** *to have to + infinitive*
tener razón *to be right*
tener sueño *to be sleepy*
todo(a) *all*
vamos a ver *let's see*

VOCABULARIO ADICIONAL

OTROS ESPECIALISTAS

el (la) endocrinólogo(a) *endocrinologist*
el (la) especialista de garganta, nariz y oídos; el (la) otorrinolaringólogo(a) *throat, nose, and ear specialist*
el (la) especialista de la piel, el (la) dermatólogo(a) *dermatologist*
el (la) geriatra *geriatrician, geriatrist*
el (la) internista *internist*
el (la) obstetra *obstetrician*
el (la) oculista *oculist*
el (la) oftalmólogo(a) *ophthalmologist*
el (la) oncólogo(a) *oncologist*
el (la) ortopeda, el (la) ortopedista *orthopedist*
el (la) podiatra *podiatrist*
el (la) psiquiatra *psychiatrist*
el (la) pulmonólogo(a) *pulmonologist*
el (la) radiólogo(a) *radiologist*
el (la) urólogo(a) *urologist*

---

[1] **Tener relaciones sexuales, acostarse con** = *to have sex*
[2] Irregular first person: **yo reconozco**
[3] Colloquialism: **preñada, en estado** (*Cuba*)

Nombre ______________________ Sección ____________ Fecha ____________

NOTAS CULTURALES

Search

- Like most women, many Latina females may feel uncomfortable or embarrassed discussing matters of sex and reproduction, especially with a male doctor. This reaction may be due in part to cultural taboos, the patient's level of education, or both. In some cultures, it is not possible or it is considered socially unacceptable to talk about any aspect of sexuality. Therefore, it is important to be sensitive and diplomatic when dealing with these topics.
- A 1998 National Center for Health Statistics study shows the following trends regarding births of Hispanic American origin and maternal healthcare between 1989 and 1995:

The fertility rate of Hispanic American women continues to be higher than that of non-Hispanic American women. Mexican American women account for 70 percent of all births of Hispanic American origin.

In the six-year period, there was a major increase (19 percent) in timely prenatal care for Hispanic American women. However, just over 70 percent of Latina women began prenatal care in the first trimester of pregnancy, compared to 87 percent of non-Hispanic white women.

The low-birth weight rate of Latino infants is 6.3 percent. This rate varies significantly among the subgroups of Hispanic Americans: from 5.8 percent for Mexican Americans to 9.4 percent for Puerto Ricans.

Cesarean delivery rates vary considerably among the subgroups of Hispanic American women: from 20 percent (Mexican American) to 30 percent (Cuban American). The rate for Cuban American women is decreasing, but it is still higher than the national average (21 percent).

Actividades

Dígame... Answer the following questions, basing your answers on the dialogue.

1. ¿Por qué va la Sra. Soto al consultorio del Dr. Aranda?

____

2. ¿Desde qué mes no tiene la menstruación la Sra. Soto?

____

3. ¿Tiene dolor en los senos? ¿Qué otros problemas tiene?

____

4. ¿Qué tiene la Sra. Soto todas las mañanas?

____

5. ¿Qué otros síntomas tiene ella?

____

6. ¿Tiene ella dolores durante las relaciones sexuales?

____

7. ¿Qué necesitan para estar seguros de que la señora está embarazada?

____

8. ¿Qué tiene que hacer (*do*) ella?

____

9. ¿Qué no debe hacer la Sra. Soto?

____

10. ¿Por qué tiene que dejar de fumar?

____

Hablemos Interview a classmate, using the following questions. When you have finished, switch roles.

1. ¿Tiene Ud. los tobillos hinchados?
2. ¿Tiene Ud. mareos o náusea?
3. ¿Está Ud. cansado(a)? ¿Débil?
4. ¿Tiene Ud. dolor de espalda?
5. ¿Orina Ud. con frecuencia?
6. ¿Toma Ud. bebidas alcohólicas?
7. Yo creo que es malo fumar. ¿Tengo razón o no?
8. ¿Es fácil (*easy*) dejar de fumar?
9. Si una mujer (*woman*) está embarazada, ¿qué síntomas tiene?
10. Estoy muy cansado(a). ¿Qué tengo que hacer (*do*)?

Nombre ______________________ Sección ____________ Fecha ____________

Vamos a practicar

A Write two comparative or superlative statements for each situation.

MODELO Raquel pesa 140 libras, Alicia pesa 120 libras y Silvia pesa 110 libras.
(a) Alicia es más delgada que Raquel.
(b) Silvia es la más delgada de las tres.

1. La temperatura de José es de noventa y nueve grados pero la temperatura de Rosa es de más de ciento dos grados.

(a) ______________________________

(b) ______________________________

2. Mi bebé pesa siete libras, el bebé de Ana pesa ocho libras y el bebé de Carmen pesa nueve libras.

(a) ______________________________

(b) ______________________________

3. Alfredo tiene once años, María tiene trece años y Miguel tiene dieciséis años.

(a) ______________________________

(b) ______________________________

4. La Clínica La Cruz Azul tiene diez doctores y la Clínica Alvarado tiene tres doctores.

(a) ______________________________

(b) ______________________________

B Complete the following dialogues with the Spanish equivalent of the words in parentheses.

1. —¿____________ al ginecólogo frecuentemente? (*Does Mrs. Aguilera come*)

—Sí, ella ____________ frecuentemente. (*has to come*)

2. —Ud. tiene que ____________, Sr. Carreras. (*to stop smoking*)

—Ud. ____________, doctor. (*are right*)

3. —¿Estás ____________, Anita? (*tired*)

—Sí, y ____________. (*I'm very sleepy*)

Nombre ______________________ Sección ____________ Fecha ____________

Conversaciones breves

Complete the following dialogue, using your imagination and the vocabulary from this lesson.

La Sra. Peña y el ginecólogo:

Doctor —¿Desde cuándo no tiene la menstruación?

Sra. Peña —______________________

Doctor —¿Tiene los tobillos hinchados? ¿Tiene mareos por la mañana?

Sra. Peña —______________________

Doctor —¿Tiene dolor de espalda?

Sra. Peña —______________________

Doctor —¿Tiene otros dolores?

Sra. Peña —______________________

Doctor —¿Orina con frecuencia?

Sra. Peña —______________________

Doctor —¿Algún aborto o malparto?

Sra. Peña —______________________

En estas situaciones

What would you say in the following situations? What might the other person say?

1. You are the doctor and your patient thinks she is pregnant. Ask her if her breasts are swollen or hard, and if she feels dizzy or nauseated in the morning.
2. You are the patient. Tell your doctor that you are always tired and weak, and that you feel (have) a great deal of pain during sexual intercourse. Also tell your doctor that you urinate frequently.
3. You are a nurse. Tell your patient that he/she must eat well and avoid heavy work. Advise him/her to stop smoking and to not drink alcoholic beverages.

Casos

Act out the following scenarios with a partner.

1. You are a doctor and one of your patients thinks she is pregnant.
2. You are a doctor and have to give instructions to a pregnant patient about what she must and must not do.
3. You are serving as an interpreter for a Spanish-speaking person who is pregnant. Tell the doctor her symptoms.

Nombre ______________________ Sección ______________ Fecha ______________

Un paso más

A Review the **Vocabulario adicional** in this lesson. Which specialist would you consult if you had the following medical conditions?

1. a fracture ______________________
2. frequent chest pains ______________________
3. a recurrent ear infection ______________________
4. blurred vision ______________________
5. a large kidney stone ______________________
6. cancer ______________________
7. a severe case of depression ______________________
8. a severely ingrown toenail ______________________
9. a bad case of acne ______________________

B Read the instructions for pregnant women on the following page. Then write all of the Spanish words or phrases that are cognates and their English meanings.

ESPAÑOL	INGLÉS
______________________	______________________
______________________	______________________
______________________	______________________
______________________	______________________
______________________	______________________
______________________	______________________
______________________	______________________
______________________	______________________
______________________	______________________
______________________	______________________
______________________	______________________
______________________	______________________
______________________	______________________
______________________	______________________
______________________	______________________

Nombre ____________________ **Sección** ____________ **Fecha** ____________

ESPAÑOL	INGLÉS
____________________	____________________
____________________	____________________
____________________	____________________
____________________	____________________
____________________	____________________
____________________	____________________

INSTRUCCIONES PARA MUJERES EMBARAZADAS

Si le ocurre lo siguiente,[1] debe llamar a su doctor.

- Hemorragia vaginal
- Contracciones regulares cada diez minutos o menos durante dos horas
- Flujo sanguíneo color rojo vivo o coágulos de sangre de la vagina (*Es normal que sangre un poco después de tener relaciones sexuales o después de un examen vaginal.*)
- Fiebre alta de más de 100.4°F o 38°C
- Dificultad o dolor al orinar
- Una disminución marcada del movimiento del feto o ningún movimiento fetal en 24 horas
- Vómitos frecuentes durante 48 horas
- Dolor de cabeza severo y persistente, vista borrosa,[2] acidez estomacal o hinchazón[3] de los tobillos, los pies o la cara.[4]

LA DIETA

Las necesidades nutritivas diarias durante el embarazo:

leche..3 vasos[5] de 8 onzas
carne[6]..6 onzas o más
pan..4 o más porciones
frutas y vegetales............................4 o más porciones

[1] **Si...** *If the following happens to you*
[2] **vista...** *blurred vision*
[3] *swelling*
[4] *face*
[5] *glasses*
[6] *meat*

EN EL CONSULTORIO DEL PEDIATRA (II)

OBJECTIVES

Structures

- Stem-changing verbs **(e:ie)**
- Some uses of the definite article
- The present progressive
- Ordinal numbers

Communication

- More on children's health

EN EL CONSULTORIO DEL PEDIATRA (II)

1–16 La Sra. Gómez lleva a su hija a la clínica. La niña tiene diarrea, una temperatura de 102 grados y las nalgas muy irritadas. Ahora la señora está hablando con la enfermera.

Enfermera —¿La niña está vacunada contra la difteria, la tos ferina y el tétano?

Sra. Gómez —No... ¿es necesario todo eso?

Enfermera: —Sí, señora, es muy importante. ¿Y contra la poliomielitis?

Sra. Gómez —No, no...

Enfermera —Bueno, la semana próxima vamos a vacunar a su hija contra la difteria, la tos ferina y el tétano.

Sra. Gómez —¿Todo junto?

Enfermera —Sí, es una vacuna contra las tres enfermedades. Más adelante vamos a vacunar a la niña contra las paperas, el sarampión y la rubéola.

Sra. Gómez —Está bien.

Enfermera —También vamos a hacer una prueba de tuberculina.

Sra. Gómez —¿Para qué es eso?

Enfermera —Para ver si hay tuberculosis. Es sólo una precaución. No se preocupe.

Sra. Gómez —Muy bien... ¡Ah! La niña tiene sarpullido en las nalgas. ¿La vaselina es buena para eso?

Enfermera —Si hay diarrea, lo mejor es limpiar a la niña en seguida y cubrir la piel con un ungüento especial. ¡Ah! Aquí está el doctor Vivar.

Con el Dr. Vivar:

Sra. Gómez —Mi hija tiene mucha diarrea, doctor, y en estos días está comiendo muy poco.
Dr. Vivar —¿Hay pus o sangre en el excremento?
Sra. Gómez —Creo que no... Pero tiene mucha fiebre.
Dr. Vivar —(*Revisa a la niña.*) Tiene una infección en el oído. Voy a recetar Kaopectate para la diarrea, unas gotas para el oído y un antibiótico para la infección.
Sra. Gómez —Muy bien.
Dr. Vivar —La niña está deshidratada. Déle Pedialyte.
Sra. Gómez —Sí, doctor. ¿Cuándo debemos regresar?
Dr. Vivar —Si todavía hay fiebre, quiero ver a la niña mañana por la tarde. Si no, la semana que viene.

Con la recepcionista:

Sra. Gómez —Quiero pedir turno para la semana próxima, por favor.
Recepcionista —A ver... ¿El miércoles, primero de mayo a las diez y veinte está bien?
Sra. Gómez —Prefiero venir por la tarde, si es posible. ¿A qué hora cierran?
Recepcionista —A las cinco. ¿Quiere venir a las tres y media?
Sra. Gómez —Sí. Muchas gracias.

1-16

¡Escuchemos! While listening to the dialogue, circle **V (verdadero)** if the statement is true or **F (falso)** if it is false.

1. La Sra. Gómez está hablando con la enfermera.
2. Tienen que vacunar a la hija de la señora contra la difteria, la tos ferina y el tétano.
3. La prueba de tuberculina es para ver si hay sarampión.
4. La niña tiene sarpullido en las nalgas.
5. La niña no tiene fiebre.
6. La niña tiene una infección en el oído.
7. El Dr. Vivar receta un ungüento especial para el oído.
8. El Dr. no receta un antibiótico.
9. Un problema que tiene la niña es que está deshidratada.
10. Si hay fiebre, el doctor quiere ver a la niña la semana que viene.

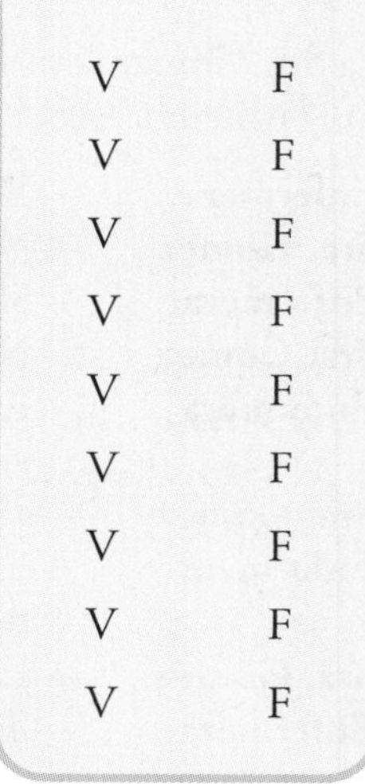

Nombre ______________________ Sección ____________ Fecha ____________

Audio

VOCABULARIO

COGNADOS

la clínica
deshidratado(a)
la diarrea
la difteria
especial
importante
la infección
irritado(a)
necesario(a)
la poliomielitis
la precaución
el pus, la supuración
el tétano, el tétanos
la tuberculina
la tuberculosis
la vaselina

NOMBRES

la enfermedad *disease, sickness*
la gota *drop*
las nalgas, las asentaderas *buttocks*
las paperas, las farfallotas (*Puerto Rican colloquialism*) *mumps*
la piel *skin*
el (la) primero(a) *first one*
la prueba *test*
la rubéola *rubella*
el sarampión *measles*
el sarpullido, el salpullido *rash*
la tos ferina *whooping cough, pertussis*
el turno, la cita *appointment*
el ungüento, la pomada *ointment*

VERBOS

cerrar (e:ie) *to close*
cubrir *to cover*
hacer (yo hago) *to do, to make*
limpiar *to clean*
preferir (e:ie) *to prefer*
querer (e:ie) *to want, to wish*
recetar *to prescribe*
revisar, chequear *to check*
vacunar *to vaccinate*
venir *to come*
ver (yo veo) *to see*

ADJETIVOS

junto(a) *together*
vacunado(a) *vaccinated*

OTRAS PALABRAS Y EXPRESIONES

¿a qué hora...? *(at) what time...?*
contra *against*
Creo que no. *I don't think so.*
en estos días *these days, lately*
en seguida *right away*
lo mejor *the best (thing)*
más adelante *later on*
No se preocupe. *Don't worry.*
¿para qué...? *what... for?*
pedir turno, pedir hora *to make an appointment*
la próxima vez *next time*
la semana que viene, la semana próxima, la semana entrante *next week*
todo eso *all that*

Nombre ______________________ Sección ____________ Fecha ____________

VOCABULARIO ADICIONAL

ALGUNAS ENFERMEDADES COMUNES Y OTROS PROBLEMAS

la alergia *allergy*
la amigdalitis, la infección de la garganta *tonsilitis*
el aneurisma *aneurysm, aneurism*
las ampollas *blisters*
la apendicitis *appendicitis*
la artritis *arthritis*
el cólico *colic*
la colitis, la inflamación del intestino grueso *colitis*
la conjuntivitis *conjunctivitis*
las convulsiones *convulsions*
el crup, el garrotillo *croup*
el eccema *eczema*
la endometriosis *endometriosis*
los escalofríos *chills*
la fiebre del heno *hay fever*
la fiebre escarlatina *scarlet fever*
la fiebre reumática *rheumatic fever*
la gastritis *gastritis*
la gripe[1] *influenza*
la insolación *sunstroke*
la intoxicación *intoxication*
la(s) jaqueca(s), la migraña *migraine*
la laringitis *laryngitis*
la leucemia *leukemia*
la meningitis *meningitis*
el orzuelo *sty*
la pulmonía, la pneumonía *pneumonia*
el reumatismo *rheumatism*
la sarna *scabies*
la urticaria *hives*
la varicela *chickenpox*
la viruela *smallpox*

NOTAS CULTURALES

- According to the National Institute of Allergy and Infectious Diseases, asthma is a growing concern in the U.S., particularly in inner-city African American and Latino communities. Several factors contribute to the disproportionate rates among African Americans and Latinos at risk of having a severe asthma attack or of dying from asthma: poverty, substandard housing that results in increased exposure to certain indoor allergens, inadequate access to health care, and the failure to take appropriate medications.
- Due to general poverty, the number of children without vaccinations is still a serious problem in some Spanish-speaking countries. In addition, some people may have misconceptions about vaccinations. For example, they may believe that as a result of vaccinations certain diseases such as polio, diphtheria, and whooping cough have been eradicated or that it is not necessary to vaccinate a child until he/she is of school age. Moreover, some Hispanic Americans, particularly those who are migrant workers, find it difficult to maintain vaccination schedules because they are constantly moving their place of residence. In these situations, parents should be informed of the importance of each type of vaccination, and they should be encouraged to keep a written record of their child's vaccinations.

---

[1]Colloquialism: **la monga** (*Puerto Rico*)

Nombre ______________________ Sección ____________ Fecha ____________

- The Office of Hispanic Affairs of the Chicago Department of Public Health found that a percentage of the Chicago Hispanic population uses mercury for religious and domestic purposes and as a form of folk medicine (press release 9/27/2000). Mercury is used in creams or candles. It can be ingested or sprinkled in children's cribs or throughout the home for good luck, to rid the house of bad spirits, or to treat nervousness or alcoholism.

Actividades

Dígame... Answer the following questions, basing your answers on the dialogues.

1. ¿Qué problemas tiene la hija de la Sra. Gómez?

____

2. ¿Contra qué enfermedades van a vacunar a la niña la próxima vez? ¿Y más adelante?

____

3. ¿Para qué es la prueba de tuberculina?

____

4. Si hay diarrea, ¿qué es lo mejor?

____

5. ¿La niña está comiendo bien en estos días?

____

6. ¿Qué va a recetar el doctor Vivar?

____

7. ¿Por qué debe tomar Pedialyte la niña?

____

8. Si la fiebre no baja, ¿cuándo quiere ver el doctor a la niña?

____

9. ¿Para qué día es el turno de la Sra. Gómez?

____

10. ¿A qué hora prefiere venir la Sra. Gómez?

____

Nombre ______________________ **Sección** ____________ **Fecha** ____________

Hablemos Interview a classmate, using the following questions. When you have finished, switch roles.

1. ¿Qué quiere comer Ud.?
2. Para el desayuno, ¿prefiere Ud. comer fruta o cereal?
3. ¿Tiene Ud. turno para ver al médico? ¿Cuándo?
4. ¿Qué toma Ud. cuando tiene diarrea?
5. ¿Es importante vacunar a los niños contra la poliomielitis?
6. ¿Contra qué enfermedades está vacunado(a) Ud.?
7. Tengo 102 grados de fiebre. ¿Qué debo hacer?
8. Tengo una infección en el oído. ¿Qué cree Ud. que me va a recetar el doctor?
9. ¿Qué toma Ud. si está deshidratado(a)?
10. ¿Qué debo hacer si un niño tiene las nalgas irritadas?

Vamos a practicar

A Complete the following sentences, using the present progressive of the verbs given.

Modelo Luis __________ (comer).
Luis **está comiendo.**

1. La enfermera ______________________ (hablar) con el médico.
2. ¿Tú ______________________ (leer) la hoja clínica?
3. Nosotros ______________________ (vacunar) a los niños.
4. Ellos ______________________ (beber) jugo de naranja.
5. Yo ______________________ (examinar) al paciente.

Nombre ______________________ Sección ____________ Fecha ____________

B Give the Spanish equivalent of the words in parentheses.

1. —¿Cuándo ____________ a mi hija? (*do you want to see*)
   —Necesita ____________ para la semana entrante. (*make an appointment*)
2. —¿Tú ____________ al hospital mañana? (*want to go*)
   —No, ____________ hoy. (*I prefer to go*)
3. —¿A qué hora ____________ hoy? (*do you close*)
   —Los lunes nosotros ____________ a las seis. (*close*)

Conversaciones breves

Complete the following dialogues, using your imagination and the vocabulary from this lesson.

A La enfermera y la madre de un paciente:

Enfermera —____

Sra. Ruiz —Sí, el niño está vacunado contra esas tres enfermedades.

Enfermera —____

Sra. Ruiz —No, no está vacunado contra la poliomielitis.

Enfermera —____

Sra. Ruiz —¿Una prueba de tuberculina? ¿Para qué es eso?

Enfermera —____

B El doctor y la madre de una paciente:

Sra. Rojas —Mi hija tiene las nalgas muy irritadas. ¿Qué debo hacer?

Doctor —____

Sra. Rojas —¿Cuándo tengo que regresar?

Doctor —____

Nombre ______________________ Sección ____________ Fecha ____________

En estas situaciones

What would you say in the following situations? What might the other person say?

1. You are a doctor. Tell your patient that he/she has an ear infection and prescribe the proper medication.
2. You are a patient. Make an appointment with the receptionist to see the doctor on July 2 at two-thirty in the afternoon.
3. You are a nurse. Tell a patient that you are going to do a tuberculin test and explain its purpose. Then tell the patient that you want to see him/her in forty-eight hours to check the test.

Casos

Act out the following scenarios with a partner.

1. A pediatrician and a parent confer about a child who has the following symptoms: diarrhea, a rash on the buttocks, and a high temperature.
2. A nurse and a parent discuss a child's vaccination record. Use the immunization record on page 64 as a basis for your conversation.

Un paso más

A Review the **Vocabulario adicional** in this lesson. Then work with a partner to classify all the medical conditions named in the **Vocabulario adicional** list according to whether they are related to the skin, the blood, the bones, the eyes, etc. Also write the type of doctor or specialist to whom you would refer a patient who has each condition.

Los huesos (*Bones*)

____________________ ____________________

Especialista: ____

Los ojos (*Eyes*)

______________ ______________ ______________

Especialista: ____

La piel

____________________ ____________________

____________________ ____________________

____________________ ____________________

Especialista: ____

Nombre ______________________ Sección ____________ Fecha ____________

El aparato respiratorio (*Respiratory system*)

______________________ ______________________
______________________ ______________________
______________________ ______________________
______________________ ______________________

Especialista: ______________________

El sistema nervioso (*Nervous system*)

______________________ ______________________
______________________ ______________________
______________________ ______________________

Especialista: ______________________

La sangre

______________ ______________ ______________

Especialista: ______________________

B Read the following information from a brochure that was published as part of the National Campaign of Immunization to educate people in the United States about the need for vaccinations. Remember to guess the meaning of the cognates.

Algunas vacunas protegen[1] contra más de una enfermedad, pero su niño necesita todas las siguientes vacunas para mantenerse saludable.

- **M-M-R** *Lo protege contra el sarampión, las paperas y la rubéola.*
- **Vacuna de polio** *Lo protege contra la poliomielitis.*
- **DTP** *Lo protege contra la difteria, el tétano y la pertusis* (tos ferina).
- **Hib** *Lo protege contra "haemophilus influenzae" tipo b, una de las causas principales de la meningitis.*
- **Hepatitis B** *Lo protege contra infecciones del hígado,[2] una de las causas de la cirrosis y del cáncer del hígado.*

A los dos años de edad, su niño debe haber recibido[3] las siguientes vacunas.

- 1 vacuna contra el sarampión
- 4 vacunas contra la difteria, el tétano y la pertusis (tos ferina)
- 3 vacunas contra la Hepatitis B
- 3-4 vacunas contra el "haemophilus influenzae b"

---

[1] *protect*
[2] *liver*
[3] ***haber...*** *have received*

Nombre ______________________ Sección ______________ Fecha ______________

C With a partner, discuss at what age(s) the vaccinations listed are normally administered to children. Then write the information so it can be distributed to your Spanish-speaking patients.

____

____

____

____

____

____

____

____

____

____

____

____

____

Nombre ______________________ Sección ____________ Fecha ____________

RÉCORD DE INMUNIZACIONES (Vacunas)

Paciente: ______________________ **Fecha de nacimiento:** ______________________

Inmunizaciones

Vacuna contra la viruela ______________________

Fecha

Resultados

❑ Prendió[1] ❑ No prendió ❑ Contraindicado

Firma del doctor

Revacunación contra la viruela ______________________

Fecha

Resultados

❑ Prendió ❑ No prendió ❑ Contraindicado

Firma del doctor

Difteria, tos ferina, tétano

Tratamiento[2]	Fecha	Dosis	Firma del doctor
1a Dosis			
2a Dosis			
3a Dosis			
1a Reacción			
2a Reacción			
3a Reacción			

Poliomielitis

Tratamiento	Tipo usado	Dosis	Fecha	Firma del doctor
1a Dosis				
2a Dosis				
3a Dosis				
1a Reacción				
2a Reacción				
3a Reacción				

Otras inmunizaciones o pruebas

Nombre	Fecha	Resultado	Firma del doctor

Enfermedades y fechas

Tos ferina ____________ Paperas ____________

Rubéola ____________ Sarampión ____________

Varicela ____________ Difteria ____________

Escarlatina ____________ Poliomielitis ____________

Accidentes (dar fechas y especificar) ______________________

Impedimentos y anomalías (especificar) ______________________

Otras enfermedades (especificar) ______________________

Operaciones (especificar) ______________________

Defectos de los sentidos[3] (especificar) ______________________

---

[1] *It reacted*
[2] *Treatment*
[3] *senses*

Nombre ______________________________ Sección ______________ Fecha ______________

Lecciones 1-5 Repaso

Práctica de vocabulario

A Circle the word or phrase that best completes each sentence.

1. El doctor receta (gotas / pus / tostadas) para el oído.
2. Fumo una (frazada/ cajetilla / almohada) al día.
3. Voy a orinar. Necesito (la chata / la mantequilla / la dentadura postiza).
4. Mañana, para el desayuno, deseo sólo (receta / planilla / cereal).
5. Deseo beber (pastilla / agua / pollo).
6. La enfermera mira la hoja (clínica / aventada / estreñida).
7. Tose mucho. Necesita tomar (sangre / letra / jarabe) para la tos.
8. Para ver si es anémico, necesitamos un análisis de (materia fecal / orina / sangre).
9. Ella sufre, pero yo sufro (también / todavía / bueno).
10. El catarro es una (enfermedad / pulgada / clínica).
11. No ve bien. Necesita (anteojos / fotocopias / calentura).
12. Yo pago (la cuenta / la letra de imprenta / la rubéola).
13. ¿Tiene Ud. su (segundo nombre / firma / tarjeta) de seguro médico?
14. En caso de (emergencia / comida / seguro social), debe llamar a mi esposo.
15. Mi mamá (entra / llena / cubre) la planilla.

B Circle the word or phrase that does not belong in each group.

1. la próxima vez la semana que viene ahora
2. aceite mineral tarjeta ungüento
3. póliza análisis muestra
4. compañía de seguro póliza almohada
5. antibiótico cuarto penicilina
6. evitar dormir descansar
7. a menudo con frecuencia tanto
8. cajetilla comida cigarrillo
9. por qué para qué cuánto
10. trabajo senos tobillos
11. mareo náusea espalda
12. poco mucho quizá
13. desear querer dar
14. ahora mismo al rato después
15. diarrea tétano excremento
16. pies pulgadas ninguno
17. taza sarpullido piel
18. estar cansado tener sueño llamar
19. ahora en esos días adónde
20. laboratorio cucharadita orden

Nombre ________________ Sección ________ Fecha ________

C Match the questions in column **A** with the answers in column **B.**

A		B
1. ¿No quiere comer?	______	a. Sí, voy a usar un ungüento especial.
2. ¿Cuánto mide?	______	b. La planilla.
3. ¿Cuál es su ocupación?	______	c. Sí, tiene una temperatura de 102 grados.
4. ¿Cuándo debo tomar las cápsulas?	______	d. No, va a tener un aborto.
5. ¿Eva tiene fiebre todavía?	______	e. No, de orina.
6. ¿Tiene las nalgas irritadas?	______	f. Dos de mayo de 1985.
7. ¿No va a tener el bebé?	______	g. No, de uvas.
8. ¿Cuál es su estado civil?	______	h. Soy médica.
9. ¿Quién paga la cuenta?	______	i. Tengo turno para la semana entrante.
10. ¿Cuál es su fecha de nacimiento?	______	j. Sí, voy a tomar Tylenol.
11. ¿Cuánto pesa?	______	k. A las cinco.
12. ¿Desea jugo de naranja?	______	l. En su consultorio.
13. ¿Qué debo llenar?	______	m. No, no tiene apetito.
14. ¿Quieres un cigarrillo?	______	n. Sí, necesita un dermatólogo.
15. ¿Tienes dolor de cabeza?	______	o. Ciento cincuenta libras.
16. ¿Dónde está el médico?	______	p. El seguro.
17. ¿Necesita un análisis de materia fecal?	______	q. Después de las comidas.
18. ¿Tiene eccema?	______	r. Cinco pies, dos pulgadas.
19. ¿Cuándo regresas?	______	s. No, gracias. No fumo.
20. ¿A qué hora cierran?	______	t. Soy casado.

D **¿Verdadero o falso?** Read each statement and decide if it is true **(V)** or false **(F).**

______ 1. Es importante tomar precauciones.

______ 2. Tiene una temperatura de noventa y ocho grados. Es muy alta.

______ 3. Estoy un poco acatarrado. Eso es muy grave.

______ 4. Si está aventado, debe tomar mucho líquido y descansar.

______ 5. Algunas personas son alérgicas a la penicilina.

______ 6. Aquí está la hoja clínica. Tiene información sobre el paciente.

Nombre ______________________ Sección ____________ Fecha ____________

_________ **7.** Lo mejor es no dejar de fumar.

_________ **8.** Si está embarazada, debe evitar los trabajos pesados y las bebidas alcohólicas.

_________ **9.** Como tengo una infección, necesito un postre.

_________ **10.** Cada vez que un niño come algo, debemos llamar al médico.

_________ **11.** El Sr. Vega no tiene la menstruación desde enero.

_________ **12.** Quiero agua porque tengo mucha hambre.

_________ **13.** El doctor receta jarabe para la tos.

_________ **14.** Los niños deben ser vacunados contra la poliomielitis.

_________ **15.** El niño tiene dolor de cabeza. Debe usar aceite mineral.

_________ **16.** Hacen las radiografías en la sala de espera.

_________ **17.** Más adelante vamos a vacunar a la niña contra las paperas, la rubéola y el sarampión.

_________ **18.** El médico va a recetar Kaopectate para la tos ferina.

E Crucigrama

Across

1. con frecuencia: a ___________
6. lentes
7. examinar
9. Estoy muy nerviosa. Necesito un ___________.
10. luego
12. ungüento
15. pastilla para el dolor
20. garrotillo
22. especialista de garganta, nariz y oído
24. ¿Tiene su tarjeta de ___________ médico?
28. resfriado
29. vomitar
30. pneumonía
31. calentura
32. inflamación del intestino grueso
33. penicilina (por ejemplo)

Down

2. Usa ___________ postiza.
3. pan tostado
4. remedio
5. *measles* (en español)
8. especialista de la piel
11. Tengo que llenar la ___________.
13. *blisters* (en español)
14. embarazada
16. cita
17. pechos
18. esposo
19. inflamado
21. cobija
23. aborto natural
25. opuesto de **frío**
26. migraña
27. melocotón

Nombre ______________________ **Sección** __________ **Fecha** __________

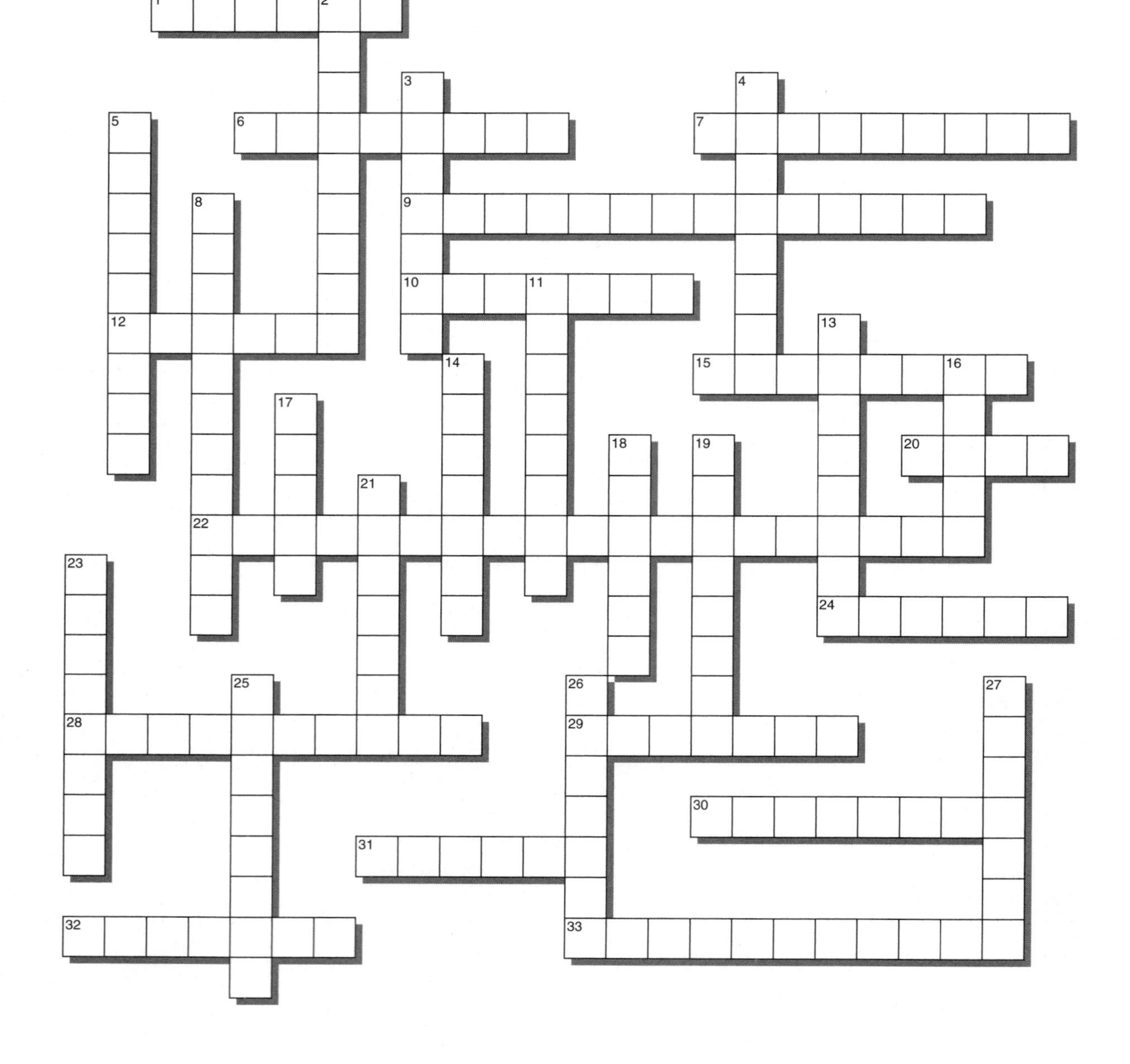

Nombre ______________________ Sección ____________ Fecha ____________

Práctica oral

1–17 Listen to the following exercise on the audio program. The speaker will ask you some questions. Answer the questions, using the cues provided. The speaker will verify the correct answer. Repeat the correct answer.

1–18

1. ¿Es Ud. de Arizona? (no, de California)
2. ¿Cuánto mide Ud.? (cinco pies, ocho pulgadas)
3. ¿Cuánto pesa Ud.? (ciento cincuenta libras)
4. ¿Ud. tiene seguro médico? (sí)
5. ¿Usa Ud. anteojos? (no, lentes de contacto)
6. ¿Su hijo es alérgico a alguna medicina? (sí, a la penicilina)
7. ¿Con quién necesita hablar Ud.? (con el médico)
8. ¿Su médico es el Dr. Ruiz? (no, el Dr. Molina)
9. ¿A qué hora debe Ud. regresar a la oficina? (a la una)
10. ¿Qué necesita Ud.? (una planilla)
11. ¿Tiene Ud. dolor de espalda? (no)
12. ¿Tiene Ud. los tobillos hinchados? (sí)
13. ¿Quiere Ud. pedir turno con el médico? (sí)
14. ¿Prefiere ir al médico por la mañana o por la tarde? (por la tarde)
15. ¿A qué hora cierran Uds. el consultorio? (a las cinco y media)
16. ¿Qué necesitan Uds.? (una muestra de orina)
17. Cuando Ud. tiene fiebre, ¿qué toma? (aspirinas)
18. ¿Qué come Ud. cuando tiene hambre? (pollo)
19. ¿Qué desea comer hoy? (cereal y pan tostado)
20. ¿Qué desea beber? (café)
21. ¿Bebe Ud. jugo de naranja? (sí)

Lección 6 Con la dietista

Objectives

Structures

- Stem-changing verbs **(o:ue)**
- Affirmative and negative expressions
- Pronouns as object of a preposition
- Direct object pronouns

Communication

- The importance of diet

Con la dietista

1–19

La Sra. Rivas está hablando con la dietista sobre los problemas de su hijo Ramón.

Dietista —Sra. Rivas, su hijo Ramón necesita perder peso.

Sra. Rivas —Ya lo sé, pero come constantemente, especialmente dulces. Además toma muchos refrescos y nunca toma leche.

Dietista —Si no quiere tomar leche, Ud. puede usar leche descremada en las comidas que prepara para él.

Sra. Rivas —Estoy muy preocupada porque Ramón está muy gordo. Pesa 140 libras y sólo tiene diez años.

Dietista —Tiene que bajar de peso, porque la obesidad es peligrosa.

Sra. Rivas —¿Necesita seguir una dieta estricta? Eso va a ser muy difícil.

Dietista —No estamos hablando de una dieta estricta, pero el niño debe adelgazar porque más tarde puede tener problemas con el corazón.

Sra. Rivas —Yo siempre tengo miedo porque mi padre padece del corazón y mi madre es diabética.

Dietista: —Por eso tiene que tener mucho cuidado. Aquí tengo una lista de alimentos que su hijo debe comer. Es importante tener variedad. Muchos de los alimentos de la lista tienen pocas calorías.

Sra. Rivas —A ver si ahora puede adelgazar en vez de engordar.

Dietista —Tiene que comer por lo menos una cosa de cada grupo, pero en pequeñas cantidades.

Sra. Rivas —¿Tengo que contar las calorías?

Nombre ______________________ Sección ____________ Fecha ____________

Dietista —No, no es necesario contarlas, pero Ramón tiene que hacer ejercicio y comer sólo la mitad de lo que come ahora y, sobre todo, debe evitar comer mucha grasa.
Sra. Rivas —Pero Ramón almuerza en la escuela y generalmente come hamburguesas y papas fritas.
Dietista —Puede comerlas a veces, pero no muy a menudo.
Sra. Rivas —¿Cuándo volvemos?
Dietista —En dos semanas; y aquí tiene la lista de alimentos. Si necesita hablar conmigo me puede llamar por teléfono después de las tres.
Sra. Rivas —Muchas gracias. Si tengo preguntas, la llamo.

GRUPO 1

leche descremada
queso
yogur
margarina (un poco)

GRUPO 2

pescado
pollo
hígado
huevos (blanquillos)
frijoles, habichuelas
mantequilla de cacahuete[1] (maní) (un poco)

GRUPO 3

naranjas
toronjas
chiles (pimientos) verdes y rojos
fresas
melón
repollo, col
bróculi
tomates

GRUPO 4

tortillas
cereal
pan
macarrones
espaguetis
arroz

¡Escuchemos!

While listening to the dialogue, circle **V (verdadero)** if the statement is true or **F (falso)** if it is false.

1. Ramón tiene que adelgazar. V F
2. Ramón debe comer menos. V F
3. Ramón pesa 114 libras. V F
4. Una persona obesa puede tener problemas con el corazón. V F
5. El padre de la Sra. Rivas es diabético. V F

[1] **cacahuate** (*Méx. y Honduras*)

Nombre ______________________ Sección ____________ Fecha ____________

6. La Sra. Rivas padece del corazón.	V	F
7. Ramón necesita hacer ejercicio y comer solamente la mitad de lo que come ahora.	V	F
8. Es necesario comer mucha grasa.	V	F
9. En la escuela, Ramón come pollo.	V	F
10. Si la Sra. Rivas necesita hablar con la dietista, puede llamarla por teléfono.	V	F

Vocabulario

COGNADOS

el bróculi
la caloría
constantemente
diabético(a)
la dieta
los espaguetis
especialmente
estricto(a)
generalmente
el grupo
la hamburguesa
la lista
los macarrones
la margarina
el melón
la obesidad, la gordura
el tomate
la tortilla
la variedad
el yogur

NOMBRES

el alimento *food, nourishment*
el arroz *rice*
la cantidad *quantity*
el chile, el pimiento *pepper*
la cosa *thing*
el dulce *sweet, candy*
la escuela *school*
la fresa *strawberry*
los frijoles, las habichuelas (*Puerto Rico*) *beans*
la grasa *fat*
el hígado *liver*
el huevo, el blanquillo (*Méx.*) *egg*
la leche descremada *skim milk*
la mantequilla de cacahuete (maní) *peanut butter*
la mitad *half*
la naranja *orange*
el padre, el papá *father*
las papas fritas *French fries*
el pescado *fish*
el peso *weight*
la pregunta *question*
el queso *cheese*
el refresco *soft drink, soda pop*
el repollo, la col *cabbage*
la toronja *grapefruit*

VERBOS

adelgazar, rebajar (*Méx.*) *to lose weight*
almorzar (o:ue) *to have lunch*
contar (o:ue) *to count*
engordar[1] *to gain weight*

---

[1]Also: **subir de peso** or **ganar peso**

Nombre ______________________ Sección ______________ Fecha ______________

padecer (yo padezco) *to suffer*
poder (o:ue) *to be able to, can*
preparar *to prepare*
volver (o:ue) *to come (go) back, to return*

ADJETIVOS

difícil *difficult*
gordo(a) *fat*
peligroso(a) *dangerous*
pequeño(a) *small, little*
pocos(as) *few*
preocupado(a) *worried*
rojo(a) *red*
verde *green*

OTRAS PALABRAS Y EXPRESIONES

a veces, algunas veces *sometimes*
además *besides, in addition*
conmigo *with me*
en vez de *instead of*
eso *that*
perder (e:ie) peso, bajar de peso *to lose weight*
hacer ejercicio *to exercise*
más tarde *later*
nunca *never*
padecer del corazón, estar enfermo(a) del corazón, sufrir del corazón *to have heart problems*
por eso *that's why, for that reason*
por lo menos *at least*
seguir (e:i) una dieta *to go on a diet*
sobre todo *above all*
tener (diez) años *to be (ten) years old*
tener cuidado *to be careful*
Ya lo sé. *I know (it).*

Audio

VOCABULARIO ADICIONAL

LAS DIETAS

No debe comer
- **azúcar** *sugar*
- **grasas** *fats*
- **comidas picantes, comidas muy condimentadas** *spicy food*

Debe comer
- **fibras** *fiber, roughage*
- **vegetales** *vegetables*
- **una porción más pequeña** *a smaller portion*

Debe tomar
- **mucho líquido** *a lot of liquids*
- **caldos claros** *clear broths*

Debe seguir una dieta
- **especial** *special*
- **balanceada** *balanced*
- **con poca grasa** *low-fat*
- **sin sal** *salt-free*
- **con pocos carbohidratos** *low in carbohydrates*
- **con poca pasta o harina** *with little pasta or flour*

Nombre ______________________ Sección ____________ Fecha ____________

Modos de preparar la comida
- **asar** *to roast, to grill*
- **freír**[1] *to fry*
- **hervir (e:ie)** *to boil*
- **cocinar al vapor** *to steam*
- **cocinar al horno, hornear** *to bake*

- Hispanic Americans have a higher prevalence of diabetes than non-Hispanic people, with the highest rates for type 2 diabetes among Puerto Ricans and Hispanics living in the Southwest, and the lowest rate among Cubans (Carter JS, Pugh JA, Monterrosa A. Non-insulin-dependent diabetes mellitus in minorities in the United States. Ann Intern Med 1996; 125(3):221–32(AHRQ Grant HS07397).
- 10.6 percent of Mexican Americans have diabetes, compared with 6.2% of whites (Mokdad AH, Ford ES, Bowman Ba, et al. Diabetes trends in the U.S.: 1990–1998. *Diabetes Care* 2000; 23(9): 1278–83).
- AHRQ-funded research has shown that Hispanics with diabetes often face economic barriers to treatment and are reluctant to place their own medical needs over the needs of family members. Other common barriers include:
  - A distrust of insulin therapy
  - A preference for more familiar traditional remedies
  - A fatalistic acceptance of the course of the disease

  (Noel PH, Larme AC, Meyer I, et al. Patient choice in diabetes education curriculum. *Diabetes Care* 1998;21(6):986–991. (AHRAQ Grant HS07397) & (Lipton RB, Losey LM, Giachello A, et al. Attitudes and issues in treating Latino patients with Type 2 diabetes: views of healthcare providers. *DiabetesEduc* 1998;24(1);67–71. (AHRQ Grant HS07376-03).

Actividades

Dígame... Answer the following questions, basing your answers on the dialogue.

1. ¿Con quién está hablando la Sra. Rivas sobre los problemas de Ramón?

   ____

2. ¿Ramón toma mucha leche? ¿Qué toma?

   ____

[1]**frío, fríes, fríe freímos, fríen**

3. ¿Qué puede usar la Sra. Rivas en las comidas que prepara para Ramón?

____

4. ¿Por qué está preocupada la Sra. Rivas? ¿Cuánto pesa Ramón?

____

5. ¿Quién padece del corazón? ¿Quién es diabética?

____

6. ¿Qué debe hacer Ramón para adelgazar en vez de engordar?

____

7. Sobre todo, ¿qué debe evitar Ramón?

____

8. ¿Dónde almuerza Ramón y qué come generalmente?

____

9. ¿Cuándo vuelven Ramón y su mamá a ver a la dietista?

____

10. ¿Qué puede hacer la Sra. Rivas si desea hablar con la dietista?

____

Hablemos Interview a classmate, using the following questions. When you have finished, switch roles.

1. ¿Necesita Ud. perder peso? ¿Por qué o por qué no?
2. ¿Come Ud. muchos dulces? ¿Toma muchos refrescos?
3. ¿Necesita Ud. seguir una dieta estricta?
4. ¿Alguien de su familia padece del corazón? ¿Alguien es diabético?
5. ¿Cuenta Ud. siempre las calorías cuando come?
6. ¿Qué cantidad de leche toma Ud. cada día? ¿Toma leche descremada?
7. ¿Qué alimentos tienen mucha proteína?
8. ¿Qué frutas tienen vitamina C?

9. ¿Qué alimentos de la lista tienen muchas calorías?

10. ¿Qué es necesario hacer para adelgazar?

Quiz

Vamos a practicar

A Answer the following questions in the negative.

MODELO ¿Llama Ud. a alguien (*someone*)?
No, **no** llamo a **nadie.**

1. ¿Uds. pueden hacer algo por mi hijo?

____

2. ¿Ud. va a hablar con alguien?

____

3. ¿Hay algunas personas diabéticas aquí?

____

4. ¿Ud. padece del corazón o de los riñones (*kidneys*)?

____

5. ¿Ud. siempre vuelve a su casa por la mañana?

____

B Answer the questions in the affirmative, using direct object pronouns.

MODELO ¿Ud. siempre toma **leche descremada**?
Sí, siempre **la** tomo.

1. ¿Ud. siempre cuenta **las calorías**?

____

2. ¿Puede Ud. llamar**me** mañana? (*Answer with **tú** form*)

____

3. ¿Llama Ud. **a su médico** a menudo?

____

Nombre ______________________ Sección ____________ Fecha ____________

4. ¿El médico **los** llama **a Uds.**?

____

5. ¿Lleva Ud. **a los niños** al médico con frecuencia?

____

C Complete the following exchanges with the Spanish equivalent of the words in parentheses.

1. —¿Paquito, ______________________ al hospital ______________________ ?
   (*can you go/with me*)
   —No, Carlos, ____________________ porque tengo que esperar a Diego. (*I can't go with you*)
2. —¿La mantequilla de maní es ____________________? (*for me*)
   —Sí, Anita, es ____________________. (*for you*)

Conversaciones breves

Complete the following dialogue, using your imagination and the vocabulary from this lesson.

La Sra. Pérez y la dietista:

Sra. Pérez —Estoy muy preocupada porque mi hija Rosa está muy gorda.

Dietista —¿____?

Sra. Pérez —Pesa 150 libras.

Dietista —¿____?

Sra. Pérez —Tiene sólo doce años.

Dietista —____

Sra. Pérez —Sí, ya sé que debe perder peso, pero ella come mucho.

Dietista —____

Sra. Pérez —Sí, come muchos dulces y además toma muchos refrescos.

Dietista —____

Sra. Pérez —No, nunca toma leche.

Dietista —____

Sra. Pérez —Yo sé que ella necesita tomar leche, pero no quiere. ¿Qué otros alimentos necesita comer?

Dietista —____

Sra. Pérez —¿Tengo que contar las calorías?

Dietista —____

Nombre ______________________ Sección ____________ Fecha ____________

Sra. Pérez —Bueno, a ver si Rosa puede adelgazar ahora. La obesidad es peligrosa. Muchas gracias, señora. ¿Cuándo debo volver?

Dietista —____

En estas situaciones

What would you say in the following situations? What might the other person say?

1. You are a patient. Tell the dietician that you want to lose weight, but that you eat lots of sweets and foods that have many calories. Tell him/her how much you weigh.
2. You are a dietician. Tell your patient that obesity is very dangerous and he/she needs to go on a diet. Also, tell the person to eat only half the amount he/she eats now and to drink skim milk. Finally, tell your patient that it is necessary to exercise.
3. You are a doctor. Tell your patient that he/she has to be careful, because he/she is a diabetic and has heart problems.
4. Make a shopping list of foods you are going to buy at the market to prepare healthy meals.

Casos

Act out the following scenarios with a partner.

1. A dietician and a patient discuss the patient's need to lose weight because of potential health problems. Discuss also what may be causing the weight gain and come up with ideas for substitution of ingredients.
2. A dietician and a patient discuss the importance of a balanced diet and what foods the person should eat.

Un paso más

Review the **Vocabulario adicional** in this lesson. Then work with a partner and decide what advice you would give the following people in each situation. Recommend what the person should or should not eat and what type of diet the person should follow.

1. Una persona obesa

____

____

____

____

____

____

Nombre ______________________ Sección ____________ Fecha ____________

2. Una persona que tiene hipertensión

____

____

____

____

____

____

3. Una persona que siempre está estreñida

____

____

____

____

____

____

4. Una persona diabética

____

____

____

____

____

____

5. Una persona que tiene gastritis

____

____

____

____

____

____

La dieta para diabéticos

(Adapted from TEL MED, tape #611)

Hay tres principios básicos que se deben tener en cuenta[1] con respecto a las dietas para los diabéticos.

El primero y el más importante es el control de las calorías que la persona consume. El control del peso[2] es el factor más importante para controlar la diabetes porque el exceso de tejido graso[3] puede[4] interferir con la absorción de insulina por el cuerpo.

El segundo principio de la dieta consiste en no comer dulces[5] concentrados. La persona diabética debe evitar el azúcar de mesa,[6] la miel,[7] las gelatinas y todos los alimentos que contengan mucho azúcar, como por ejemplo[8] ciertos refrescos,[9] los pasteles[10] y las galletitas.[11]

El tercer principio básico es la forma[12] en que comen los diabéticos. Una persona que tiene diabetes debe comer por lo menos[13] tres comidas al día. El desayuno debe ser la comida más importante. El almuerzo[14] y la cena[15] deben ser en cantidades moderadas. Si comen algo ligero[16] entre[17] comidas, deben limitar las cantidades en las comidas principales.

Conversaciones

1-20 —Doctor, mi esposo es diabético. ¿Qué no debe comer?
—Debe evitar comer dulces.
—¿Puede tomar refrescos?
—Sí, si no están endulzados con azúcar.

1-21 —¿Qué es lo más importante para controlar la diabetes?
—Lo más importante es controlar el peso.
—¿Por qué?
—Porque el tejido graso interfiere con la absorción de la insulina.

1-22 —Doctor, ¿cuántas comidas puedo comer al día?
—Debe comer por lo menos tres comidas.

---

[1]**tener...** *keep in mind*
[2]*weight*
[3]**tejido...** *fatty tissue*
[4]*can*
[5]*sweets*
[6]**azúcar...** *table sugar*
[7]*honey*
[8]**por...** *for example*
[9]*soft drinks*
[10]*pies or cakes*
[11]*cookies*
[12]*way*
[13]**por...** *at least*
[14]*lunch*
[15]*dinner*
[16]*light*
[17]*between*

—¿Cuál debe ser la comida principal?
—La comida principal debe ser el desayuno.

1-23 —Mi hijo es diabético. ¿Qué alimentos puede comer?
—Puede comer solamente los alimentos especificados en su dieta.
—¿Puede comer huevos?
—Sí, pero no todos los días.

Dígame... Answer the following questions, basing your answers on the reading and the conversations.

1. ¿Cuántos principios básicos hay que tener en cuenta con respecto a las dietas para los diabéticos?

   ____

2. ¿Cuál es el más importante?

   ____

3. ¿Cuál es el factor más importante para controlar la diabetes?

   ____

4. ¿Qué puede interferir con la absorción de la insulina por el cuerpo?

   ____

5. ¿Qué no debe comer la persona diabética?

   ____

6. ¿Cuántas comidas debe comer una persona que tiene diabetes?

   ____

7. ¿Cuál debe ser la comida más importante?

   ____

8. ¿Cómo debe ser la cantidad de comida en la cena?

   ____

9. ¿Qué deben limitar las personas diabéticas cuando comen algo ligero entre comidas?

   ____

10. ¿Deben las personas diabéticas comer mucha grasa (*fat*)?

    ____

11. ¿Qué no deben comer todos los días las personas diabéticas?

    ____

12. ¿Qué tipos de alimentos deben comer las personas diabéticas?

    ____

EN EL CENTRO DE PLANIFICACIÓN FAMILIAR

OBJECTIVES

Structures

- Stem-changing verbs (**e:i**)
- Irregular first-person forms
- **Saber** contrasted with **conocer**
- Indirect object pronouns

Communication

- Family planning

EN EL CENTRO DE PLANIFICACIÓN FAMILIAR

1-24 La Sra. Reyes está en el Centro de Planificación Familiar. Es recién casada y, como es muy joven, no quiere tener hijos todavía. Le pide información a la Dra. Fabio sobre los distintos métodos usados para el control de la natalidad.

Sra. Reyes —Dra. Fabio, yo sé que puedo tomar pastillas anticonceptivas, pero muchos dicen que causan cáncer.

Dra. Fabio —Si Ud. no quiere usar la pastilla, hay distintos métodos que puede probar para evitar el embarazo.

Sra. Reyes —Pero, ¿son efectivos también?

Dra. Fabio —De todos los métodos, la pastilla es el más efectivo, pero muchas mujeres prefieren no tomarla.

Sra. Reyes —Conozco a una señora que usa un aparato intrauterino. Ella dice que no tiene problemas, pero ¿no son peligrosos los aparatos intrauterinos?

Dra. Fabio —No necesariamente. El ginecólogo lo inserta en el útero... pero a veces pueden causar molestias...

Sra. Reyes —¿Hay algún otro método?

Dra. Fabio —Sí, puede usar un diafragma que sirve para cubrir la entrada del útero y parte de la vagina.
Sra. Reyes —¿Debe insertarlo el médico?
Dra. Fabio —No. El médico mide la vagina para determinar el tamaño correcto, pero Ud. lo inserta.
Sra. Reyes —¿Cuándo debo insertarlo?
Dra. Fabio —Antes de tener relaciones sexuales.
Sra. Reyes —Veo que no es muy fácil tampoco.
Dra. Fabio —No... Además, debe cubrir el diafragma con jalea o crema por dentro y por fuera.
Sra. Reyes —¿Y el condón? ¿Es efectivo?
Dra. Fabio —Sí, si lo usa correctamente.
Sra. Reyes —¿Y qué piensa Ud. sobre los implantes que se pueden colocar en el brazo de la mujer?
Dra. Fabio —Voy a darle unos folletos que tienen información sobre ese método. Puede leerlos. Además, hay una inyección que pueden ponerle una vez al mes.
Sra. Reyes —¿Y si sigo el método del ritmo, doctora?
Dra. Fabio —Bueno, en ese caso, Ud. debe saber cuál es su período fértil.
Sra. Reyes —¿El período fértil...?
Dra. Fabio —Sí, unos días antes, durante y después de la ovulación.
Sra. Reyes —Bueno, voy a pensarlo, doctora. Gracias por todo.
Dra. Fabio —De nada. Buena suerte.
Sra. Reyes —¿Qué hago ahora? ¿Le pido turno a la recepcionista para la semana que viene?
Dra. Fabio —Sí, yo puedo verla la semana entrante.

1-24

¡Escuchemos!

While listening to the dialogue, circle **V (verdadero)** if the statement is true or **F (falso)** if it is false.

1. La Sra. Reyes es muy joven. V F
2. La Dra. Fabio dice que la pastilla anticonceptiva es el método más efectivo. V F
3. El médico tiene que insertar el diafragma. V F
4. La Sra. Reyes tiene que medir la vagina. V F
5. La Dra. Fabio dice que el condón no es efectivo. V F
6. La Dra. Fabio le va a dar unos folletos a la Sra. Reyes. V F
7. La Sra. Reyes le pregunta a la Dra. Fabio sobre el método del ritmo. V F
8. Para seguir el método del ritmo, la Sra. Reyes necesita usar jalea o crema. V F
9. El período fértil es unos días antes, durante o unos días después de la ovulación. V F
10. La Dra. Fabio puede ver a la Sra. Reyes mañana. V F

Nombre ______________________ Sección ____________ Fecha ____________

Vocabulario

Cognados

el centro
el condón
el control
correctamente
correcto(a)
la crema
el diafragma
efectivo(a)
la familia
familiar
fértil
el implante
el método
necesariamente
la ovulación
la parte
el útero
la vagina

Nombres

el aparato intrauterino *intrauterine device (I.U.D.)*
el embarazo *pregnancy*
la entrada *opening, entry*
el folleto *brochure, pamphlet*
la inyección *shot*
la jalea *jelly*
la molestia *trouble, discomfort*
la mujer *woman*
la natalidad *birth*
la planificación *planning*
el (la) recién casado(a) *newlywed*
el ritmo *rhythm*
el tamaño *size*
la vez *time (in a series)*

Verbos

colocar *to place*
conocer (yo conozco) *to know, to be acquainted with*
decir (yo digo) *to say, to tell*
determinar *to determine*
insertar *to insert*
medir (e:i) *to measure*
pedir (e:i) *to ask for; to request*
pensar (e:ie) *to think (about)*
probar (o:ue) *to try*
saber (yo sé) *to know*
seguir (e:i)[1] *to follow, to continue*
servir (e:i) *to serve*

Adjetivos

anticonceptivo(a) *for birth control, contraceptive*
distinto(a), diferente *different*
fácil *easy*
joven *young*
mejor *better, best*
usado(a) *used*

Otras palabras y expresiones

al mes, por mes *a month, per month*
buena suerte *good luck*
en ese caso *in that case*
poner una inyección *to give a shot*
por dentro *on the inside*
por fuera *on the outside*
tampoco *either, neither*
una vez *once*

[1]First person: **yo sigo**

Nombre ______________________ Sección ____________ Fecha ____________

VOCABULARIO ADICIONAL

OTROS TÉRMINOS RELACIONADOS CON LA CONCEPCIÓN

la abstinencia *abstinence*
el bebé de probeta *test-tube baby*
concebir (e:i) *to conceive*
la esperma *sperm*
la esterilidad *sterility*
esterilizar *to sterilize*
eyacular *to ejaculate*
la impotencia *impotence*
la inseminación artificial *artificial insemination*
ligar los tubos, amarrar los tubos *to tie the tubes*
lubricar *to lubricate*
(no) tener familia *(not) to have children*
el óvulo *ovum*
por vía bucal, por vía oral *orally*
el semen *semen*
la vasectomía *vasectomy*

¡OJO! For additional anatomical terms related to the reproductive organs, see the diagrams on page xxi.

NOTAS CULTURALES

- Latino attitudes toward contraception and reproduction are very complex, and they are greatly influenced by many factors: socioeconomic status, level of education, religious beliefs, and cultural beliefs. For example, as a group Latinos are predominantly Roman Catholic, and the teachings of the Church may affect their decision. Two other concepts that may influence their decisions are the cultural importance given to motherhood and childrearing, and the cultural notion of **machismo,** which is associated with proving one's virility, manliness, or masculinity. One example of **machismo** in practice relates to those Hispanic men who don't want to have a baby, but they will not permit their wives to use contraceptives and they refuse to use condoms. In these cases, the women are faced with a dilemma and don't know what to do because very few alternatives remain.
- According to a recent study based on data from the Hispanic Health and Nutrition Examination Survey, there are also differences regarding contraceptive/reproductive decisions among the three major Hispanic American ethnic groups. This study indicated that Mexican American females are almost twice as likely to be using oral contraceptives as Cuban American or Puerto Rican females. In addition, Mexican American women show a higher rate of hysterectomies and oophorectomies than the other two groups, while the largest percentage of tubal ligations is among Puerto Rican women. In fact, 58 percent of all contraception in Puerto Rico is due to female sterilization.

Nombre ______________________ Sección ____________ Fecha ____________

Actividades

Dígame... Answer the following questions, basing your answers on the dialogue.

1. ¿Por qué va la Sra. Reyes al Centro de Planificación Familiar?

____

2. ¿Por qué no quiere tener hijos todavía?

____

3. ¿Qué le pide la Sra. Reyes a la Dra. Fabio?

____

4. ¿Qué le dice la médica sobre la pastilla?

____

5. ¿Son peligrosos los aparatos intrauterinos?

____

6. ¿Dónde inserta el ginecólogo el aparato intrauterino?

____

7. ¿Para qué sirve el diafragma? ¿Cuándo se debe insertar?

____

8. ¿Con qué se debe cubrir el diafragma antes de insertarlo?

____

9. ¿Qué va a darle la Dra. Fabio a la Sra. Reyes?

____

10. ¿Qué debe saber la Sra. Reyes para seguir el método del ritmo?

____

11. ¿Qué le va a pedir la señora a la recepcionista?

____

12. ¿Cuándo puede verla la Dra. Fabio?

____

Nombre ______________________ **Sección** ______________ **Fecha** ______________

Hablemos Interview a classmate, using the following questions. When you have finished switch roles.

1. ¿Cuál cree Ud. que es el método más fácil para el control de la natalidad?
2. ¿Cuál cree Ud. que es el método más efectivo?
3. ¿Si una mujer quiere usar el diafragma? ¿Debe ver antes a un ginecólogo? ¿Por qué?
4. ¿Es fácil seguir el método del ritmo? ¿Por qué o por qué no?
5. ¿Es efectivo el condón?
6. ¿Conoce Ud. a una pareja (*couple*) de recién casados?
7. ¿Cuánto tiempo (*How long*) cree Ud. que debe esperar una pareja de recién casados para tener hijos?
8. ¿Cuántos hijos cree Ud. que debe tener una pareja?

Vamos a practicar

A Complete the following sentences, using the present indicative of the verbs listed.

pedir	hacer	decir
saber	poner	conocer
servir	medir	seguir

Modelo María _____ turno para la semana que viene.
María **pide** turno para la semana que viene.

1. Mamá ______________________ que las pastillas anticonceptivas causan cáncer.
2. ¿Para qué ______________________ las jaleas y las cremas? ¿Para evitar el embarazo?
3. Yo ______________________ a una mujer que tiene un implante en el brazo.
4. Yo no ______________________ nada para evitar el embarazo.
5. El médico ______________________ la vagina para determinar el tamaño correcto.
6. ¿______________________ Uds. el método del ritmo? ¿Es efectivo eso?
7. Yo ______________________ la crema por dentro y por fuera.
8. Yo ______________________ que el aparato intrauterino puede causar molestias.

Nombre ______________________ **Sección** ____________ **Fecha** ____________

B Complete the following sentences with the Spanish equivalent of the words in parentheses.

MODELO Ella _____ el folleto. (*gives them*)
Ella **les da** el folleto.

1. Yo voy a ____________________ información. (*ask her for*)
2. La médica ____________________ de las pastillas anticonceptivas. (*speaks to us*)
3. ¿Qué vas a ____________________? (*tell them*)
4. Yo puedo ____________________ la crema, señora. (*give you*)
5. Ella siempre ____________________ que son peligrosos. (*tells me*)

Conversaciones breves Complete the following dialogue, using your imagination and the vocabulary from this lesson.

El doctor y la paciente:

Paciente —Yo no quiero tomar la pastilla.

Doctor —____

Paciente —Pero no son muy efectivos.

Doctor —____

Paciente —Pero, ¿no son peligrosos los aparatos intrauterinos?

Doctor —____

Paciente —¿Cuándo debo insertar el diafragma?

Doctor —____

Paciente —¿También debo usar alguna crema o jalea con el diafragma?

Doctor —____

Paciente —Yo creo que mi esposo puede usar un condón.

Doctor —____

Paciente —Sí, prefiero eso.

En estas situaciones What would you say in the following situations? What might the other person say?

1. You are a doctor and your patient does not want to have children yet. Explain to your patient that her fertile period is before, during, and after ovulation. Then tell your patient that if she doesn't want to use birth control pills, there are other methods she can use to avoid pregnancy.

2. You are a doctor and your patient wants a diaphragm. Tell your patient that you have to measure her vagina to determine the right size and that she should insert the diaphragm before having sexual intercourse. Describe the placement of the diaphragm to her.
3. You are a patient. Tell your doctor that your husband doesn't want to use a condom. Ask him/her if the rhythm method is effective.
4. You are a doctor. Explain to a patient that, to avoid pregnancy, she can have an implant in her arm or that they can give her a shot once a month.

Casos Act out the following scenario with a partner.

A doctor and a patient discuss the nature and use of the following birth control methods.

1. the pill
2. the I.U.D.
3. the diaphragm
4. the rhythm method
5. the implant
6. Depo Provera shots

Un paso más Review the **Vocabulario adicional** in this lesson. Then write the words or phrases related to the following.

1. Lo que (*What*) se puede hacer para evitar tener hijos:

____

____

____

____

____

____

____

____

Nombre ______________________ **Sección** __________ **Fecha** __________

2. Términos relacionados con los órganos reproductivos del hombre (*man*):

____

____

____

____

____

____

3. Métodos artificiales para tener hijos:

____

____

____

4. Términos relacionados con la infertilidad:

____

____

____

____

5. Forma en que se toma una medicina:

____

____

Lección 8 Un examen físico

Objectives

Structures

- **Pedir** contrasted with **preguntar**
- Special construction with **gustar, doler,** and **hacer falta**
- Demonstrative adjectives and pronouns
- Direct and indirect object pronouns used together

Communication

- Getting your annual physical exam

Un examen físico

1-25 Carlos está en el consultorio del Dr. Díaz. El doctor le está haciendo un examen general. La enfermera trae la hoja clínica del paciente y se la da al médico. Carlos tiene la presión normal y parece muy sano.

Dr. Díaz —¿Tiene dolores de cabeza a menudo?
Carlos —Sí, a veces, cuando leo mucho o trabajo con la computadora muchas horas.
Dr. Díaz —¿Puede doblar la cabeza hacia adelante, hasta tocar el pecho con la barbilla?
Carlos —¿Así?
Dr. Díaz —Sí. Ahora hacia atrás. ¿Le duele cuando hace eso?
Carlos —No, no me duele, pero me molesta un poco.
Dr. Díaz —¿Tiene algún ruido en los oídos?
Carlos —Sí, en este oído, a veces.
Dr. Díaz —¿Tiene tos o está ronco sin estar resfriado?
Carlos —No, nunca.
Dr. Díaz —¿Puede respirar, por la boca, por favor? Respire hondo... lentamente. ¿Tiene dificultad para respirar a veces?
Carlos —Solamente después de correr mucho o de hacer algún ejercicio violento.

Nombre ______________________ **Sección** ____________ **Fecha** ____________

Dr. Díaz —¿Siente algún dolor en el pecho?
Carlos —No.
Dr. Díaz —¿Tiene a veces la presión alta o baja?
Carlos —Siempre es normal cuando me la toman.
Dr. Díaz —¿Le duele algunas veces el estómago después de comer?
Carlos —Cuando como mucho y de prisa, tengo gases y a veces me duele.
Dr. Díaz —¿Le duele cuando le aprieto el estómago así?
Carlos —Me duele un poco...
Dr. Díaz —¿Le duele el pene cuando orina?
Carlos —No.
Dr. Díaz —¿Puede doblar las rodillas...? Otra vez, separándolas... ¿Siente algún dolor en los huesos?
Carlos —No, doctor.
Dr. Díaz —¿Siente comezón o ardor a veces?
Carlos —No, nada fuera de lo común...
Dr. Díaz —¿Duerme bien?
Carlos —Algunas veces tengo insomnio.
Dr. Díaz —¿Sube y baja de peso con frecuencia?
Carlos —No, siempre peso más o menos lo mismo.
Dr. Díaz —Bueno. Vamos a hacerle un análisis de sangre para ver si hay diabetes o si tiene el colesterol alto. Debe ir al laboratorio en ayunas y darle esta orden a la enfermera.
Carlos —Muy bien, doctor. ¿Cuándo vuelvo?
Dr. Díaz —Si el resultado del análisis es negativo, dentro de seis meses. Si es positivo, nosotros lo llamamos.
Carlos —Gracias.

1-25

¡Escuchemos!

While listening to the dialogue, circle **V (verdadero)** if the statement is true or **F (falso)** if it is false.

1. A veces Carlos tiene dolores de cabeza.
2. A veces Carlos tiene ruido en un oído.
3. A veces, Carlos está ronco sin estar resfriado.
4. Después de correr mucho o de hacer un ejercicio violento, Carlos tiene dificultad para respirar.
5. Carlos tiene la presión alta.
6. Carlos nunca come de prisa.
7. A veces, Carlos siente ardor.
8. Carlos está subiendo mucho de peso.
9. Le van a hacer un análisis de sangre a Carlos.
10. Carlos no debe comer antes de ir al laboratorio.

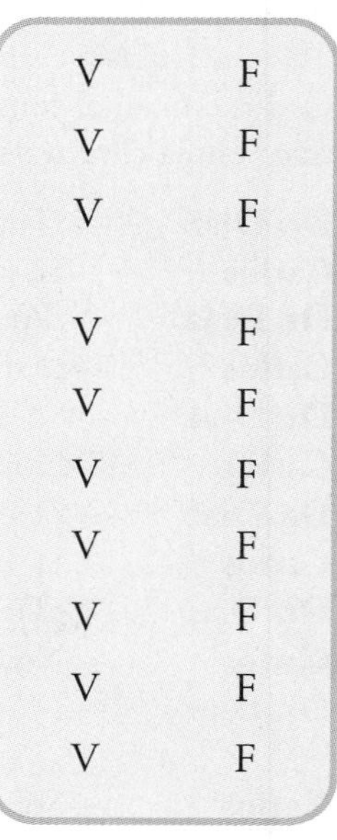

Nombre ______________________ Sección ____________ Fecha ____________

Audio

Vocabulario

COGNADOS

el colesterol
la computadora
el examen, el chequeo
físico(a)
gas
general
insomnio
negativo(a)
normal
positivo(a)
violento(a)

NOMBRES

el ardor *burning*
la barbilla *chin*
la comezón, la picazón *itching*
la dificultad *difficulty*
el hueso *bone*
el pene *penis*
la presión, la presión arterial *pressure, blood pressure*
el resultado *result*
el ruido *noise, ringing*

VERBOS

apretar (e:ie) *to press (down)*
correr *to run*
doblar *to bend*
doler (o:ue)[1] *to hurt, to ache*
dormir (o:ue) *to sleep*
molestar *to bother*
parecer (yo parezco) *to seem*
respirar, resollar *to breathe*
sentir (e:ie) *to feel*
separar *to separate*
tocar *to touch*
trabajar *to work*
traer (yo traigo) *to bring*

ADJETIVOS

ronco(a) *hoarse*
sano(a) *healthy*

OTRAS PALABRAS Y EXPRESIONES

así *like this, so*
de prisa *in a hurry*
dentro de *in, within*
el ejercicio violento *strenuous exercise*
en ayunas *with an empty stomach, fasting*
fuera de lo común *out of the ordinary*
hacer un análisis, hacer una prueba *to run a test*
hacer un examen *to give a checkup*
hacia adelante *forward*
hacia atrás *backward*
hasta *until, till*
lentamente *slowly*
lo mismo *the same (thing)*
más o menos *more or less*
muchos(as) *a lot*
nada *nothing*
otra vez *again*
por la boca *through the mouth*
Respire hondo. *Take a deep breath, Breathe deeply.*
un poco *a little*

---

[1]**Doler** is used with indirect object pronouns. **Me duele el estómago.** *My stomach hurts.* (literally, *The stomach is hurting me.*)

Nombre ______________________ Sección ____________ Fecha ____________

Audio

VOCABULARIO ADICIONAL

LOS SIGNOS VITALES (*Vital Signs*)

la temperatura del cuerpo *body temperature*
la presión (la tensión) arterial *blood pressure*
el pulso *pulse*

EL EXAMEN FÍSICO

¿Tiene Ud.
- **dificultad al tragar?** *difficulty swallowing*
- **fatiga?** *fatigue*
- **mucha flema?** *a lot of phlegm*
- **gases intestinales (flato)?** *intestinal gas (flatus)*
- **malestar? molestias?** *discomfort*
- **tendencia a sangrar?** *tendency to bleed*
- **tos seca?** *dry cough*
- **urticaria? ronchas?** *hives*

¿Alguien de su familia tiene
- **bocio?** *goiter*
- **esclerosis múltiple?** *multiple sclerosis*
- **hidropesía?** *dropsy*
- **malaria?** *malaria*
- **pleuresía?** *pleurisy*

NOTAS CULTURALES

Search

- The use of health care services by Hispanic Americans depends greatly upon socioeconomic status and type of employment because these affect access to comprehensive and preventive medical care. Data from the Hispanic Health and Nutrition Examination Survey indicates that one-third of the Mexican American population, one-fifth of the Puerto Rican population, and one-fourth of the Cuban American population are uninsured for medical expenditures. Furthermore, compared with Hispanic Americans with private health insurance, uninsured Hispanic Americans are less likely to have a regular source of health care, less likely to have visited a physician in the past year, and less likely to have had a routine physical examination. Mexican Americans, who have the least insurance, visit physicians least often. The highest rate in number of physician visits is among Puerto Ricans, which may be due in part to the fact that they have greater access to Medicaid.

Nombre ______________________ Sección ____________ Fecha ____________

Actividades

Dígame... Answer the following questions, basing your answers on the dialogue.

1. ¿Qué le está haciendo el doctor a Carlos?
   ____
2. ¿Qué le da la enfermera al médico?
   ____
3. ¿Cuándo le duele la cabeza a Carlos?
   ____
4. ¿Cuándo tiene Carlos dificultad para respirar?
   ____
5. ¿Tiene Carlos la presión alta?
   ____
6. ¿Carlos siempre duerme bien?
   ____
7. ¿Para qué le van a hacer un análisis a Carlos?
   ____
8. ¿Por qué no puede comer Carlos antes de ir al laboratorio?
   ____

Hablemos Interview a classmate, using the following questions. When you have finished, switch roles.

1. ¿Tiene Ud. la presión normal?
2. ¿Tiene Ud. dolores de cabeza a veces? ¿Cuándo?
3. ¿Le duele cuando dobla la cabeza hacia atrás?
4. ¿Tiene algún ruido en los oídos a veces? ¿Cuándo?
5. ¿Tiene tos? ¿Está ronco(a)?
6. ¿Tiene Ud. dificultad para respirar? ¿Cuándo?

Nombre ______________________ Sección ____________ Fecha ____________

7. ¿Le duele algo?

8. ¿Siente algún dolor en los huesos?

9. ¿Siente comezón o ardor a veces?

10. ¿Sube y baja de peso con frecuencia?

11. ¿Duerme bien o tiene insomnio?

12. ¿Alguien (*Someone*) en su familia tiene el colesterol alto? ¿Diabetes?

Vamos a practicar

A Rewrite the following sentences, replacing the words in boldface with the corresponding direct object pronouns.

MODELO Me pide **la orden.**
Me **la** pide.

1. Le doy **el resultado** mañana.

____

2. Te traen **los alimentos** después.

____

3. Nos toman **la presión** con frecuencia.

____

4. Me dan **las pastillas.**

____

5. Les piden **el análisis de sangre.**

____

B Complete the following exchanges with the Spanish equivalent of the words in parentheses.

1. —¿Cuándo voy a saber ____________, doctor? (*the test results*)
—____________ mañana. (*We can give it to you*)

2. —____________, Sr. Nieto? (*Does your stomach hurt*)
—Sí, ____________ mucho. (*it hurts*)

3. —¿Le doy __________ al paciente? (*these pills*)
   —Sí, Ud. tiene que __________ esta tarde. (*give them to him*)

Conversaciones breves

Complete the following dialogue, using your imagination and the vocabulary from this lesson.

El Dr. Ríos y el paciente:

Dr. Ríos —¿______________________________?

Paciente —Sí, a veces tengo dolores de cabeza.

Dr. Ríos —¿______________________________?

Paciente —No, no siento ruido en los oídos, pero a veces me duelen.

Dr. Ríos —¿______________________________?

Paciente —No, nunca siento dolor en el pecho.

Dr. Ríos —¿______________________________?

Paciente —No, nunca me duele el pene cuando orino.

Dr. Ríos —¿______________________________?

Paciente —Ardor no, pero a veces siento comezón.

Dr. Ríos —¿______________________________?

Paciente —Sólo cuando como de prisa.

Dr. Ríos —¿______________________________?

Paciente —Sí, mi padre tiene diabetes.

En estas situaciones

What would you say in the following situations? What might the other person say?

1. You are the patient. Tell your doctor you want a checkup because you sometimes have headaches and difficulty breathing.
2. You are a doctor. Tell your patient to take a deep breath through the mouth. Ask the person if his/her stomach hurts when you press it.
3. You are the doctor. Tell your patient he/she seems healthy, but that you want to run some tests. Tell your patient that he/she must not eat anything before coming to the lab.

Nombre ______________ Sección ______________ Fecha ______________

Casos Act out the following scenario with a partner.
A doctor gives a patient a complete checkup.

Un paso más

A Review the **Vocabulario adicional** in this lesson. Then write the symptoms you associate with the following medical conditions.

1. gastritis: ______________
2. anemia: ______________
3. tuberculosis: ______________
4. alergia: ______________
5. catarro: ______________
6. hemofilia: ______________
7. cáncer de la garganta (*throat*): ______________

B Read the following symptoms of diabetes. Then write six questions you would ask a patient whom you suspect might have diabetes.

¿CUÁLES SON ALGUNOS DE LOS SIGNOS COMUNES DE UNA DIABETES SEVERA?

1. Orinar frecuentemente, aún durante la noche
2. Sed[1]
3. Pérdida de peso
4. Apetito constante
5. Cansancio y debilidad
6. Comezón en la piel
7. Piel seca[2]
8. Visión borrosa[3]
9. Infecciones de la piel (*llagas*[4])

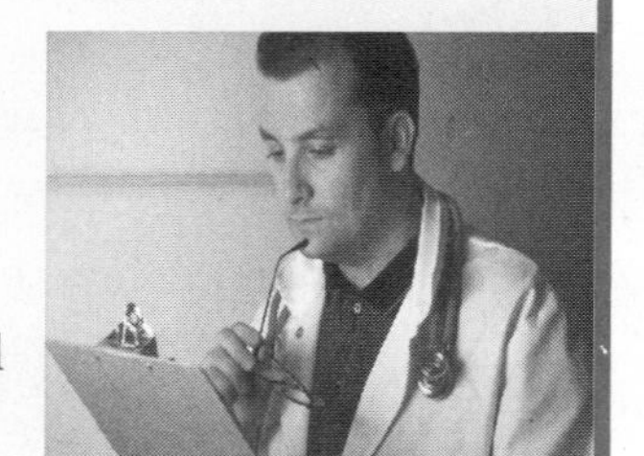

¿CUÁLES SON ALGUNOS DE LOS SIGNOS COMUNES DE UNA DIABETES MENOS SEVERA?

1. Cansancio y debilidad
2. Dolor
3. Entumecimiento[5] u hormigueo[6] en los dedos de las manos o en los pies
4. Visión borrosa
5. Infecciones de la piel (*llagas*)
6. Es posible que no haya[7] signos de ninguna clase

---

[1] *Thirst*
[2] *dry*
[3] *blurred*
[4] *wounds*
[5] *Numbness*
[6] *pins and needles, tingling*
[7] *there may be*

Nombre ______________________ Sección ____________ Fecha ____________

1. ____

2. ____

3. ____

4. ____

5. ____

6. ____

Now interview a classmate, using the questions you have written.

Lección 9 Con el dentista

Objectives

Structures

- Possessive pronouns
- Reflexive constructions
- Command forms: **Ud.** and **Uds.**
- Uses of object pronouns with command forms

Communication

- Dental hygiene and general oral health

Con el dentista

1-26

Anita va al dentista porque le duele una muela. Después de entrar en el consultorio, se sienta y la asistente le hace unas radiografías. Ahora el dentista viene para examinarle los dientes.

Dentista —Abra la boca, por favor. ¿Cuál es la muela que le duele? Tóquela.

Anita —Ésta. No puedo morder nada, y si como algo muy frío o muy caliente, el dolor es insoportable.

Dentista —Vamos a ver. (*Mira la radiografía.*) Necesito extraerle la muela. No voy a poder salvarla porque tiene un absceso. Otro día vamos a extraerle las muelas del juicio porque no tienen espacio suficiente.

Anita —Muy bien. Doctor, para sacarme la muela, ¿me va a dar anestesia local o general?

Dentista —Es una extracción simple. Voy a darle novocaína.

Anita —¿Tengo algún diente picado?

Dentista —Sí, tiene dos caries, y tiene una muela que necesita una corona.

Anita —¿Todo eso?

Dentista —Sí, lo siento.

Anita —Doctor, me sangran mucho las encías cuando me cepillo los dientes...

Dentista —Sí, veo que las tiene muy inflamadas, y tiene mucho sarro. Eso puede causar piorrea y mal aliento.

Nombre ______________________ Sección ____________ Fecha ____________

Anita —Entonces, ¿debo pedir turno para la higienista?
Dentista —Sí, pida turno para dentro de dos semanas para la higienista, y también para empastarle los dientes.
Anita —Y para el problema de las encías, ¿qué hago?
Dentista —Cepíllese los dientes después de cada comida con un buen cepillo y una pasta de dientes para controlar el sarro. Ah, y no se olvide de usar el hilo dental todos los días.

El dentista le extrae la muela.

Dentista —Enjuáguese la boca.
Anita —Si me duele, ¿puedo tomar aspirina?
Dentista —No, tome Tylenol 3. Si le sigue doliendo, llámeme por teléfono y yo le voy a recetar otro calmante. Si tiene la cara inflamada, póngase una bolsa de hielo al llegar a su casa.
Anita —¿Algo más?
Dentista —Si sangra un poco, use dos almohadas para dormir. Si sangra mucho, llámeme.

Al salir del consultorio, la asistente la llama.

Asistente —Señorita, ¿esta cartera es suya?
Anita —Sí, es mía. Gracias.

1-26

¡Escuchemos!

While listening to the dialogue, circle **V (verdadero)** if the statement is true or **F (falso)** if it is false.

1. A Anita le duele mucho la muela cuando come algo muy frío o muy caliente.
2. El dentista dice que puede salvar la muela.
3. El dentista no necesita extraerle las muelas del juicio.
4. Anita no tiene caries.
5. Una de las muelas de Anita necesita una corona.
6. A Anita le sangran las encías cuando come.
7. Las encías de Anita están muy inflamadas.
8. El sarro puede causar piorrea.
9. Anita debe usar hilo dental todos los días.
10. Si Anita tiene la cara inflamada, tiene que tomar dos aspirinas.

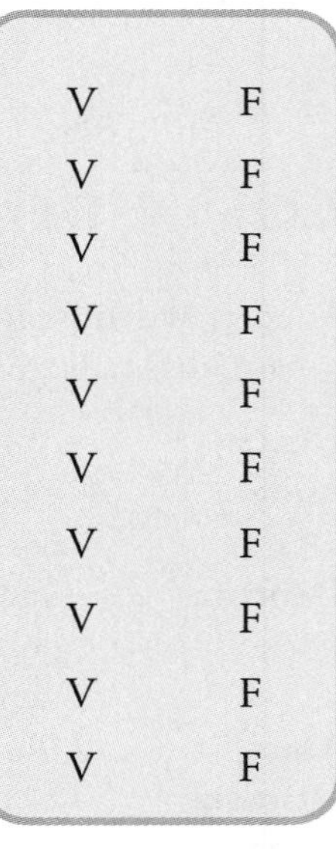

Nombre ______________________ Sección ____________ Fecha ____________

Audio

VOCABULARIO

COGNADOS

el absceso
la anestesia
el (la) asistente
el (la) dentista
el espacio
la extracción
el (la) higienista
local
la novocaína
la piorrea
simple

NOMBRES

el aliento *breath*
la boca *mouth*
la bolsa, la cartera *handbag, purse*
la bolsa de hielo *ice pack*
la caries, la picadura *cavity*
la casa *house*
el cepillo *brush*
la corona *crown*
la encía[1] *gum (of mouth)*
el hielo *ice*
el hilo dental, la seda dental *dental floss*
la muela *tooth, molar*
la muela del juicio, el cordal *wisdom tooth*
la pasta de dientes, la pasta dentífrica *toothpaste*
el sarro *tartar*

VERBOS

abrir *to open*
cepillar(se) *to brush (oneself)*
controlar *to control*
empastar, emplomar *to fill (a tooth)*
enjuagar(se) *to rinse (out)*
morder (o:ue) *to bite*
olvidarse (de) *to forget*
sacar, extraer[2] *to take out, to pull out, to extract*
salir[3] *to leave, to go out*
salvar *to save*
sentarse (e:ie) *to sit (down)*

ADJETIVOS

insoportable *unbearable*
picado(a), cariado(a) *decayed, carious*

OTRAS PALABRAS Y EXPRESIONES

ah *oh*
al llegar *upon arriving*
cepillarse los dientes *to brush one's teeth*
entonces *then*
Me sangran las encías. *My gums bleed.*
mío(a) *mine*
suficiente *enough, sufficient*
suyo(a) *yours*

---

[1]**Pus en las encías** (*Pus in the gums*)
[2]Irregular first person: **yo extraigo**
[3]Irregular first person: **yo salgo**

Nombre ____________________ Sección ____________ Fecha ____________

VOCABULARIO ADICIONAL

EL CUIDADO (*Care*) DE LOS DIENTES

Cepíllese los dientes
- **después de cada comida**
- **con un cepillo**
  - **duro** *hard*
  - **blando** *soft*
  - **semiduro** *medium*
- **con una buena pasta dentífrica con fluoruro** *with a good fluoride toothpaste*

el canal en la raíz *root canal*
el enjuague *mouthwash*
los frenos *dental braces*
el (la) odontólogo(a) *odontologist, dental surgeon, dentist*
la ortodoncia *orthodontia*
el (la) ortodoncista *orthodontist*
la placa *plaque*
el puente *(dental) bridge*

LAS PARTES DE UN DIENTE

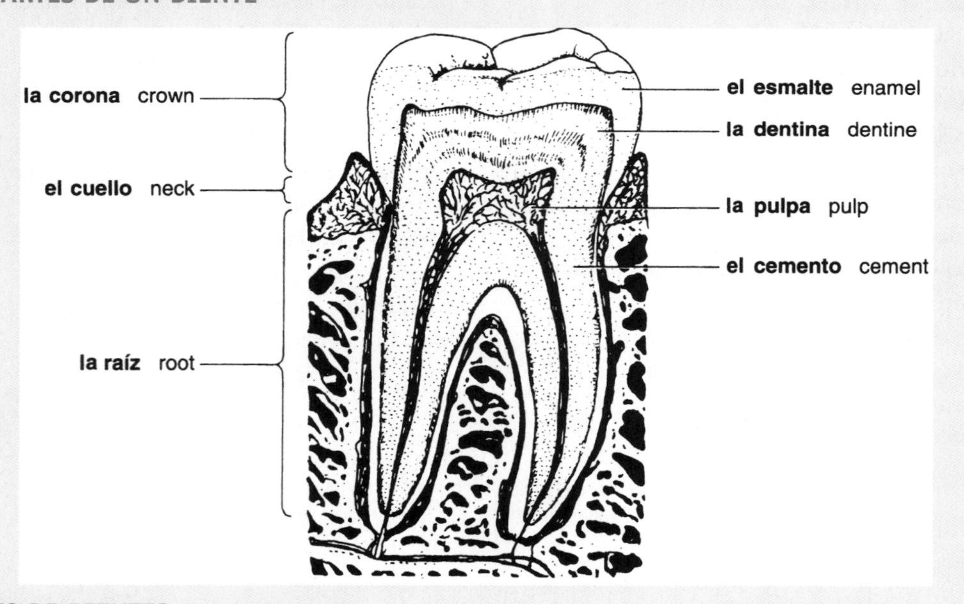

CLASES DE DIENTES

el canino, el colmillo *canine*
el incisivo *incisor*
el molar, la muela *molar*
la muela del juicio, la (muela) cordal *wisdom tooth*

¡OJO! For additional terms related to parts of the mouth, see the diagram on page xxii.

Nombre ______________________ Sección ____________ Fecha ____________

NOTAS CULTURALES

Search

- Recent research suggests that many members of the Spanish-speaking community are at greater risk of oral disease due to social conditions such as limited access to education, lower-paying jobs, and the absence of culturally sensitive health care services. Solutions to some of these problems have been proposed in the literature: increased efforts in educating both the general public and oral-health practitioners; national and public coalitions to promote oral health; legislative and regulatory initiatives; and further study of the impact that the interaction of behavioral, psychosocial, and biological factors in the individual has in attaining better oral health. [See John P. Brown, "Oral Health of Hispanics: Epidemiology and Risk Factors." In *Health Policy and Hispanics* (Boulder: Westview Press, 1992).]
- Preventive care is very important to stress to patients. Sometimes preventive dental care, and investing in their oral health before they feel a high level of pain, will help them in the end to save their own teeth. Some patients are reluctant to do work unless they feel a great deal of pain. It is important to take the time to explain the consequences.
- In an effort to inform the Spanish-speaking population about dental care, the National Institute of Dental Research, in conjunction with the U.S. Department of Health and Human Services, publishes the following pamphlets in Spanish as a public service. These brochures may also be obtained from state and local health departments.

  Rx para dientes sanos—La placa: ¿Qué es la placa dental y cómo puede quitársela? (*Rx for Sound Teeth—Plaque: What it is and how to get rid of it*)

  Evite las caries dentales (*Avoid Dental Decay*)

  Meriendas sanas para dientes y cuerpos sanos (*Smart Snacks for Healthy Teeth and Bodies*)

  Prevenga el daño que causa el biberón (*Prevent Baby Bottle Tooth Decay*)

  Consejos de cuidado dental para diabéticos (*Dental Care Tips for Diabetics*)

  Enfermedad periodontal en los diabéticos: Guía para los pacientes (*Periodontal Disease in Diabetics: Patient Guide*)

Actividades

Dígame... Answer the following questions, basing your answers on the dialogue.

1. ¿Por qué va Anita al dentista?

   ____

2. ¿Cuándo tiene Anita un dolor insoportable?

   ____

3. ¿Por qué no va a poder salvar la muela el dentista?

______

4. ¿Por qué le va a sacar las muelas del juicio?

______

5. ¿Cuántas caries tiene Anita? ¿Qué otro problema tiene?

______

6. ¿Qué problemas tiene Anita con las encías?

______

7. Para extraerle la muela, ¿el dentista le va a dar anestesia local o anestesia general?

______

8. ¿Qué puede hacer Anita si tiene dolor? ¿Y si le sigue doliendo?

______

9. ¿Qué debe hacer Anita si tiene la cara inflamada?

______

10. ¿La cartera es de Anita?

______

Hablemos Interview a classmate, using the following questions. When you have finished, switch roles.

1. ¿Tiene Ud. alguna muela picada?
2. ¿Siente Ud. dolor cuando muerde o cuando come algo muy caliente?
3. ¿Tiene Ud. un absceso?
4. ¿Cuántas veces al día se cepilla Ud. los dientes? ¿Cuándo lo hace?
5. ¿Qué pasta dentífrica usa Ud.?
6. ¿Usa Ud. hilo dental? ¿Cuántas veces a la semana?
7. ¿Cuántas veces al año le hace su higienista una limpieza (*cleaning*)?
8. ¿Tiene Ud. alguna corona?

9. ¿Qué puedo hacer si me duele mucho la muela?

10. Si una persona tiene mucho sarro, ¿qué problemas puede tener?

Vamos a practicar

A Answer the questions, using the affirmative or negative commands according to the cues given.

Modelo ¿Debo abrir la boca ahora? (sí)
Sí, **abra** la boca ahora.

¿Puedo cerrar la boca ahora? (no)
No, no **cierre** la boca ahora.

1. ¿Puedo comer algo después de salir del consultorio? (no)
______
2. ¿Debemos cepillarnos los dientes después de las comidas? (sí)
______
3. ¿Debemos usar seda dental? (sí)
______
4. ¿Debo darle anestesia general, doctor? (no)
______
5. ¿Debo empastarla ahora mismo? (sí)
______
6. ¿Debo enjuagarme la boca? (sí)
______
7. ¿Puedo ponerme una bolsa de hielo si tengo dolor? (sí)
______
8. ¿Debemos tomar aspirinas? (no)
______
9. ¿Debemos usar una pasta de dientes para controlar el sarro? (sí)
______
10. ¿Debemos ir al dentista una vez al año? (sí)
______

Nombre ______________________ **Sección** ____________ **Fecha** ____________

B Complete the following exchanges, giving the Spanish equivalent of the words in parentheses.

1. —Éste no es mi cepillo de dientes. ¿____________, señorita? (*Is it yours*)
   —Sí, es ____________, gracias. (*mine*)
2. —Me sangran mucho las encías ____________. (*when I brush my teeth*)
   —____________ no me sangran nunca. (*Mine*)
3. —¿Ésta es la ____________ de Sergio? (*toothpaste*)
   —No, no es ________; es ________. (*his / mine*)

Conversaciones breves

Complete the following dialogues, using your imagination and the vocabulary from this lesson.

A El Sr. Paz y su dentista:

Sr. Paz —Doctor, tengo un dolor de muelas insoportable.

Dentista —____________________________

Sr. Paz —Ésta es la muela que me duele: la muela del juicio.

Dentista —____________________________

Sr. Paz —Sí, me duele cuando tomo algo muy frío.

Dentista —____________________________

Sr. Paz —¿Extraerla? ¿No me la puede salvar?

Dentista —____________________________

Sr. Paz —¿Me va a dar anestesia general o local?

Dentista —____________________________

B Jorge y su dentista:

Jorge —Doctora, cada vez que me cepillo los dientes, las encías me sangran.

Dentista —____________________________

Jorge —Sí, doctora, ya sé que tengo las encías hinchadas.

Dentista —____________________________

Jorge —Tengo mucho sarro. ¿Es malo eso?

Dentista —____________________________

Jorge —¿Qué puedo hacer para evitar la piorrea?

Dentista —____________________________

Jorge —¿Es necesario usar el hilo dental?

Dentista —____________________________

Nombre ______________________ Sección ____________ Fecha ____________

En estas situaciones

What would you say in the following situations? What might the other person say?

1. You are a dentist. Ask your patient which tooth hurts and then tell the person to touch it. Ask your patient to open his/her mouth so you can examine the tooth.
2. You are a patient. Explain to your dentist that when you bite on something very hot or very cold the pain is unbearable and that your gums bleed when you brush your teeth.
3. You are a dentist. Explain to your patient that you have to pull out a wisdom tooth because there isn't enough room in his/her mouth for the tooth. Tell the person to make an appointment with the receptionist.

Casos

Act out the following scenarios with a partner.

1. You are a dentist and a patient comes to you with a toothache. Examine the person's teeth to find out what is causing the problem. Then inform your patient of the results of your examination and propose suitable solutions.
2. A patient comes to you with a number of abscessed teeth. After examining the person's teeth, explain to him/her that he/she needs dentures.
3. Explain to a patient how to take care of his/her teeth properly so that the person can avoid having dental problems in the future.
4. Discuss flossing and why it's important.

Un paso más

A Review the **Vocabulario adicional** in this lesson and answer the following questions.

1. ¿Qué enjuague usa Ud.?

   ____

2. ¿Es mejor usar un cepillo duro, blando o semiduro?

   ____

3. ¿Qué ventaja (*advantage*) tiene usar una pasta de dientes con fluoruro?

   ____

4. Si una persona tiene los dientes torcidos (*crooked*), ¿a qué especialista debe ir? ¿Qué van a ponerle?

   ____

5. ¿Cuál es la especialización de ese dentista?

   ____

Nombre ______________________ Sección ______________ Fecha ______________

6. Si tengo una caries muy profunda, ¿qué tiene que hacerme el dentista antes de ponerme una corona?

____

B Label the following diagrams in Spanish. For the diagram of the mouth, you may want to refer to the diagram on page 108.

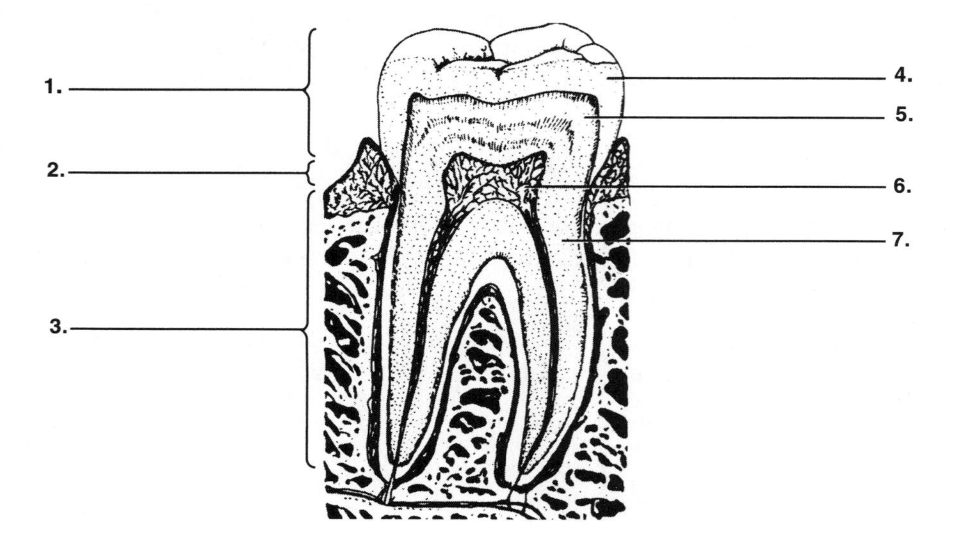

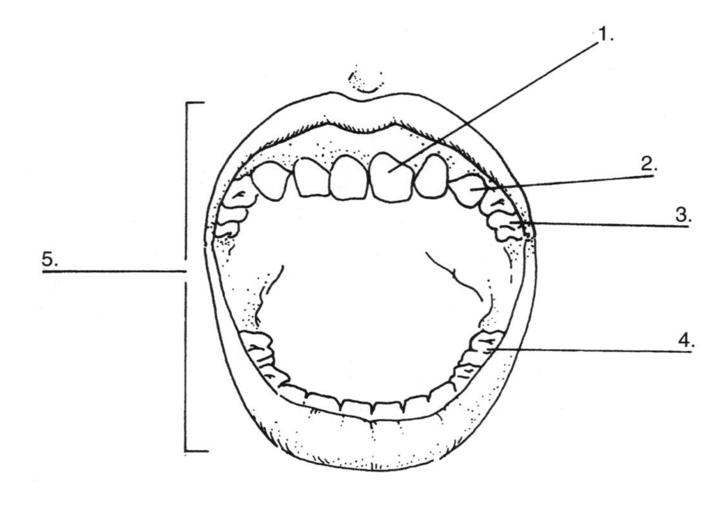

Nombre ______________________ Sección ______________ Fecha ______________

C Read the ad for Miami Dental Care Centers and answer the questions. Remember to guess the meaning of all cognates.

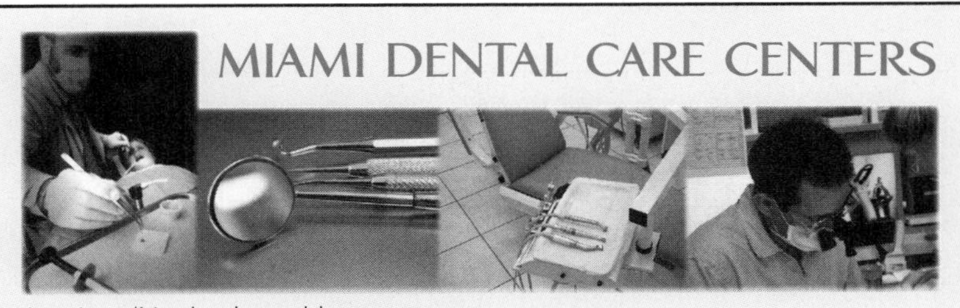

Anuncia su clínica dental cerca del aeropuerto.
GRATIS: Examen completo de su boca incluyendo radiografías.

Aproveche[1] esta oportunidad para cambiar esos dientes torcidos[2] que desde hace tanto tiempo le afean[3] su apariencia. Le podemos solucionar cualquier[4] problema dental, garantizándole su tratamiento[5] y utilizando materiales de alta calidad aprobados por la ADA.

Dentaduras completas	$500.00
Coronas de porcelana	$300.00
Limpieza[6]	$38.00
Empastes	$30.00

- Un laboratorio instalado en la misma clínica nos permite ofrecer los últimos adelantos[7] de la odontología moderna a precios de descuento[8].
- Abierto seis días a la semana.
- Servicio de emergencia las veinticuatro horas.
- Flexibilidad de horario[9] para su mayor comodidad[10].
- Se aceptan Visa, MasterCard y toda clase de seguros.

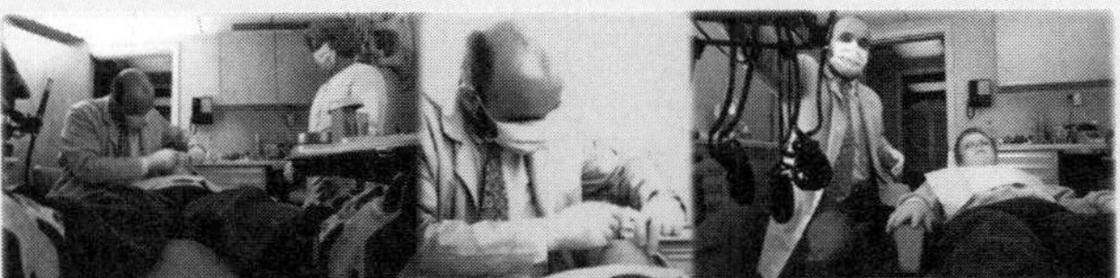

Permita que profesionales con largos años de experiencia le atiendan[11] su boca en forma amena[12], con equipos[13] modernos.

Pedro Urbino D.D.S.
José Martínez D.D.S.
Sylvia Madrigal D.D.S.
Eduardo Castellanos D.D.S.

Llame hoy mismo para una cita

695-4301

---

[1] *Take advantage of*
[2] *crooked*
[3] *disfigure*
[4] *any*
[5] *treatment*
[6] *Cleaning*
[7] *advances*
[8] *discount*
[9] *hours, schedule*
[10] *convenience*
[11] *attend to*
[12] *pleasant, agreeable*
[13] *equipment*

Nombre ______________________ Sección ____________ Fecha ____________

1. ¿Qué puede Ud. recibir gratis (*free*) en la clínica dental?

____

2. Según (*According to*) el anuncio, ¿qué puede cambiar?

____

3. ¿Cómo son los materiales que usan en la clínica dental?

____

4. ¿Cuánto va a pagar por una dentadura completa?

____

5. Si Ud. necesita una limpieza y un empaste, ¿cuánto va a pagar?

____

6. ¿Qué material usan en la clínica dental para las coronas?

____

7. ¿Cuántos dentistas trabajan (*work*) en la clínica?

____

8. Si Ud. tiene dolor de muelas a las once de la noche (*night*), ¿puede ir a la clínica dental? ¿Por qué?

____

Lectura 3 ¿Qué es la planificación familiar?

La planificación familiar es decidir cuándo se quiere tener un bebé. Si una mujer no quiere quedar embarazada, tiene que usar un método anticonceptivo.

¿Qué método es mejor para usted?

Al escoger[1] un método anticonceptivo, debe saber cuál es el mejor para usted. Hágase estas preguntas:

1. ¿Es un método saludable?[2] Quizás voy a necesitar la ayuda de mi médico para escoger un buen método.
2. ¿Voy a poder usar el método correctamente cada vez?
3. ¿Puede este método protegerme de enfermedades transmitidas sexualmente? Las enfermedades transmitidas sexualmente son las que se contagian al tener relaciones sexuales.

Tipos de métodos anticonceptivos:

1. Algunos no le permiten al óvulo de la mujer salir de los ovarios. Si los óvulos no salen de los ovarios, no pueden unirse al esperma para causar un embarazo.
2. Con otros métodos, el esperma del hombre no entra en el útero de la mujer y la mujer no puede quedar embarazada.
3. Algunos métodos matan[3] el esperma para prevenir la unión con el óvulo.

Recuerde lo siguiente:

1. Algunos métodos anticonceptivos funcionan mejor que otros.
2. Usar cualquier[4] método es mejor que no usar ninguno.
3. Los condones sirven para proteger contra el SIDA[5] y otras enfermedades transmitidas sexualmente. Si usa un condón con cualquier otro método ayuda a prevenir la transmisión del VIH[6] y de otras enfermedades que se transmiten sexualmente.
4. Debe visitar a su médico para obtener más información sobre la planificación familiar y de los diferentes métodos anticonceptivos. Con su ayuda, usted puede escoger el mejor método.

---

[1] **Al...** *When choosing*
[2] *healthy*
[3] *kill*
[4] *any*
[5] *AIDS*
[6] *HIV*

Nombre ______________________ Sección ____________ Fecha ____________

Conversaciones

1–27 —Doctor, yo no quiero tener un bebé todavía.
—Señora Silva, si usted no quiere quedar embarazada ahora, debe escoger un buen método anticonceptivo.
—¿Cuál es el más efectivo?
—La pastilla.
—¿Es un método seguro?
—Si lo usa correctamente, sí. Yo puedo darle una receta hoy mismo.

1–28 —Doctor, mi esposo no quiere usar condón y yo tengo problemas cuando tomo la pastilla. No sé qué hacer.
—Hay otros métodos, señora Lascano, como el diafragma, por ejemplo.
—No me gustan los diafragmas.
—Bueno... está el método del ritmo...
—Pero no es muy seguro.
—Es mejor usar cualquier método que no usar ninguno.

Dígame... Answer the following questions, basing your answers on the reading and the conversations.

1. ¿Qué es la planificación familiar?

   ____

2. ¿Qué pasa cuando los óvulos no salen de los ovarios?

   ____

3. ¿Cuál de los métodos anticonceptivos protege contra las enfermedades venéreas?

   ____

4. ¿Qué no quiere tener todavía la señora Silva?

   ____

5. ¿Cuál es el método anticonceptivo más efectivo?

   ____

6. ¿Es un método seguro?

   ____

7. ¿Cuándo puede darle el doctor la receta?

   ____

Nombre ______________________ Sección ____________ Fecha ____________

8. ¿Qué no quiere usar el Sr. Lascano?

____

9. ¿Por qué no puede usar su esposa la pastilla?

____

10. ¿Qué otros métodos recomienda el médico?

____

11. ¿Qué dice la señora del método del ritmo?

____

12. ¿Qué dice el doctor que es mejor?

____

Lección 10

En la sala de emergencia

Objectives

Structures

- The preterit of regular verbs
- The preterit of **ser, ir,** and **dar**
- Uses of **por** and **para**
- Seasons of the year and weather expressions

Communication

- Dealing with various health emergencies

En la sala de emergencia

1-29 Un accidente: Llega una ambulancia al hospital... Traen a un herido. Llevan la camilla a la sala de emergencia.

Doctor —¿Qué pasó?

Paciente —¡Ay...! Mi carro chocó con un árbol, me golpeé el hombro y me corté el brazo. Fue horrible.

Doctor —¿Perdió el conocimiento?

Paciente —Yo creo que sí, pero fue sólo por unos segundos.

Doctor —¿Cómo se siente ahora?

Paciente —Me duele mucho el hombro.

Doctor —Bueno, voy a limpiarle y desinfectarle la herida. Luego voy a tener que darle puntos y vendarle el brazo.

Paciente —¿Me va a poner una inyección antes?

Doctor —Sí, después vamos a hacerle una radiografía para ver si hay fractura. La enfermera lo va a llevar a la sala de rayos X.

Como el paciente necesita una inyección antitetánica, la enfermera se la pone.

Nombre ______________________ Sección ____________ Fecha ____________

Un caso de envenenamiento: Una madre trae a su hijo a la sala de emergencia. El niño tomó veneno.

Doctor —¿Qué cantidad de veneno tomó el niño, señora?
Madre —No sé... aquí está el frasco... está casi vacío...
Doctor —¿Vomitó o le dio Ud. algún líquido?
Madre —No, no vomitó ni tomó nada.
Doctor —Vamos a hacerle un lavado de estómago. No debe preocuparse. Pronto va a estar bien. Espere afuera, por favor.

Una fractura: La Sra. García se cayó en la escalera, y su esposo la trae a la sala de emergencia.

Doctor —¿Dónde le duele, señora?
Sra. García —Me duele mucho el tobillo; creo que me lo torcí.
Doctor —A ver... No, yo creo que es una fractura.

Los enfermeros llevan a la Sra. García a la sala de rayos X en una silla de ruedas. Después de ver las radiografías, el doctor confirma su diagnóstico y le explica a la Sra. García lo que va a hacer.

Doctor —Pues sí, Sra. García, Ud. se fracturó el tobillo. Vamos a tener que enyesárselo.
Sra. García —¿Por cuánto tiempo tengo que usar el yeso?
Doctor —Por seis semanas.
Sra. García —¿Voy a tener que usar muletas para caminar?
Doctor —Sí, señora.

Una quemadura: Una niña se quemó y su papá la trae a la sala de emergencia.

Doctor —¿Con qué se quemó la niña? ¿Con algo eléctrico, con algún ácido o con algo caliente?
El papá —Se quemó con agua hirviendo.
Doctor —La niña tiene una quemadura de tercer grado. Vamos a tener que ingresarla.

1-29

¡Escuchemos! While listening to the dialogue, circle **V (verdadero)** if the statement is true or **F (falso)** if it is false.

1. El carro de la primera paciente chocó con un árbol.
2. A la paciente le duele mucho el hombro.
3. Le van a hacer un análisis de sangre.
4. La paciente necesita una inyección antitetánica.
5. Una madre trae a su hijo a la sala de emergencia porque el niño tomó veneno.
6. El niño vomitó.
7. Van a llevar al niño a la sala de rayos equis.
8. La Sra. García cree que se torció el tobillo, pero el doctor cree que es una fractura.

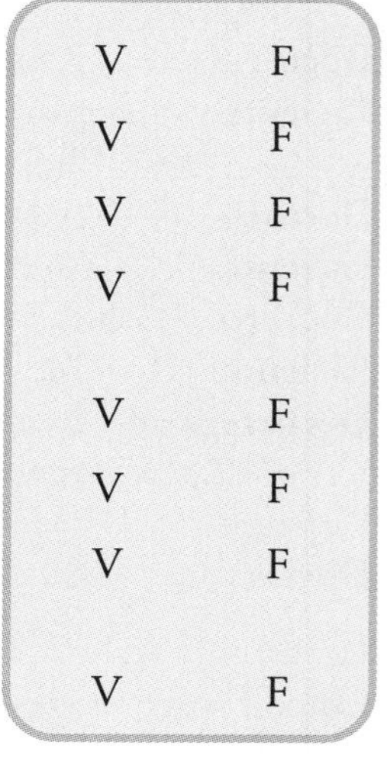

Nombre ______________________ Sección ____________ Fecha ____________

9. La Sra. García va a tener que usar muletas. V F

10. El señor que viene a la sala de emergencia se quemó con agua hirviendo. V F

Vocabulario

Cognados

el accidente
el ácido
la ambulancia
el caso
el diagnóstico
eléctrico(a)
la fractura
terrible

Nombres

el árbol *tree*
la camilla *gurney, stretcher*
el carro, el coche, el auto, la máquina (*Cuba*) *car*
el envenenamiento *poisoning*
la escalera *staircase*
el frasco, la botella, el pomo (*Cuba*) *bottle*
la frente *forehead*
la herida *wound*
el (la) herido(a) *injured person*
la inyección antitetánica *tetanus shot*
la muleta *crutch*
el punto, la puntada *stitch*
la quemadura *burn*
la sala de rayos X (equis) *X-ray room*
el segundo *second*
la silla de ruedas *wheelchair*
el veneno *poison*
el yeso, la escayola (*España*) *cast*

Verbos

caer(se)[1] *to fall*
caminar *to walk*
confirmar *to confirm*
chocar *to run into, to collide*
cortar(se) *to cut* (*oneself*)
desinfectar *to disinfect*
enyesar, escayolar (*España*) *to put a cast on*
explicar *to explain*
fracturarse, quebrarse (e:ie) (*Méx.*), **romperse** *to fracture, to break*
golpear(se) *to hit* (*oneself*)
ingresar *to admit* (*to a hospital*)
limpiar[2] *to clean*
llegar *to arrive*
pasar *to happen*
preocuparse (por) *to worry* (*about*)
quemar(se) *to burn* (*oneself*)
torcer(se)[3] **(o:ue)** *to twist*
vendar *to bandage*

Adjetivos

hirviendo *boiling*
tercero(a) *third*
vacío(a) *empty*

---

[1]Irregular first person: **yo (me) caigo.**
[2]**Lavar la herida** (*To wash the wound*) is also used.
[3]Irregular first person: **yo (me) tuerzo**

Nombre ______________________ **Sección** ____________ **Fecha** ____________

OTRAS PALABRAS Y EXPRESIONES

afuera *outside*
antes *first, before*
¡ay! *oh!*
casi *almost*
como *since, being that*
Creo que sí. *I think so.*
hacer un lavado de estómago *to pump the stomach*
lo que *that which*
perder (e:ie) el conocimiento, desmayarse *to lose consciousness, to faint, to be unconscious*
¿Por cuánto tiempo...? *For how long...?*
por unos segundos *for a few seconds*
pronto *soon*
pues *well*

VOCABULARIO ADICIONAL

ALGUNAS EXPRESIONES RELACIONADAS CON ACCIDENTES Y EMERGENCIAS

Tenga siempre a mano el número de teléfono *Always keep at hand the telephone number*
- **de su médico**
- **del centro de envenenamiento** *poison center*
- **de la policía** *police*
- **del hospital**
- **del departamento de bomberos** *fire department*
- **de la ambulancia**
- **de los paramédicos** *paramedics*

Para evitar el riesgo de envenenamiento, *To avoid the risk of poisoning,*
- **lea bien las instrucciones antes de tomar una medicina.** *read instructions carefully before taking (any) medicine.*
- **nunca tome medicinas en la oscuridad.** *never take (any) medicine in the dark.*
- **guarde las medicinas fuera del alcance de los niños pequeños.** *keep medicines out of small children's reach.*
- **nunca le diga a un niño que la medicina es "caramelo (dulce)".** *never tell a child that medicine is "candy."*

Nombre ______________________ **Sección** __________ **Fecha** __________

Está en la sala de emergencia porque
He/She is in the emergency room because

- **le dieron (pegaron) un tiro.** *they shot him/her.*
- **le dieron dos puñaladas.** *they stabbed him/her twice.*
- **tiene una herida de bala.** *he/she has a guhshot wound.*
- **tomó una sobredosis de cocaína (heroína).** *he/she took an overdose of cocaine (heroin)*
- **tuvo una reacción adversa a la medicina.** *he/she had an adverse reaction to the medication.*
- **sufrió un efecto secundario severo.** *he/she had a severe side effect.*
- **intentó suicidarse (matarse).** *he/she tried to commit suicide [kill himself (herself)].*

NOTAS CULTURALES

- In many Spanish-speaking countries, people are taken to special centers called **Casa de Socorros** (literally, *House of Help*) or **Casa de Primeros Auxilios** (*House of First Aid*) when they have medical emergencies. The staff at these centers treats the patient's problem and either releases the patient or sends him/her to a hospital for further treatment.
- In large urban areas in the U.S., economically disadvantaged Hispanic Americans receive a large portion of their health care services from big, public hospitals that have rotating staffs. In this type of setting, they rarely experience continuity of health care. Also, data from the HHANES study reveals that many Hispanic Americans use the emergency department as a source of primary care and that they are more likely to enter hospitals via emergency rooms rather than by other means. In a paper published in 1996, Llewellyn J. Cornelius and Zulema E. Suárez discuss the factors that account for such dependency of Hispanic Americans (and African Americans) on the outpatient care departments and the emergency room. This research was based on the National Medical Expenditure Survey. (See *Achieving Equitable Access: Studies of Health Care Issues Affecting Hispanics and African Americans.* Joint Center for Political and Economic Studies.)
- Some Hispanic patients are unsure how to access the American healthcare system other than through the emergency room. By the time they arrive in the emergency room, after trying to avoid medical attention, a simple condition may have become more serious.

Nombre ______________________ Sección ____________ Fecha ____________

Actividades

Dígame... Answer the following questions, basing your answers on the dialogues.

1. ¿Traen al herido en un coche o en una ambulancia?

   ____

2. ¿Qué le pasó al paciente cuando chocó contra un árbol?

   ____

3. ¿Por cuánto tiempo perdió el conocimiento?

   ____

4. ¿Para qué van a hacerle una radiografía al paciente?

   ____

5. ¿Por qué le van a hacer un lavado de estómago al niño?

   ____

6. ¿Dónde se cayó la Sra. García?

   ____

7. ¿Por qué van a enyesarle el tobillo?

   ____

8. ¿Por cuánto tiempo va a tener que usar el yeso, y qué va a necesitar para caminar?

   ____

9. ¿Con qué se quemó la niña?

   ____

10. ¿Por qué van a tener que ingresar a la niña?

    ____

Hablemos Interview a classmate, using the following questions. When you have finished, switch roles.

1. ¿Chocó Ud. con un auto alguna vez (*ever*)? ¿Qué le pasó?
2. ¿Se golpeó la cabeza alguna vez?
3. ¿Perdió Ud. el conocimiento alguna vez?

Nombre ______________________ Sección ____________ Fecha ____________

4. ¿Se quemó Ud. alguna vez? ¿Con qué?
5. ¿Se torció Ud. el tobillo alguna vez?
6. ¿Cómo se siente hoy?
7. Yo me fracturé la pierna. ¿Qué me van a hacer?
8. Yo me corté el dedo (*finger*). ¿Qué debo hacer?
9. Tengo una quemadura de primer grado. ¿Tienen que ingresarme en el hospital?
10. ¿Qué cree Ud. que va a hacer el médico?
11. ¿Qué hacen los médicos generalmente cuando una persona toma veneno?
12. ¿Cómo llevan a un herido de la ambulancia a la sala de emergencia?

Vamos a practicar

A Complete the following sentences, using the preterit of the verbs listed.

tomar	perder	romperse
golpearse	torcerse	quemarse
ir (2)	desinfectar	dar
llegar	ser	enyesar

Modelo Yo __________ a la clínica.
Yo **fui** a la clínica.

1. Mi papá __________ la cabeza.
2. La doctora me __________ la herida y me __________ cinco puntos.
3. La ambulancia __________ con un herido.
4. Yo __________ con agua hirviendo.
5. El Dr. López __________ el médico de mi esposo.
6. Mi papá __________ una pierna (*leg*) y el médico se la __________.
7. ¿__________ tú el conocimiento?
8. ¿Qué cantidad de veneno __________ él?
9. ¿Adónde __________ Uds. después del accidente? Nosotros __________ al hospital.
10. ¿Cuándo __________ Ud. el tobillo?

Nombre ______________________ Sección ____________ Fecha ____________

B Complete the following sentences with the Spanish equivalent of the words in parentheses.

MODELO Las muletas son __________. (*for my daughter*)
Las muletas son **para mi hija.**

1. ¿Cuánto pagaste ____________________? (*for the crutches*)
2. Lo llevaron a la sala de rayos X ____________________. (*to take an X-ray*)
3. Perdió el conocimiento ____________________. (*for a few seconds*)
4. Necesitamos los análisis ____________________. (*by tomorrow morning*)
5. Mi esposo tiene que estar en el hospital ____________________. (*for three days*)
6. Estos frascos son ____________________. (*for Dr. Soto*)

Conversaciones breves

Complete the following dialogues, using your imagination and the vocabulary from this lesson.

A El herido y la doctora:

Doctora —____________________

Herido —Me siento mal; la herida me duele mucho. ¿Tiene que darme puntos?

Doctora —____________________

Herido —¿Me va a doler?

Doctora —____________________

Herido —La pierna (*leg*) también me duele mucho. ¿Cree Ud. que tengo una fractura?

Doctora —____________________

Herido —¿Cuándo van a hacerme las radiografías?

Doctora —____________________

B La madre de un niño y el doctor:

Madre —Mi hijo tomó veneno.

Doctor —____________________

Madre —Sí, aquí está el frasco. Está casi vacío.

Doctor —____________________

Madre —¿Un lavado de estómago? ¿Va a estar bien después?

Doctor —____________________

Madre —Muchas gracias, doctor.

C El doctor y un paciente:

Paciente —Doctor, me quemé el brazo con ácido. Me duele mucho.

Doctor —____

Paciente —¿Una quemadura de tercer grado?

Doctor —____

Paciente —¿Por cuánto tiempo tengo que estar en el hospital?

Doctor —____

En estas situaciones

What would you say in the following situations? What might the other person say?

1. You have been hurt in a car accident. Tell the doctor that your car ran into a bus, and you hit your head on the windshield (**el parabrisas**) and cut your face. Also tell the doctor that you were unconscious for a few moments.

   The doctor explains that he/she is going to wash and disinfect the wound and give you three stitches and a tetanus shot.
2. You are a doctor. A parent with a child who has taken poison comes to the emergency room. Ask the parent how much poison the child took and whether he/she has the bottle. Tell the parent you are going to pump the child's stomach.
3. You are a doctor. A parent with a child who fell out of a tree and broke his/her arm comes to the emergency room. Tell the parent you are going to have X-rays taken and then put the child's arm in a cast.
4. You are a nurse. You tell a patient that since he broke his ankle, you are going to take him to the X-ray room in a wheelchair.

Casos

Act out the following emergency room scenes with a partner who plays the role of the patient needing medical treatment as a result of the situations listed.

1. a car accident
2. a case of poisoning
3. a fracture
4. a burn

Un paso más

A Review the **Vocabulario adicional** in this lesson. Then write whom you would call (the police, the fire department, etc.).

1. Ud. ve un accidente. ____

2. Hay un ladrón (*burglar*) en su casa. ______________________

3. Una mujer está lista (*ready*) para tener un bebé. ______________________

4. Hay un incendio (*fire*) en su casa. ______________________

5. Su hijo tomó veneno. ______________________

B Give the following people advice so that they can avoid the risk of poisoning.

1. una madre que tiene niños pequeños

____

____

____

____

2. una persona que siempre toma medicinas por la noche

____

____

____

____

3. una persona que tiene varios problemas de salud (*health*)

____

____

____

____

C The families of three patients who are in the emergency room ask you what happened. Since they only speak Spanish, you have to give them the following news in Spanish.

1. Their son took an overdose of cocaine.

____

2. Someone shot their mother twice.

____

3. Their daughter's husband stabbed her five times.

____

Nombre ______________________ Sección ____________ Fecha ____________

D Read the description of the emergency medical care unit at the Hospital Edgardo Rebagliati Martins in Lima, Perú, and answer the questions. Remember to guess the meaning of all cognates.

UNIDAD[1] DE EMERGENCIAS

• Es una de las más modernas y equipadas del país,[2] donde se atienden[3] aproximadamente 375 pacientes diariamente.[4] La unidad cuenta con treinta médicos permanentes de todas las especialidades, además de tres ambulancias que operan las veinticuatro horas del día. La unidad está habilitada con una moderna sala de reanimación[5] y shock-trauma para atender a los pacientes en estado[6] de shock y una unidad de monitoreo para controlar a aquéllos en estado crítico. Los pacientes que requieren una intervención quirúrgica[7] de emergencia son operados en una de las dos salas de operaciones de uso exclusivo con las que cuenta esta unidad.

1. ¿Cuántos pacientes pueden atender en un día en esta unidad?

   ____

2. ¿Cuántas ambulancias tienen? ¿Cuándo puede Ud. conseguir (*obtain*) una?

   ____

3. ¿Qué hacen con los pacientes en estado de shock?

   ____

4. ¿Cuántas salas de operaciones tiene esta unidad de emergencias?

   ____

5. ¿Cómo se compara (*compare*) esta unidad de emergencias con una en los Estados Unidos?

   ____

   ____

[1] *Unit*
[2] *country*
[3] **se ...** *are tended*
[4] *daily*
[5] *revival*
[6] *state*
[7] *surgical*

Nombre ______________________ Sección ____________ Fecha ____________

Repaso

Práctica de vocabulario

A Circle the word or phrase that best completes each sentence.

1. Tiene que comer por lo menos una cosa de cada (fruta / grupo / hígado).
2. Debe comer cantidades más (pequeñas / jóvenes / peligrosas).
3. Traen al herido en una (escalera / quemadura / camilla).
4. Quiero beber (un yeso / un refresco / una cartera).
5. El dentista dice que necesito una limpieza porque tengo mucho (sarro / espacio / ritmo).
6. Tomó veneno. Por eso le van a hacer un lavado de (boca / jalea / estómago).
7. Estos alimentos tienen pocas (calorías / coronas / dificultades).
8. Abra la boca y tóquese la muela que le duele cuando (saca / salva / muerde).
9. El médico le está haciendo un examen físico. Le pregunta si tiene ardor o (comezón / control / fractura) a veces.
10. Cuando corro, tengo dificultad para (doblar / apretar / respirar).
11. No comí nada. Estoy (ronco / sano / en ayunas).
12. Para tocarme el pecho con la barbilla, debo doblar la cabeza (hondo / hacia adelante / hacia atrás).
13. ¿Tiene Ud. la presión normal, alta o (baja / general / distinta)?
14. No hay nada (lentamente / de prisa / fuera de lo común).
15. Respire hondo. Respire por (el pie / la cabeza / la boca).
16. Para evitar la obesidad, hay que (torcerse el tobillo / hacer ejercicio / parecer sano).
17. Mi carro chocó con (un árbol / una pastilla / un chequeo).
18. Doble la cabeza hacia adelante hasta tocar (la espalda / las nalgas / el pecho) con la barbilla.
19. Me caí (en la escalera / correctamente / dentro de dos semanas).
20. ¿Eso se hace así? (¡Yo creo que sí! / ¿Qué pasó? / ¡En ese caso!)
21. En la escuela él come (preguntas / papas fritas / boca).
22. Ellos piden (caries / hamburguesas / sarro).

Nombre ______________________ **Sección** __________ **Fecha** __________

B Circle the word or phrase that does not belong in each group.

1. padezco, me duele, otra vez
2. sin comer, más o menos, en ayunas
3. no mucho, lo mismo, un poco
4. entrada, examen general, análisis
5. medir, ruido, tamaño
6. aparato intrauterino, condón, lista
7. chiles verdes, mantequilla de maní, melón
8. pescado, frijoles, naranjas
9. quemarse, pensar, fracturarse
10. probar, desinfectar, limpiar
11. vendar, variedad, herida
12. agua hirviendo, quemadura, árbol
13. tener insomnio, no poder dormir, perder el conocimiento
14. el condón, el control de la natalidad, el colesterol
15. leche, toronja, queso
16. espacio, cepillo de dientes, muela
17. adelgazar, bajar de peso, sentir
18. diabetes, azúcar, muleta
19. silla de ruedas, hombro, camilla
20. llegar, doler, molestar

C Complete the following sentences with the appropriate word or phrase from column **B.**

A	B
1. Tiene mal __________	a. encía.
2. Póngase una bolsa __________	b. preocupada.
3. Enjuáguese __________	c. posible.
4. Me sangra la __________	d. es insoportable.
5. El dolor __________	e. cuidado.
6. No coma muchos __________	f. dele yogur.
7. Estoy muy __________	g. de hielo.
8. Eso no es __________	h. más tarde.
9. Ella padece __________	i. sé.
10. Vuelva __________	j. la boca.
11. Si no quiere leche, __________	k. del corazón.
12. Hay que tener __________	l. calorías.
13. Tiene que contar las __________	m. aliento.
14. Se rompió __________	n. la pierna.
15. Ya lo __________	o. dulces.
16. Buena __________	p. con frecuencia.
17. No como dulces __________	q. las rodillas.
18. Separe __________	r. suerte.

Nombre ______________________ Sección ______________ Fecha ______________

D Crucigrama

Across

2. Quiero comer ____________ fritas.
4. Le van a ____________ la pierna porque tiene una fractura.
6. No sé el ____________ del análisis todavía.
11. Para hacer un sándwich, necesito ____________.
13. No quiero tener hijos. Uso un aparato ____________.
14. Está enfermo. No se ____________ bien.
15. Necesito un examen ____________.
21. Su ____________ es 150 libras.
22. Tengo piorrea. Debo ir al ____________.
24. Voy a ponerle una ____________ de penicilina.
26. Voy a la sala de rayos ____________.
28. Debe comer una cosa de cada ____________ de alimentos.
30. Necesita ____________ para caminar porque le enyesaron la pierna.
32. picadura
33. Para limpiarse entre los dientes usa hilo ____________.
34. La pastilla ____________ es un método efectivo para evitar el embarazo.
37. to happen, en español
39. Quiero jugo de ____________.
42. Tomó veneno. Es un caso de ____________.
44. Necesito un ____________ de estómago.
45. Aquí tiene una ____________ de los alimentos que debe comer.
46. ¿Su hijo tomó veneno? ¿Tiene el ____________ vacío?
47. Ellos ____________ al hospital a las tres.
48. No puedo dormir. Tengo ____________.

Down

1. Voy al dentista porque me duele una ____________.
2. opuesto de madre
3. Centro de ____________ de la familia.
5. El resultado no es positivo. Es ____________.
7. Tengo problemas para seguir una dieta. Es muy ____________.
8. Debe poner la crema por dentro y por ____________.
9. diferente
10. en seguida; muy ____________
12. Antes de extraerme la muela, el dentista me da ____________. Es una anestesia local.
14. Tengo que sacarle le muela porque no tiene ____________ espacio.
16. Debe comer la ____________ de lo que come ahora, si quiere perder peso.
17. No está frío. Está ____________.
18. El médico limpia y ____________ la herida.
19. En México es un blanquillo.
20. Tiene que seguir una ____________ estricta porque está muy gordo.
23. a veces, ____________ veces
25. No es incorrecto. Es ____________.
27. Tiene diabetes. Es ____________.
29. El dentista va a empastarme el diente porque está ____________.
31. El pollo, el arroz y las toronjas son ____________.
35. Me cepillo los ____________ con pasta dentífrica.
36. Me corté el dedo (*finger*) y el médico dice que necesito cinco ____________.
38. perder peso
40. Para el mal ____________ use Scope.
41. col
43. No tiene hijos. Está recién ____________.

Nombre ______________________ **Sección** ____________ **Fecha** ____________

1 2 3 4 5 6 7 8 9 10 11 12 13 14 15 16 17 18 19 20 21 22 23 24 25 26 27 28 29 30 31 32 33 34 35 36 37 38 39 40 41 42 43 44 45 46 47 48

Nombre ______________________ Sección ____________ Fecha ____________

Práctica oral

1-30 Listen to the following exercise on the audio program. The speaker will ask you some questions. Answer the questions, using the cues provided. The speaker will confirm the correct answer. Repeat the correct answer.

1-31

1. ¿Cuánto pesa Ud.? (180 libras)
2. ¿Cuánto peso necesita perder Ud.? (20 libras)
3. ¿Ud. sube y baja de peso con frecuencia? (no)
4. ¿Es difícil para Ud. seguir una dieta estricta? (sí)
5. ¿Come Ud. muchos dulces? (no)
6. ¿Qué frutas prefiere comer Ud.? (naranjas y fresas)
7. ¿Padece Ud. del corazón? (no)
8. ¿Tiene Ud. dolor de cabeza frecuentemente? (sí)
9. ¿Qué toma Ud. cuando le duele la cabeza? (aspirinas)
10. ¿Tiene Ud. ruido en los oídos? (sí, a veces)
11. ¿Tiene Ud. dificultad para respirar? (sí, cuando corro)
12. ¿Tiene Ud. dolor o ardor cuando orina? (no, nunca)
13. ¿Tiene Ud. la presión alta? (no, normal)
14. ¿Tiene Ud. el colesterol normal? (no, alto)
15. ¿Necesita Ud. hacerse algún análisis? (sí, de sangre)
16. ¿Qué pasta de dientes usa Ud.? (Colgate)
17. ¿Le sangran las encías cuando se cepilla los dientes? (a veces)
18. ¿Perdió Ud. el conocimiento alguna vez? (no, nunca)
19. ¿Se cayó Ud. ayer? (sí, en la escalera)
20. ¿Se quemó Ud. alguna vez? (sí, con agua hirviendo)
21. ¿Cuál cree Ud. que es el mejor método para evitar el embarazo? (la pastilla)
22. ¿Son peligrosos los aparatos intrauterinos? (no)

NACE UN BEBÉ

OBJECTIVES

Structures

- Time expressions with **hacer**
- Irregular preterits
- The preterit of stem-changing verbs (**e:i** and **o:u**)
- Command forms: **tú**

Communication

- Giving birth–infant care

NACE UN BEBÉ

El Sr. Guerra llama por teléfono al médico porque su esposa comenzó a tener los dolores de parto.

Dr. Peña —¿Cuánto tiempo hace que tiene los dolores?
Sr. Guerra —Hace unas dos horas. Comenzaron a las cuatro de la tarde.
Dr. Peña —¿Cada cuánto tiempo le vienen?
Sr. Guerra —Cada cinco minutos.
Dr. Peña —¿Siente los dolores en la espalda primero y después en el vientre?
Sr. Guerra —Sí.
Dr. Peña —Tráigala al hospital en seguida.

Veinte minutos más tarde, la Sra. Guerra está en el hospital. Su esposo la trajo y una amiga de la Sra. Guerra vino con ellos. Ya se le rompió la bolsa de agua.

Dr. Peña —Abra las piernas y doble las rodillas. Ponga los pies en los estribos. Relájese. No se ponga tensa. (*Después de examinarla*) Bueno, Ud. tiene que quedarse en el hospital. ¿A qué hora movió el vientre?
Sra. Guerra —Esta tarde, después de comer.
Dr. Peña —Vamos a llevarla a la sala de parto ahora mismo.

En la sala de parto, el Sr. Guerra está con su esposa.

Dr. Peña —No puje si no siente los dolores. Cálmese. Respire normalmente.
Sra. Guerra —Déme algo para calmar el dolor... por favor... ¿Voy a necesitar una operación cesárea?
Dr. Peña —No. Ud. es un poco estrecha, pero todo va bien. Vamos a ponerle una epidural y Ud. no va a sentir los dolores. (*Le ponen la inyección.*) Ahora tiene Ud. una contracción. Puje. Muy bien. Voy a tener que usar fórceps para sacar al bebé. (*A la enfermera*) Dame los fórceps.
Sra. Guerra —¿Va a usar fórceps? ¡Eso puede lastimar al bebé!
Dr. Peña —No, no se preocupe. Puje... Ya está saliendo... ¡Es un varón!
Sr. Guerra —¡Tenemos un hijo!
Sra. Guerra —¿Tuve un varón... ?
Dr. Peña —Sí, y todo salió muy bien. No sintió mucho dolor, ¿verdad? Ahora tiene que salir la placenta. Puje otra vez. Así... eso es...

Más tarde:

Dr. Peña —¿Va a darle de mamar al bebé o piensa darle biberón?
Sra. Guerra —Pienso darle biberón.
Dr. Peña —En ese caso, para no tener leche Ud., debe ponerse bolsas de hielo en los senos y debe tomar Tylenol si siente dolor. Ah, ¿ya eligieron un nombre para el niño?
Sra. Guerra —Sí, se va a llamar Gustavo Adolfo.

La Sra. Guerra habla con su esposo en la habitación.

Sra. Guerra —(*A su esposo*) Ve a ver al niño en la sala de bebés. Es muy bonito, ¿verdad? Hazme un favor, dile a la enfermera que queremos tener al bebé con nosotros un rato.

2–2

¡Escuchemos!

While listening to the dialogue, circle **V (verdadero)** if the statement is true or **F (falso)** if it is false.

1. Hace cuatro horas que la Sra. Guerra tiene dolores de parto.
2. La señora tiene dolores cada cinco minutos.
3. El médico dice que la Sra. puede regresar a su casa.
4. El doctor va a ponerle una epidural a la señora.
5. La señora debe pujar con cada contracción.
6. La señora cree que los fórceps van a lastimar al bebé.
7. La señora tuvo una hija.
8. La señora. le va a dar de mamar a su bebé.
9. Los padres ya eligieron el nombre del bebé.
10. La señora. va a ir ahora a ver a su bebé.

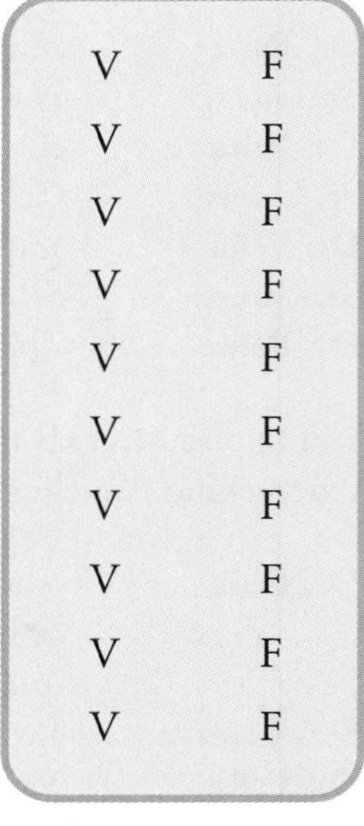

Nombre ______________ Sección ______________ Fecha ______________

Audio

Vocabulario

COGNADOS

cesárea
la contracción
la epidural
el favor
los fórceps
normalmente
la operación
la placenta

NOMBRES

el (la) amigo(a) *friend*
el biberón, la mamadera, la mamila (*Méx.*) *baby bottle*
la bolsa de agua, la fuente de agua *water bag*
el dolor de parto *labor pain*
los estribos *stirrups*
la habitación *room*
el parto, el alumbramiento *delivery*
la pierna *leg*
la sala de bebés *nursery*
la sala de parto *delivery room*
la tarde *afternoon*
el varón[1] *male, boy*
el vientre, la barriga *abdomen*

VERBOS

calmar(se) *to calm down*
comenzar (e:ie) *to begin, to start*
elegir (e:i)[2] *to choose, to select*
lastimar(se) *to hurt* (*oneself*)
llamarse *to be named*
nacer[3] *to be born*
pensar (e:ie) *to plan*
pujar *to push* (*in the case of labor or defecation*)
quedarse *to remain, to stay*
relajarse *to relax* (*oneself*)

ADJETIVOS

bonito(a) *pretty*
estrecho(a) *narrow*

OTRAS PALABRAS Y EXPRESIONES

así *like that, that way*
dar de mamar, dar el pecho, amamantar *to nurse*
mover (o:ue) el vientre, obrar, defecar, evacuar (*Méx.*)[4] *to have a bowel movement*
ponerse tenso(a) *to tense up*
un rato *a while*
¿verdad? *right?, true?*
ya *already, now*

---

[1]Colloquialism: **la mujercita** (*Méx.*) = *female, girl*
[2]First person: **yo elijo**
[3]Irregular first person: **yo nazco**
[4]Colloquialisms: **hacer caca, corregir (e:i)** (*Cuba*)

Nombre ______________________ Sección ____________ Fecha ____________

VOCABULARIO ADICIONAL

OTROS TÉRMINOS RELACIONADOS CON EL PARTO Y EL CUIDADO DEL BEBÉ

el bebé prematuro *premature baby*
el cordón umbilical *umbilical cord*
el cuidado postnatal *postnatal care*
el cuidado prenatal *prenatal care*
el chupete, el chupón (*Méx.*), **el tete** (*Cuba*) *pacifier*
dar a luz, parir *to give birth*
dilatado(a) *dilated*
estar de parto *to be in labor*
el feto *fetus*
la fórmula *formula*
hacer un sonograma *to do a sonogram*
la incubadora *incubator*
los (las) mellizos(as), los (las) gemelos(as)[1] *twins*
el nacimiento *birth*
la partera, la comadrona *midwife*
el parto natural *natural childbirth*
el pezón *nipple*
la raquídea, la anestesia espinal *spinal anesthesia*
el (la) recién nacido(a) *newborn*
romperse la fuente *to break water*
la sala de maternidad *maternity ward*

NOTAS CULTURALES

- In small towns and rural regions of Latin America, midwives play an important role because there are relatively few doctors. Even in large cities, some women prefer to give birth in their homes with the help of a midwife in spite of the fact that care in large hospitals may be free of charge.
- The actual percentage of Hispanic American mothers who breast-feed for any duration varies widely among the three major ethnic groups. Generally, Mexican Americans are more likely to breast-feed than Cuban Americans or Puerto Ricans. For example, studies have shown that breast-feeding rates among Mexican American women range from 31% to 60%, whereas those among Puerto Rican women are from 10% to 11%, and the rate among Cuban American women is 12%. Two reasons for the overall low rate of breast-feeding have been proposed. The first one reflects cultural attitudes. Some Latinos with little education believe that a fat baby is healthy, and bottle-fed babies tend to be fatter than breast-fed babies. The second one involves the manner in which the obstetrician approaches the topic of breast-feeding versus bottle-feeding and the mother's compliance with the physician's recommendations.

[1]Colloquialisms: **los (las) cuates** (*Méx.*), **los (las) jimaguas** (*Cuba*)

Nombre ______________________ Sección ____________ Fecha ____________

Actividades

Dígame... Answer the following questions, basing your answers on the dialogue.

1. ¿Cuánto tiempo hace que la Sra. Guerra tiene dolores?

2. ¿Cada cuánto tiempo le vienen los dolores?

3. ¿Dónde siente los dolores?

4. ¿Se le rompió la bolsa de agua?

5. ¿Tiene que quedarse la Sra. Guerra en el hospital?

6. ¿Adónde van a llevarla?

7. ¿Va a necesitar la Sra. Guerra una operación cesárea? ¿Qué va a necesitar?

8. ¿Tuvo la Sra. Guerra un varón o una niña? ¿Qué nombre eligieron para el bebé?

9. ¿Va a darle de mamar al bebé la Sra. Guerra?

10. ¿Qué debe hacer la Sra. Guerra si siente dolor en los senos?

Hablemos Interview a classmate, using the following questions. When you have finished, switch roles.

1. ¿En qué año nació Ud.?
2. Cuando Ud. nació, ¿estuvo su padre en la sala de parto?
3. ¿Estuvo Ud. ingresado(a) en el hospital alguna vez? ¿Por qué?

4. ¿Cuánto tiempo se quedó en el hospital?

5. ¿Cuánto tiempo se queda Ud. en clase normalmente?

6. ¿Trabaja Ud. (*Do you work*) en la sala de partos?

7. Si una mujer tiene dolores de parto cada tres minutos, ¿qué debe hacer?

8. ¿Cuántas operaciones cesáreas puede tener una mujer?

9. ¿Qué es mejor para el bebé, darle de mamar o darle el biberón?

10. ¿Es necesario mover el vientre todos los días?

11. ¿Se pone Ud. tenso(a) a veces?

12. ¿Qué hace Ud. para calmarse?

Vamos a practicar

A Rewrite the following sentences, changing the verbs to the preterit.

Modelo Él no sabe qué decir.
Él no **supo** qué decir.

1. Ella viene al hospital y trae los biberones.

____

2. Nosotros no estamos en la sala de parto.

____

3. Ellos tienen que hablar con su vecino.

____

4. Tú no quieres ir al hospital.

____

5. El médico no puede calmarla.

____

6. Ella pone los pies en los estribos.

____

7. ¿Qué dicen los médicos?

____

8. Ella no hace nada.

____

9. Él siente mucho dolor.

____

10. Ellos eligen un nombre para su hijo.

____

B Give instructions, using familiar (**tú**) commands and the cues provided.

MODELO hacer los análisis
Haz los análisis.

1. venir a la una y traer las muestras

____

2. ir al hospital y llevar a la señora a la sala de parto

____

3. decirle al médico que el niño está enfermo

____

4. relajarse; no preocuparse

____

5. tener cuidado; no lastimarse

____

6. no quedarse en casa

____

7. comprar un biberón y ponerlo en el cuarto

____

8. darle la mamadera al bebé

____

9. ponerse una bolsa de hielo

____

10. no caerse

____

Nombre ______________________ **Sección** ____________ **Fecha** ____________

C Write the following exchange in Spanish.

"How long have you had the pain, Mrs. Cabrera?"
"I've had it for three hours."

____

____

Conversaciones breves

Complete the following dialogue, using your imagination and the vocabulary from this lesson.

A La paciente y el doctor:

Paciente —Hola, ¿Dr. Paz? Comencé a tener dolores...

Doctor —____

Paciente —Hace una hora.

Doctor —____

Paciente —Cada seis minutos.

Doctor —____

Paciente —Primero en la espalda y después en el vientre.

Doctor —____

Paciente —Muy bien, doctor. En seguida vamos.

B En la sala de parto:

Paciente —¿Pujo ahora, doctor?

Doctor —____

Paciente —¿Voy a necesitar una operación cesárea?

Doctor —____

Paciente —¿Va a usar fórceps? ¿No va a lastimar eso al bebé?

Doctor —____

Paciente —¡Estoy pujando!

Doctor —____

Paciente —¡Un varón! ¿Está bien?

Doctor —____

Paciente —Doctor. Yo quiero darle biberón al bebé. No voy a darle el pecho.

Doctor —____

Nombre ______________________ Sección ____________ Fecha ____________

En estas situaciones What would you say in the following situations? What might the other person say?

1. Tell someone that your friend is having labor pains every five minutes and to please call the doctor.
2. You are a doctor, examining a patient in labor. Tell your patient to open her legs and bend her knees and put her feet on the stirrups. Tell her not to be tense and to relax. Ask her what time she had a bowel movement.
3. You are a doctor. Tell your patient to breathe normally and not to push if she doesn't feel a contraction. Explain to her that she is a little narrow, so you are going to take the baby out with forceps.
4. You are a nurse. Ask Mrs. Paz whether she felt a lot of pain. Ask her also how she slept last night.

Casos Act out the following scenarios with a partner.

1. A patient calls her obstetrician to find out if it's time to go to the hospital because she thinks she is having labor pains.
2. A doctor examines a patient to see whether or not she's ready to be admitted to the hospital.
3. A patient and her obstetrician are in the birthing room; the patient is giving birth.

Un paso más

A Review the **Vocabulario adicional** in this lesson. Then complete the following conversations.

1. —Ayer me hicieron un ____________.

   —¿Qué te dijo el médico? ¿Que es un varón?

   —No, que es una niña.

   —¿Cuántas semanas tiene el ____________?

   —Tiene tres semanas.

2. —¿De qué les habló la partera?

   —Nos habló del cuidado prenatal y ____________ de los bebés.

3. —¿El bebé nació antes de los nueve meses?

   —Sí, fue un bebé ____________. Lo pusieron en la ____________.

   —¿Dónde está la mamá ahora?

   —Está en la sala de ____________.

   —¿A qué hora dio a ____________?

   —A las cinco de la tarde.

   —¿Le dieron anestesia?

   —Sí, le pusieron ____________.

4. —¿Ya le cortaron el ____________ umbilical a su hijo?

—Sí.

5. —¿La Sra. García tuvo ____________?

—Sí. ¡Son idénticos!

—¿Fue un ____________ natural?

—No, tuvieron que hacerle cesárea.

—¿Dónde están ahora los recién ____________?

—En su casa (*home*).

—¿Ella les va a dar de mamar?

—No, les va a dar ____________.

6. —¿Por qué llora (*cry*) el niño?

—Porque no tiene su ____________.

B Read these suggestions on the care of newborns and answer the following questions. Remember to guess the meaning of all cognates.

Algunas sugerencias útiles[1]

La mayoría de los bebés al principio[2] comen cada tres o cuatro horas. Si el bebé duerme por más de cinco horas durante el día, debe despertarlo y darle de comer. No es necesario despertar al bebé durante la noche para darle de comer.

No es necesario calentar[3] la fórmula antes de usarla. Sólo tiene que colocar el biberón en agua tibia para que la leche no esté muy fría y ponerla a la temperatura ambiente.[4] Si el bebé no toma toda la fórmula en el biberón, no debe forzarlo. Si queda un poco de fórmula, puede refrigerarla y usarla sólo una vez[5] más. Una vez que haya usado[6] un biberón nunca le añada[7] más fórmula. Puede darle la fórmula usada primero, y después continúe dándole fórmula de un biberón nuevo.[8]

La fórmula con hierro tiene todas las vitaminas y minerales que el bebé necesita durante los primeros meses de vida.[9] Es buena idea darle al bebé fórmula fortificada con hierro durante los primeros seis meses de vida. Luego puede cambiar a leche natural.

Su bebé no necesita comidas sólidas, jugos de fruta ni agua adicional hasta que no tenga[10] por lo menos cinco o seis meses. Debe consultar con el pediatra antes de darle comidas sólidas. Antes de salir del hospital, el médico o la enfermera puede contestar cualquier[11] pregunta que Ud. tenga sobre el cuidado del bebé. Una vez en su casa, puede llamar al doctor, a la clínica o a la asociación de enfermeras de salud[12] pública si tiene alguna pregunta.

---

[1] *useful*
[2] **al...** *in the beginning*
[3] *to heat up*
[4] *room*
[5] **una...** *once*
[6] **haya...** *you have used*
[7] *add*
[8] *new*
[9] *life*
[10] **hasta...** *until he is*
[11] **contestar...** *answer any*
[12] *health*

Nombre ______________________ **Sección** __________ **Fecha** __________

1. ¿Cuándo comen los recién nacidos?

____

2. ¿Debe despertar al bebé durante la noche para darle de comer?

____

3. ¿Qué debe hacer con la fórmula antes de dársela al bebé?

____

4. ¿Por qué debe darle al bebé fórmula con hierro?

____

5. ¿Con quién debe consultar antes de darle al bebé comidas sólidas?

____

6. ¿A qué edad (*age*) debe darle al bebé comidas sólidas?

____

Lección 12 En el centro médico

Objectives

Structures

- **En** and **a** as equivalents of *at*
- The imperfect tense
- The past progressive
- The preterit contrasted with the imperfect

Communication

- In the specialist's office

En el centro médico

2-3

Una mañana en los consultorios de algunos especialistas

En el consultorio del oculista:

Oculista —Voy a hacerle un examen de la vista. Mire a la pared. ¿Puede leer las letras más grandes?
Paciente —Sí, las veo claramente.
Oculista —¿Y la línea siguiente?
Paciente —También. (*Lee las letras.*)
Oculista —¿La próxima línea?
Paciente —Ésa no, las letras están un poco borrosas.
Oculista —Ahora mire directamente a la luz en este aparato. Dígame ahora cuántas luces ve. ¿Están cerca o lejos una de otra?
Paciente —Veo dos; están cerca.
Oculista —Siga el punto rojo. Ahora lea las letras con estos lentes. ¿Qué letras ve mejor? ¿Las letras del lado rojo o las letras del lado verde?
Paciente —Las letras que están en el lado verde.
Oculista —Ahora voy a hacerle la prueba del glaucoma. Ponga la barbilla aquí y mire directamente a la luz.

Nombre ______________________ Sección ____________ Fecha ____________

En el consultorio del urólogo:

Sr. Paz —Doctor, mi esposa tuvo otro bebé y nosotros no queríamos más hijos... Ella me dijo que podía ligarse los tubos o que yo podía hacerme una vasectomía.
Doctor —La decisión es de Uds.
Sr. Paz —Si yo me hago una vasectomía, ¿cuánto tiempo tengo que estar en el hospital?
Doctor —Puedo operarlo aquí mismo, y sólo tiene que dejar de trabajar dos días. No es una cirugía mayor.
Sr. Paz —¡Ah!, es una cirugía menor. Yo no sabía que era tan fácil. Voy a pensarlo antes de tomar una decisión. Ah, ¿la operación es reversible?
Doctor —Sí, es reversible, pero puede haber complicaciones.

En el consultorio del cirujano:

Doctor —¿Cuándo fue la última vez que se hizo una mamografía?
Sra. Mena —El año pasado, pero el otro día, cuando me estaba revisando los senos, encontré una bolita en el pecho izquierdo.
Doctor: —Vamos a ver.

Después de examinarla:

Doctor —Sí, encontré algo duro en el seno.
Sra. Mena —Puede ser cáncer, ¿verdad?
Doctor —No necesariamente. Puede ser un quiste o un tumor, pero la mayoría de los tumores son benignos. Para asegurarnos de que no es maligno, vamos a hacerle una biopsia.

En el consultorio de la dermatóloga:

Paciente —Doctora, tengo mucho acné. Usé una crema pero no me dio resultado.
Doctora —Sí, tiene muchos granos y espinillas. Es un problema frecuente en las personas jóvenes.
Paciente —Cuando yo era adolescente comía mucha grasa y mucho chocolate, pero ahora me cuido más.
Doctora —La alimentación no tiene mucha importancia en este caso, pero Ud. necesita tratamiento.
Paciente —¿Qué tengo que hacer?
Doctora —Yo voy a sacarle las espinillas y el pus de los granos. Además, Ud. debe usar un jabón medicinal y una loción.
Paciente —Muy bien. ¡Ah! Tengo una verruga en el cuello. Traté de cortármela pero me sangraba mucho.
Doctora —Eso es peligroso. Yo puedo quitársela la próxima vez.

2–3

¡Escuchemos!

While listening to the dialogue, circle **V (verdadero)** if the statement is true or **F (falso)** if it is false.

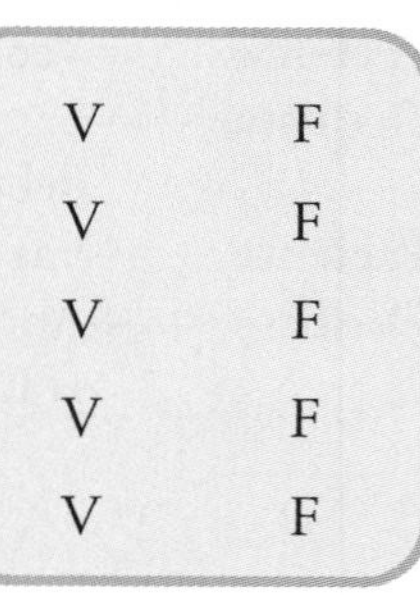

1. El paciente no ve bien las letras más grandes porque están borrosas. V F
2. El paciente ve tres luces. V F
3. El paciente ve las luces cerca una de otra. V F
4. El Sr. Paz y su esposa desean tener más hijos. V F
5. El Sr. Paz debe ir al hospital para hacerse una vasectomía. V F

6. La vasectomía es una operación muy difícil.
7. La Sra. Mena puede tener un tumor en el seno.
8. El médico dice que la mayoría de los tumores son malignos.
9. El acné es un problema frecuente en los adolescentes.
10. El paciente tiene muchas espinillas y granos.

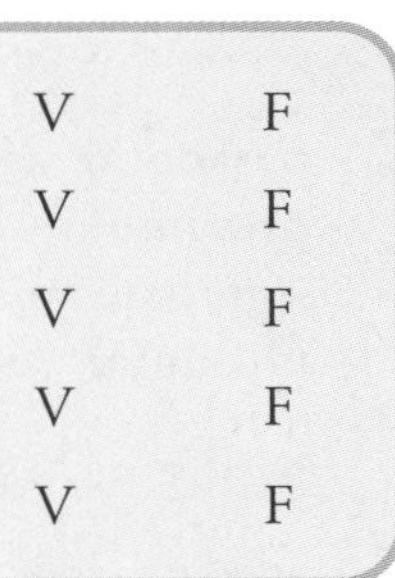

Vocabulario

Cognados

el acné
benigno(a)
la biopsia
la complicación
la decisión
el (la) dermatólogo(a)
directamente
el (la) especialista
frecuente
el glaucoma
la importancia
la loción
maligno(a)
la mamografía
medicinal
el (la) oculista
la persona
reversible
el tumor
el (la) urólogo(a)
la vasectomía

Nombres

el (la) adolescente *teenager*
la alimentación *food*
el aparato *apparatus, instrument*
la bolita[1] *lump, little ball*
la cirugía *surgery*
el día *day*
la espinilla *blackhead*
el grano *pimple*
el jabón *soap*
el lado *side*
la línea *line*
la luz *light*
la mayoría *majority*
la pared *wall*
el punto *dot*
el quiste *cyst*
el tratamiento *treatment*
la verruga *wart*
la vista *vision*

Verbos

asegurarse *to make sure*
cuidar(se) *to take care (of oneself)*
encontrar (o:ue) *to find*
operar *to operate*
quitar *to take out, to remove*

Adjetivos

borroso(a) *blurry*
izquierdo(a) *left*
mayor *major*
menor *minor*

[1]Colloquialism: **la masa** (*mass*)

pasado(a) *last*
próximo(a) *next*
siguiente *following, next*
último(a) *last* (in a series)

OTRAS PALABRAS Y EXPRESIONES

aquí mismo *right here*
cerca (de) *near, close*
claramente *clearly*
dar resultado *to work, to produce results*
lejos (de) *far (away)*
ligar los tubos *to tie the tubes*
no tener importancia *to not matter*
puede haber *there can be*
tomar una decisión *to make a decision*
la última vez *the last time*

Vocabulario adicional

ALGUNOS TÉRMINOS RELACIONADOS CON LA UROLOGÍA

El paciente tiene
- **cálculos (piedras) en el riñón** *kidney stones*
- **infección en la vejiga** *infection in the urinary bladder*
- **irritación y dolor al orinar** *irritation and pain when urinating*

ALGUNOS TÉRMINOS RELACIONADOS CON LA DERMATOLOGÍA

Ud. tiene
- **el cutis**[1] *skin*
  - **seco** *dry*
  - **grasiento** *oily*
  - **normal** *normal*
- **eccema** *eczema*
- **hongos** *fungus*
- **soriasis** *psoriasis*
- **una infección en el cuero cabelludo** *an infection in the scalp*

ALGUNOS TÉRMINOS RELACIONADOS CON LA VISTA

Ud. tiene
- **astigmatismo** *astigmatism*
- **desprendimiento de la retina** *a detached retina*
- **miopía** *nearsightedness*
- **daltonismo** *color blindness*
- **hiperopía** *farsightedness*
- **cataratas** *cataracts*

Él es
- **bizco** *cross-eyed*
- **ciego** *blind*
- **miope, corto de vista** *nearsighted*
- **présbita, présbite** *farsighted*

¡OJO! For additional terms related to the eye, see the diagram on page xxii.

---

[1]This term is used to refer to facial skin.

Nombre ______________________ Sección ____________ Fecha ____________

NOTAS CULTURALES

Search

- A vasectomy is the least common means of birth control used by Latino men for two cultural reasons: the concept of **machismo** and the belief that women are responsible for birth control.
- In most Spanish-speaking countries, the use of **curanderos** or folk healers has a long tradition that dates back to pre-Columbian times. **Curanderos** use their knowledge of medicinal herbs and plants to treat all types of illnesses, and they sometimes utter prayers when they administer their remedies.

Although controversy exists among Latino health experts concerning the frequency with which **curanderos** are used in the United States, it is true that some Hispanic Americans, who have little or no formal education, may consult both a **curandero** and a physician for the same ailment. The physician's response to the use of the **curandero** can greatly influence a patient's decision regarding treatment. To establish trust, it is not necessary to give credence to folk healing; instead it is better to inquire about the use of a **curandero** (if they exist in your area) during the diagnostic process by asking, "Have you visited a **curandero** recently and, if so, what were you given?" In this manner, the doctor acknowledges the importance of this cultural practice in the patient's life. The question is also valid from a clinical standpoint since some of the herbs or medications dispensed by the **curandero** may have negative interactions with the medication prescribed by the physician.

Actividades

Dígame... Answer the following questions, basing your answers on the dialogues.

1. ¿Cómo ve el paciente del oculista las dos primeras líneas?

   ____

2. ¿Qué letras ve mejor el paciente: las del lado verde o las del lado rojo?

   ____

3. ¿Qué prueba va a hacerle el oculista al paciente?

   ____

4. ¿Qué le dijo la Sra. Paz a su esposo?

   ____

5. ¿Cuánto tiempo debe dejar de trabajar el Sr. Paz después de la vasectomía?

   ____

6. ¿Cuándo fue la última vez que le hicieron una mamografía a la Sra. Mena?

   ____

Nombre ______________________ Sección ____________ Fecha ____________

7. ¿Qué encontró la Sra. Mena cuando se estaba revisando los senos?

____

8. ¿Qué va a hacer el doctor para asegurarse de que el tumor no es maligno?

____

9. ¿Qué problemas tiene el paciente de la dermatóloga?

____

10. ¿Qué comía él cuando era adolescente?

____

11. ¿Se cuida más ahora?

____

12. ¿Qué no es importante en este caso?

____

13. ¿Qué debe usar el paciente para el acné?

____

14. ¿Qué le pasó al paciente cuando trató de cortarse la verruga? ¿Quién se la va a quitar?

____

Hablemos Interview a classmate, using the following questions. When you have finished, switch roles.

1. ¿Le hizo el oculista la prueba del glaucoma la última vez que Ud. fue a verlo?
2. Si las letras son pequeñas, ¿las ve Ud. claramente?
3. ¿La vasectomía es una cirugía mayor o menor? ¿Es reversible?
4. ¿Son malignos todos los tumores?
5. ¿Qué puede hacer el cirujano para saber si un tumor es benigno o maligno?
6. ¿Tuvo Ud. acné alguna vez?
7. ¿Tiene Ud. espinillas? ¿Granos?
8. ¿Come Ud. mucha grasa? ¿Mucho chocolate?
9. ¿Está Ud. siguiendo algún tratamiento?

Nombre ______________________ **Sección** ____________ **Fecha** ____________

10. ¿Qué debe hacer una persona que tiene muchas espinillas?

11. ¿Tiene Ud. verrugas?

12. ¿Le sangra a veces la nariz (*nose*)?

13. ¿Lo (La) operaron alguna vez? ¿De qué?

Quiz

Vamos a practicar

A Write sentences telling what the following people were doing at four o'clock yesterday, using the past progressive and the elements given.

MODELO él / comer / chocolate
Él **estaba comiendo** chocolate.

1. Carlos / trabajar / y yo / dormir
____

2. nosotros / hablar / con el oculista
____

3. los médicos / examinar / a sus pacientes
____

4. tú / servir / café
____

5. Uds. / pedir turno / con el dermatólogo
____

B Complete the following exchanges, using the preterit or the imperfect of the verbs given.

MODELO ¿Dónde __________ (vivir) él cuando __________(ser) niño?
¿Dónde **vivía** él cuando **era** niño?

1. —¿Qué te __________(decir) el médico ayer?
—Me __________(decir) que yo __________(tener) un tumor benigno.
2. —¿Qué hora __________(ser) cuando tú __________(ver) al especialista ayer?
—__________(Ser) las dos.

3. —¿Por qué no ___________(venir) ellos al hospital el martes pasado?
—Porque no ___________(poder). ___________(Tener) que ir al dermatólogo.
4. —¿Tú ___________(comer) mucha grasa cuando ___________(ser) adolescente?
—No, yo me ___________(cuidar) mucho.
5. —¿Cuántos años ___________(tener) tú cuando ___________(venir) a California?
—Yo ___________(tener) 20 años.
6. —¿Adónde ___________(ir) Uds. cuando yo los ___________(ver)?
—___________(Ir) al consultorio del urólogo.

Conversaciones breves

Complete the following dialogues, using your imagination and the vocabulary from this lesson.

A En el consultorio de la oculista:

Oculista —¿______________________________________?
Paciente —No, están borrosas.
Oculista —¿______________________________________?
Paciente —Esas sí. P X T V L.
Oculista —¿______________________________________?
Paciente —Veo dos luces.
Oculista —¿______________________________________?
Paciente —Veo mejor las letras que están en el lado rojo.

B En el consultorio del urólogo:

Paciente —Doctor, mi esposa y yo no queremos tener más hijos. ¿Qué puedo hacer?
Urólogo —______________________________________
Paciente —Pero, una vasectomía es una cirugía mayor...
Urólogo —______________________________________
Paciente —¿Tengo que ir al hospital para hacerme la operación?
Urólogo —______________________________________
Paciente —Muy bien, entonces voy a hablar con mi esposa.

C En el consultorio del cirujano:

Paciente —Cuando me revisé los senos, encontré una bolita.
Doctor —______________________________________

Nombre ______________________ Sección ______________ Fecha ______________

Paciente —¿La encuentra, doctor?

Doctor —______________________________

Paciente —¿Puede ser un tumor maligno?

Doctor —______________________________

D En el consultorio del dermatólogo:

Doctor —Ud. tiene mucho acné.

Paciente —______________________________

Doctor —La alimentación no tiene importancia, pero Ud. necesita tratamiento.

Paciente —______________________________

Doctor —Voy a sacarle las espinillas y el pus de los granos.

Paciente —______________________________

Doctor —Sí, puede usar un jabón medicinal y una loción.

En estas situaciones

What would you say in the following situations? What might the other person say?

1. You are an eye doctor. Explain to your patient that you are going to do a glaucoma test. Then tell the person to place his/her chin on this instrument and look straight at the light.
2. You are a patient. Ask your doctor if he/she can perform a vasectomy in his/her office, and how long you have to take off from work.
3. You are the doctor. Ask your patient if she examines her breasts frequently and when the last time was she had a mammogram.
4. You are a patient. Ask your dermatologist if you can cut off a wart.

Casos

Act out the following scenarios with a partner.

1. An ophthalmologist examines a patient's vision.
2. A urologist and a patient discuss a vasectomy as an alternative means of birth control.
3. A doctor and a patient discuss the lump in the patient's breast and what measures should be taken.
4. A dermatologist examines a patient who has acne, and they discuss treatment for the problem.

Un paso más

A Review the **Vocabulario adicional** in this lesson. Then complete the following sentences.

1. El urólogo me dijo que tenía ____________ en el riñón y una infección en la ____________.
2. No tengo el cutis ____________ ni ____________; mi cutis es normal.
3. No es présbite; es ____________.

4. Tiene una infección en el cuero ___________.

5. Tengo ___________ y dolor al orinar.

6. No distingue ciertos (*distinguish certain*) colores porque tiene ___________.

7. No ve nada. Es ___________.

8. No lo operaron de ___________. Lo operaron de un ___________ de la retina.

9. No tiene astigmatismo; tiene ___________.

10. Desenex es una medicina que se usa para los ___________.

B Read the announcement on the next page, then answer the following questions. Remember to guess the meaning of all cognates.

1. ¿Para quiénes es importante este anuncio?

____

2. Según el anuncio, ¿qué enfermedad es curable si se detecta a tiempo?

____

3. En Puerto Vallarta, ¿quiénes tienen el único equipo especial para hacer mamografías?

____

4. ¿Dónde tienen estos médicos su consultorio?

____

Nombre ______________________ Sección ____________ Fecha ____________

Hospital Aralias

AVISO IMPORTANTE

El cáncer ya es curable...

¿Pertenece al sexo femenino?

¿Es usted mayor de 30 años?

¿Sabía usted que el cáncer es curable si se detecta a tiempo?

¿Sabía usted que con un estudio especial de mamografía se puede detectar el cáncer en un 78%?

LO MÁS IMPORTANTE ES QUE YA CONTAMOS CON EL ÚNICO EQUIPO ESPECIAL PARA MAMOGRAFÍA EN PUERTO VALLARTA

Consulte a su ginecólogo
Con gusto[1] la atenderemos en:

Paseo del Marlin 155
Tel: 4-51-29

Y

Juárez 688
Tel: 2-18-35 y 3-04-10

MÉDICOS RADIÓLOGOS
Dra. Ma. Aceves Amaya y Dr. M. Zarkin T.

[1] *pleasure*

EL CÁNCER

(*Adapted from TEL MED, tape #1083*)

El cáncer mata[1] a miles de personas todos los años y si esto no cambia,[2] cerca de[3] 80 millones—o una de cada tres personas que viven actualmente[4] en los Estados Unidos—tendrá[5] cáncer en algún momento de su vida.[6]

Hay tres cosas que se pueden hacer para protegerse[7] contra el cáncer:

1. Evitar fumar o exponerse[8] demasiado[9] al sol.
2. Hacerse exámenes médicos periódicamente. Los hombres de menos de cuarenta años deben hacerlo cada dos años, y una vez[10] al año después de los cuarenta años. Las mujeres de menos de treinta y cinco años deben hacerlo una vez cada dos años, y una vez al año después de los treinta y cinco años.
3. Aprender a reconocer[11] las señales[12] que indican la presencia de cáncer y ver al médico si alguno de estos síntomas persiste por más de dos semanas.

Hay siete señales que pueden indicar la existencia de cáncer:

1. Una pérdida de sangre[13] no usual.
2. Un abultamiento o endurecimiento[14] en el seno o cualquier[15] otra parte del cuerpo.
3. Una llaga[16] que no se cura.
4. Un cambio[17] en los hábitos de defecar u orinar.
5. Ronquera[18] o tos persistente.
6. Problemas de indigestión o dificultad para tragar.[19]
7. Cualquier cambio en el tamaño o color de una verruga,[20] lunar[21] o mancha[22] en la piel.

El cáncer puede tratarse[23] con algunas drogas, con radiación, con quimioterapia o con cirugía,[24] pero es importante ver al médico en seguida si se descubren[25] algunos de los síntomas indicados.

---

[1] *kills*
[2] **si...** *if this doesn't change*
[3] **cerca...** *about*
[4] *at the present time*
[5] *will have*
[6] *life*
[7] *protect oneself*
[8] *exposing oneself*
[9] *too much*
[10] **una...** *once*
[11] *to recognize*
[12] *signs*
[13] **pérdida...** *bleeding*
[14] *lump or hardening*
[15] *any*
[16] *sore*
[17] *change*
[18] *hoarseness*
[19] *to swallow*
[20] *wart*
[21] *mole*
[22] *birthmark*
[23] *can be treated*
[24] *surgery*
[25] *are discovered*

Nombre ______________________ Sección ______________ Fecha ______________

Conversaciones

2-4 —¿Qué puedo hacer para evitar el cáncer?
—No debe fumar y no debe exponerse mucho al sol.

2-5 —¿Cada cuánto tiempo debo hacerme un examen médico?
—Si tiene menos de treinta y cinco años, cada dos años.
—Yo tengo cuarenta y cinco años.
—Entonces, debe hacerlo cada año.

2-6 —Tengo dificultad para tragar.
—Eso puede ser una señal de cáncer.
—¿Qué debo hacer?
—Debe ver a su médico si el problema persiste por más de dos semanas.

Dígame... Answer the following questions, basing your answers on the reading and the conversations.

1. ¿Qué enfermedad mata a miles de personas todos los años?

   ____

2. ¿Cuántas personas en los Estados Unidos tendrán cáncer?

   ____

3. ¿Qué debemos evitar para protegernos contra el cáncer?

   ____

4. ¿Con qué frecuencia deben hacerse chequeos los hombres de menos de cuarenta años? ¿De más de cuarenta?

   ____

5. ¿Con qué frecuencia deben hacerse exámenes las mujeres antes de los treinta y cinco años? ¿Después?

   ____

6. ¿Cuál es una señal de cáncer?

   ____

7. ¿Cuáles son otras señales que pueden indicar cáncer?

   ____

8. ¿Cómo puede tratarse el cáncer?

   ____

9. ¿Qué es importante hacer si tiene algunos de los síntomas que indican la presencia de cáncer?

   ____

Lección 13 En el hospital (II)

Objectives

Structures

- Changes in meaning with the imperfect and preterit of **conocer, saber,** and **querer**
- **Hace** meaning *ago*
- Uses of **se**
- **¿Qué?** and **¿cuál?** used with **ser**

Communication

- As a patient in the hospital

En el hospital (II)

2-7

La Sra. Peña tuvo una hemorragia hace dos días. La trajeron al hospital anteanoche y le hicieron una transfusión de sangre. Acaba de visitarla su médico y ahora está hablando con la enfermera.

Enfermera —Buenos días, señora. Hoy se ve mucho mejor. ¿Cómo durmió anoche?
Sra. Peña —Dormí mejor con las tabletas que me dio el médico.
Enfermera —Sí, eran calmantes. ¿Le duele el brazo donde le pusieron la sangre?
Sra. Peña —Sí. ¿Cuándo me quitan el suero? Tengo unos moretones alrededor de la vena y me duele mucho el brazo.
Enfermera —Ah, no sabía que tenía problemas. Voy a quitárselo ahora mismo. Pero antes voy a tomarle el pulso y la temperatura. Póngase el termómetro debajo de la lengua, por favor.

Después de un rato:

Sra. Peña —Por favor, necesito la chata.
Enfermera —Aquí está. Levante las nalgas para ponérsela, pero la próxima vez tiene que ir al baño y usar el inodoro. Más tarde voy a darle un baño de esponja aquí, en la cama.
Sra. Peña —Señorita, todavía me duele el brazo.
Enfermera —Le voy a poner unas compresas de agua fría.

La enfermera baña a la paciente, la ayuda a cambiarse de ropa y le da unas fricciones en la espalda.

Sra. Peña —Ahora me siento mucho mejor. ¿Puede subirme un poco la cama?

Enfermera —¡Cómo no! ¿Así está cómoda? En seguida le traigo el almuerzo. Pero antes voy a darle una cucharada de este líquido.

Sra. Peña —¡Ay! A mí no me gusta esta medicina. ¡Ah!... estaba preocupada... Yo tenía un reloj y dos anillos cuando vine...

Enfermera —No se preocupe. Las joyas se guardan en la caja de seguridad del hospital. Si necesita algo más, avíseme. Apriete este botón que está al lado de la cama.

Sra. Peña —Muy amable. Gracias. ¡Ah! ¿Cuáles son las horas de visita?

Enfermera —De dos a tres y de siete a nueve.

Sra. Peña —¿Cuándo cree usted que me van a dar de alta?

Enfermera —No sé. Tiene que preguntárselo a su médico. Necesitamos una orden de él. Además, antes de darle de alta, tenemos que darle unas instrucciones.

Sra. Peña —¡Ay, yo no quería quedarme en el hospital por tanto tiemp...!

2–7

¡Escuchemos!

While listening to the dialogue, circle **V (verdadero)** if the statement is true or **F (falso)** if it is false.

1. A la Sra. Peña la llevaron al hospital porque tuvo una hemorragia.
2. Hoy la Sra. Peña está peor.
3. El médico le dio un calmante a la señora.
4. A la señora le duele el brazo donde tiene un suero.
5. La Sra. Peña va a bañarse sola.
6. La enfermera le da fricciones en el brazo a la señora.
7. La señora va a ir a la cafetería para almorzar.
8. El reloj de la señora está en la caja de seguridad del hospital.
9. Si la señora necesita llamar a la enfermera puede usar el teléfono que está al lado de la cama.
10. La señora puede recibir visitas por la noche.

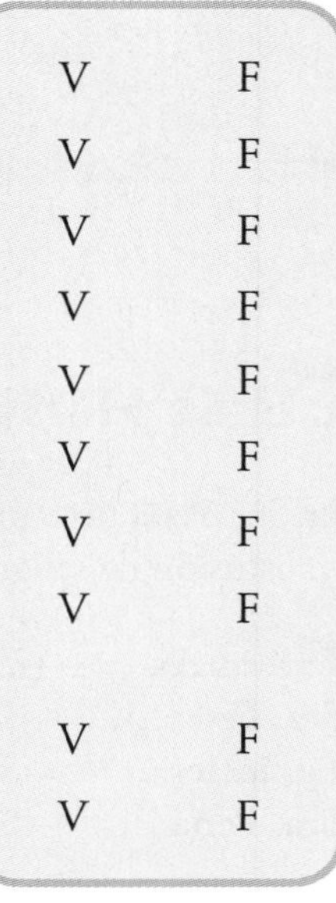

Nombre ______________________ Sección ____________ Fecha ____________

Vocabulario

Cognados

la hemorragia
las instrucciones
el pulso
la tableta
el termómetro
la transfusión

Nombres

el almuerzo[1] *lunch*
el anillo *ring*
el baño de esponja *sponge bath*
el botón *button*
la caja de seguridad, la caja fuerte *safe*
la cama *bed*
la compresa de agua fría *cold water compress*
la cucharada (*table*)*spoonful*
la fricción *rub, rubbing, massage*
las horas de visita *visiting hours*
el inodoro *toilet*
las joyas *jewelry*
la lengua *tongue*
el moretón, el morado, el cardenal (*Cuba*) *bruise*
el reloj *watch*
la ropa *clothes, clothing*
el suero *I.V.* (*serum*)
la vena *vein*

Verbos

acabar de (+ *inf.*) *to have just* (*done something*)
avisar *to let know*
ayudar *to help*
bañar *to bathe*
guardar *to put away, to keep*
gustar[2] *to like, to be pleasing to*
levantar *to lift, to raise*
preguntar *to ask* (*a question*)
subir *to lift, to go up*
verse *to look, to seem*
visitar *to visit*

Adjetivos

cómodo(a) *comfortable*
escrito(a) *written*
varios(as) *several*

Otras palabras y expresiones

al lado de *at the side of*
alrededor de *around*
anoche *last night*
anteanoche[3] *the night before last*
cómo no *of course, sure*
dar de alta *to release* (*from a hospital*)
debajo de *under*
más tarde *later*
muy amable *very kind* (*of you*)

---

[1]Colloquialism: **el lonche** (*Méx.*)
[2]**Gustar** is used with indirect object pronouns: **No me gusta esa medicina.** *I don't like that medicine.* (literally, *That medicine is not pleasing to me.*)
[3]**anteayer** *the day before yesterday*

Nombre ____________________ Sección ____________ Fecha ____________

VOCABULARIO ADICIONAL

EN EL HOSPITAL

¿Dónde está
- **el ascensor, el elevador?** *elevator*
- **la oficina de pagos?** *business (payment) office*
- **el cajero?** *cashier*
- **la tienda de regalos?** *gift shop*
- **la unidad de cuidados intensivos?** *intensive care unit*
- **el banco de sangre?** *the blood bank*
- **el departamento de personal?** *personnel department*
- **el estacionamiento?** *parking*

Busco el departamento de
- **archivo clínico**[1] *medical records*
- **radiología** *radiology*
- **ortopedia** *orthopedics*
- **enfermedades mentales y siquiatría** *mental health and psychiatry*
- **anestesiología** *anesthesiology*
- **pediatría** *pediatrics*
- **neurología** *neurology*
- **medicina nuclear** *nuclear medicine*

Busco la sala de
- **cardiología** *cardiology*
- **cirugía (operaciones)** *surgery, operating room*
- **recuperación** *recovery room*
- **terapia física** *physical therapy*

- While relatively few hospitals in the United States have well-established interpreter services, in August of 2000, a policy guide related to Title VI of the Civil Rights Act of 1964 was issued. It states that "...in order to avoid discrimination against Limited English Proficiency (LEP) persons, health and social service providers must take adequate steps to ensure that such persons received the language assistance necessary to afford them *meaningful* access to their services, free of charge." Family members, friends, and other untrained bilingual individuals are not considered competent interpreters since they may be unfamiliar with medical terminology. They may omit or edit information, which would provide incomplete communication between the health care provider and the patient.

[1] **el expediente médico** *patient's medical record*

Nombre ______________________ **Sección** ____________ **Fecha** ____________

- Latinos living in the United States speak many different dialects of Spanish. Parts of the body, physiological functions, symptoms of illness, and many names of foods are just a few areas in which dialects differ. For example, **constipación** may mean a *cold, nasal congestion,* or *intestinal congestion;* and the word *peas* can be translated as **guisantes, arvejas,** or **chícharos.**

Actividades

Dígame... Answer the following questions, basing your answers on the dialogue.

1. ¿Por qué trajeron a la Sra. Peña al hospital? ¿Cuánto tiempo hace que la trajeron?
____
2. ¿Quién acaba de visitarla y con quién está hablando ahora?
____
3. ¿Por qué durmió mejor la Sra. Peña?
____
4. ¿Dónde tiene la señora unos moretones? ¿Qué le duele mucho?
____
5. ¿Qué va a hacer la enfermera antes de quitarle el suero?
____
6. ¿Dónde debe ponerse el termómetro la Sra. Peña?
____
7. ¿Qué hace la enfermera después de darle un baño de esponja a la paciente?
____
8. ¿Qué le da antes de traerle el almuerzo?
____
9. ¿Por qué estaba preocupada la Sra. Peña?
____
10. ¿Dónde se guardan las joyas en el hospital?
____

11. ¿Qué debe hacer la señora si necesita algo?

____

12. ¿Cuáles son las horas de visita?

____

13. ¿Sabe la enfermera cuándo van a dar de alta a la Sra. Peña? ¿Qué deben darle antes?

____

14. ¿Qué no quería hacer la Sra. Peña?

____

Hablemos Interview a classmate, using the following questions. When you have finished, switch roles.

1. ¿Cómo durmió Ud. anoche?
2. ¿Está cómodo(a)?
3. ¿Qué calmante toma Ud. cuando le duele la cabeza?
4. ¿Tuvo Ud. una hemorragia alguna vez?
5. ¿Le hicieron a Ud. una transfusión de sangre alguna vez? ¿Por qué?
6. ¿Les da Ud. baños de esponja a sus pacientes?
7. ¿Les da Ud. fricciones a sus pacientes? ¿Cuándo?
8. ¿Los ayuda a cambiarse de ropa?
9. ¿Hay una caja de seguridad en el hospital donde Ud. trabaja?
10. ¿Cuáles son las horas de visita en el hospital donde Ud. trabaja?

Vamos a practicar

A Complete the following exchanges, using the preterit or the imperfect of **conocer, saber,** or **querer.**

MODELO —Yo ______________ al Dr. Mena ayer.
—Yo **conocí** al Dr. Mena ayer.

1. —¿Tú ______________ que el hospital tenía caja de seguridad?

—No, lo ______________ ayer, cuando me lo dijo la enfermera.

Nombre ______________________ **Sección** __________ **Fecha** __________

2. —¿Oscar no __________________ venir hoy?

   —No, prefirió quedarse en casa.

3. —¿Tú __________________ al doctor Basulto?

   —No, lo__________________ ayer, en la clínica.

4. —Ellos no __________________ venir hoy.

   —No, pero tuvieron que venir para terminar el trabajo.

B Complete the following exchanges, using the Spanish equivalent of the words in parentheses.

1. —¿A qué hora __________? (*does the hospital cafeteria open*)

   —__________ a las siete de la mañana y __________ a las nueve de la noche.
   (*It opens / it closes*)

2. —¿__________ la hemorragia? (*How long ago did Mrs. Torres have*)

   —La tuvo __________. (*three days ago*)

3. —¿__________ el número de teléfono del médico? (*What is*)

   —No sé.

Conversaciones breves

Complete the following dialogues, using your imagination and the vocabulary from this lesson.

A La Sra. Orta y la enfermera:

Enfermera —______________________________________

Sra. Orta —Dormí mucho mejor, gracias.

Enfermera —______________________________________

Sra. Orta —Sí, me duele mucho y tengo unos morados.

Enfermera —______________________________________

Sra. Orta —Sí, en el brazo, alrededor de la vena.

B La enfermera y la Srta. Rojas:

Enfermera —Voy a darle un baño de esponja.

Srta. Rojas —______________________________________

Enfermera —Sí, aquí en la cama.

Nombre ______________________ Sección ____________ Fecha ____________

Srta. Rojas —______________________________

Enfermera —No, no puedo subirle la cama ahora.

Srta. Rojas —______________________________

Enfermera —Le traigo el almuerzo después, pero antes debe tomar este líquido.

Srta. Rojas —______________________________

Enfermera —No, sólo tiene que tomar una cucharada.

Srta. Rojas —______________________________

Enfermera —Las horas de visita son de doce a dos y de siete a nueve.

En estas situaciones

What would you say in the following situations? What might the other person say?

1. You are a patient. Tell the nurse that you did not sleep very well last night and that you want some painkillers. Ask the nurse when he/she is going to take out the I.V.
2. You are a nurse and a patient asks for a bedpan. Tell the person to lift his/her buttocks so you can place the bedpan. Then inform the patient that you are going to give him/her a sponge bath later.
3. You are a nurse. Tell your patient that you are going to take his/her pulse and temperature. Tell the patient to place the thermometer under his/her tongue. Explain to the patient that he/she has to take two spoonfuls of his/her medication before lunch.
4. You are a nurse. Tell your patient that you are going to help him/her change clothes and then you are going to give him/her a back rub. Before you leave the room, tell your patient to press the button if he/she needs you.
5. You are a doctor. Tell your patient that he/she is much better and that you are going to release him/her from the hospital tomorrow. Add that the nurse is going to give him/her instructions.
6. You are a nurse. Tell a patient that visiting hours are from seven to nine.
7. You are a nurse. Tell your patient that he/she has to go to the bathroom and use the toilet.

Casos

Act out the following scenarios with a partner.

1. A nurse and a patient discuss visiting hours, the safekeeping of items, and the patient's release from the hospital.
2. A nurse is monitoring a patient who had a blood transfusion and is now feeling some discomfort.

Un paso más

A Review the **Vocabulario adicional** in this lesson. Then write what hospital service or facility the following people need according to each situation.

1. Ana necesita ir a la habitación número 528.

____

2. Sergio tiene cáncer del estómago y está muy grave.

____

3. Raúl necesita ver al siquiatra.

____

4. Teresa va a donar (*to donate*) sangre.

____

5. Jorge tiene problemas con el corazón (*heart*).

____

6. Daniel quiere comprar un regalo.

____

7. María tiene que pagar la cuenta del hospital.

____

8. Raquel acaba de tener una operación y necesita recuperarse (*recover*) de la anestesia.

____

9. Alina no camina bien después del accidente.

____

10. El bebé de Julia necesita un examen.

____

11. La Sra. Torres tiene una fractura.

____

12. Luis quiere trabajar en el hospital.

____

13. La recepcionista busca la hoja clínica de un paciente.

____

14. Margarita tiene esquizofrenia (*schizophrenia*).

____

15. Están operando al Sr. Montenegro.

____

Nombre ______________________ Sección ____________ Fecha ____________

B Read the following announcement of services offered by the Hospital Rebagliati and then list five points of comparison between this hospital and one in your city or town. Remember to guess the meaning of all cognates.

CAPACIDAD DE ATENCIÓN HOSPITALARIA

El Hospital Rebagliati pertenece a la Categoría-Nivel IV por su alta especialización. Brinda[1] atención a aquellos pacientes transferidos por los policlínicos de Lima y provincias, que requieren alta cirugía o tratamientos rigurosos.

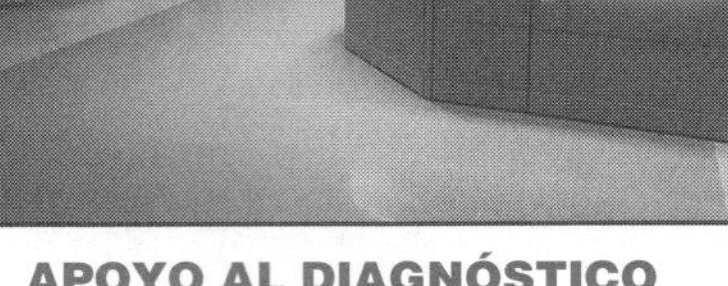

ESPECIALIDADES MÉDICAS

- Medicina interna
- Cardiología
- Dermatología y Alergia
- Nefrología
- Neumología
- Neurología
- Endocrinología
- Psiquiatría
- Genética
- Gastroenterología
- Oncología
- Hematología

ESPECIALIDADES QUIRÚRGICAS

- Cirugía general
- Neurocirugía
- Ortopedias
- Traumatología
- Cirugía cardiovascular
- Urología
- Otorrino
- Oftalmología
- Cirugía de cabeza y cuello

OTROS SERVICIOS

- Obstetricia
- Pediatría
- Cuidados intensivos
- Emergencia

APOYO AL DIAGNÓSTICO Y TRATAMIENTO

- Laboratorio
- Imágenes (Rayos X, Resonancia Magnética, Ecografía y otros)
- Rehabilitación
- Cobaltoterapia
- Diálisis

GENERALIDADES (Datos aproximados)

- Intervenciones quirúrgicas: 68 diarias[2]
- Staff de médicos permanentes: 600
- Total de médicos: 900
- Número de enfermeras: 800
- Número de camas: 1,300
- Promedio[3] de hospitalización: 13 días
- Consultas externas: 1,500 diarias
- Lavado de prendas y sábanas:[4] 4,000 kg. diarios
- Trasplantes renales por año: 50
- Unidad de emergencia: 375 pacientes diarios
- Presupuesto[5] del hospital: 100 millones de nuevos soles[6]

---

[1] *It offers*
[2] *daily*
[3] *Average*
[4] **Lavado...** *Washing clothing and sheets*
[5] *Budget*
[6] *monetary unit of Peru*

Nombre ____________________ Sección __________ Fecha __________

1. ______________________________

2. ______________________________

3. ______________________________

4. ______________________________

5. ______________________________

Objectives

Structures

- The past participle
- The present perfect tense
- The past perfect (pluperfect) tense

Communication

- Diagnostic evaluations

En el laboratorio y en la sala de rayos X

2–8

La Sra. Pérez ha venido hoy al laboratorio porque hace tres días que su médico le ordenó unos análisis.

Un análisis de sangre:

Técnica —¿Cuánto tiempo hace que comió?
Sra. Pérez —Estoy en ayunas. No he comido nada desde anoche.
Técnica —Muy bien. Voy a sacarle una muestra de sangre para el análisis de tiroides y para el conteo.
Sra. Pérez —¿Me va a sacar sangre de la vena?
Técnica —Sí. Le voy a poner una ligadura. Va a apretarle un poco. Súbase la manga y extienda el brazo.
Sra. Pérez —¿Así?
Técnica —Sí. Abra y cierre la mano. Ahora déjela cerrada.
Sra. Pérez —¿Me va a doler?
Técnica —No, abra la mano poco a poco. (*Le saca la sangre.*) Ya está. Ahora voy a ponerle una curita. Puede quitársela dentro de una hora.

Un análisis de orina:

Técnica —Necesito una muestra de orina. Vaya al baño y orine en este vasito.
Sra. Pérez —¿Dónde está el baño?
Técnica —Es el segundo cuarto a la derecha. Límpiese bien los genitales con estas toallitas.

Sra. Pérez —¿Necesita toda la orina?
Técnica —No. Comience a orinar en el inodoro, y después de unos segundos, termine de orinar en el vasito. Luego, tape bien el vasito.
Sra. Pérez —Está bien. ¿Dónde debo dejar la muestra?
Técnica —Llévela al cuarto que está al final del pasillo, a la izquierda.
Sra. Pérez —¿Cuándo van a estar listos los análisis?
Técnica —Su doctor le va a avisar.

Una radiografía del pecho:

El Sr. Franco fue a la sala de rayos X porque su doctor le había ordenado una radiografía del pecho.

Técnico —Quítese la ropa y póngase esta bata.

Pocos minutos después.

Técnico —Párese aquí y ponga los brazos a los costados.
Sr. Franco —¿Así?
Técnico —No, acérquese un poco más. No se mueva... Respire hondo... aguante la respiración... no respire ahora... respire...
Sr. Franco —¿Ya puedo irme?
Técnico —No, espere un momento.
Sr. Franco —Creía que ya habíamos terminado.
Técnico —Tengo que ver si la radiografía ha salido bien.

Una radiografía del colon:

El Sr. Barrios necesita hacerse una radiografía del colon.

Técnico —Acuéstese en la mesa. Vamos a insertarle este tubo en el recto.
Sr. Barrios —¿Eso me va a doler?
Técnico —No, no le va a doler. Relájese. No se ponga tenso. Respire por la boca.
Sr. Barrios —¿Esto es como un enema?
Técnico —Algo similar. Vuélvase sobre el lado derecho... ahora sobre el lado izquierdo. Ya está.

Una fluoroscopía del estómago:

La Sra. Sosa va al laboratorio a hacerse una fluoroscopía del estómago.

Técnico —Por favor, párese aquí y tome este líquido.
Sra. Sosa —¿Lo tomo todo ahora?
Técnico —No, yo le voy a avisar cuando puede tomarlo.
Sra. Sosa —Muy bien.
Técnico —Tome un poco... trague ahora...
Sra. Sosa —Esto es muy malo. No me gusta...
Técnico —Tome un poco más, por favor... trague ahora... no trague...
Sra. Sosa —¿Ya hemos terminado? ¿Puedo vestirme?
Técnico —Sí, ya puede irse.

Nombre ______________________ Sección ____________ Fecha ____________

2-8

¡Escuchemos! While listening to the dialogue, circle **V (verdadero)** if the statement is true or **F (falso)** if it is false.

1.	La señora Pérez necesita hacerse dos tipos de análisis.	V	F
2.	La señora desayunó antes de ir al laboratorio.	V	F
3.	A la señora le van a sacar sangre de la vena.	V	F
4.	La técnica le va a poner una ligadura en el brazo.	V	F
5.	Para el análisis de orina necesitan toda la orina.	V	F
6.	Al Sr. Franco le van a hacer una radiografía del pecho.	V	F
7.	El Sr. Franco necesita vestirse antes de hacerse la radiografía.	V	F
8.	El Sr. Barrios necesita una radiografía del estómago.	V	F
9.	Antes de hacerse la fluoroscopía la Sra. Sosa debe tomar un líquido.	V	F
10.	A la señora le gusta el líquido que debe tomar.	V	F

Audio

Vocabulario

COGNADOS

el colon
el enema[1]
la fluoroscopía
los genitales, las partes privadas
el recto
similar
el (la) tiroides
el tubo

NOMBRES

la bata *robe*
el conteo *blood count, count*
el costado *side*
la curita *adhesive bandage*
la ligadura, el torniquete *tourniquet*
la manga *sleeve*
la mano *hand*
la mesa *table*
el pasillo *hallway*
el (la) técnico(a) *technician*
la toallita *towelette*
el vasito *little glass, cup*

VERBOS

acercarse *to get close, to approach*
acostarse (o:ue) *to lie down, to go to bed*
apretar (e:ie) *to be tight*
dejar *to leave (behind)*
extender (e:ie) *to stretch, to extend*
irse *to leave, to go away*
moverse (o:ue) *to move*
ordenar *to order*
pararse *to stand*
tapar *to cover*
terminar *to finish, to be done*
tragar *to swallow*
vestirse (e:i) *to get dressed*
volverse (o:ue), darse vuelta, voltearse (*Méx.*) *to turn over*

---

[1]Also **la lavativa, el lavado intestinal**

ADJETIVOS

cerrado(a) *closed*
derecho(a) *right*
listo(a) *ready*
segundo(a) *second*

OTRAS PALABRAS Y EXPRESIONES

a los costados, a los lados *to (at) the sides*
aguantar la respiración *to hold one's breath*
al final *at the end*
¿Cuánto tiempo hace... ? *How long ago...?*
poco a poco *little by little*
quitarse la ropa *to take off one's clothes*
salir bien *to turn out okay*
subirse la manga, remangarse *to roll up one's sleeve*
Ya está. *That's it.*
¿Ya hemos terminado? *Have we finished (already)?*

VOCABULARIO ADICIONAL

LA ROPA

el abrigo *coat*
la blusa *blouse*
los calcetines *socks*
la camisa *shirt*
el camisón *nightgown*
la chaqueta *jacket*
la falda *skirt*
las medias *stockings, hose*
los pantalones *pants*
las pantimedias *pantyhose*
el pijama *pajamas*
la ropa interior *underwear*
el vestido *dress*
las zapatillas, las babuchas *slippers*
los zapatos *shoes*

OTROS TIPOS DE PRUEBAS DIAGNÓSTICAS

Voy a hacerle
- **una broncoscopia** *bronchoscopy*
- **una colonoscopia** *colonoscopy, coloscopy*
- **un electrocardiograma** *electrocardiogram (EKG)*
- **un electroencefalograma** *electroencephalogram (EEG)*
- **una endoscopia** *endoscopy*
- **una laparoscopia** *laparoscopy*
- **una tomografía axial computarizada** *computer axial tomography (C.A.T.)*
- **una imagen de resonancia magnética** *computer resonance imaging (M.R.I.)*
- **un ultrasonido (una ultrasonografía)** *ultrasound*

Nombre ______________________ **Sección** ____________ **Fecha** ____________

NOTAS CULTURALES

Search

- The following table indicates the percentage of use of certain screening tests by the Hispanic American population. With the exception of the Pap smear, the persons surveyed were age 40 and over. In many instances, the percentage of Latinos who had had the procedure is somewhat lower than that of other ethnic groups.

NEVER HAD PROCEDURE (%)			HAD PROCEDURE (%)		
Test	Never heard of	Heard of but never had	For health problem	For screening purposes	
				Less than 1 year ago	1–3 years ago
Digital rectal exam (males)	29.3	28.5	10.5	8.4	7.2
Digital rectal exam (females)	31.5	28.5	5.3	15.1	6.9
Mammography	31.6	42.2	3.1	12.9	3.1
Clinical breast exam	13.4	14.7	4.0	45.0	11.7
Pap smear (Age 18–39)	13.8	10.4	8.8	50.2	11.8
Pap smear (Age 40 or over)	17.1	8.5	5.3	36.8	14.5

Source: The American Cancer Society

Actividades

Dígame... Answer the following questions, basing your answers on the dialogues.

1. ¿Cuánto tiempo hace que el doctor le ordenó unos análisis a la Sra. Pérez?

____

2. ¿Ha comido hoy algo la Sra. Pérez?

____

3. ¿Para qué le van a sacar sangre de la vena? ¿Qué le van a poner en el brazo?

____

Nombre ______________________ Sección ____________ Fecha ____________

4. ¿Qué debe hacer la Sra. Pérez antes de orinar en el vasito?

____

5. ¿Dónde debe dejar la señora la muestra de orina?

____

6. ¿Qué le había ordenado el doctor al Sr. Franco?

____

7. ¿Qué le van a hacer al Sr. Barrios para la radiografía del colon?

____

8. ¿Qué le han hecho a la Sra. Sosa?

____

Hablemos Interview a classmate, using the following questions. When you have finished, switch roles.

1. ¿Dónde está el baño?
2. ¿Cuánto tiempo hace que Ud. comió?
3. ¿Le han hecho alguna vez (*ever*) un análisis de tiroides?
4. ¿Le han hecho alguna vez una radiografía del colon?
5. ¿Le han hecho un conteo? ¿Cuándo?
6. Si me van a sacar sangre de la vena, ¿qué debo hacer?
7. ¿Cuándo fue la última vez que le hicieron un análisis de orina?
8. Para hacerme una radiografía del pecho, ¿debo quitarme toda la ropa? ¿Qué me pongo?
9. Para la radiografía del colon, ¿tengo que acostarme?
10. ¿Ya hemos terminado? ¿Puedo irme?

Vamos a practicar

A Rewrite the following sentences, first in the present perfect and then in the pluperfect.

MODELO Ellos hablan con él.
Ellos **han hablado** con él.
Ellos **habían hablado** con él.

Nombre ______________________ Sección ____________ Fecha ____________

1. Tengo problemas de tiroides.

____

____

2. Se limpia los genitales.

____

____

3. Usan el excusado.

____

____

4. ¿Le pones una ligadura en el brazo?

____

____

5. El doctor ordena una radiografía.

____

____

6. Nosotros no hacemos nada.

____

____

B Complete the following sentences with the Spanish equivalent of the words in parentheses.

MODELO Los niños están ____________ (*bathed*).
Los niños están **bañados**.

1. Tiene las manos ____________________ (*closed*).
2. La puerta (*door*) del baño estaba ____________________ (*open*).
3. Ellos están ____________________ (*standing*) en el pasillo.
4. El doctor no me dio ninguna orden ____________________ (*written*).
5. El análisis está ____________________ (*done*).

Nombre ____________________ Sección ____________ Fecha ____________

Conversaciones breves

Complete the following dialogues, using your imagination and the vocabulary from this lesson.

A Un análisis de sangre:

Técnico —¿Cuánto tiempo hace que comió?

Paciente —______________________________

Técnico —Muy bien. Voy a sacarle sangre de la vena.

Paciente —______________________________

Técnico —Sí, es para el análisis de tiroides.

Paciente —______________________________

Técnico —Sí, súbase la manga, por favor. Extienda el brazo y abra y cierre la mano.

Paciente —______________________________

Técnico —Sí, así está bien.

B Un análisis de orina:

Técnico —______________________________

Paciente —¿Dónde está el baño?

Técnico —______________________________

Paciente —¿Orino en este vasito?

Técnico —______________________________

Paciente —¿Necesita toda la orina?

Técnico —______________________________

Paciente —Cuándo va estar listo el análisis?

Técnico —______________________________

C Una fluoroscopia del estómago:

Paciente —¿Tengo que quitarme la ropa?

Técnico —______________________________

Paciente —¿Dónde me paro?

Técnico —______________________________

Paciente —¿Tengo que tomarlo todo?

Técnico —______________________________

Paciente —Muy bien.

Nombre ______________________ **Sección** ____________ **Fecha** ____________

Técnico —____

Paciente —¡No me gusta este líquido! ¡Es horrible!

Técnico —____

Paciente —¿Ya terminamos?

Técnico —____

En estas situaciones

What would you say in the following situations? What might the other person say?

1. You are a lab technician. Tell your patient that you are going to draw blood from the vein in order to check the blood count.
2. You are a lab technician. Inform your patient that you are going to take an X-ray of the spinal column (**columna vertebral**). Tell your patient where to stand and then tell the person not to move, to take a deep breath, and to hold it. Then tell the person to wait outside.
3. You are a lab technician, doing an X-ray of the colon. Tell your patient to lie down on the table and then explain that you are going to insert a tube in the rectum. Tell the person not to tense up; the procedure is similar to an enema. Then ask the person to turn over on his/her left side.
4. You are a lab technician. Tell a patient she has to go to the bathroom (give directions) and urinate in a cup. You give her some towelettes and tell her to clean her genitals well.

Casos

Act out the following scenarios with a partner.

1. A medical technician performs a blood test to check how a patient's thyroid gland is functioning.
2. A medical technician gives a patient a chest X-ray.
3. A nurse asks a patient to take a urine test.
4. A medical technician performs a stomach fluoroscopy on a patient.

Un paso más

A Review the **Vocabulario adicional** in this lesson. Then complete the following sentences.

1. Van a hacerle una ____________ antes de la operación.
2. Quítese la ____________ y póngase la bata.
3. No van a hacerle un ultrasonido; van a hacerle una ____________.

Nombre ______________________ Sección ______________ Fecha ______________

B Write the corresponding word for each numbered item.

1. ______________________
2. ______________________
3. ______________________
4. ______________________
5. ______________________
6. ______________________

7. ______________________
8. ______________________
9. ______________________
10. ______________________
11. ______________________
12. ______________________

Lección 15 Enfermedades venéreas

Objectives

Structures

- The future tense
- The conditional tense
- Some uses of the prepositions **a, de,** and **en**

Communication

- Dealing with sexually transmitted diseases

Enfermedades venéreas

2–9

La Srta. Ramos sospecha que tiene una enfermedad venérea. Por fin hoy va al Departmento de Salud Pública y ahora está hablando de sus problemas con una enfermera.

Srta. Ramos —Me gustaría hablar con un médico porque creo que tengo una enfermedad venérea.

Sra. Méndez —Bueno, pero primero tendré que hacerle algunas preguntas. ¿Qué síntomas tiene? ¿Tiene alguna llaga o lesión?

Srta. Ramos —No, pero cuando orino me arde mucho la vagina, y además me sale un líquido...

Sra. Méndez —¿Tiene el líquido un color amarillento o verdoso?

Srta. Ramos —Sí, es verdoso y tiene mal olor.

Sra. Méndez —¿Cuándo empezó todo esto?

Srta. Ramos —Empecé a tener mucho ardor hace dos semanas.

Sra. Méndez —¿Sabe Ud. si el hombre con quien Ud. ha tenido relaciones sexuales tiene también esos síntomas?

Srta. Ramos —Bueno... no sé... Creo que uno de ellos tiene sífilis o gonorrea... o herpes.

Sra. Méndez —Srta. Ramos, Ud. tendrá que ir a la Clínica de Enfermedades Venéreas. Allí le dirán si necesita tratamiento.

Al día siguiente la Srta. Ramos va a la Clínica de Enfermedades Venéreas. Uno de los médicos la revisa y ve que tiene varios síntomas que indican gonorrea. Una prueba confirma el diagnóstico y el médico le da un antibiótico. Momentos después, la Srta. Ramos llega a la oficina de la Sra. Alba, investigadora de enfermedades venéreas.

Nombre ______________________ Sección ______________ Fecha ______________

Sra. Alba	—¿Cuánto tiempo hace que tiene estos síntomas, Srta. Ramos?
Srta. Ramos	—Unas dos semanas...
Sra. Alba	—¿Cuándo fue la última vez que tuvo relaciones sexuales?
Srta. Ramos	—Hace una semana.
Sra. Alba	—Necesitamos saber el nombre y la dirección del hombre con quien tuvo relaciones sexuales, Srta. Ramos.
Srta. Ramos	—¿Para qué?
Sra. Alba	—Si él tiene gonorrea, necesitará tratamiento, y cuanto antes mejor.
Srta. Ramos	—Pues... yo me había acostado con otros hombres antes.
Sra. Alba	—Necesitamos el nombre y la dirección de todos ellos. Es muy importante. La gonorrea es muy contagiosa.
Srta. Ramos	—Bueno, yo creo que podré conseguirlos... Desgraciadamente, dos de ellos son bisexuales, de modo que ahora tengo que pensar en la posibilidad del SIDA...
Sra. Alba	—El único modo de saber con certeza si usted tiene el virus del SIDA es haciéndose el análisis del VIH.
Srta. Ramos	—Entonces, voy a hacérmelo.
Sra. Alba	—Buena idea. Mientras tanto, no tome ninguna bebida alcohólica ni se acueste con nadie hasta estar completamente curada de la gonorrea.
Srta. Ramos	—Está bien. ¿Tendré que volver la semana que viene?
Sra. Alba	—Sí. ¿Podría venir el lunes a las tres de la tarde o preferiría venir el martes por la mañana?
Srta. Ramos	—Vendré el lunes, sin falta.

2–9

¡Escuchemos!

While listening to the dialogue, circle **V (verdadero)** if the statement is true or **F (falso)** if it is false.

1. La Srta. Ramos está segura de que tiene sífilis.
2. La señorita no tiene ninguna lesión.
3. Cuando la señorita orina le sale un líquido amarillento.
4. Los síntomas de la señorita indican que tiene gonorrea.
5. El médico le receta un calmante.
6. La Sra. Alba necesita los nombres de los hombres que tuvieron relaciones sexuales con la Srta. Ramos.
7. La gonorrea no es una enfermedad contagiosa.
8. Para saber si la señorita tiene SIDA necesita hacerse un análisis.
9. La señorita no debe tener relaciones sexuales hasta estar curada de la gonorrea.
10. La señorita no necesita volver a hablar con la Sra Alba.

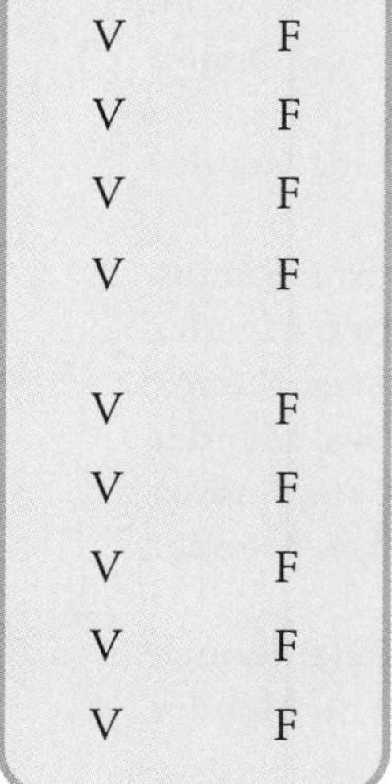

Nombre ______________________ Sección ____________ Fecha ____________

Audio

VOCABULARIO

COGNADOS

bisexual
completamente
contagioso(a)
la gonorrea
el herpes
la idea
el (la) investigador(a)
la lesión
el momento
la posibilidad
público(a)
la sífilis
venéreo(a)
el virus

NOMBRES

la certeza, la seguridad *certainty*
el hombre *man*
la llaga *sore, wound*
el modo, la manera *way*
el olor *odor, smell*
la salud *health*
el SIDA[1] *AIDS*

VERBOS

arder *to burn*
conseguir (e:i) *to obtain, to get*
empezar (e:ie) *to begin, to start*
indicar *to indicate*
sospechar *to suspect*

ADJETIVOS

amarillento(a) *yellowish*
curado(a) *cured*
único(a) *only*
verdoso(a) *grenish*

OTRAS PALABRAS Y EXPRESIONES

al día siguiente *on the following day*
allí *there*
cuanto antes mejor *the sooner the better*
de modo que (de manera que) *so*
desgraciadamente *unfortunately*
hacer una pregunta *to ask a question*
momentos después *moments later*
nadie *nobody, no one*
por fin, finalmente *finally*
primero *first*
salirle un líquido a uno, tener un flujo *to have a discharge*
sin falta *without fail*
tener mal olor, tener peste, apestar *to have a bad odor*

---

[1]**síndrome de inmunodeficiencia adquirida**

Nombre ______________________ Sección ____________ Fecha ____________

Vocabulario adicional

EFECTOS DE LA SÍFILIS

La sífilis puede causar
- **daño permanente al corazón** *permanent heart damage*
- **parálisis** *paralysis*
- **locura** *insanity*
- **ceguera** *blindness*
- **sordera** *deafness*
- **muerte** *death*

SÍNTOMAS DE LA SÍFILIS

Primarios (*Primary*)
- **chancro sifilítico (en los genitales o en la boca)** *syphilis chancre*
- **secreción** *secretion*

Secundarios (*Secondary*)
- **erupciones de la piel** *skin rashes*
- **lesiones en las mucosas** *lesions in the mucous membranes*
- **el pelo se cae en mechones** *hair falls out in patches*
- **malestar general** *general malaise*
- **dolor de garganta y de cabeza** *sore throat and headache*
- **fiebre** *fever*
- **inflamación de los ganglios linfáticos** *swelling of the lymph glands*

OTRAS ENFERMEDADES TRANSMITIDAS A TRAVÉS DEL CONTACTO SEXUAL (*Other sexually transmitted diseases*)

la clamidia *chlamydia*
la enfermedad inflamatoria de la pelvis *pelvic inflammatory disease*
la hepatitis B *hepatitis B*
la prostatitis *prostatitis*
la vaginitis *vaginitis*
el virus de inmunodeficiencia humana (VIH) *human immunodeficiency virus (HIV)*
el virus de papiloma *papilloma virus*

OTROS TÉRMINOS IMPORTANTES

confidencial *confidential*
heterosexual *heterosexual*
homosexual *homosexual*
el período de incubación *incubation period*

¡OJO! For additional terms related to the reproductive organs, see the diagram on page xxi.

Nombre ______________________ **Sección** ____________ **Fecha** ____________

NOTAS CULTURALES

Search

- Sexually transmitted diseases are present in all racial groups; however, the STD rate has been higher in Hispanics when compared to whites. Rates of STDs such as gonorrhea and syphillis are two to three times higher among Hispanics, likely due to the disparity in access to health care.
- HIV/AIDS

  Hispanics have been increasingly impacted by HIV. As of 1999, while Hispanics make up approximately 13% of the United States population, they are estimated to account for 18% of all AIDS cases ever reported, and 20% of all new HIV infections estimated to occur among men.

  For Hispanic adult men in the United States the annual incidence rate for AIDS is 3.2 times that of non-Hispanic men, and for Hispanic women, the annual incidence rate is 6.1 times that of non-Hipanic women (Centers for Disease Control "HIV/AIDS Surveillance Report, 1999 special data run," 2000).

  It is estimated that 110,000 to 170,000 Hispanics are infected with HIV, and more than 58,000 of these individuals are living with AIDS. CDC studies have confirmed that risk behaviors differ depending on which region the Hispanic person is from. HIV infected Hispanics born in the United States or Puerto Rico are most likely to have contracted HIV due to injected drug use, while most of the cases from those born in Mexico, Cuba, and Central and South America are the result of sex between men.

Actividades

Dígame... Answer the following questions, basing your answers on the dialogue.

1. ¿Qué sospecha la Srta. Ramos? ¿Con quién habla de sus problemas?

   ____

2. ¿Qué síntomas tiene la Srta. Ramos?

   ____

3. ¿Cómo es el líquido que le sale de la vagina?

   ____

4. ¿Cuánto tiempo hace que comenzaron los síntomas?

   ____

5. ¿Adónde tendrá que ir la Srta. Ramos al día siguiente?

   ____

6. ¿Qué hace uno de los médicos?

   ____

Nombre ______________________ Sección ____________ Fecha ____________

7. ¿Con quién habla después la Srta. Ramos?

____

8. ¿Cuándo fue la última vez que la Srta. Ramos tuvo relaciones sexuales?

____

9. ¿Qué dice la Sra. Alba que necesitan? ¿Por qué?

____

10. ¿Se había acostado la Srta. Ramos con otros hombres antes?

____

11. ¿Por qué piensa ella que puede tener el virus del SIDA?

____

12. ¿Cuál es el único modo de saber con certeza si lo tiene o no?

____

13. ¿Qué debe evitar la Srta. Ramos hasta estar completamente curada?

____

14. ¿Cuándo tendrá que volver a la clínica?

____

Hablemos Interview a classmate, using the following questions. When you have finished, switch roles.

1. ¿Cuál es la dirección del Departamento de Salud Pública?
2. ¿Le gustaría trabajar en una clínica de enfermedades venéreas? ¿Por qué o por qué no?
3. De las enfermedades venéreas, ¿cuál es la más peligrosa?
4. ¿Qué síntomas tiene una persona que tiene herpes?
5. ¿Cómo se puede diagnosticar (*diagnose*) un caso de sífilis?
6. ¿Qué tratamiento necesita una persona que tiene sífilis?
7. ¿Por qué debe evitar tener relaciones sexuales una persona que tiene una enfermedad venérea?
8. ¿Se puede curar (*cure*) el herpes? ¿Y la sífilis?

Nombre ______________________ Sección ____________ Fecha ____________

Vamos a practicar

A Rewrite the following sentences, first in the future and then in the conditional.

Modelo Ella sale el lunes.
Ella **saldrá** el lunes.
Ella **saldría** el lunes.

1. Dice que está curado.

____

____

2. El médico confirma el diagnóstico.

____

____

3. Los hombres vienen mañana.

____

____

4. Hablamos con la investigadora.

____

____

5. Tú debes hacerte un análisis.

____

____

6. Yo puedo conseguir los nombres.

____

____

B Complete the following sentences with the prepositions **a, de,** or **en.**

Modelo ¿A qué hora empiezas ____________ trabajar?
¿A qué hora empiezas **a** trabajar?

1. La radiografía estará lista ____________ la una ____________ la tarde.

2. Empezaré ____________ hacer el análisis ahora mismo.

3. Dejaré los resultados ______________ los análisis ______________ la mesa.

4. Este señor tiene llagas ______________ el pene; creo que tiene herpes. Él necesita ir ______________ la Clínica de Enfermedades Venéreas.

5. El Dr. Sosa es el mejor urólogo ______________ la clínica. ¿______________ dónde es?

C Complete the following exchanges, using the Spanish equivalent of the words in parentheses.

1. —¿Él investigador ______________ los hombres? (*will begin calling*)

—Sí, ______________. (*the sooner the better*)

2. —______________ mañana, Srta. Peña. Él ______________ el diagnóstico. (*Call / will confirm*)

—¿Él ______________ el hospital? (*will be at*)

—Sí, él ______________ a las nueve ______________. (*will be here / in the morning*)

Conversaciones breves

Complete the following dialogues, using your imagination and the vocabulary from this lesson.

A En el Departmento de Salud Pública:

Enfermera —______________________________

Paciente —Sí, señorita. Tengo una llaga y me arde mucho cuando orino.

Enfermera —______________________________

Paciente —Sí, me sale un líquido amarillento.

Enfermera —______________________________

Paciente —Sí, tiene mal olor.

Enfermera —______________________________

Paciente —No sé si él también tiene estos síntomas. Él no me ha dicho nada.

Enfermera —______________________________

Paciente —¿Tiene Ud. la dirección de la clínica?

Enfermera —______________________________

B En la Clínica de Enfermedades Venéreas:

Investigador —______________________________

Paciente —No sé la dirección, pero le puedo dar el nombre. ¿Para qué quiere saberlo?

Investigador —______________________________

Nombre ______________________ Sección ______________ Fecha ______________

Paciente —Yo creía que solamente la sífilis era contagiosa. ¿Hasta cuándo debo esperar para tener relaciones sexuales?

Investigador —____

En estas situaciones

What would you say in the following situations? What might the other person say?

1. You are the patient. Tell the nurse that you have a sore on your genitals. Then explain that it burns when you urinate and that you have a discharge—a greenish liquid with a bad odor.
2. You are the doctor. Tell the patient that the symptoms indicate gonorrhea and explain that he/she needs treatment, because gonorrhea is a very contagious disease. Say that you are going to administer treatment and then tell the person to make an appointment for next week.
3. You are a social worker talking to a client who thinks he might have AIDS. Encourage him to be tested for HIV. Add that that is the only way to find out for sure.

Casos

Act out the following scenarios with a partner.

1. A public health nurse interviews a patient who thinks he/she has a venereal disease.
2. A V.D. investigator gives instructions to a patient who has gonorrhea, regarding what he/she must and must not do.

Un paso más

A Review the **Vocabulario adicional** in this lesson. Then write the names of the different parts of the body that can be affected by syphilis.

1. ______________________ 5. ______________________
2. ______________________ 6. ______________________
3. ______________________ 7. ______________________
4. ______________________ 8. ______________________

B Complete the following sentences.

1. El ___________ y la ___________ son enfermedades transmitidas a través del contacto sexual.
2. Las mujeres deben hacerse un ___________ todos los años.
3. ¿Cuál es el período de ___________ de la hepatitis B?
4. El ___________ sifilítico es un síntoma ___________ de la sífilis.
5. La sífilis afecta el cerebro (*brain*) y puede causar la ___________ y la muerte.

Nombre ______________________ **Sección** ____________ **Fecha** ____________

C How much do you know about AIDS? Complete the following questionnaire published by the U.S. Department of Health and Human Services. Remember to guess the meaning of all cognates.

¿Sabe usted lo suficiente como para hablar del SIDA? Tome este test.

Es importante para cada uno de nosotros compartir[1] nuestros conocimientos acerca del[2] SIDA con los miembros de nuestra familia y con otros seres queridos.[3]

El conocimiento y la comprensión son las mejores armas que tenemos contra la enfermedad. Señale[4] su respuesta marcando el cuadro[5] que corresponde.

1. Usted debe preocuparse por el SIDA, aun[6] cuando usted no esté dentro del grupo de alto riesgo.[7]

   ❑ Cierto ❑ Falso

2. El virus del SIDA no se propaga por

   ❑ A. picaduras[8] de insecto.
   ❑ B. contacto casual.
   ❑ C. compartir agujas[9] para inyectarse drogas.
   ❑ D. relaciones sexuales.

3. Los condones son una forma eficaz,[10] pero no absolutamente segura, para prevenir la transmisión del virus del SIDA.

   ❑ Cierto ❑ Falso

4. Usted no puede decir a simple vista que alguien tiene el virus del SIDA.

   ❑ Cierto ❑ Falso

5. Si usted piensa que ha estado expuesto al virus del SIDA, usted debería hacerse una prueba de SIDA.

   ❑ Cierto ❑ Falso

6. La gente[11] que proporciona[12] ayuda a alguien que tiene SIDA no se está arriesgando[13] a contraer la enfermedad.

   ❑ Cierto ❑ Falso

---

[1] *to share*
[2] **conocimientos...** *knowledge about*
[3] **seres...** *loved ones*
[4] *Indicate*
[5] *box*
[6] *even*
[7] *risk*
[8] *bites*
[9] *needles*
[10] *effective*
[11] *people*
[12] *provide*
[13] *risking*

Nombre ______________________ Sección ____________ Fecha ____________

With a partner, discuss your answers and then write two questions you think should be included on the questionnaire on page 196.

____

____

____

____

El SIDA

(*Adapted from TEL MED, tape #571*)

La enfermedad llamada[1] *AIDS* en inglés, se conoce en español con el nombre de SIDA (Síndrome de Inmunodeficiencia Adquirida). Las primeras personas que padecieron de esta enfermedad en los Estados Unidos fueron hombres homosexuales y drogadictos. Hoy se sabe que es un virus el que transmite la enfermedad.

El contacto físico íntimo (el contacto sexual vaginal, anal y también oral), las transfusiones de sangre, las agujas y jeringas[2] que usan los drogadictos para inyectarse las drogas y la leche de los senos de la madre, son las formas en que el virus puede propagarse. Este virus destruye[3] las defensas del cuerpo y cuando esto sucede[4] se desarrollan[5] infecciones y cánceres que de otra forma serían destruidos.

La lista de personas que pueden ser infectadas por el SIDA incluye a los hemofílicos que requieren frecuentes transfusiones de sangre, a las prostitutas, a las compañeras sexuales[6] de hombres homosexuales o bisexuales y a los bebés de madres infectadas. También ahora el SIDA se ha extendido a los heterosexuales; la enfermedad ya no es solamente "un problema de los homosexuales".

La mayoría de la gente[7] infectada con el virus tendrá una reacción positiva al análisis de sangre para el VIH (virus de inmunodeficiencia humana) a los tres o seis meses de exponerse[8] pero los síntomas del SIDA no se manifestarán[9] por muchos años. Los síntomas de esta enfermedad al principio[10] son muy similares a los de la influenza común, y entre ellos están la fiebre, la inflamación de los ganglios linfáticos, la pérdida[11] de peso sin explicación, diarrea, pérdida del apetito, cansancio[12] por más de un par[13] de días y tos crónica.

En este momento no existe ninguna vacuna o cura y la mejor manera de evitar la enfermedad es la prevención o no exponerse al virus. El uso de condones hechos de "latex" con un lubricante es altamente recomendado.

Conversaciones

2–10

—¿Cómo se transmite el SIDA?

—Por contacto sexual si no se usa un condón en una penetración anal o vaginal, o si se tiene sexo oral sin protección.

---

[1] *called* [2] **agujas...** *needles and syringes* [3] *destroys* [4] *happens* [5] **se...** *develop* [6] **compañeras...** *sexual partners* [7] *people* [8] *exposing themselves* [9] **no...** *will not manifest* [10] **al...** *at the beginning* [11] *loss* [12] *fatigue* [13] *couple*

—¿Uno puede contagiarse donando sangre?
—No, y tampoco por medio de abrazos, por contacto con asientos de inodoros o en las albercas.

2-11 —El SIDA es una enfermedad exclusiva de los homosexuales, ¿no?
—No, se ha extendido a los hemofílicos y a los heterosexuales.
—Si una mujer embarazada tiene SIDA, ¿se lo transmite al bebé?
—Sí.

2-12 —¿Cuáles son algunos de los síntomas del SIDA?
—Los mismos de la gripe; también pérdida de peso, diarrea y cansancio prolongado.

2-13 —¿Existe alguna vacuna contra el SIDA?
—No, la mejor forma de evitar la enfermedad es la prevención.

Dígame... Answer the following questions, basing your answers on the reading and the conversations.

1. ¿Cómo se llama en español el *AIDS?*

____

2. ¿Quiénes fueron las primeras personas que tuvieron el SIDA?

____

3. ¿Cómo se transmite la enfermedad?

____

4. ¿Cuáles son tres formas en las que se puede propagar?

____

5. ¿Qué sucede cuando el virus del SIDA destruye las defensas del cuerpo?

____

6. Además de los hombres homosexuales, ¿qué otras personas pueden ser infectadas por el SIDA?

____

7. ¿Cuándo tendrá una persona una reacción positiva a una prueba de VIH?

____

8. ¿Cuáles son algunos de los síntomas del SIDA?

____

9. ¿Existe cura para el SIDA?

____

10. ¿De qué forma puede evitarse el SIDA?

Nombre ______________________ Sección ____________ Fecha ____________

REPASO

Práctica de vocabulario

A Circle the word or phrase that best completes each sentence.

1. No veo las letras claramente. Están (cansadas / borrosas / verdosas).
2. Hoy no. Vamos a hacerle los análisis (anoche / aquí mismo / la próxima vez).
3. Usé una loción para el acné, pero no me (miró / dio resultado / dio de alta).
4. Quiero hacerle una (pregunta / posibilidad / curita).
5. El paciente se ve (muy bien / peligroso / siguiente).
6. Tome una (llaga / luz / cucharada) de jarabe para la tos.
7. Si necesita algo, apriete este (botón / moretón / reloj).
8. Cuando me estaba examinando los senos, encontré (un enema / una bolita / una certeza). Estoy muy preocupada.
9. Mire el punto que está en (la pared / el pasillo / el vasito).
10. Tengo una (vez / barbilla / verruga) en el cuello.
11. Voy a darle un baño de (biberón / esponja / tratamiento).
12. ¿Puede ayudarme a (cambiarme / avisarme / indicarme) de ropa?
13. Tiene acné, pero la dieta (es muy importante / no tiene importancia / es difícil) en este caso.
14. No puede irse todavía. Tengo que ver si la radiografía (está enferma / salió bien / es confidencial).
15. Por fin hoy ella fue al (herpes / urólogo / acné).
16. El baño está (en la pared / en la esponja / al final del pasillo).
17. Debe (dejar / terminar / extender) el brazo.
18. Aguante (la vasectomía / la respiración / el momento).
19. Esto es (amarillento / tenso / similar) a un enema.
20. Cuando orino, me arde mucho (el recto / el colon / la vagina).

B Circle the word or phrase that does not belong in each group.

1. biopsia, mamografía, vasectomía
2. mayor, menor, siguiente
3. grasa, quiste, chocolate

4. modo, único, manera
5. moverse, darse vuelta, tragar
6. a los hombres, a los costados, a los lados
7. muy bueno, muy amable, muy cómodo
8. subir, bajar, ayudar
9. cómo no, no, sí
10. senos, estribos, pezón
11. obrar, hacer caca, lastimarse
12. ponerse tenso, calmarse, relajarse
13. tableta, pastilla, líquido
14. desayuno, glaucoma, almuerzo
15. vasectomía, fluoroscopía, radiografía
16. dar el pecho, dar la medicina, dar de mamar
17. mañana, ayer, anteanoche
18. niño, adolescente, joyas
19. decidir, tomar una decisión, hacer una pregunta
20. después, más tarde, entonces

C Complete the following sentences with the appropriate word or phrase in column **B.**

A

1. Me sale un ____________.
2. Volvió momentos ____________.
3. Ésta es la última ____________.
4. Venga dentro de ____________.
5. Ellos no están ____________.
6. El doctor confirma ____________.
7. Es una buena ____________.
8. No tiene gonorrea; ____________.
9. Tiene una lesión ____________.
10. Todo esto indica ____________.
11. Ya estoy completamente ____________.
12. Ella es la ____________.

a. idea
b. de la vena
c. tiene sífilis
d. debajo de la lengua
e. tratamiento
f. en el pene
g. una fricción
h. investigadora
i. líquido verdoso
j. unos días
k. en la vena
l. vez

Nombre ______________________________ Sección ______________ Fecha ______________

A		B
13. Necesita ____________.	**m.**	una enfermedad venérea
14. Le ponen una inyección ____________.	**n.**	el diagnóstico
15. Le voy a dar ____________.	**o.**	después
16. ¿Hay un botón al lado ____________?	**p.**	el suero
17. ¿Cuáles son las horas ____________?	**q.**	curada
18. ¿Tiene moretones alrededor ____________?	**r.**	de visita
19. Póngase el termómetro ____________.	**s.**	allí
20. ¿Cuándo me van a quitar ____________?	**t.**	de la cama

D **¿Verdadero o falso?** Read each statement and decide if it is true (V) or false (F).

_______ **1.** Primero sale el bebé y después la placenta.

_______ **2.** Cuando la mujer es estrecha, a veces el doctor tiene que sacar al bebé con fórceps.

_______ **3.** Cuando una mujer tiene los dolores de parto y las contracciones vienen cada cinco minutos, debe ir al hospital.

_______ **4.** Para tomarle el pulso, necesito un termómetro.

_______ **5.** Si una persona tiene una hemorragia, puede necesitar una transfusión de sangre.

_______ **6.** Le van a poner una inyección de penicilina.

_______ **7.** Una operación cesárea es un parto normal.

_______ **8.** Me van a poner una inyección en la nalga. Tengo que subirme la manga.

_______ **9.** Debo limpiarme los genitales antes de orinar en el vasito.

_______ **10.** Voy a llevar a mi hijo al médico porque tiene problemas de salud.

_______ **11.** Tiene cinco años. Nació ayer.

_______ **12.** Necesito la cuña porque quiero defecar.

_______ **13.** Ya eligieron un nombre para la niña. Se va a llamar Ana María.

_______ **14.** Tiene que quedarse en el hospital por un minuto, pero eso es mucho tiempo.

_______ **15.** Voy a guardar la llaga en la caja de seguridad del hospital.

_______ **16.** La niña está muy enferma. Su mamá tiene que llevarla al médico sin falta.

_______ **17.** La vasectomía es una operación reversible.

_______ **18.** Debe vestirse antes de bañarse.

_______ **19.** Le va a dar biberón al bebé porque no puede amamantarlo.

_______ **20.** El inodoro está en la sala de espera.

Nombre ______________________ Sección ____________ Fecha ____________

E Crucigrama

Across

1. Es enfermera del Departamento de Salud ____________.
3. No quiere más hijos. Se va a hacer una ____________.
5. *he suspects,* en español
6. Voy a tomarle el ____________ y la temperatura.
10. No está cerca. Está ____________.
12. *thyroid,* en español
15. Tengo una ____________ en el seno izquierdo.
16. Va a sentirse mejor poco a ____________.
19. Relájese. No se ponga ____________.
20. El cáncer es un tumor ____________.
21. *mouth,* en español
24. Va a tener un bebé. Está en la sala de ____________.
25. No es una mujer. Es un ____________.
27. *to stretch,* en español
28. *odor,* en español
29. *cured,* en español
31. *line,* en español
33. *pimple,* en español
34. mamila
37. *hallway,* en español
39. Su ____________ está en la caja de seguridad.
41. opuesto de primero
42. *It is better.* Es ____________.
44. niño
46. Las joyas están en la ____________ fuerte.
47. cirugía
48. enfermedad venérea
50. Para hacerle la radiografía voy a insertarle este ____________ en el recto.
51. Le di un ____________ de esponja.
52. Necesito una muestra de sangre para el ____________.
53. *wall,* en español

Down

2. *ready,* en español
4. *blackhead,* en español
7. Ayer el médico ____________ varios análisis y radiografías.
8. Tomó veneno. Necesita un lavado de ____________.
9. *chocolate,* en español
10. costado
11. Para el acné, puede usar ____________ medicinal.
13. parte del cuarto de baño
14. Quítese la ropa y póngase esta ____________.
17. los genitales o las ____________ privadas
18. *the next day;* al día ____________
22. La ____________ de los tumores son benignos.
23. No se va. Tiene que ____________.
26. No le voy a dar biberón. Le voy a dar de ____________.
30. Tiene sólo diecisiete años. Es muy ____________.
32. Es un bebé recién ____________.
35. El doctor la examinó. Ya se le rompió la ____________ de agua.
36. *greenish,* en español
38. *to get close,* en español
40. No es la derecha; es la ____________.
43. barriga
45. *rectum,* en español
49. *that way,* en español

Nombre ______________________ **Sección** ____________ **Fecha** ____________

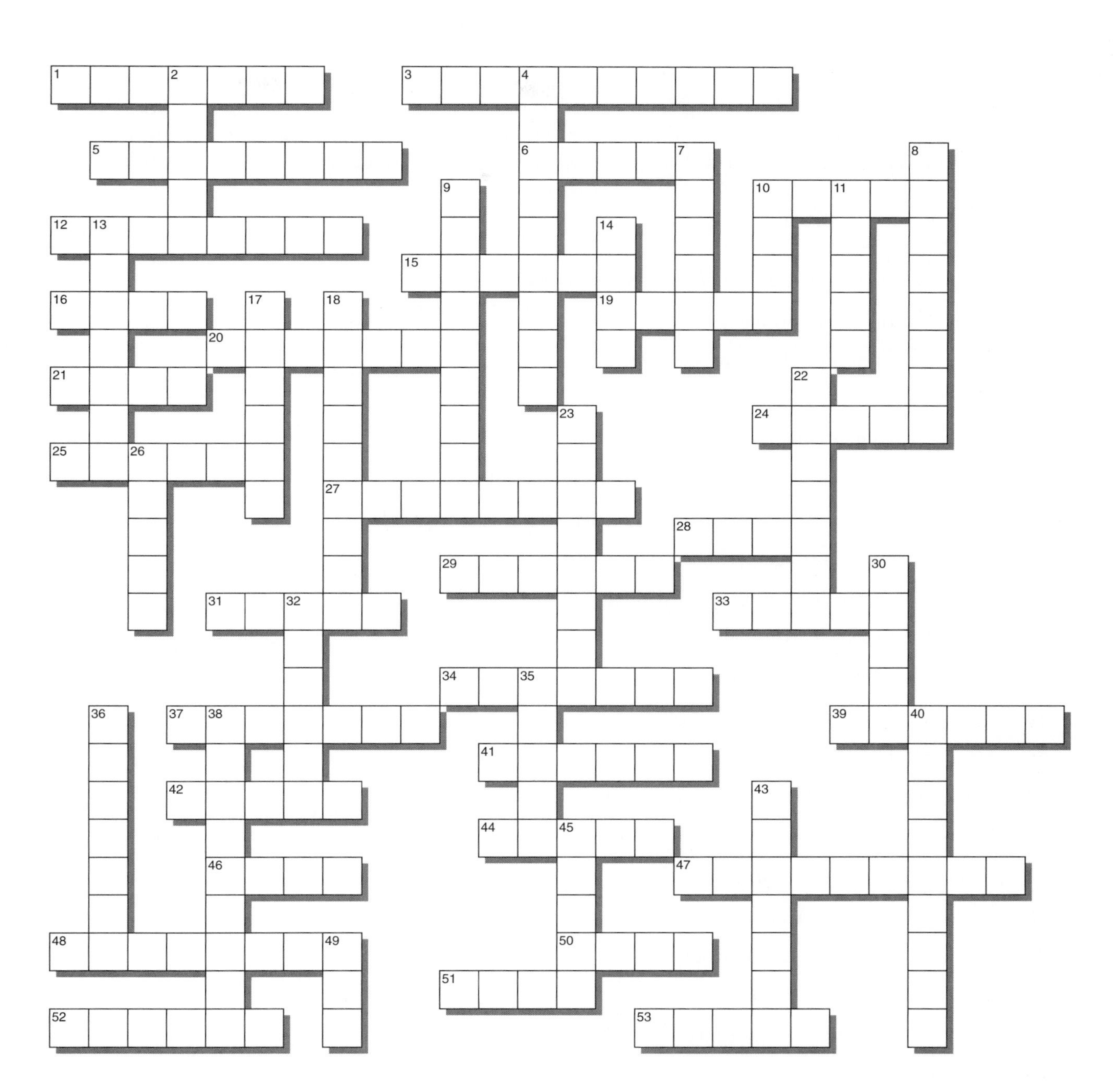

Nombre ______________________ Sección ____________ Fecha ____________

Práctica oral

2–14 Listen to the following exercise on the audio program. The speaker will ask you some questions. Answer the questions, using the cues provided. The speaker will confirm the correct answer. Repeat the correct answer.

2–15

1. ¿Lo operaron recientemente? (sí)
2. ¿Tuvo Ud. que quedarse en el hospital? (sí, por cinco días)
3. Cuando estuvo en el hospital, ¿le dieron baños en la cama? (sí, de esponja)
4. ¿Tiene Ud. dolores en el vientre? (sí, a veces)
5. ¿Movió Ud. el vientre hoy? (sí, por la tarde)
6. ¿Le han hecho una radiografía del colon? (no, nunca)
7. ¿Cuándo fue la última vez que le hicieron un conteo? (el año pasado)
8. ¿Le hicieron un análisis de orina recientemente? (sí, la semana pasada)
9. ¿Tuvo Ud. una hemorragia alguna vez? (no, nunca)
10. ¿Le hicieron una transfusión alguna vez? (sí, una vez)
11. ¿Tuvo moretones alrededor de la vena? (sí)
12. ¿Qué se puso? (compresas frías)
13. ¿Tiene Ud. problemas de tiroides? (no)
14. ¿Tuvo Ud. acné cuando era joven? (sí)
15. ¿Qué usó para el acné? (un jabón medicinal)
16. ¿Usó Ud. alguna loción para los granos? (sí)
17. ¿Tiene Ud. alguna verruga? (sí, en el cuello)
18. ¿Fue Ud. al oculista? (sí, la semana pasada)
19. ¿Le hicieron la prueba del glaucoma? (sí)
20. ¿Ve Ud. bien las letras pequeñas? (sí)
21. ¿Trabaja Ud. en la sala de parto? (no, de bebés)
22. ¿Le gustaría trabajar en una clínica de enfermedades venéreas? (no)
23. ¿Son malignos todos los tumores del seno? (no)
24. ¿Qué cree Ud. que es mejor para el bebé: darle biberón o darle de mamar? (darle de mamar)
25. ¿Tiene Ud. hijos? (sí, dos varones)

Lección 16

Problemas de la hipertensión

Objectives

Structures

- The present subjunctive
- The subjunctive with verbs of volition
- The absolute superlative

Communication

- Dealing with high blood pressure in patients

Problemas de la hipertensión

2-16 El Sr. Castro está en el consultorio del Dr. Rivas. La enfermera le toma la presión y ve que es altísima. Tiene 200 sobre 98.

Dr. Rivas —Sr. Castro, Ud. tiene la presión muy alta.
Sr. Castro —Yo sólo tengo treinta años, doctor. ¿No es ése un problema de los viejos?
Dr. Rivas —No, no solamente las personas mayores tienen ese problema. Puede ocurrir a cualquier edad.
Sr. Castro —Mi padre tiene la presión alta también.
Dr. Rivas —Sí, a veces eso es hereditario.
Sr. Castro —Pero yo tengo una vida tranquila, sin estrés... me siento bien. No estoy nervioso. No tengo palpitaciones...
Dr. Rivas —Bueno, porque el problema está apenas comenzando... Pero es importantísimo tratarlo ahora. Yo le aconsejo que no espere porque esto puede afectarle el corazón.
Sr. Castro —Entonces esto es grave.
Dr. Rivas —Sí, podría causarle un derrame.
Sr. Castro —¡Pero eso me puede dejar paralítico!
Dr. Rivas —Sí, un derrame puede causar parálisis total o parcial.
Sr. Castro —Mi padre ha tenido muchos problemas con los riñones.
Dr. Rivas —Pues Ud. podrá evitar todo esto si sigue un tratamiento para controlar la presión.
Sr. Castro —Eso es lo que me gustaría hacer, por supuesto. ¿Qué me sugiere Ud. que haga?
Dr. Rivas —Le aconsejo que elimine o por lo menos disminuya la cantidad de sal que Ud. usa en la comida. Es importante que evite, por ejemplo, las carnes enlatadas, el tocino y otros alimentos de ese tipo que tienen mucho sodio.

Sr. Castro —Será difícil, pero trataré de hacerlo. ¿Qué más me recomienda que haga?

Dr. Rivas —Quiero que evite el alcohol y el tabaco. También es necesario bajar de peso y hacer ejercicio por lo menos tres veces por semana.

Sr. Castro —¿Me va a recetar alguna medicina?

Dr. Rivas —Sí, le voy a dar unas pastillas. Si se siente peor después de tomarlas, llámeme para cambiarle la dosis o recetarle otra medicina.

Sr. Castro —¿Por cuánto tiempo quiere que tome la medicina?

Dr. Rivas —Depende; muchas veces el problema se puede resolver con el cambio en la dieta y el ejercicio. Si es necesario, podemos hacerle una angiografía de la arteria renal.

Sr. Castro —Muy bien. Quiero empezar el tratamiento lo más pronto posible.

2–16

¡Escuchemos! While listening to the dialogue, circle **V (verdadero)** if the statement is true or **F (falso)** if it is false.

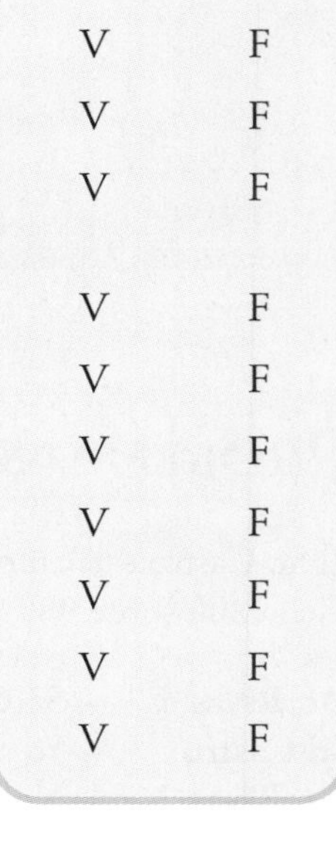

1.	La presión del Sr. Castro es normal.	V	F
2.	La hipertensión es un problema de los viejos.	V	F
3.	La hipertensión puede ser hereditaria.	V	F
4.	El doctor le aconseja al Sr. Castro que empiece un tratamiento para controlar la presión.	V	F
5.	Si el señor tiene un derrame puede quedar paralítico.	V	F
6.	El señor Castro tiene problemas con los riñones.	V	F
7.	Es necesario que el señor disminuya el uso de la sal.	V	F
8.	El Sr. Castro debe evitar fumar.	V	F
9.	El médico no va a recetarle nada al paciente.	V	F
10.	El médico quiere que el señor haga ejercicio.	V	F

Audio

Vocabulario

Cognados

el alcohol
la angiografía
la arteria
la dosis
el estrés
hereditario(a)
la hipertensión
la palpitación
la parálisis
parcial
probablemente
renal
el resto
el sodio
el tabaco
el tipo
total

Nombre ______________________ Sección ____________ Fecha ____________

NOMBRES

el cambio *change*
la carne *meat*
la comida *food*
el corazón *heart*
el derrame, la hemorragia cerebral, la embolia *stroke*
el riñón *kidney*
el tocino *bacon*
la vida *life*
el (la) viejo(a), la persona mayor[1] *elderly man, elderly woman*

VERBOS

aconsejar *to advise*
afectar *to affect*
cambiar *to change*
depender *to depend*
disminuir[2] *to cut down, to diminish*
eliminar *to eliminate*
ocurrir, suceder *to happen, to occur*
recomendar (e:ie) *to recommend*
resolver (o:ue) *to solve*
sugerir (e:ie) *to suggest*
tratar *to try, to treat*

ADJETIVOS

cualquier(a) *any*
enlatado(a) *canned*
medio(a) *half*
nervioso(a) *nervous*
paralítico(a) *paralyzed*
peor *worse, worst*
tranquilo(a) *quiet, peaceful*

OTRAS PALABRAS Y EXPRESIONES

apenas *barely*
lo más pronto posible *as soon as possible*
muchas veces *many times*
por ejemplo *for example*
por supuesto, claro *of course*
¿Qué más? *What else?*
tomar la presión, tomar la tensión *to take the blood pressure*

Audio

VOCABULARIO ADICIONAL

Ud. debe evitar
- **la cafeína** *caffeine*
- **las medicinas que contienen...** *medicines that contain...*
- **los ejercicios violentos** *strenuous exercises*
- **el estrés** *stress*

Ud. debe
- **aumentar la dosis** *increase the dosage*
- **mantener la misma dosis** *maintain the same dosage*

El paciente necesita
- **diálisis** *dyalisis*
- **un transplante de**
  - **riñón** *kidneys*
  - **corazón** *heart*
  - **pulmón** *lung*

---

[1]A more polite way to refer to an older person.
[2]Present tense: **disminuyo, disminuyes, disminuye, disminuimos, disminuís disminuyen**

Nombre ______________________ Sección ______________ Fecha ______________

NOTAS CULTURALES

Search

- In general, there is a high incidence of hypertension among the Latino population. Also, Latinos who are economically disadvantaged exhibit a higher risk for unrecognized and untreated hypertension. Data from the Hispanic Health and Nutrition Examination Survey indicate that almost half of the Puerto Ricans surveyed with hypertension did not know they had it.
- Looking at hypertension from a folk medicine perspective, it is defined as a "hot illness." In 60% of the cases, the etiology is thought to be due to *corajes* (anger) or *susto* (fear); the remaining 40% are felt to be due to "thick blood." Cool remedies such as bananas and lemon juice are popular, as well as teas of passion flowers (**pasionaria, pasiflora**), linden [**tilo(a)**], or sapodilla (**zapote blanco**).

  Nancy Neff, M.D., Assistant Professor, Department of Community Medicine, Baylor College of Medicine (http://www.rice.edu/projects/HispanicHealth/Courses/mod7/mo).
- It seems that diet does not have a big impact on hypertension. Despite the fact that Mexican Americans have a lower fat intake and higher fiber intake than other Americans, they tend to suffer more from hypertension. The average daily intake of total fat in the United States is 81.4 grams. For Mexican Americans the average is 77.6 grams (88.0 for males and 66.5 for females). The recommended daily intake of dietary fiber is 25 grams or more. Americans consume a daily average of 15.6 grams of dietary fiber. For Mexican Americans the average is 18.5 grams (21.0 grams for males and 15.9 for females).
  NHANES III (National Health an Nutrition Examination Survey) (1988–94), (CDC/NCHS) (Centers for Disease Control and Prevention/National Center for Health Statistics).

Actividades

Dígame... Answer the following questions, basing your answers on the dialogue.

1. ¿Qué problema tiene el Sr. Castro?

   ____

2. ¿Por qué cree el Sr. Castro que él no debería tener la presión alta?

   ____

3. ¿A qué edad dice el médico que puede ocurrir ese problema?

   ____

4. ¿Qué dice el Dr. Rivas que es importantísimo hacer?

   ____

5. ¿Qué problemas puede causar la presión alta?

   ____

Nombre ______________________ Sección ____________ Fecha ____________

6. ¿Cómo podrá evitar el Sr. Castro estos problemas?

____

7. ¿Qué quiere el Dr. Rivas que elimine o disminuya el paciente? ¿Qué tipos de alimentos le aconseja que evite?

____

8. ¿Qué más le sugiere que haga?

____

9. ¿Qué debe hacer el Sr. Castro si se siente peor después de tomar las pastillas?

____

10. Muchas veces, ¿cómo se puede resolver el problema de la hipertensión?

____

11. ¿Qué pueden hacerle al Sr. Castro si es necesario?

____

12. ¿Cuándo quiere empezar el tratamiento el Sr. Castro?

____

Hablemos Interview a classmate, using the following questions. When you have finished, switch roles.

1. ¿Usa Ud. mucha sal en la comida?
2. ¿Tiene Ud. palpitaciones?
3. ¿Ha tenido Ud. problemas con los riñones? ¿Cuándo?
4. ¿Tiene Ud. la presión alta, baja o normal?
5. ¿Les toma Ud. la presión a sus pacientes?
6. ¿Puede la presión alta afectar el corazón?
7. ¿Podría la presión alta causar una embolia?
8. ¿Podría un derrame causar parálisis total o parcial?
9. ¿Es hereditaria la hipertensión? ¿Y la diabetes?
10. Si una persona tiene la presión altísima, ¿qué le aconseja Ud. que haga?

Nombre ______________________ **Sección** ____________ **Fecha** ____________

Vamos a practicar

A Complete the following sentences, using the infinitive or the present subjunctive of the verbs given.

Modelo Yo le aconsejo que __________ (comer) menos.
Yo le aconsejo que **coma** menos.

1. Yo deseo __________ (hablar) sobre los problemas que trae el alcohol.
2. Nosotros no queremos que nuestros hijos __________ (fumar).
3. Les aconsejo que __________ (ir) al hospital en seguida.
4. Ud. necesita __________ (disminuir) la cantidad de sal que usa en las comidas.
5. Quiero que la enfermera me __________ (tomar) la presión.
6. Es importante __________ (seguir) una dieta baja en colesterol.
7. Te sugiero que __________ (hacer) ejercicio todos los días.
8. Es necesario __________ (evitar) el alcohol y el tabaco.
9. El médico quiere que yo le __________ (dar) esta medicina a mi padre lo más pronto posible.
10. Es necesario que Uds. __________ (estar) en el hospital a las ocho de la mañana.

B Complete the following exchanges, using the Spanish equivalent of the words in parentheses.

1. —¿Qué __________, Sr. Vega? (*does the doctor want you to do*)

   —Él __________ mañana, pero yo prefiero __________ esta tarde. (*wants me to come / to come*)
2. —__________ la sal de su dieta, señora. (*I advise you to eliminate*)

   —__________ muy fácil. (*It's not going to be*)

   —Es importantísimo __________. (*that you do it*)

Conversaciones breves

Complete the following dialogue, using your imagination and the vocabulary from this lesson.

Un paciente y una doctora:

Doctora —______________________________

Paciente —¿Tengo la presión alta? ¡Pero yo me siento bien...!

Doctora —______________________________

Paciente —Sí, debe estar apenas comenzando, porque yo no tengo ningún síntoma.

Doctora —____

Paciente —Además de afectar el corazón, ¿qué otros problemas podría causar la presión alta?

Doctora —____

Paciente —¡Un derrame! ¿A mi edad?

Doctora —____

Paciente —Pues yo ya he tenido problemas con los riñones.

Doctora —____

Paciente —Sí, uso mucha sal.

Doctora —____

Paciente —Puedo disminuir la cantidad, pero no puedo eliminarla completamente de mi dieta.

Doctora —____

Paciente —Pues yo no tomo ni fumo. ¿Me va a recetar algo?

Doctora —____

Paciente —¿Por cuánto tiempo tendré que tomar la medicina?

Doctora —____

En estas situaciones

What would you say in the following situations? What might the other person say?

1. You are a nurse. Tell your patient that you're going to take his/her blood pressure.
2. You are a patient. Tell your doctor that you are very nervous, that you have palpitations, and that you don't sleep very well.
3. You are the doctor. Tell your patient that high blood pressure can happen at any age and that it is important to treat it now. If he/she waits, it can affect his/her heart and a stroke could leave a person paralyzed.
4. You are the doctor, and your patient says he/she is feeling worse after taking his/her medication for high blood pressure. Tell your patient to diminish the dosage and to take only half a pill.
5. You are the doctor. Tell your patient that you suggest he/she start treatment as soon as possible.
6. You are a patient. Ask the doctor if he can prescribe another medicine for you, because you are feeling worse.

Casos

Act out the following scenarios with a partner.

1. A doctor explains to a patient the problems high blood pressure can cause.
2. A doctor and a patient discuss how the patient can control high blood pressure.

Nombre ______________________ Sección ____________ Fecha ____________

Un paso más

A Review the **Vocabulario adicional** in this lesson and then give advice to the following people.

1. Olga tiene palpitaciones y está muy nerviosa.

   ____

2. Rafael está tomando una pastilla al día y tiene que tomar tres.

   ____

3. Oscar tiene la presión arterial muy alta.

   ____

4. Teresa es alérgica a la codeina (*codeine*).

   ____

5. Graciela tiene problemas con el corazón.

   ____

6. Los riñones del Sr. Pérez no funcionan.

   ____

7. Cuando Roberto toma café, se pone (*becomes*) muy nervioso.

   ____

8. Magaly tiene que seguir tomando cuatro pastillas al día.

   ____

Nombre ______________________ Sección ____________ Fecha ____________

B Read the following announcement and answer the questions. Remember to guess the meaning of all cognates.

Receta para una larga vida

- Mantenga un peso apropiado.
- Use una dieta variada en su alimentación.
- Incluya una variedad de legumbres[1] y frutas en su dieta diaria.
- Coma una mayor cantidad de alimentos con alto contenido de fibra.
- Reduzca el consumo total de grasas (30% o menos de las calorías totales).
- Tome bebidas alcohólicas con moderación.
- Coma menos cantidad de alimentos curados con sal o ahumados,[2] o preservados con nitritos.

Para mayor información:
ÁREA METROPOLITANA
764-2295

1. ¿A quiénes está dirigido (*directed*) este anuncio?

____

2. ¿Qué organización publicó (*published*) esta información?

____

[1] *vegetables*
[2] *smoked*

3. Según el anuncio, ¿qué tipo de alimentos debemos incluir en la dieta diaria?

____

4. ¿Qué por ciento (*percent*) de las calorías que consumimos debe ser de grasas?

____

5. ¿Qué sugiere el anuncio con respecto a las bebidas alcohólicas?

____

6. De los consejos (*advice*) que dan en el anuncio, ¿cuáles sigue Ud.?

____

7. ¿Qué otras sugerencias (*suggestions*) le gustaría a Ud. incluir en esta lista?

____

En el consultorio del Dr. Gómez, clínico

Objectives

Structures

- The subjunctive to express emotion
- The subjunctive with some impersonal expressions
- Formation of adverbs

Communication

- Consulting a doctor about common ailments

En el consultorio del Dr. Gómez, clínico

2-17

El Dr. Gómez habla con tres de sus pacientes.

Con el Sr. Navas, que tiene diabetes:

Sr. Navas —He estado sintiendo mucho cansancio y debilidad últimamente, doctor, y orino con mucha frecuencia.
Dr. Gómez —Por los análisis veo que tiene muy alta el azúcar.
Sr. Navas —¿Entonces tengo diabetes, doctor?
Dr. Gómez —Sí, y es importante que Ud. siga fielmente las instrucciones que voy a darle.
Sr. Navas —¿Voy a tener que seguir una dieta especial?
Dr. Gómez —Sí, y quiero que pierda peso.
Sr. Navas —¿Voy a tener que inyectarme insulina?
Dr. Gómez —No, vamos a empezar con unas pastillas.

Con la Sra. Ordaz, que tiene una úlcera:

Sra. Ordaz —Yo creo que tengo una úlcera, doctor. Tengo mucha acidez, y generalmente, cuando tengo el estómago vacío, me duele. Se me alivia cuando como.
Dr. Gómez —¿Toma algún antiácido o leche?
Sra. Ordaz —Sí, tomo un vaso de leche y el dolor se me pasa. A veces vomito. He tomado algunos remedios caseros, pero no me han ayudado mucho.

Dr. Gómez —¿Ha notado alguna vez sangre en el vómito, o la materia fecal negra?
Sra. Ordaz —No, nunca.
Dr. Gómez —Vamos a hacerle una endoscopia porque temo que tenga una úlcera.
Sra. Ordaz —¿Puedo comer cualquier cosa?
Dr. Gómez —No, es necesario que evite los alimentos muy condimentados y las bebidas con cafeína. No tome bebidas alcohólicas y no fume.
Sra. Ordaz —¿Va a recetarme alguna medicina?
Dr. Gómez —Sí, voy a recetarle Prilosec, una medicina que cura las úlceras.

Con el Sr. Rosas, anciano de ochenta y dos años:

Sr. Rosas —Doctor, tengo muchos problemas con las hemorroides. Estoy muy estreñido. ¿Debo tomar un laxante o un purgante?
Dr. Gómez —Puede tomar un laxante de vez en cuando, pero no regularmente.
Sr. Rosas —Está bien.
Dr. Gómez —Vamos a hacerle una colonoscopia para estar seguros de que no tiene un problema del intestino grueso.
Sr. Rosas —También me duele el estómago.
Dr. Gómez —Podemos hacerle un ultrasonido para ver si tiene piedras en la vesícula biliar, pero antes voy a examinarlo. Abra la boca y saque la lengua. Diga "Ah".
Sr. Rosas —Doctor, no lo oigo bien. Creo que me estoy quedando sordo.
Dr. Gómez —Ud. necesita usar un audífono.
Sr. Rosas —Está bien. Ojalá que mi hijo me compre uno. Ah, doctor, me duelen mucho las piernas. ¿No podría recetarme algo para las várices?
Dr. Gómez —Compre un par de medias elásticas. Espero que eso lo ayude.

2–17

¡Escuchemos!

While listening to the dialogue, circle **V (verdadero)** if the statement is true or **F (falso)** if it is false.

1. El Sr. Navas tiene síntomas que indican diabetes.
2. El Sr. Navas debe perder peso.
3. El médico va a recetarle insulina al Sr. Navas.
4. La Sra. Ordaz tiene mucha acidez y le duele el estómago.
5. Cuando la señora come tiene más dolor.
6. A la Sra. Ordaz no le gusta tomar remedios caseros.
7. El Dr. Gómez teme que la señora tenga una úlcera.
8. La Sra. Ordaz no necesita tomar ninguna medicina.
9. El Dr. Gómez va a hacerle una colonoscopia al Sr. Rosas.
10. El Sr. Rosas espera que su hijo le compre un audífono.

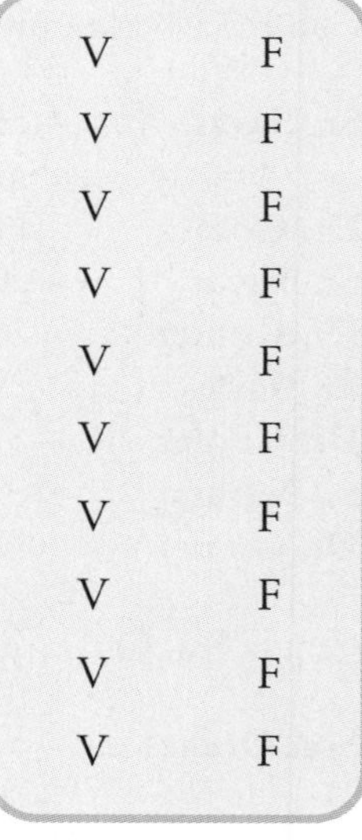

Nombre ______________________ Sección ____________ Fecha ____________

Audio

VOCABULARIO

COGNADOS

el antiácido
la colonoscopia
comercial
elástico(a)
la endoscopia
la hemorroide, la almorrana
la instrucción
la insulina
el laxante
regularmente
la úlcera
el ultrasonido

NOMBRES

la acidez *acidity, heartburn*
el (la) anciano(a) *elderly man, elderly woman*
el audífono *hearing aid*
el azúcar *sugar*
la bebida *drink, beverage*
el cansancio, la fatiga *tiredness, exhaustion*
el clínico, el (la) internista *general practitioner, internist*
la debilidad *weakness*
el intestino grueso *large intestine*
las medias *stockings, hose*
  las medias elásticas *support stockings*
el par *pair*
la piedra, el cálculo *stone*
el purgante *purgative, cathartic*
el remedio casero *home remedy*
las várices, las venas varicosas *varicose veins*
el vaso *glass*
la vesícula biliar *gallbladder*

VERBOS

aliviarse[1] *to feel better, to diminish (a pain)*
curar *to cure*
esperar *to hope*
inyectar(se) *to inject (oneself)*
notar *to notice*
oír[2] *to hear*
pasársele a uno *to pass*
temer *to be afraid, to fear*

ADJETIVOS

condimentado(a) *spiced, spicy*
negro(a) *black*
sordo(a) *deaf*

OTRAS PALABRAS Y EXPRESIONES

alguna vez *ever*
de vez en cuando *from time to time*
diariamente *daily*
el dolor se me pasa *the pain goes away*
fielmente *faithfully*
ojalá *I hope, if only...*
quedarse sordo(a) *to go deaf*
sacar la lengua *to stick out one's tongue*
últimamente *lately*

---

[1]Irregular verb: **oigo, oyes, oye, oímos, oís, oyen.**
[2]In Mexico, **aliviarse** means *to give birth.*

Nombre ______________________ Sección ____________ Fecha ____________

VOCABULARIO ADICIONAL

¿Ud. ha tenido alguna vez

- **trastornos nerviosos?** *nervous disorders*
- **depresión?** *depression*
- **psicosis?** *psychosis*
- **ansiedad o angustia?** *anxiety*
- **ronquera?** *hoarseness*
- **problemas de los riñones?** *kidney problems*
- **las piernas inflamadas (hinchadas)?** *swollen legs*
- **retención de líquido?** *liquid retention*
- **insomnio?** *insomnia*
- **convulsiones?** *convulsions*
- **una embolia?** *embolism, clot*
- **entumecimiento en los brazos (las piernas)?** *numbness in your arms (legs)*
- **una infección de hongo vaginal?** *vaginal infection*

NOTAS CULTURALES

- Gastrointestinal problems are very common among Latinos as a result of their diet and their lifestyle. The high incidence rate of gallstones is a health issue of major concern for the Latino population.
- Some stomach discomfort may be attributed to *empacho,* which literally means an impacted stomach. While all ages may be prone to **empacho**, it is much more common in young children. Symptoms are anorexia, stomachache, vomiting, pain with diarrhea, and generalized abdominal fullness. Remedies include rubbing the stomach or back, popping of the skin, and teas of wormwood [**ajenjo, estafiate** (Méx.)] or chamomile (**manzanilla**). Red lead (**azarcón, minio**) or a compound of mercury [**greta** (Méx.)] powders are still occasionally given.

  Nancy Nett, MoDo, Assistant Professor, Department of Community Medicine, Baylor College of Medicine (http:www. rice.edu/projects/Hispanic/Health/Courses/mod7/mod7.html)
- Some Spanish-speaking patients with little or no formal education may describe their illnesses according to their cultural understanding. For example, they may confuse neurological problems with nervous problems and use the term **problemas de los nervios** (*nervous problems*) to refer to mental health. Other mental illnesses and conditions may be described as a **susto** (*fright*) or **mal de ojo** (*evil eye*). Some Mexican Americans use the term **ataques** (*attacks*) to refer to seizures or epilepsy. Often these cases have biological bases and need careful and sensitive exploration by the attending physician to diagnose the illness accurately.

Nombre ______________________ Sección ____________ Fecha ____________

Actividades

Dígame... Answer the following questions, basing your answers on the dialogues.

1. ¿Qué problemas ha tenido últimamente el Sr. Navas?

____

2. ¿Qué debe seguir fielmente el Sr. Navas?

____

3. ¿Debe inyectarse insulina el Sr. Navas? ¿Qué le va a recetar el médico?

____

4. ¿Por qué cree la Sra. Ordaz que tiene una úlcera?

____

5. ¿Cuándo se le pasa el dolor a la Sra. Ordaz? ¿Qué más ha tomado?

____

6. ¿Qué va a hacerle el doctor a la Sra. Ordaz? ¿Por qué?

____

7. ¿Qué es necesario que evite comer la señora? ¿Qué le va a recetar el médico?

____

8. ¿Debe el Sr. Rosas tomar un laxante regularmente?

____

9. ¿Qué va a hacerle el doctor? ¿Para qué?

____

10. ¿Por qué quiere el doctor hacerle un ultrasonido al Sr. Rosas?

____

11. ¿Qué debe usar él para poder oír mejor? ¿Qué espera que haga su hijo?

____

12. ¿Qué le recomienda el doctor que use para las várices?

____

Nombre ______________________ Sección ____________ Fecha ____________

Hablemos Interview a classmate, using the following questions. When you have finished, switch roles.

1. ¿Toma Ud. remedios caseros a veces? ¿Cuáles?
2. ¿Le han hecho un ultrasonido alguna vez? ¿Por qué?
3. ¿Tiene Ud. azúcar en la sangre? ¿En la orina?
4. ¿Ha sentido Ud. mucho cansancio o debilidad últimamente?
5. ¿Tiene Ud. acidez?
6. ¿Consume Ud. (*Do you consume*) mucha cafeína? ¿Cuántas tazas de café toma al día?
7. ¿Cuáles son algunos de los alimentos que Ud. no debe comer?
8. ¿Sigue Ud. fielmente las instrucciones de su médico?
9. Si Ud. tiene dolor de cabeza, ¿se le pasa el dolor cuando toma aspirinas?
10. Tengo mucha acidez. ¿Qué debo tomar?
11. ¿Es malo tomar purgantes regularmente?
12. Una amiga mía tiene várices. ¿Qué le recomienda Ud. que haga?

Vamos a practicar

A Complete the following sentences, using the subjunctive, the indicative, or the infinitive of the verbs given.

Modelo Temo que él no ____________ (poder) venir hoy.
Temo que él no **pueda** venir hoy.

1. Temo que ella ____________________ (tener) diabetes.
2. Es mejor que Ud. ____________________ (seguir) una dieta especial.
3. Temo no ____________________ (poder) comprarte un audífono.
4. Es necesario ____________________ (inyectarse) insulina diariamente.
5. Ojalá que ellos no ____________________ (desmayarse).
6. Es importante que nosotros no ____________________ (comer) nada condimentado.
7. El doctor teme que yo ____________________ (tener) cálculos en la vesícula biliar.
8. Es difícil ____________________ (evitar) eso.
9. No es necesario que Ud. ____________________ (tomar) purgante diariamente.

Nombre ______________________ **Sección** __________ **Fecha** __________

10. Es seguro que ellos ______________ (necesitar) medias elásticas.

11. Es importante que tú ______________ (seguir) un tratamiento.

12. Ojalá que se le ______________ (pasar) el dolor.

B Change the following adjectives to adverbs.

MODELO raro (*rare*)
raramente

1. fácil ______________

2. necesario ______________

3. general ______________

4. especial ______________

5. frecuente ______________

6. total ______________

7. regular ______________

8. completo ______________

9. normal ______________

10. directo ______________

C Use the adverbs you wrote in Exercise B to complete the following sentences.

MODELO Ella __________ me visita.
Ella **raramente** me visita.

1. Ella puede hacer eso ______________.

2. ______________ tomo la medicina después de las comidas.

3. A veces me duele el estómago, ______________ cuando tengo hambre.

4. El señor es ______________ sordo.

5. Tiene que hablar ______________ con el médico. No hable con la recepcionista.

6. Ella habla con el especialista ______________. Habla dos o tres veces por semana.

7. El cuarto está ______________ vacío.

8. Tienes que ir al hospital, pero no ______________ los lunes.

Nombre ______________________ Sección ____________ Fecha ____________

Conversaciones breves

Complete the following dialogues, using your imagination and the vocabulary from this lesson.

A Una doctora y un paciente que tiene diabetes:

Doctora —______________________

Paciente —Sí, últimamente he sentido mucho cansancio.

Doctora —______________________

Paciente —¿Una dieta especial? ¿Es para perder peso?

B Un médico y una paciente que cree tener úlceras:

Doctor —______________________

Paciente —Sí, tengo mucha acidez y dolor de estómago.

Doctor —______________________

Paciente —Tomo un antiácido o un vaso de leche, y el dolor se me pasa.

Doctor —______________________

Paciente —No, nunca vomito.

Doctor —______________________

Paciente —Sí, ayer noté un poco de sangre en la materia fecal.

En estas situaciones

What would you say in the following situations? What might the other person say?

1. You are the doctor. Tell your patient to stick out his/her tongue and say "Ah."
2. You are a patient. Tell your doctor your left side hurts sometimes. Ask the doctor if the pain could be caused by gallstones because your mother had them.
3. You are the doctor. Tell your patient that you think he/she has a gallbladder problem and you're going to do an ultrasound. Explain to the person that he/she should avoid spicy food and that it is better not to drink alcoholic beverages.
4. You are a patient. Tell your doctor that you don't hear people well when they speak. Ask him/her if you are going deaf.
5. You are a doctor. Ask your patient if he/she has been drinking any special teas for his/her stomach discomfort and ask about other home remedies.

Casos

Act out the following scenarios with a partner.

1. A doctor examines a patient who might be diabetic.
2. A doctor examines and prescribes treatment for a patient who has an ulcer.

Nombre ______________________ Sección ______________ Fecha ______________

Un paso más

A Review the **Vocabulario adicional** in this lesson and then write what medical conditions the following people have.

1. Rosa no puede dormir por la noche.

   ____

2. El niño tiene epilepsia (*epilepsy*).

   ____

3. A Celita le recetaron calmantes.

   ____

4. Carmen tiene que sentarse con las piernas en alto (*up*).

   ____

5. A Luis le duele la garganta (*throat*) y tiene dificultad para hablar.

   ____

6. El médico le recetó un diurético (*diuretic*) a Gloria.

   ____

7. Guillermo tiene problemas cuando orina.

   ____

8. A Carlos muchas veces se le duermen los pies.

   ____

9. El médico le recetó Monistat a Marta.

   ____

Nombre ______________ Sección ______________ Fecha ______________

B Read these descriptions of services offered at the Hospital Edgardo Rebagliati Martins and answer the questions on page 227. Remember to guess the meaning of all cognates.

Unidad de hemorragia digestiva

Es una unidad operativa de cuidados intermedios para aquellos pacientes que ingresan al hospital con hemorragias digestivas provocadas por úlcera duodenal, gastritis hemorrágica y úlcera gástrica. En esta unidad, con capacidad para seis pacientes, se atienden[1] 600 casos de hemorragia digestiva al año. La unidad cuenta con una sala especial para llevar a cabo[2] laparoscopia diagnóstica y terapéutica. Asimismo,[3] cuenta con un ambiente[4] altamente técnico para realizar endoscopia digestiva diagnóstica (por ejemplo: biopsias) y terapéutica (por ejemplo: extracción de pequeños tumores en el estómago). El equipo[5] de endoscopia computarizado es uno de los más modernos del país.[6]

Servicio de sonografía

Este servicio médico cuenta con seis ecógrafos de tiempo real: equipos muy sofisticados y entre los más completos del medio. El ecógrafo se emplea[7] para diagnosticar diversas patologías mediante la técnica del ultrasonido. Permite descubrir[8] tumores, lesiones inflamatorias y detectar a tiempo[9] un cáncer del ovario o de la próstata. También tiene aplicación en el área ginecológica y obstétrica, y sirve como guía[10] para realizar biopsias de tumores y drenajes[11] de abscesos. El servicio está considerado entre los más modernos de América Latina y atiende a cien pacientes diariamente.

---

[1]**se...** *are attended*
[2]**llevar...** *to carry out*
[3]*Also*
[4]*atmosphere*
[5]*equipment*
[6]*country*
[7]**se...** *is employed*
[8]*to discover*
[9]**a...** *on time*
[10]*guide*
[11]*drainage*

Nombre ______________________ Sección ______________ Fecha ______________

1. ¿Qué problemas médicos pueden causar una hemorragia digestiva?

____

2. ¿Qué tipo de cirugía pueden hacer en la sala especial?

____

3. ¿Para qué usan el equipo de endoscopia?

____

4. ¿Cuántos ecógrafos tiene este hospital? ¿Y cuántos tiene su hospital?

____

5. ¿Qué problemas se pueden detectar con el ultrasonido?

____

6. ¿Se usa mucho el servicio de sonografía? ¿Cómo lo sabe?

____

Lección 18 En la clínica de drogadictos

Objectives

Structures

- The subjunctive to express doubt, disbelief, and denial
- The subjunctive to express indefiniteness and nonexistence
- Diminutive suffixes

Communication

- Discussing drugs and drug addiction

En la clínica de drogadictos

2–18

La Srta. Muñoz, coordinadora del Programa Antidrogas, está hablando con Mario Acosta, un muchachito de quince años.

Srta. Muñoz —Dime, ¿cuánto tiempo hace que tomas drogas, Mario?
Mario —No sé... unos dos años.
Srta. Muñoz —¿Alguna vez tuviste hepatitis o alguna otra enfermedad del hígado?
Mario —No sé, pero creo que no.
Srta. Muñoz —¿Cuándo fue la última vez que fuiste al médico?
Mario —Hace como un año. Tuve convulsiones.
Srta. Muñoz —¿Tomas bebidas alcohólicas?
Mario —Sí, cerveza o vino... a veces, pero no creo que eso me haga daño...
Srta. Muñoz —¿Usas anfetaminas?
Mario —Sí.
Srta. Muñoz —¿Cuándo empezaste a usar drogas diariamente?
Mario —Cuando tenía trece años.
Srta. Muñoz —¿Cuántas veces por día?
Mario —Tres veces.
Srta. Muñoz —¿Cuál es la dosis? ¿Cuántos globos compras?
Mario —Seis... a veces ocho o nueve...

Nombre ______________________ Sección ______________ Fecha ______________

Srta. Muñoz	—Dime, ¿te inyectas la droga en la vena o la fumas?
Mario	—La fumo y también me la inyecto. A veces comparto jeringuillas con mis amigos.
Srta. Muñoz	—¿Te han hecho la prueba del SIDA?
Mario	—No.
Srta. Muñoz	—¿Cuándo fue la última vez que trataste de dejar las drogas?
Mario	—La semana pasada.
Srta. Muñoz	—¿Y cuánto tiempo pudiste estar sin usar drogas?
Mario	—Un día y medio... Dudo que pueda aguantar más tiempo. ¿Hay algo que me puedan dar para ayudarme?
Srta. Muñoz	—Estoy segura de que aquí podremos ayudarte. Ven conmigo.
Mario	—No hay nadie que pueda hacer nada por mí.
Srta. Muñoz	—No digas eso. Llena esta planilla y el médico te verá en seguida.
Mario	—Mi hermanita, que tiene 12 años, empezó a fumar mariguana. ¿Puedo traerla?
Srta. Muñoz	—Sí, tráela cuanto antes.

2–18

¡Escuchemos! While listening to the dialogue, circle **V (verdadero)** if the statement is true or **F (falso)** if it is false.

1.	Mario es drogadicto.	V	F
2.	Mario tuvo hepatitis hace dos años.	V	F
3.	Mario no toma ninguna bebida alcohólica.	V	F
4.	Mario empezó a usar drogas cuando tenía 13 años.	V	F
5.	Mario niega que comparta jeringuillas con sus amigos.	V	F
6.	Mario pudo estar solamente un día y medio sin tomar drogas.	V	F
7.	Mario duda que pueda dejar de tomar drogas.	V	F
8.	Mario cree que no hay nadie que pueda ayudarlo.	V	F
9.	La hermanita de Mario nunca ha usado drogas.	V	F
10.	La Srta. Muñoz quiere hablar con la hermanita de Mario.	V	F

Nombre ______________________ Sección ____________ Fecha ____________

PLANILLA

Favor de contestar las siguientes preguntas:

1. ¿Está siguiendo tratamiento médico? *Sí*
2. ¿Tiene Ud. algunas limitaciones o incapacidades físicas? *No*
3. ¿Está recibiendo actualmente algún tratamiento por problemas mentales? *No*
4. ¿Estuvo Ud. alguna vez en algún hospital para enfermos mentales o bajo tratamiento psiquiátrico por otros problemas? *No*
5. **PARA MUJERES**: Fecha de su última visita al ginecólogo. *2/13/05*

HISTORIA CLÍNICA

	SÍ	NO	Fecha y lugar del tratamiento
Hepatitis		X	
Ataques al corazón		X	
Epilepsia		X	
Tuberculosis		X	
Diabetes		X	
Úlcera	X		*Hospital General 3/24/99*
Abortos		X	
Aborto natural	X		*5/12/94*
Problemas de alcoholismo		X	
Abscesos		X	
Enfermedades venéreas		X	
Problemas dentales	X		*Clínica Dental Fabio 8/23/95*
Alergias		X	

Resumen: ____________________

Nombre ____________________ Sección ____________ Fecha ____________

Audio

VOCABULARIO

COGNADOS

la alergia
la anfetamina
antidroga
las convulsiones
el (la) coordinador(a)
dental
la droga
el (la) drogadicto(a)
la epilepsia
la hepatitis
la limitación
la mariguana, marihuana[1]
mental
el programa

NOMBRES

el ataque al corazón, el infarto *heart attack*
la cerveza *beer*
el (la) enfermo(a) *sick person*
la fecha *date*
el globo *balloon (drug dosage)*
el (la) hermano(a) *brother, sister*
la incapacidad *disability*
la jeringuilla *hypodermic syringe*
el lugar *place*
el (la) muchacho(a) *boy, young man, girl, young woman*
el resumen *summary*
el vino *wine*

VERBOS

aguantar *to stand, to tolerate, to bear*
compartir *to share*
decidir *to decide*
dudar *to doubt*
recibir *to receive*

OTRAS PALABRAS Y EXPRESIONES

actualmente *currently, at the present time*
bajo tratamiento psiquiátrico *under psychiatric treatment*
favor de *please*
hace como (cinco años) *about (five years) ago*
hacer daño *to hurt*
por mí *for me, on my behalf*
¿Te (Le) han hecho la prueba de... ? *Have you been tested for... ?*

VOCABULARIO ADICIONAL

TIPOS DE DROGAS

el ácido *LSD*
la cocaína, la coca[2] *cocaine*
el crac[3] *crack*
los esteroides anabólicos *anabolic steroids*
el éxtasis *ecstasy*
el hachich, el hachis *hashish*
la heroína[4] *heroin*
el leño, la cucaracha, el porro *joint*
la metadona *methadone*
la morfina *morphine*
el opio *opium*
el PCP, el polvo de ángel *angel dust*
el porro mortal *killer joint*

---

[1]Colloquialisms: **el perico, el polvo**
[2]Colloquialisms: **la yerba, el pito, el pasto**
[3]Colloquialisms: **la piedra, la roca, la coca cocinada**
[4]Colloquialism: **la manteca** (*Caribe*)

Nombre ______________________ Sección ____________ Fecha ____________

adicto(a) *addicted*
la aguja *needle*
las alucinaciones *hallucinations*
el delirium tremens *DT's*
la desintoxicación *detoxification*
endrogarse[1] *to take drugs, to become addicted to drugs*
pullar (*Caribe*) *to shoot up*
la sobredosis *overdose*

NOTAS CULTURALES

- Drug addiction and alcoholism are important health issues that affect the Hispanic American population; the incidence rate is particularly high among Mexican Americans and Puerto Ricans. In addition, Hispanic Americans have a disproportionate number of deaths due to narcotic addictions. In the Hispanic Health and Nutrition Survey, 21.5% of Puerto Ricans reported having used cocaine, while the figure was 11.1% for Mexican Americans and 9.2% for Cuban Americans.
- In Spanish, the word **droga** does not mean *medicine* as in English. Latinos use this term to refer to narcotics and other illegal drugs. Similarly, a **droguero(a)** is a person who uses or sells illicit drugs.

Actividades

Dígame... Answer the following questions, basing your answers on the dialogue.

1. ¿Cuánto tiempo hace que Mario toma drogas?

   ____

2. ¿Ha tenido Mario hepatitis o alguna otra enfermedad del hígado? ¿Qué tuvo hace un año?

   ____

3. ¿Qué bebidas alcohólicas toma Mario?

   ____

4. ¿Cuándo empezó Mario a tomar drogas diariamente?

   ____

5. ¿Cuántos globos compra Mario?

   ____

[1]Colloquialism: **dar un viaje, tripear**

6. ¿Mario fuma la droga o se la inyecta? ¿Qué comparte con sus amigos?

____

7. ¿Cuándo fue la última vez que Mario trató de dejar las drogas?

____

8. ¿Cuánto tiempo pudo estar sin tomar drogas?

____

9. ¿Hay alguien en la clínica que pueda ayudar a Mario?

____

10. ¿Qué debe llenar Mario?

____

11. ¿Qué problema tiene la hermanita de Mario? ¿Cuántos años tiene?

____

12. ¿Qué le dice la Srta. Muñoz a Mario que haga?

____

Hablemos Interview a classmate, using the following questions. When you have finished, switch roles.

1. ¿Toma Ud. bebidas alcohólicas? ¿Cuáles?
2. ¿Ha tenido Ud. alguna vez una enfermedad del hígado? ¿Cuál?
3. ¿Conoce Ud. a alguien que use drogas?
4. ¿Es peligroso tomar bebidas alcohólicas y drogas al mismo tiempo? ¿Por qué?
5. ¿Qué drogas hacen más daño: las que se fuman o las que se inyectan?
6. ¿Cuál cree Ud. que es la droga más peligrosa? ¿Por qué?
7. ¿Cree Ud. que es fácil dejar de usar drogas? ¿Por qué?
8. ¿Conoce Ud. algún programa especial para ayudar a los drogadictos? ¿Cómo se llama?

Nombre ______________________ Sección ____________ Fecha ____________

Vamos a practicar

A Complete the following sentences, using the present subjunctive or the present indicative of the verbs given.

MODELO Yo no creo que él ____________ (saber) mi dirección.
Yo no creo que él **sepa** mi dirección.

1. Yo creo que él ____________ (tomar) anfetaminas, pero dudo que ____________ (ser) drogadicto.
2. Estoy seguro de que ella ____________ (estar) bajo tratamiento psiquiátrico.
3. El médico duda que estas medicinas te ____________ (hacer) daño.
4. Es verdad que ella ____________ (ser) la coordinadora del programa, pero no es verdad que ____________ (venir) a la clínica todos los días.
5. No creo que Ud. ____________ (tener) hepatitis.
6. Yo no dudo que él ____________ (comprar) ocho o nueve globos.
7. ¿Hay alguien que ____________ (poder) ayudar a ese muchachito?
8. Conozco a alguien que ____________ (saber) tratar las incapacidades físicas.
9. Aquí hay muchas personas que ____________ (beber) cerveza, pero no hay nadie que ____________ (beber) vino.
10. No hay ninguna enfermera que ____________ (querer) trabajar con ese médico.

B Complete the following exchanges, using the Spanish equivalent of the words in parentheses.

1. —¿Hay alguien en su familia ____________? (*who has epilepsy*)
   —Sí, tengo un primo que ____________. (*has epilepsy*)
2. —¿Hay alguien que ____________ la dirección de Eva? (*knows*)
   —No, y no hay nadie que ____________ su número de teléfono. (*has*)
3. —Es verdad que yo ____________, pero no es verdad que ____________ sin el alcohol. (*drink a little / I can't live*)
   —Es mejor no ____________. (*drink*)

Nombre ______________________ Sección ____________ Fecha ____________

Conversaciones breves

Complete the following dialogue, using your imagination and the vocabulary from this lesson.

Una drogadicta y la coordinadora del programa:

Coordinadora —______________________________

Paciente —Hace unos tres años que tomo drogas.

Coordinadora —______________________________

Paciente —Sí, tuve hepatitis.

Coordinadora —______________________________

Paciente —La última vez que fui al médico fue hace dos años.

Coordinadora —______________________________

Paciente —Empecé a tomar drogas cuando tenía catorce años.

Coordinadora —______________________________

Paciente —No, nunca traté de dejar las drogas.

Coordinadora —______________________________

Paciente —No creo que nadie pueda ayudarme.

En estas situaciones

What would you say in the following situations? What might the other person say?

1. You work in a drug abuse clinic. Ask your patient how long he/she has been on drugs and what drugs he/she is taking. Then find out if the person has tried to quit taking drugs.
2. You are interpreting for a drug addict. Tell the doctor that the patient takes amphetamines daily and drinks beer often. Add that he shares hypodermic syringes with his friends.
3. You are a doctor. Ask your patient if he/she has been tested for AIDS and if he/she has ever had hepatitis.

Casos

Act out the following scenarios with a partner.

1. A coordinator in a drug abuse clinic interviews a drug addict about his/her addiction.
2. A coordinator takes the clinical history of a drug addict. Use the form on page 237 as a basis for your conversation.

Nombre ______________________ Sección ____________ Fecha ____________

PLANILLA

Favor de contestar las siguientes preguntas:

1. ¿Está siguiendo tratamiento médico? ______________________

____

2. ¿Tiene Ud. algunas limitaciones o incapacidades físicas? ______________________

____

3. ¿Está recibiendo actualmente algún tratamiento por problemas mentales? ______________________

____

4. ¿Estuvo Ud. alguna vez en algún hospital para enfermos mentales o bajo tratamiento psiquiátrico por otros problemas? ______________________

____

5. **PARA MUJERES**: Fecha de su última visita al ginecólogo. ______________________

HISTORIA CLÍNICA

	SÍ	NO	Fecha y lugar del tratamiento
Hepatitis			
Ataques al corazón			
Epilepsia			
Tuberculosis			
Diabetes			
Úlcera			
Abortos			
Aborto natural			
Problemas alcohólicos			
Abscesos			
Enfermedades venéreas			
Problemas dentales			
Alergias			

Resumen: ______________________

____

____

____

____

Nombre ______________________ Sección ____________ Fecha ____________

Un paso más

A Review the **Vocabulario adicional** in this lesson and then complete the sentences.

1. El __________ y el __________ son drogas que se fuman.
2. El médico me inyectó __________ para el dolor.
3. Tiene alucinaciones porque usó __________.
4. Murió (*He died*) de una __________ de heroína.
5. Carmen es __________ a la cocaína.
6. El __________ es una droga barata (*cheap*).
7. Para inyectarme necesito una __________ y una jeringuilla.
8. Está en un programa de __________. Le están dando metadona.

B Read the following information about drugs, published by the Department of Health and Human Services and then answer the questions on page 239. Remember to guess the meaning of all cognates.

¿Cuáles son los peligros físicos de las drogas que contienen opio?

Los peligros físicos dependen del tipo de droga que se consuma, de su fuente,[1] de la dosis y de la forma en que se consuma. La mayoría de los peligros son ocasionados por consumir una cantidad excesiva de una droga, por utilizar agujas no esterilizadas, por contaminación de la propia[2] droga o por combinar la droga con otras substancias. A la larga,[3] las personas que consumen estas drogas pueden contraer infecciones de los tejidos[4] que revisten el corazón y las válvulas, abscesos de la piel y congestión pulmonar. Las infecciones ocasionadas por soluciones, jeringas y agujas no esterilizadas pueden producir enfermedades tales como el tétano, la hepatitis serosa y el SIDA.

---

[1] *source*
[2] *itself*
[3] **A...** *In the long run*
[4] *tissues*

Nombre ______________________ Sección ______________ Fecha ______________

1. Cuando se consumen drogas que contienen opio, ¿de qué dependen los peligros físicos?

____

2. ¿Es peligroso combinar las drogas con otras substancias?

____

3. ¿Cómo afectan estas drogas el corazón?

____

4. ¿Qué pueden producir en los pulmones?

____

5. ¿Qué enfermedad del hígado pueden causar?

____

6. ¿Qué producen en la piel?

____

LECTURA 6 INFORMACIÓN SOBRE LA COCAÍNA

Search

(From *National Institute on Drug Abuse*)

La cocaína es una droga derivada de la planta de la coca y generalmente tiene la apariencia de un polvo blanco. El polvo de la cocaína se inhala a menudo por la nariz o se puede disolver en agua e inyectarse en las venas. Los términos comunes para describirla en español son "talco", "nieve" y "coca". En inglés se llama "*coke*", "*snow*", "*blow*", "*lady*" y "*flake*".

La cocaína también se usa en forma de pequeños cristales que se fuman. Éstos se conocen como "*crack*", por el sonido crujiente que hacen cuando se calientan. En español se conoce como cocaína "crack" o "cocinada". En inglés se conoce como "*rock*" o "*freebase*".

La cocaína puede:

- Causar una ansiedad intensa, lo que significa que el usuario necesita usar más droga y con mayor frecuencia a fin de sentir el mismo placer que sintió en los primeros usos. Eventualmente, el usuario puede también necesitar la droga con mayor frecuencia sólo para sentirse normal o para evitar sentirse irritable o deprimido.
- Reducir los vasos sanguíneos, lo que requiere que el corazón trabaje y lata más fuerte.
- Causar espasmos musculares, dolor de pecho y ataques al corazón o derrames cerebrales.

"La cocaína puede acelerar el latido del corazón y causar un ritmo irregular, y eso puede provocar una muerte repentina."

Conversaciones

2-19

—¿De dónde se obtiene la cocaína?
—Se obtiene de la planta de la coca.
—¿Cómo es la cocaína?
—Es un polvo blanco.
—¿Cómo se usa generalmente?
—Se inhala por la nariz.

Nombre ______________________ **Sección** ____________ **Fecha** ____________

2-20 —¿Qué les produce la cocaína a las personas que la usan?
—Les produce una ansiedad intensa.
—¿Es adictiva la cocaína?
—Sí, y cada vez es necesario usarla con mayor frecuencia.

2-21 —¿Puede la cocaína provocar la muerte?
—Sí, porque puede causar un ritmo irregular del corazón, y la muerte puede ser repentina.

Dígame... Answer the following questions, basing your answers on the reading and the conversations.

1. ¿De qué color es la cocaína?

   ____

2. ¿De qué planta se deriva la cocaína?

   ____

3. ¿Qué se debe hacer con la droga para podérsela inyectar?

   ____

4. ¿Qué palabras se usan en español para hablar de la cocaína?

   ____

5. ¿Es posible fumar la cocaína? ¿En qué forma?

   ____

6. ¿Por qué se la llama "crack"?

   ____

7. ¿Qué efecto produce la cocaína en las personas que la usan?

   ____

8. ¿Por qué es necesario usar cada vez más droga y con mayor frecuencia?

   ____

9. Mencione otros problemas que puede causar la cocaína.

   ____

10. ¿Por qué puede la cocaína provocar la muerte?

   ____

Lección 19 Consejos útiles

Objectives

Structures
- The subjunctive after certain conjunctions
- The present perfect subjunctive
- Uses of the present perfect subjunctive

Communication
- Talking about child safety and first aid in the home

Consejos útiles

2–22 Una madre joven habla con el pediatra de su bebé.

Madre —Quería hacerle algunas preguntas, doctor.
Pediatra —Muy bien.
Madre —Todavía tengo miedo de dejar al bebé solo en la cuna...
Pediatra —En la cuna está seguro, si no hay en ella objetos peligrosos como alfileres, monedas, botones, bolsas de plástico, etcétera.
Madre —¿Puede usar su almohadita?
Pediatra —No use almohadas; pueden sofocar al niño.
Madre —El otro día, tomando el biberón, el bebé se atragantó; y no sé por qué... Me asusté mucho.
Pediatra —Quizás el agujero del biberón es demasiado grande.
Madre —Voy a revisarlo, pero no creo que haya sido eso... Cuando empiece a gatear y a pararse voy a tener más problemas.
Pediatra —En cuanto empiece a andar por la casa, tiene que tener mucho más cuidado porque el bebé puede envenenarse con muchas de las cosas que hay en la casa, como lejía, tintes, insecticidas, pinturas, detergentes, maquillajes, etcétera. En este folleto encontrará Ud. otras instrucciones útiles.

Nombre ______________________ Sección __________ Fecha __________

Instrucciones

1. El niño no debe estar cerca del horno, de la estufa, de la plancha, de los fósforos, de los líquidos calientes ni de los objetos eléctricos.
2. Si el niño se quema, trate la quemadura con agua, no con hielo. Nunca ponga yodo ni mantequilla en la quemadura. Si ésta es grave, lleve al niño al médico.
3. Ponga enchufes de seguridad sobre los tomacorrientes que no use y tape con muebles los que están en uso.
4. En caso de cortaduras y rasguños, limpie la herida con agua y jabón y cúbrala con un vendaje. Si la herida es profunda, llame al médico. Si sangra mucho, aplique presión sobre la herida y lleve al niño médico.
5. No deje al niño al sol por mucho tiempo, y póngale un gorro. Para un niño pequeño, dos minutos por día es suficiente.
6. No deje al niño solo en la casa, ni en la bañadera ni en la piscina, ni en el coche.
7. Haga vacunar a su niño antes de que empiece a ir a la escuela.
8. En su casa y en el carro tenga siempre un botiquín o un estuche de primeros auxilios con lo siguiente:

cinta adhesiva
curitas
gasa
pinzas
tijeras
termómetro
alcohol
agua oxigenada
crema antibacteriana
antihistamínico (líquido de *Benadryl*)
ungüento para quemaduras menores
ipecacuana
Tylenol

Tenga también los números de teléfono del centro de envenenamiento, de los paramédicos, del hospital y de su médico.

2–22

¡Escuchemos! While listening to the dialogue, circle **V (verdadero)** if the statement is true or **F (falso)** if it is false.

1. La mamá piensa que el bebé está seguro en la cuna. V F
2. El pediatra dice que es peligroso tener almohaditas en la cuna del bebé. V F
3. Si el agujero del biberón es demasiado grande el bebé se puede atragantar. V F
4. Si un niño se quema, debe ponerle hielo en la quemadura. V F

Nombre ______________________ Sección ____________ Fecha ____________

5. Si un niño tiene una cortadura pequeña deben llevarlo al médico. V F
6. No es necesario poner enchufes de seguridad en los tomacorrientes. V F
7. Un niño pequeño no debe estar al sol más de dos minutos al día. V F
8. Es peligroso dejar a un niño solo en el coche. V F
9. No es necesario vacunar al niño antes de empezar a ir a la escuela. V F
10. Es importante tener el teléfono del centro de envenenamiento cuando hay niños en la casa. V F

VOCABULARIO

COGNADOS

el antihistamínico
el detergente
el insecticida
el objeto
el (la) paramédico(a)
el plástico

NOMBRES

el agua oxigenada *hydrogen peroxide*
el agujero, el hueco *hole*
el alfiler *pin*
la bañadera, la bañera *bathtub*
el botiquín *medicine chest, medicine cabinet*
el centro de envenenamiento *poison center*
la cinta adhesiva *adhesive tape*
el consejo *advice*
la cortadura *cut*
la cuna *crib, cradle*
el enchufe de seguridad *electrical plug cover*
el estuche (el botiquín) de primeros auxilios, *first-aid kit*
la estufa, la cocina *stove*
el fósforo, la cerilla *match*
el gorro *bonnet, cap*
el horno *oven*
la ipecacuana *ipecac*
la lejía *bleach*
el maquillaje *makeup*
la moneda *coin*
el mueble *piece of furniture*
la pintura *paint*
las pinzas *tweezers*
la piscina, la alberca (*Méx.*) *swimming pool*
la plancha *iron*
los primeros auxilios *first aid*
el rasguño *scratch*
el sol *sun*
el teléfono *telephone*
las tijeras *scissors*
el tinte *dye*
el tomacorrientes *electrical outlet, socket*
el vendaje, la venda *bandage*
el yodo *iodine*

VERBOS

andar *to walk*
aplicar *to apply*
asustarse *to be scared, to be frightened*

atragantarse *to choke*
envenenar(se) *to poison (oneself)*
gatear, andar a gatas *to crawl*
sofocar(se) *to suffocate (oneself)*

ADJETIVOS

profundo(a), hondo(a) *deep*
seguro(a) *safe*
solo(a) *alone*
útil *useful*

OTRAS PALABRAS Y EXPRESIONES

en cuanto, tan pronto como *as soon as*
demasiado *too much*
hacer preguntas *to ask questions*
tener miedo *to be afraid*

Audio

Vocabulario adicional

EL CUIDADO DE LOS BEBÉS

el asiento para el auto *car seat*
el babero *bib*
cambiar el pañal *to change the diaper*
el cochecito *baby carriage*
la comidita de bebé *baby food*
la fórmula *formula*
llorar *to cry*
la loción para bebé *baby lotion*
el pañal *diaper*
  el pañal desechable *disposable diaper*
los pañuelos de papel *tissues*
la sillita alta *high chair*
el talco para bebé *baby powder*
la toallita *washcloth*

ponerse
- **rojo(a)** *to turn red*
- **azul** *to turn blue*
- **blanco(a)** *to turn white*
- **pálido(a)** *to turn pale*

Search

- Hispanic cultural traditions stress the importance of family as a social unit. Within this unit, Latino families exhibit interdependence, affiliation, and cooperation. For example, grandmothers are often involved in the daily care and raising of their grandchildren. Hispanics often include many people in their extended family such as aunts, uncles, cousins, "**compadres**" (godparents and/or close friends), close friends, and godparents (**padrinos**) of the family's children.
- When communicating with a Latino patient, health care providers should remember that they are sometimes, either directly or indirectly, speaking with the patient's family. Frequently, important decisions are made by entire families, not individuals, and patients may discuss a physician's diagnosis and recommendations for treatment with their families before deciding to follow them. In many families, it is the mother, and sometimes the grandmother, who makes the decisions regarding health and illness.

Nombre ______________________ **Sección** ____________ **Fecha** ____________

- Along with the concept of extended family, respect is very important in the Hispanic culture towards others based on the age, sex, social position, and authority. Older adults expect respect from youngsters. Health care providers, given their knowledge and healing abilities are given a high level of "**respeto**" (respect). One of the ways Hispanics show respect is to avoid eye contact with authority figures, and this should not be confused with disinterest. At the same time, health care providers may need to encourage questions, as questioning the authority figure may not come naturally for some Hispanic patients.

Actividades

Dígame... Answer the following questions, basing your answers on the dialogue.

1. ¿Por qué quiere hablar la madre con el pediatra de su bebé?

   ____

2. ¿De qué tiene miedo la madre todavía?

   ____

3. ¿Qué objetos no debe ella dejar en la cuna del bebé?

   ____

4. ¿Por qué no debe usar almohada el bebé?

   ____

5. ¿Por qué debe tener más cuidado la madre cuando el bebé comience a andar?

   ____

6. ¿Con qué cosas de la casa puede envenenarse el bebé?

   ____

7. ¿Qué le da el pediatra a la madre?

   ____

8. ¿Qué dice el folleto que es necesario hacer cuando una herida sangra mucho?

   ____

9. ¿Qué debe ponerse sobre los tomacorrientes que no se están usando?

   ____

10. ¿Qué deben hacer los padres antes de que sus hijos empiecen a ir a la escuela?

   ____

Nombre ______________________________ Sección ____________ Fecha ____________

Hablemos Interview a classmate, using the following questions. When you have finished, switch roles.

1. ¿Se atragantó Ud. alguna vez? ¿Con qué?
2. ¿Tiene Ud. un botiquín de primeros auxilios en su casa? ¿Qué cosas tiene en él?
3. ¿Qué cosas tiene Ud. en su casa que deben estar fuera del alcance (*out of reach*) de los niños?
4. Mi bebé tiene tres meses. ¿Cuánto tiempo puedo dejarlo al sol?
5. Mi hijo se quemó la mano. ¿Qué debo hacer?
6. ¿Cómo debe ser el agujero del biberón para darle leche a mi bebé?
7. Tengo un rasguño en el brazo. ¿Qué debo hacer?
8. ¿Por qué son peligrosas las bolsas de plástico para los niños pequeños?
9. ¿Con qué pueden quemarse los niños?
10. ¿Qué cosas que hay en la casa son generalmente peligrosas para un niño?

Vamos a practicar

A Complete the following sentences, using the present perfect subjunctive or the present perfect indicative of the verbs given.

MODELO No hay nadie que __________ (estar) enfermo.

No hay nadie que **haya estado** enfermo.

1. Creo que el niño ____________________ (envenenarse).
2. Temo que ellos ____________________ (dejar) al bebé al sol.
3. Dudan que nosotros ____________________ (aplicar) presión sobre la herida.
4. No es verdad que tú ____________________ (poner) yodo en la quemadura.
5. Ojalá que el bebé no ____________________ (sofocarse).
6. Es verdad que él ____________________ (tapar) todos los tomacorrientes.

Nombre ______________________ Sección ____________ Fecha ____________

B You are needed as an interpreter. Give the Spanish equivalent of the following.

1. When the child starts to crawl, I will have to be more careful.

____

2. When the baby started choking, I called the paramedics immediately.

____

3. The nurse is going to call me as soon as they know something.

____

4. I will have to treat the burn before we can take her to the hospital.

____

5. As soon as I wash the wound, I will put a bandage on it.

____

6. You will have to wait until the doctor finishes his examination, Mrs. Vega.

____

Conversaciones breves

Complete the following dialogue, using your imagination and the vocabulary from this lesson.

La pediatra y una madre:

Madre —Buenos días, doctora.

Pediatra —____

Madre —Sí, tengo varias preguntas. La primera es, ¿necesita el bebé una almohadita?

Pediatra —____

Madre —¿Es peligroso dejar al bebé solo en la cuna?

Pediatra —____

Madre —A veces el bebé se atraganta cuando toma el biberón. ¿Por qué es eso?

Pediatra —____

Madre —Voy a revisar bien el biberón. ¡Ah! El otro día mi hijo Antonio se quemó la mano y no sabía qué ponerle. ¿Qué es bueno para una quemadura?

Pediatra —____

Madre —Creo que el bebé necesita tomar sol... ¿Cuánto tiempo puedo dejarlo al sol?

Pediatra —____

Madre —Bueno... no tengo más preguntas hoy. Gracias por todo.

Nombre ______________________ Sección ____________ Fecha ____________

En estas situaciones What would you say in the following situations? What might the other person say?

1. You are a nurse. Advise a parent to keep his/her child away from the oven, stove, iron, matches, hot liquids, and electrical appliances (objects) so that the child doesn't burn himself/herself.
2. You are a parent. Tell the babysitter not to leave your daughter alone in the house or the bathtub. Remind him/her to feed the child at 6:00.
3. You are a nurse. Ask a parent if his/her children have been vaccinated. Then tell him/her they should be immunized before they start school.
4. You are a nurse. Explain to a parent with small children what items he/she should keep in the medicine cabinet.

Casos Act out the following scenarios with a partner.

1. A nurse and a young mother/father with a toddler discuss common household dangers.
2. A pediatrician and a mother/father discuss child care.

Un paso más

A Review the **Vocabulario adicional** in this lesson and then write what you would do in the following situations.

1. Después de bañar al bebé:

   ____

2. Cuando el bebé tiene hambre:

   ____

   ____

   ____

3. Cuando el bebé orina:

   ____

4. Cuando el bebé tiene la piel seca (*dry*):

   ____

5. Para limpiarle las manos y la cara al bebé:

   ____

6. Para limpiarle la nariz (*nose*) al bebé:

   ____

Nombre ______________________ Sección ____________ Fecha ____________

7. Cuando yo quiero ir a caminar y llevar al bebé:

____

8. Cuando llevan al bebé en el auto:

____

B Complete the following sentences.

1. El bebé no podía respirar y se puso ____________________.
2. El bebé lloró mucho y se puso ____________________.
3. El bebé orinó y le tuve que ____________________ el pañal.
4. No me gustan los pañales de tela (*cloth*); prefiero los pañales ____________________.
5. El bebé se asustó y se puso ____________________.

Lección 20 En el consultorio del cardiólogo

Objectives

Structures

- The imperfect subjunctive
- Uses of the imperfect subjunctive
- *If* clauses

Communication

- Dealing with heart-related ailments

En el consultorio del cardiólogo

2–23 Con el Sr. Calles:

El Sr. Calles tiene algunos problemas que podrían indicar que sufre del corazón, y su médico le dijo que viera al cardiólogo.

Doctor —¿Le ha dicho su médico que Ud. tiene problemas con el corazón?
Sr. Calles —No, pero tengo algunos síntomas que podrían indicar un problema, y mi médico me dijo que viniera a verlo a Ud.
Doctor —¿Ha tenido alguna vez fiebre reumática o temblores en las extremidades?
Sr. Calles —No, nunca.
Doctor —¿Le duele el pecho o siente alguna opresión cuando hace ejercicio?
Sr. Calles —Sí, a veces tengo dolor y me falta el aire... cuando subo una escalera, por ejemplo...
Doctor —¿Es un dolor sordo o agudo?
Sr. Calles —Es un dolor agudo.
Doctor —¿Le late el corazón muy rápidamente a veces?
Sr. Calles —Sí, cuando corro.
Doctor —¿Tiene a veces sudor frío después de un ejercicio violento?
Sr. Calles —No.
Doctor —¿Algún pariente cercano suyo ha tenido alguna vez un ataque al corazón antes de los sesenta años?
Sr. Calles —Bueno, un tío, el hermano de mi mamá, murió de un ataque al corazón a los cincuenta años.

Doctor —Ajá... ¿Tiene calambres en las piernas cuando camina varias cuadras?
Sr. Calles —Bueno, si yo caminara, tal vez tendría calambres, pero casi nunca camino.
Doctor —¿Le han encontrado el ácido úrico elevado en la sangre alguna vez?
Sr. Calles —No.
Doctor —Bueno, antes de comenzar ningún tratamiento, vamos a hacerle un electrocardiograma. También vamos a hacerle una angiografía coronaria para ver si tiene una arteria parcialmente obstruida.
Sr. Calles —¿Y si la tengo obstruida?
Doctor —Entonces le haremos una angioplastia y quizás necesitemos ponerle un *stent.*

Con el Sr. Luna:

El cardiólogo habla con el Sr. Luna sobre el marcapasos que el paciente necesita.

Doctor —Le voy a colocar en el pecho, debajo de la piel, una caja pequeña que contiene baterías.
Sr. Luna —¿Eso me va a mejorar?
Doctor —Sí, con el marcapasos su corazón va a latir mejor.
Sr. Luna —¿Voy a estar despierto o dormido cuando me lo haga?
Doctor —Eso lo decidiremos más tarde.
Sr. Luna —El otro médico me dijo que le preguntara si tendría ciertas limitaciones.
Doctor —Bueno, llámeme si le dicen que Ud. necesita una radiografía. Tiene que avisarles que Ud. tiene un marcapasos.
Sr. Luna —¿Qué otras precauciones debo tomar?
Doctor —Si va al dentista, dígale que tiene un marcapasos.
Sr. Luna —¿Cuánto tiempo me van a durar las baterías del marcapasos?
Doctor —Le van a durar entre diez y doce años.

2–23

¡Escuchemos! While listening to the dialogue, circle **V (verdadero)** if the statement is true or **F (falso)** if it is false.

1. El médico le aconsejó al Sr. Calles que viera a un urólogo.
2. Hace cinco años que el Sr. Calles tuvo fiebre reumática.
3. Cuando el Sr. Calles hace ejercicio le falta el aire.
4. Nadie en la familia del Sr. Calles ha tenido problemas del corazón.
5. El Sr. Calles no hace mucho ejercicio.
6. Al Sr. Calles le van a hacer un electrocardiograma para saber si tiene una arteria obstruida.
7. Si el Sr. Calles tiene una arteria obstruida va a necesitar una angioplastia.
8. El Sr. Luna necesita un marcapasos.
9. Con el marcapasos el corazón del Sr. Luna va a latir mejor.
10. El Sr. Luna debe informarle a su dentista que tiene un marcapasos.

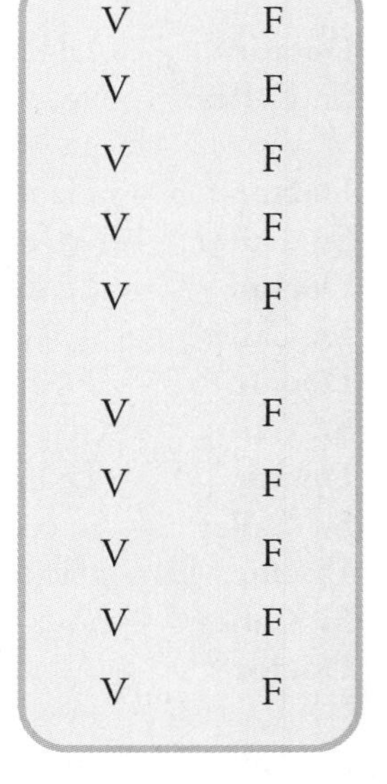

Nombre ______________________ Sección ____________ Fecha ____________

VOCABULARIO

COGNADOS

la angioplastia
la batería
el (la) cardiólogo(a)
el electrocardiograma
coronario(a)
elevado(a)
parcialmente
rápidamente
úrico(a)

NOMBRES

la caja *box*
el calambre *cramp*
la cuadra *block*
las extremidades *limbs*
la fiebre reumática *rheumatic fever*
el marcapasos *pacemaker*
la opresión *tightness*
el (la) pariente *relative*
el (la) pariente cercano(a) *close relative*
el sudor *sweat*
el temblor *tremor, shaking*
el (la) tío(a) *uncle, aunt*

VERBOS

contener[1] *to contain*
durar *to last*
latir *to beat*
mejorar *to make better, to improve*
morir (o:ue) *to die*

ADJETIVOS

agudo(a), punzante *sharp, stabbing*
cercano(a) *near*
cierto(a) *certain*
despierto(a) *awake*
dormido(a) *asleep*
obstruido(a) *clogged, obstructed*
sordo(a) *dull (pain)*

OTRAS PALABRAS Y EXPRESIONES

casi nunca *hardly ever*
entonces *then*
entre *between*
faltarle algo a uno *to be lacking something*
faltarle el aire a uno *to have shortness of breath*
tal vez *perhaps*

VOCABULARIO ADICIONAL

El (La) paciente
- **tiene un coágulo** *has a clot*
- **tiene un soplo cardíaco (cardiaco)** *has a (heart) murmur*
- **tiene taquicardia** *has tachycardia*
- **tiene la urea alta (uremia)** *has uremia*
- **tiene las arterias obstruidas** *has clogged arteries*
- **necesita ser monitorizado(a)** *needs to be monitored*

---

[1] **Contener** is conjugated like **tener.**

Nombre ______________________ Sección ____________ Fecha ____________

El (La) paciente
- **necesita una operación de corazón abierto** *needs open-heart surgery*
- **necesita nitroglicerina** *needs nitroglycerin*
- **necesita un anticoagulante** *needs an anticoagulant*
- **necesita una prueba de tolerancia al ejercicio** *needs a stress test*
- **necesita un trasplante de corazón** *needs a heart transplant*
- **necesita un puente coronario** *needs a bypass*
- **necesita un cateterismo cardíaco** *needs a cardiac catheterization*

LOS PARIENTES[1]

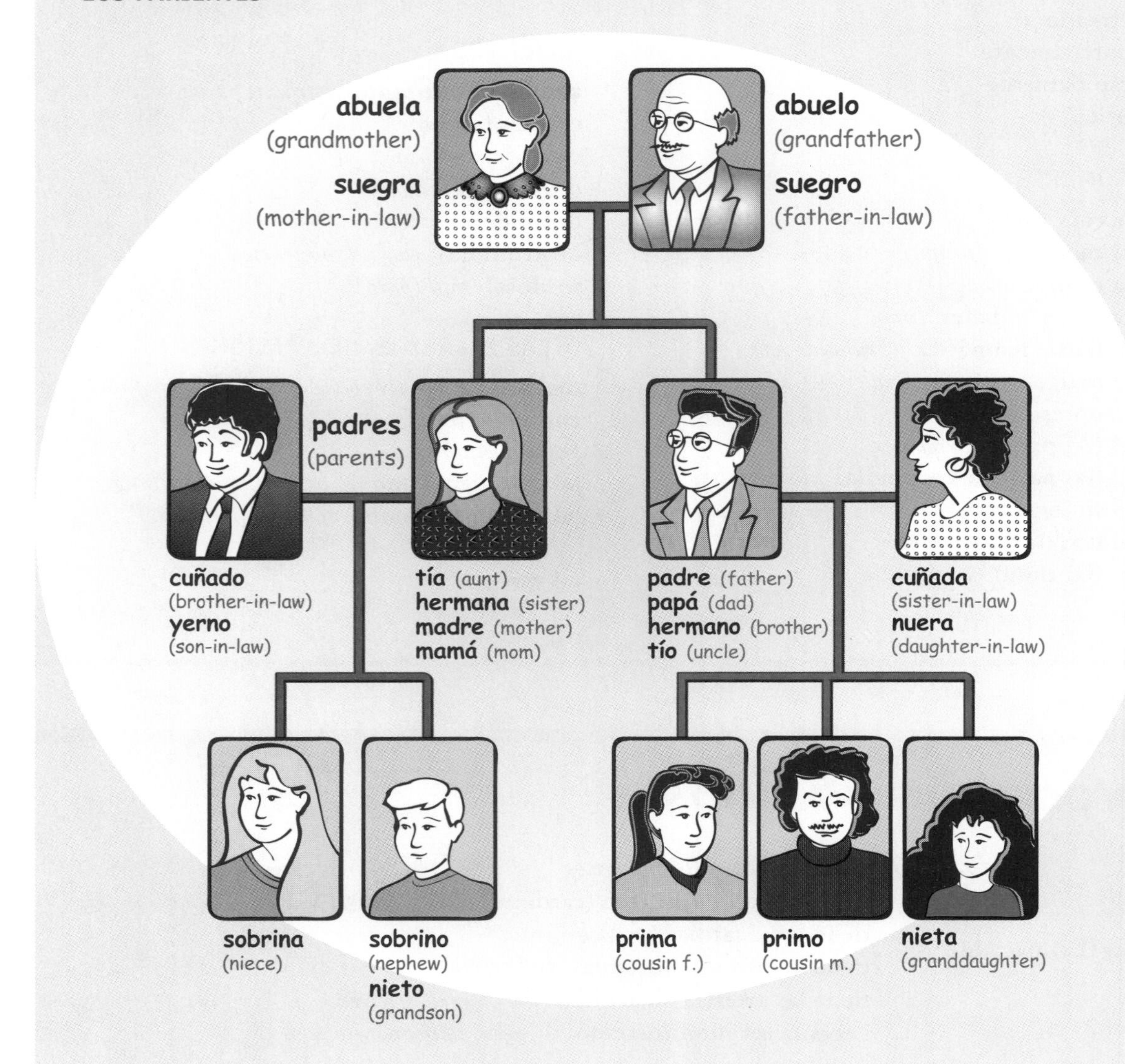

---

[1]The words in the family tree are not recorded on the audio program.

Nombre ______________________ Sección ____________ Fecha ____________

el (la) hermanastro(a) *stepbrother, stepsister*
el (la) hijastro(a) *stepchild*
la madrastra *stepmother*
el padrastro *stepfather*

NOTAS CULTURALES

Search

- Although the number of cardiovascular deaths is declining in the United States, smoking-related cancer deaths continue to rise. Of particular concern for health care professionals are the statistics revealing an increase in tobacco use among teenagers. The first-ever report on tobacco use by ethnic and racial minorities was made public by the U.S. Surgeon General in 1998 (Atlanta: U.S. Department of Health and Human Services, Office on Smoking and Health). A study carried out by the Office on Smoking and Health and by the Division of Adolescent and School Health shows that the prevalence of current cigarette smoking among high school students increased 32% from 1991 to 1997, whereas it increased 34% among Latino students. The 1995 Youth Risk Behavior Survey shows that 10% of Hispanic American students smoke frequently, whereas 5% of African American students and 20% of white students are frequent smokers.

Actividades

Dígame... Answer the following questions, basing your answers on the dialogues.

1. ¿Por qué le dijo el médico al Sr. Calles que viera al cardiólogo?

____

2. ¿Qué problemas tiene el Sr. Calles cuando sube la escalera? ¿El dolor es agudo o sordo?

____

3. ¿El señor tiene a veces sudor frío después de un ejercicio violento?

____

4. ¿De qué murió un tío del Sr. Calles?

____

5. ¿Por qué dice el Sr. Calles que no tiene calambres cuando camina?

____

6. ¿Qué va a hacer el doctor antes de comenzar ningún tratamiento?

____

Nombre ______________________ Sección ____________ Fecha ____________

7. ¿Qué le van a hacer al Sr. Calles si la arteria está obstruida?

____

8. ¿Qué le van a colocar al Sr. Luna en el pecho?

____

9. ¿Cómo va a ayudar el marcapasos al Sr. Luna?

____

10. ¿Qué le dijo el otro médico que le preguntara al cardiólogo?

____

11. ¿Qué otras precauciones debe tomar?

____

12. ¿Cuánto tiempo le van a durar las baterías del marcapasos?

____

Hablemos Interview a classmate, using the following questions. When you have finished, switch roles.

1. ¿Le dijo a Ud. su médico que consultara a un especialista?
2. Si Ud. sufriera del corazón, ¿a qué especialista iría?
3. ¿Ha tenido alguna vez fiebre reumática?
4. ¿Tiene Ud. temblores en las extremidades? ¿Cuándo?
5. ¿Le duele el pecho o siente alguna opresión cuando hace ejercicios violentos?
6. ¿Le falta el aire cuando sube una escalera?
7. ¿Le late el corazón muy rápidamente a veces? ¿Cuándo?
8. ¿Algún pariente cercano suyo murió de un ataque al corazón? ¿Quién?
9. ¿Tiene calambres en las piernas cuando camina mucho?
10. ¿Le han encontrado el ácido úrico elevado en la sangre alguna vez? ¿Cuándo?
11. ¿Le han hecho alguna vez un electrocardiograma? ¿Cuándo?
12. ¿Qué es un marcapasos? ¿Para qué sirve? ¿Cuánto tiempo duran las baterías generalmente?

Nombre ______________________ Sección ____________ Fecha ____________

Vamos a practicar

A Change the following sentences from direct to indirect speech.

MODELO El médico dijo: —Vaya al laboratorio.
El médico dijo **que fuera** al laboratorio.

1. La médica me dijo: —Consulte al cardiólogo.
____
2. El cardiólogo dijo: —Respire hondo.
____
3. Él me dijo: —Dígame si el dolor es sordo o agudo.
____
4. Él me aconsejó: —Hágase un electrocardiograma.
____
5. El técnico me dijo: —Póngase esta bata.
____
6. La enfermera me aconsejó: —Tome precauciones.
____
7. Mi hermano me dijo: —No fumes tanto.
____
8. Ellos me aconsejaron: —No corra todas las mañanas.
____

B Complete the following sentences with the Spanish equivalent of the words in parentheses.

1. Si ____________ (*you go*) al dentista, dígale que Ud. tiene un marcapasos.
2. Si su mamá ____________ (*has*) calambres, déle esta medicina.
3. Ella no podría hacer eso si ____________ (*had*) fiebre reumática.
4. Si tú ____________ (*feel*) una opresión en el pecho, llama a tu médico.
5. Si ____________ (*you ran*) como yo, el corazón te latiría muy rápido también.

6. Si mi tío no __________ (*suffered*) del corazón, podría ir a Miami conmigo.

7. Si ella __________ (*is sleeping*), no la despierte.

8. Si __________ (*you took*) la medicina, Ud. mejoraría en seguida, Sr. Rojas.

Conversaciones breves

Complete the following dialogue, using your imagination and the vocabulary from this lesson.

El cardiólogo y un paciente:

Paciente —¿Qué me va a colocar en el pecho?

Doctor —______________________________

Paciente —¿Cómo me va a ayudar el marcapasos?

Doctor —______________________________

Paciente —¿Voy a estar despierto o dormido cuando me coloquen el marcapasos?

Doctor —______________________________

Paciente —¿Qué precauciones debo tomar?

Doctor —______________________________

Paciente —¿El marcapasos me va a durar por el resto de mi vida?

Doctor —______________________________

En estas situaciones

What would you say in the following situations? What might the other person say?

1. You are a patient. Tell your doctor that you have a sharp pain in your chest and shortness of breath when you exercise. Then tell him/her that you have tightness in your chest when you climb stairs rapidly.
2. You are the doctor. Ask your patient if he/she has ever had elevated uric acid in his/her blood. Then find out if he/she has leg cramps when running or walking several blocks.
3. You are the doctor. Explain to your patient that his/her electrocardiogram is not normal and that he/she needs treatment.

Casos

Act out the following scenarios with a partner.

1. A doctor examines a patient who might have a cardiac condition.
2. A cardiologist explains the insertion and use of a pacemaker to a patient.

Nombre ______________________ Sección ____________ Fecha ____________

Un paso más

A Review the **Vocabulario adicional** in this lesson and then complete the following sentences.

1. El paciente tiene las ____________ obstruidas. Vamos a hacerle un ____________.
2. La paciente tiene la ____________ muy alta.
3. El médico me dijo que mi esposo necesitaba una operación de ____________ abierto.
4. Le van a hacer un ____________ de corazón. Están buscando un donante (*donor*).
5. El paciente necesita un ____________ coronario.

B Write the Spanish term that describes each of the following relationships.

1. La hija de mi tía es mi ____________.
2. El hijo de mi hermano es mi ____________.
3. La mamá de mi esposo(a) es mi ____________.
4. El hermano de mi esposo(a) es mi ____________.
5. El papá de mi primo es mi ____________.
6. El esposo de mi hija es mi ____________.
7. La esposa de mi hijo es mi ____________.
8. La hija de mi hijo es mi ____________.
9. La hija de mi hermana es mi ____________.
10. La mamá de mi padre es mi ____________.

Nombre ____________________ Sección ____________ Fecha ____________

C Read the following lists of the top ten causes of death in Puerto Rico. Note that they are ranked in order of importance. Remember to guess the meaning of the cognates.

CAUSAS DE MUERTE EN PUERTO RICO

1995	1998
corazón	corazón
cáncer	cáncer
diabetes	diabetes
SIDA	cerebrovasculares
cerebrovasculares	enfermedades hipertensivas
accidentes	accidentes
neumonía e influenza	enfermedades pulmonares
enfermedades hipertensivas	neumonía e influenza
enfermedades pulmonares	homicidios
enfermedades del hígado y cirrosis	enfermedades del hígado y cirrosis

Fuente (*Source*): Departamento de Salud, San Juan, Puerto Rico.

With a partner, discuss what conclusions you can draw from the information and write them in Spanish below.

____

____

____

____

____

____

____

____

____

____

____

____

LECTURA 7 SÍNTOMAS DE UN ATAQUE AL CORAZÓN

(*Adapted from TEL MED, tape #63*)

Un dolor en el pecho, especialmente si baja al brazo izquierdo, puede ser una señal[1] de un ataque al corazón; el paciente que sufre fuertes[2] dolores en el pecho deberá ver a su médico inmediatamente.

El dolor típico causado por problemas relacionados con un ataque al corazón se concentra en el medio[3] del pecho. Se siente una gran opresión, dolor y una punzada.[4] El dolor puede durar desde unos pocos minutos hasta horas y puede aliviarse y volver después. Frecuentemente estos primeros síntomas de un ataque al corazón van acompañados de debilidad, fatiga, sudor, dificultad para respirar, náuseas o indigestión, aunque a veces sólo se presenta el dolor.

Las personas que tienen mayor probabilidad de sufrir un ataque al corazón son las personas que:

1. tienen familiares que han sufrido ataques al corazón antes de los sesenta años.
2. fuman un paquete de cigarrillos o más al día.
3. tienen exceso de peso.[5]
4. tienen el colesterol alto.
5. tienen la presión alta.
6. tienen diabetes.
7. no hacen ejercicios o tienen demasiada tensión emocional.

La mitad de las personas que sufren ataques al corazón no han tenido antes ningún síntoma, pero si una persona siente alguno de los síntomas señalados,[6] debe ver a su médico inmediatamente o llamar a la sala de emergencia del hospital más cercano a su casa y debe seguir exactamente las instrucciones que le den.

Si una persona cree que tiene un ataque al corazón debe mantenerse quieto.[7] Si le falta la respiración[8] se sentirá más cómodo sentado.[9] Tampoco debe comer ni beber nada excepto líquido tomado con algún medicamento.

---

[1] *sign*
[2] *strong*
[3] **en...** *in the middle*
[4] *a sharp pain*
[5] **tienen...** *are overweight*
[6] *indicated*
[7] **mantenerse...** *keep still*
[8] **Si...** *If he/she can't breathe*
[9] *sitting*

Nombre ______________________ Sección ____________ Fecha ____________

Conversaciones

2-24 —Carlos, tengo un fuerte dolor en el pecho.
—Eso puede indicar un ataque al corazón.
—¿Qué debo hacer?
—Debes ver a tu médico en seguida.

2-25 —Doctor, mi padre murió de un ataque al corazón.
—Entonces Ud. tiene más probabilidad de sufrir un ataque al corazón.
—¿Qué puedo hacer para evitarlo?
—No fume, haga ejercicio y no aumente de peso.

2-26 —Mi esposo fuma más de dos paquetes de cigarrillos al día.
—Eso aumenta la probabilidad de tener cáncer o problemas del corazón.

2-27 —Doctor, ¿quiénes tienen más probabilidad de tener problemas del corazón, las personas delgadas o las personas gordas?
—Las personas que tienen exceso de peso tienen más probabilidad.

Dígame... Answer the following questions, basing your answers on the reading and the conversations.

1. ¿Qué puede indicar un dolor en el pecho que baja por el brazo?

   ____

2. ¿Qué debe hacer una persona que sufre fuertes dolores en el pecho?

   ____

3. ¿Dónde se concentra el dolor causado por un ataque al corazón?

   ____

4. ¿Cuáles son otros de los síntomas de un ataque al corazón?

   ____

5. ¿Cuánto puede durar el dolor?

   ____

6. ¿De qué van acompañados muchas veces los primeros síntomas de un ataque al corazón?

   ____

7. Si Ud. fuma un paquete de cigarrillos o más al día y si tiene exceso de peso, ¿tiene más o menos probabilidad de sufrir un ataque al corazón?

   ____

Nombre ______________________ Sección ____________ Fecha ____________

8. ¿Qué otras cosas pueden hacer más probable un ataque al corazón?

____

9. ¿Qué debe hacer una persona que siente uno de los síntomas de un ataque al corazón?

____

10. ¿Cómo debe mantenerse la persona?

____

11. ¿Cómo se sentirá más cómodo el paciente si tiene dificultad para respirar?

____

12. ¿Qué cosas debe evitar?

____

Nombre ______________________ Sección ______________ Fecha ______________

REPASO

Práctica de vocabulario

A Circle the word or phrase that best completes each sentence.

1. Ud. tiene la presión muy (media / alta / nerviosa).
2. Eso puede ocurrir a (apenas / peor / cualquier) edad.
3. Si sufre del corazón, debe consultar al (dermatólogo / urólogo / cardiólogo).
4. Un (derrame / riñón / viejo) puede causar parálisis total o parcial.
5. Le (aconsejo / disminuyo / afecto) que vaya a un especialista.
6. Debe (tratar / ocurrir / sugerir) de cambiar la dosis.
7. Tiene temblores en las (extremidades / cerillas / cuadras).
8. Es el hermano de mi padre. Es un pariente (agudo / sordo / cercano).
9. Me preguntó si era un dolor sordo o (despierto / dormido / agudo).
10. Debe seguir (generalmente / fielmente / lentamente) las instrucciones del médico.
11. ¿Está (bajo / entre / sobre) tratamiento psiquiátrico?
12. El médico le (resuelve / espera / recomienda) un cambio en la dieta.
13. Mi mamá sacó el pan del (tomacorrientes / horno / enchufe de seguridad).
14. Ponga al bebé en la (lejía / plancha / cuna).
15. Aquí le dejo estos (folletos / maquillajes / muebles) que puede leer.
16. La hepatitis afecta (la cabeza / el corazón / el hígado).
17. Cuando como, se me alivia el (agujero / dolor / sudor).
18. No recuerdo (la edad / la dosis / la comida) de Ana. ¿Cuántos años tiene?
19. Debe empezar el tratamiento (muchas veces / lo más pronto posible / ayer).
20. No oigo bien. Necesito (un audífono / una media / un purgante).
21. Es (una anciana / una debilidad / un cálculo). Tiene noventa años.
22. Yo hablo con ellos de vez en (cuando / donde / como).
23. Un ataque al corazón es (una cerveza / un lugar / un infarto).
24. No puedo (aguantar / decidir / dudar) el dolor.
25. Ellos no tienen (cortaduras / piscina / rasguños) en su casa.

Nombre ______________________ Sección ____________ Fecha ____________

B Circle the word or phrase that does not belong in each group.

1. en caso de, si, por suerte
2. primeros auxilios, botiquín, resumen
3. problemas del hígado, hepatitis, cortaduras
4. tapar, notar, cubrir
5. laxante, purgante, cuna
6. tres veces por semana, regularmente, casi nunca
7. curita, vendaje, plancha
8. en cuanto, más tarde, tan pronto como
9. tener miedo, asustarse, dudar
10. sugerir, aconsejar, ocurrir
11. claro, apenas, por supuesto
12. hemorroide, audífono, almorrana
13. debilidad, cansancio, media
14. cálculo, piedra, horno
15. sentirse mejor, oír, aliviarse
16. abrir la boca, notar, sacar la lengua
17. cerveza, vino, fecha
18. duele, recibe, hace daño
19. hueco, alfiler, agujero
20. fósforo, cerilla, mueble
21. carne, embolia, tocino
22. sal, tipo, sodio
23. vieja, bebé, persona mayor
24. suceder, ocurrir, compartir
25. corazón, pulmón, babero

C Complete the following questions with the appropriate word or phrase in column **B.**

	B
1. ¿Cuánto tiempo hace ____________?	a. conmigo
2. ¿Cuántos globos ____________?	b. natural
3. ¿Puedes aguantar un mes ____________?	c. problema físico
4. ¿Quieres venir ____________?	d. esa muchacha
5. ¿Tiene limitaciones o ____________?	e. coordinador
6. ¿Tiene algún ____________?	f. sin tomar anfetaminas
7. ¿Fue un aborto ____________?	g. actualmente
8. ¿Cuándo fue la ____________?	h. de epilepsia
9. ¿Conoce Ud. a ____________?	i. horno
10. ¿Tuvo otro ataque ____________?	j. que tomas drogas
11. ¿Habló Ud. con el ____________?	k. desmayó
12. ¿Podrán hacer algo ____________?	l. última vez
13. ¿Está tomando drogas ____________?	m. incapacidades físicas
14. ¿El pan está en el ____________?	n. por mí
15. ¿Se ____________?	o. compras

Nombre ____________________ Sección ____________ Fecha ____________

A	B
16. ¿Siente __________?	p. presión
17. ¿Debo aplicar __________?	q. debilidad
18. ¿Qué __________?	r. más
19. ¿Murió de un __________?	s. daño
20. ¿Eso puede hacerme __________?	t. derrame

D Crucigrama

Across

1. hondo
4. fósforo
5. opuesto de dormido
7. *summary,* en español
8. estufa
10. andar a gatas
14. recomienda
19. tener miedo
20. sufrir
24. órgano principal
27. agudo
28. tensión nerviosa
30. No oye; es __________.
31. muy viejo
32. cansancio
33. Las usamos para cortar.

Down

2. todos los días
3. inflamada
6. opuesto de mejor
9. el clínico, el __________
11. bañera
12. *cramp,* en español
13. Puse la __________ en el biberón.
15. Tengo la jeringuilla, pero necesito la __________.
16. Lo usamos para oír mejor.
17. vino, por ejemplo
18. que pasa de un padre a un hijo (*fem.*)
21. piedra
22. alberca
23. Es un remedio __________.
25. lo que hace el corazón
26. venda
29. opuesto de nacer

Nombre ______________________ Sección ____________ Fecha ____________

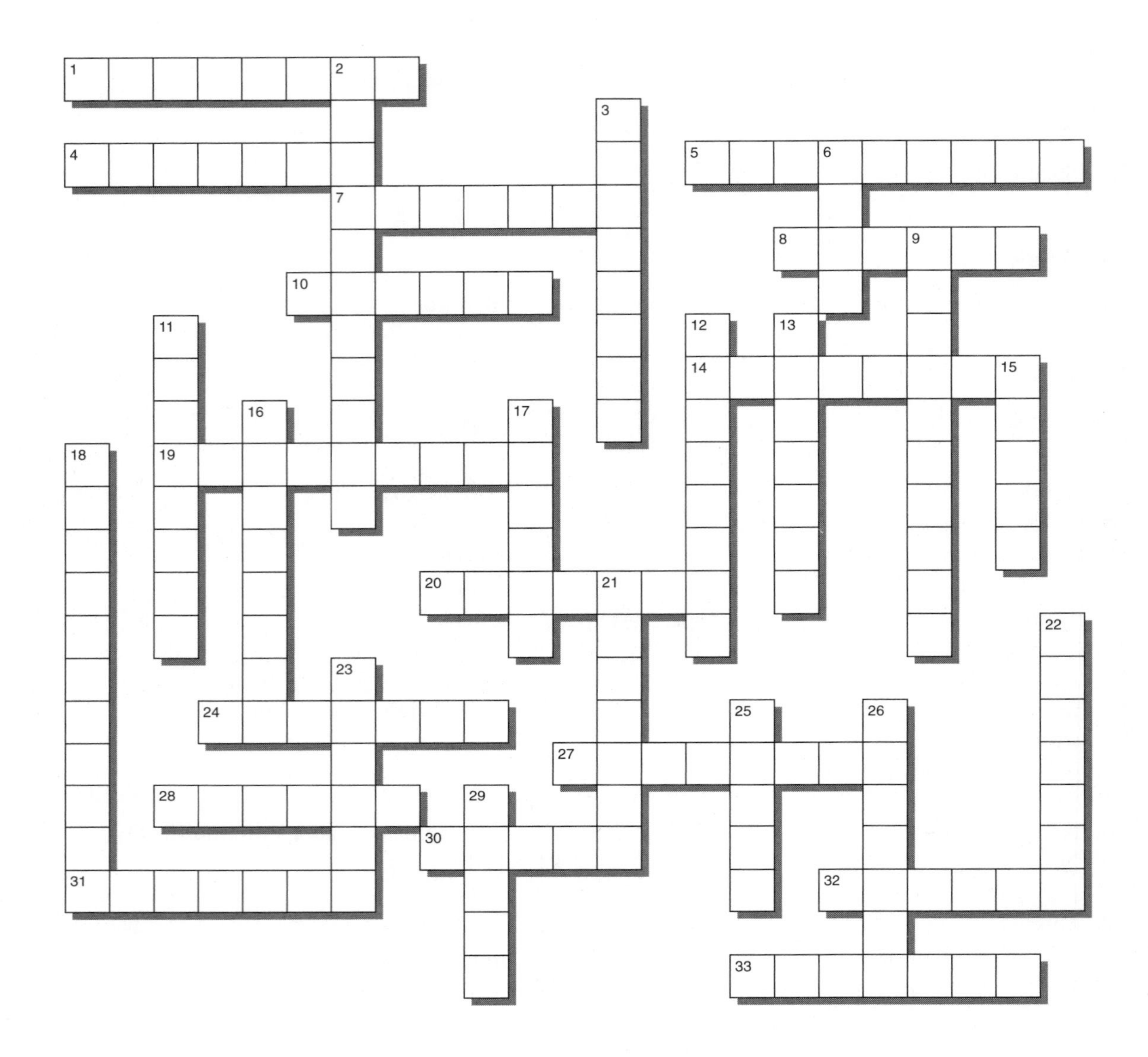

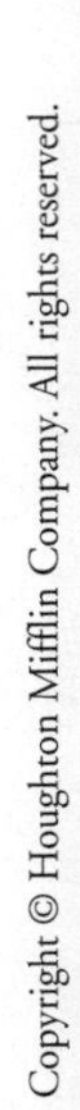

Nombre ______________________ Sección ____________ Fecha ____________

Práctica oral

2–28 Listen to the following exercise on the audio program. The speaker will ask you some questions. Answer the questions, using the cues provided. The speaker will confirm the correct answer. Repeat the correct answer.

2–29

1. ¿Qué edad tiene Ud.? (treinta años)
2. ¿Tiene Ud. la presión alta, baja o normal? (normal)
3. ¿Tiene Ud. alguna enfermedad hereditaria? (no, ninguna)
4. ¿Ha tenido Ud. un derrame alguna vez? (no, nunca)
5. ¿Ha disminuido Ud. la cantidad de sal que usa en la comida? (no)
6. ¿Ha estado sintiendo Ud. cansancio últimamente? (sí, mucho)
7. ¿Tiene Ud. acidez a veces? (sí, a veces)
8. ¿Ha notado Ud. alguna vez la materia fecal negra? (no, nunca)
9. ¿Qué le dijo su médico que debía evitar? (la cafeína)
10. ¿Le han hecho a Ud. un ultrasonido últimamente? (no)
11. ¿Ha tenido Ud. alguna enfermedad del hígado? (no)
12. ¿Cuándo fue la última vez que Ud. fue al médico? (el mes pasado)
13. ¿Es verdad que Ud. ha tomado anfetaminas? (no)
14. ¿Se atragantó Ud. alguna vez cuando comía? (sí, muchas veces)
15. ¿Se quemó Ud. alguna vez? (sí, muchas veces)
16. ¿Pone Ud. yodo o mantequilla en una quemadura? (no)
17. ¿Tiene Ud. un botiquín de primeros auxilios en su carro? (sí)
18. ¿A quién consultaría Ud. si sufriera del corazón? (a un cardiólogo)
19. ¿Es verdad que Ud. ha tenido fiebre reumática? (no)
20. ¿Le falta el aire a veces cuando hace ejercicio? (sí, a veces)
21. ¿Le late el corazón muy rápidamente a veces? (sí, cuando corro)
22. ¿Le han encontrado el ácido úrico elevado en la sangre alguna vez? (no, nunca)
23. ¿Tiene Ud. calambres a veces? (sí, en las piernas)
24. ¿Tiene Ud. algún pariente cercano que haya muerto del corazón? (no)
25. ¿Siente Ud. a veces opresión en el pecho? (no, nunca)

Introduction to Spanish Sounds and the Alphabet

Sections marked with a Web-audio icon are recorded on the website that supplements this text. Repeat each Spanish word after the speaker, imitating as closely as possible the correct pronunciation.

The Alphabet

LETTER	NAME	LETTER	NAME	LETTER	NAME	LETTER	NAME
a	a	h	hache	ñ	eñe	t	te
b	be	i	i	o	o	u	u
c	ce	j	jota	p	pe	v	ve
d	de	k	ka	q	cu	w	doble ve
e	e	l	ele	r	ere	x	equis
f	efe	m	eme	rr	erre	y	i griega
g	ge	n	ene	s	ese	z	zeta

The Vowels

1. The Spanish **a** has a sound similar to the English *a* in the word *father.* Repeat:

   Ana casa banana mala dama mata

2. The Spanish **e** is pronounced like the English *e* in the word *eight.* Repeat:

   este René teme déme entre bebe

3. The Spanish **i** is pronounced like the English *ee* in the word *see.* Repeat:

   sí difícil Mimí ir dividir Fifí

4. The Spanish **o** is similar to the English *o* in the word *no,* but without the glide. Repeat:

   solo poco como toco con monólogo

5. The Spanish **u** is similar to the English *ue* sound in the word *Sue.* Repeat:

   Lulú un su universo murciélago

The Consonants

1. The Spanish **p** is pronounced like the English *p* in the word *spot.* Repeat:

   pan papá Pepe pila poco pude

2. The Spanish **c** in front of **a, o, u, l,** or **r** sounds similar to the English *k.* Repeat:

   casa como cuna clima crimen cromo

3. The Spanish **q** is only used in the combinations **que** and **qui,** in which the **u** is silent, and also has a sound similar to the English *k.* Repeat:

   que queso Quique quinto quema quiso

4. The Spanish **t** is pronounced like the English *t* in the word *stop.* Repeat:

   toma mata tela tipo atún Tito

5. The Spanish **d** at the beginning of an utterance or after **n** or **l** sounds somewhat similar to the English *d* in the word *David.* Repeat:

   día dedo duelo anda Aldo

   In all other positions, the **d** has a sound similar to the English *th* in the word *they.* Repeat:

   medida todo nada Ana dice Eva duda

6. The Spanish **g** also has two sounds. At the beginning of an utterance and in all other positions, except before **e** or **i,** the Spanish **g** sounds similar to the English *g* in the word *sugar.* Repeat:

   goma gato tengo lago algo aguja

   In the combinations **gue** and **gui,** the **u** is silent. Repeat:

   Águeda guineo guiso ligue la guía

7. The Spanish **j,** and **g** before **e** or **i,** sounds similar to the English *h* in the word *home.* Repeat:

   jamás juego jota Julio gente Genaro gime

8. The Spanish **b** and the **v** have no difference in sound. Both are pronounced alike. At the beginning of the utterance or after **m** or **n,** they sound similar to the English *b* in the word *obey.* Repeat:

   Beto vaga bote vela también un vaso

   Between vowels, they are pronounced with the lips barely closed. Repeat:

   sábado yo voy sabe Ávalos Eso vale

9. In most Spanish-speaking countries, the **y** and the **ll** are similar to the English *y* in the word *yet.* Repeat:

   yo llama yema lleno ya lluvia llega

10. The Spanish **r (ere)** is pronounced like the English *tt* in the word *gutter.* Repeat:

cara	pero	arena	carie	Laredo	Aruba

The Spanish **r** in an initial position and after **l, n,** or **s,** and **rr (erre)** in the middle of a word are pronounced with a strong trill. Repeat:

Rita	Rosa	torre	ruina	Enrique	Israel
perro	parra	rubio	alrededor	derrama	

11. The Spanish **s** sound is represented in most of the Spanish-speaking world by the letters **s, z,** and **c** before **e** or **i.** The sound is very similar to the English sibilant *s* in the word *sink.* Repeat:

sale	sitio	solo	seda	suelo
zapato	cerveza	ciudad	cena	

In most of Spain, the **z,** and **c** before **e** or **i,** is pronounced like the English *th* in the word *think.* Repeat:

zarzuela	cielo	docena

12. The letter **h** is silent in Spanish. Repeat:

hilo	Hugo	ahora	Hilda	almohada	hermano

13. The Spanish **ch** is pronounced like the English *ch* in the word *chief.* Repeat:

muchacho	chico	coche	chueco	chaparro

14. The Spanish **f** is identical in sound to the English *f.* Repeat:

famoso	feo	difícil	fuego	foto

15. The Spanish **l** is pronounced like the English *l* in the word *lean.* Repeat:

dolor	ángel	fácil	sueldo	salgo	chaval

16. The Spanish **m** is pronounced like the English *m* in the word *mother.* Repeat:

mamá	moda	multa	médico	mima

17. In most cases, the Spanish **n** has a sound similar to the English *n.* Repeat:

nada	norte	nunca	entra	nene

The sound of the Spanish **n** is often affected by the sounds that occur around it. When it appears before **b, v,** or **p,** it is pronounced like the English *m.* Repeat:

invierno	tan bueno	un vaso	un bebé	un perro

18. The Spanish **ñ (eñe)** has a sound similar to the English *ny* in the word *canyon.* Repeat:

muñeca	leña	año	señorita	piña	señor

19. The Spanish **x** has two pronunciations, depending on its position. Between vowels, the sound is similar to the English *ks.* Repeat:

examen   boxeo   exigente   éxito

Before a consonant, the Spanish **x** sounds like the English *s.* Repeat:

expreso   excusa   exquisito   extraño

Linking

In spoken Spanish, the various words in a phrase or sentence are not pronounced as isolated elements, but they are combined. This is called *linking.*

1. The final consonant of a word is pronounced together with the initial vowel of the following word. Repeat:

   Carlos‿anda   un‿ángel   el‿otoño   unos‿estudiantes

2. The final vowel of a word is pronounced together with the initial vowel of the following word. Repeat:

   su‿esposo   la‿hermana   ardua‿empresa   la‿invita

3. When the final vowel of a word and the initial vowel of the following word are identical, they are pronounced slightly longer than one vowel. Repeat:

   Ana‿alcanza   me‿espera   mi‿hijo   lo‿olvida

   The same rule applies when two identical vowels appear within a word. Repeat:

   cooperación   crees   leemos   coordinación

4. When the final consonant of a word and the initial consonant of the following word are the same, they are pronounced as one consonant with slightly longer-than-normal duration. Repeat:

   el‿lado   un‿novio   Carlos‿salta   tienes‿sed   al‿leer

Rhythm

Rhythm is the variation of sound intensity that we usually associate with music. Spanish and English each regulate these variations in speech differently, because they have different patterns of syllable length. In Spanish the length of the stressed and unstressed syllables remains almost the same, while in English stressed syllables are considerably longer than unstressed ones. Pronounce the following Spanish words, enunciating each syllable clearly.

es-tu-dian-te   bue-no   Úr-su-la
com-po-si-ción   di-fí-cil   ki-ló-me-tro
po-li-cí-a   Pa-ra-guay

Because the length of the Spanish syllables remains constant, the greater the number of syllables in a given word or phrase, the longer the phrase will be.

Intonation

Intonation is the rise and fall of pitch in the delivery of a phrase or a sentence. In general, Spanish pitch tends to change less than English, giving the impression that the language is less emphatic.

As a rule, the intonation for normal statements in Spanish starts in a low tone, raises to a higher one on the first stressed syllable, maintains that tone until the last stressed syllable, and then goes back to the initial low tone, with still another drop at the very end.

Tu amigo viene mañana. José come pan.
Ada está en casa. Carlos toma café.

Syllable Formation in Spanish

General rules for dividing words into syllables are as follows.

Vowels

1. A vowel or a vowel combination can constitute a syllable.

   a-lum-no a-bue-la Eu-ro-pa

2. Diphthongs and triphthongs are considered single vowels and cannot be divided.

   bai-le puen-te Dia-na es-tu-diáis an-ti-guo

3. Two strong vowels **(a, e, o)** do not form a diphthong and are separated into two syllables.

   em-ple-ar vol-te-ar lo-a

4. A written accent on a weak vowel **(i** or **u)** breaks the diphthong, thus the vowels are separated into two syllables.

   trí-o dú-o Ma-rí-a

Consonants

1. A single consonant forms a syllable with the vowel that follows it.

   po-der ma-no mi-nu-to

   NOTE: **rr** is considered a single consonant: **pe-rro.**

2. When two consonants appear between two vowels, they are separated into two syllables.

   al-fa-be-to cam-pe-ón me-ter-se mo-les-tia

   EXCEPTION: When a consonant cluster composed of **b, c, d, f, g, p,** or **t** with **l** or **r** appears between two vowels, the cluster joins the following vowel: **so-bre, o-tros, ca-ble, te-lé-gra-fo.**

3. When three consonants appear between two vowels, only the last one goes with the following vowel.

ins-pec-tor   trans-por-te   trans-for-mar

EXCEPTION: When there is a cluster of three consonants in the combinations described in rule 2, the first consonant joins the preceding vowel, and the cluster joins the following vowel: **es-cri-bir, ex-tran-je-ro, im-plo-rar, es-tre-cho.**

Accentuation

In Spanish, all words are stressed according to specific rules. Words that do not follow the rules must have a written accent to indicate the change of stress. The basic rules for accentuation are as follows.

1. Words ending in a vowel, **n,** or **s** are stressed on the next-to-the-last syllable.

hi-jo	**ca**-lle	**me**-sa	fa-**mo**-sos
flo-**re**-cen	**pla**-ya	**ve**-ces	

2. Words ending in a consonant, except **n** or **s,** are stressed on the last syllable.

ma-**yor**   a-**mor**   tro-pi-**cal**   na-**riz**   re-**loj**   co-rre-**dor**

3. All words that do not follow these rules must have the written accent.

ca-**fé**	**lá**-piz	**mú**-si-ca	sa-**lón**
án-gel	**lí**-qui-do	fran-**cés**	**Víc**-tor
sim-**pá**-ti-co	rin-**cón**	a-**zú**-car	**dár**-se-lo
sa-**lió**	**dé**-bil	e-**xá**-me-nes	**dí**-me-lo

4. Pronouns and adverbs of interrogation and exclamation have a written accent to distinguish them from relative pronouns.

—**¿Qué** comes?	*"What are you eating?"*
—La pera que él no comió.	*"The pear that he did not eat."*
—**¿Quién** está ahí?	*"Who is there?"*
—El hombre a quien tú llamaste.	*"The man whom you called."*
—**¿Dónde** está?	*"Where is he?"*
—En el lugar donde trabaja.	*"At the place where he works."*

5. Words that have the same spelling but different meanings take a written accent to differentiate one from the other.

el	*the*	**él**	*he, him*	**te**	*you*	té	*tea*
mi	*my*	**mí**	*me*	**si**	*if*	sí	*yes*
tu	*your*	**tú**	*you*	**mas**	*but*	más	*more*

Verbs

Regular Verbs

Model -ar, -er, -ir *verbs*

INFINITIVE		
amar (*to love*)	**comer** (*to eat*)	**vivir** (*to live*)
GERUND		
amando (*loving*)	**comiendo** (*eating*)	**viviendo** (*living*)
PAST PARTICIPLE		
amado (*loved*)	**comido** (*eaten*)	**vivido** (*lived*)

SIMPLE TENSES

Indicative Mood

PRESENT		
(*I love*)	(*I eat*)	(*I live*)
am**o**	com**o**	viv**o**
am**as**	com**es**	viv**es**
am**a**	com**e**	viv**e**
am**amos**	com**emos**	viv**imos**
am**áis**[1]	com**éis**	viv**ís**
am**an**	com**en**	viv**en**
IMPERFECT		
(*I used to love*)	(*I used to eat*)	(*I used to live*)
am**aba**	com**ía**	viv**ía**
am**abas**	com**ías**	viv**ías**
am**aba**	com**ía**	viv**ía**
am**ábamos**	com**íamos**	viv**íamos**
am**abais**	com**íais**	viv**íais**
am**aban**	com**ían**	viv**ían**

[1] **Vosotros amáis:** The **vosotros** form of the verb is used primarily in Spain. This form has not been used in this text.

	PRETERIT	
(*I love*)	(*I ate*)	(*I lived*)
am**é**	com**í**	viv**í**
am**aste**	com**iste**	viv**iste**
am**ó**	com**ió**	viv**ió**
am**amos**	com**imos**	viv**imos**
am**asteis**	com**isteis**	viv**isteis**
am**aron**	com**ieron**	viv**ieron**

	FUTURE	
(*I will love*)	(*I will eat*)	(*I will live*)
amar**é**	comer**é**	vivir**é**
amar**ás**	comer**ás**	vivir**ás**
amar**á**	comer**á**	vivir**á**
amar**emos**	comer**emos**	vivir**emos**
amar**éis**	comer**éis**	vivir**éis**
amar**án**	comer**án**	vivir**án**

	CONDITIONAL	
(*I would love*)	(*I would eat*)	(*I would live*)
amar**ía**	comer**ía**	vivir**ía**
amar**ías**	comer**ías**	vivir**ías**
amar**ía**	comer**ía**	vivir**ía**
amar**íamos**	comer**íamos**	vivir**íamos**
amar**íais**	comer**íais**	vivir**íais**
amar**ían**	comer**ían**	vivir**ían**

Subjunctive Mood

	PRESENT	
([*that*] *I* [*may*] *love*)	([*that*] *I* [*may*] *eat*)	([*that*] *I* [*may*] *live*)
am**e**	com**a**	viv**a**
am**es**	com**as**	viv**as**
am**e**	com**a**	viv**a**
am**emo**s	com**amos**	viv**amos**
am**éis**	com**áis**	viv**áis**
am**en**	com**an**	viv**an**

IMPERFECT (two forms: **-ra**, **-se**)		
([*that*] *I* [*might*] *love*)	([*that*] *I* [*might*] *eat*)	([*that*] *I* [*might*] *live*)
am**ara(-ase)**	com**iera(-iese)**	viv**iera(-iese)**
am**aras(-ases)**	com**ieras(-ieses)**	viv**ieras(-ieses)**
am**ara(-ase)**	com**iera(-iese)**	viv**iera(-iese)**
am**áramos (-ásemos)**	com**iéramos (-iésemos)**	viv**iéramos (-iésemos)**
am**arais(-aseis)**	com**ierais(-ieseis)**	viv**ierais(-ieseis)**
am**aran(-asen)**	com**ieran(-iesen)**	viv**ieran(-iesen)**

Imperative Mood (*Command Forms*)

(*love*)	(*eat*)	(*live*)
am**a** (tú)	com**e** (tú)	viv**e** (tú)
am**e** (Ud.)	com**a** (Ud.)	viv**a** (Ud.)
am**emos** (nosotros)	com**amos** (nosotros)	viv**amos** (nosotros)
am**ad** (vosotros)	com**ed** (vosotros)	viv**id** (vosotros)
am**en** (Uds.)	com**an** (Uds.)	viv**an** (Uds.)

COMPOUND TENSES

PERFECT INFINITIVE		
haber amado	**haber comido**	**haber vivido**

PERFECT PARTICIPLE		
habiendo amado	**habiendo comido**	**habiendo vivido**

Indicative Mood

PRESENT PERFECT		
(*I have loved*)	(*I have eaten*)	(*I have lived*)
he amado	he comido	he vivido
has amado	has comido	has vivido
ha amado	ha comido	ha vivido
hemos amado	hemos comido	hemos vivido
habéis amado	habéis comido	habéis vivido
han amado	han comido	han vivido

	PLUPERFECT	
(*I had loved*)	(*I had eaten*)	(*I had lived*)
había amado	había comido	había vivido
habías amado	habías comido	habías vivido
había amado	había comido	había vivido
habíamos amado	habíamos comido	habíamos vivido
habíais amado	habíais comido	habíais vivido
habían amado	habían comido	habían vivido

	FUTURE PERFECT	
(*I will have loved*)	(*I will have eaten*)	(*I will have lived*)
habré amado	habré comido	habré vivido
habrás amado	habrás comido	habrás vivido
habrá amado	habrá comido	habrá vivido
habremos amado	habremos comido	habremos vivido
habréis amado	habréis comido	habréis vivido
habrán amado	habrán comido	habrán vivido

	CONDITIONAL PERFECT	
(*I would have loved*)	(*I would have eaten*)	(*I would have lived*)
habría amado	habría comido	habría vivido
habrías amado	habrías comido	habrías vivido
habría amado	habría comido	habría vivido
habríamos amado	habríamos comido	habríamos vivido
habríais amado	habríais comido	habríais vivido
habrían amado	habrían comido	habrían vivido

Subjunctive Mood

	PRESENT PERFECT	
([*that*] *I* [*may*] *have loved*)	([*that*] *I* [*may*] *have eaten*)	([*that*] *I* [*may*] *have lived*)
haya amado	haya comido	haya vivido
hayas amado	hayas comido	hayas vivido
haya amado	haya comido	haya vivido
hayamos amado	hayamos comido	hayamos vivido
hayáis amado	hayáis comido	hayáis vivido
hayan amado	hayan comido	hayan vivido

PLUPERFECT (two forms: **-ra, -se**)		
([*that*] *I* [*might*] *have loved*)	([*that*] *I* [*might*] *have eaten*)	([*that*] *I* [*might*] *have lived*)
hubiera(-iese) amado	hubiera(-iese) comido	hubiera(-iese) vivido
hubieras(-ieses) amado	hubieras(-ieses) comido	hubieras(-ieses) vivido
hubiera(-iese) amado	hubiera(-iese) comido	hubiera(-iese) vivido
hubiéramos(-iésemos) amado	hubiéramos(-iésemos) comido	hubiéramos(-iésemos) vivido
hubierais(-ieseis) amado	hubierais(-ieseis) comido	hubierais(-ieseis) vivido
hubieran(-iesen) amado	hubieran(-iesen) comido	hubieran(-iesen) vivido

Stem-Changing Verbs

The -ar *and* -er *stem-changing verbs*

Stem-changing verbs are those that have a change in the root of the verb. Verbs that end in **-ar** and **-er** change the stressed vowel **e** to **ie** and the stressed **o** to **ue.** These changes occur in all persons, except the first and second persons plural of the present indicative, present subjunctive, and command.

INFINITIVE	PRESENT INDICATIVE	IMPERATIVE	PRESENT SUBJUNCTIVE
cerrar (*to close*)	**cie**rro	—	**cie**rre
	cierras	**cie**rra	**cie**rres
	cierra	(Ud.) **cie**rre	**cie**rre
	cerramos	cerremos	cerremos
	cerráis	cerrad	cerréis
	cierran	(Uds.) **cie**rren	**cie**rren

INFINITIVE	PRESENT INDICATIVE	IMPERATIVE	PRESENT SUBJUNCTIVE
perder (*to lose*)	**pie**rdo **pie**rdes **pie**rde perdemos perdéis **pie**rden	— **pie**rde (Ud.) **pie**rda perdamos perded (Uds.) **pie**rdan	**pie**rda **pie**rdas **pie**rda perdamos perdáis **pie**rdan
contar (*to count, to tell*)	**cue**nto **cue**ntas **cue**nta contamos contáis **cue**ntan	— **cue**nta (Ud.) **cue**nte contemos contad (Uds.) **cue**nten	**cue**nte **cue**ntes **cue**nte contemos contéis **cue**nten
volver (*to return*)	**vue**lvo **vue**lves **vue**lve volvemos volvéis **vue**lven	— **vue**lve (Ud.) **vue**lva volvamos volved (Uds.) **vue**lvan	**vue**lva **vue**lvas **vue**lva volvamos volváis **vue**lvan

Verbs that follow the same pattern include the following.

acertar	*to guess right*	**entender**	*to understand*
acordarse	*to remember*	**llover**	*to rain*
acostar(se)	*to go to bed*	**mostrar**	*to show*
almorzar	*to have lunch*	**mover**	*to move*
atravesar	*to go through*	**negar**	*to deny*
cegar	*to blind*	**nevar**	*to snow*
cocer	*to cook*	**pensar**	*to think, to plan*
colgar	*to hang*	**probar**	*to prove, to taste*
comenzar	*to begin*	**recordar**	*to remember*
confesar	*to confess*	**resolver**	*to decide on*
costar	*to cost*	**rogar**	*to beg*
demostrar	*to demonstrate, to show*	**sentar(se)**	*to sit down*
despertar(se)	*to wake up*	**soler**	*to be in the habit of*
empezar	*to begin*	**soñar**	*to dream*
encender	*to light, to turn on*	**tender**	*to stretch, to unfold*
encontrar	*to find*	**torcer**	*to twist*

The* -ir *stem-changing verbs

There are two types of stem-changing verbs that end in **-ir:** one type changes stressed **e** to **ie** in some tenses and to **i** in others and stressed **o** to **ue** or **u;** the second type always changes stressed **e** to **i** in the irregular forms of the verb.

Type I				
		e:ie	or	**i**
	-ir:			
		o:ue	or	**u**

These changes occur as follows.

Present Indicative: all persons except the first and second plural change **e** to **ie** and **o** to **ue.** *Preterit:* third person, singular and plural, changes **e** to **i** and **o** to **u.** *Present Subjunctive:* all persons change **e** to **ie** and **o** to **ue,** except the first and second persons plural, which change **e** to **i** and **o** to **u.** *Imperfect Subjunctive:* all persons change **e** to **i** and **o** to **u.** *Imperative:* all persons except the second person plural change **e** to **ie** and **o** to **ue;** first person plural changes **e** to **i** and **o** to **u.** *Present Participle:* changes **e** to **i** and **o** to **u.**

	Indicative		*Imperative*	*Subjunctive*	
INFINITIVE	**PRESENT**	**PRETERIT**		**PRESENT**	**IMPERFECT**
sentir	s**ie**nto	sentí	—	s**ie**nta	s**i**ntiera(-iese)
(*to feel*)	s**ie**ntes	sentiste	s**ie**nte	s**ie**ntas	s**i**ntieras
	s**ie**nte	s**i**ntió	(Ud.) s**ie**nta	s**ie**nta	s**i**ntiera
PRESENT	sentimos	sentimos	s**i**ntamos	s**i**ntamos	s**i**ntiéramos
PARTICIPLE	sentís	sentisteis	sentid	s**i**ntáis	s**i**ntierais
s**i**ntiendo	s**ie**nten	s**i**ntieron	(Uds.) s**ie**ntan	s**ie**ntan	s**i**ntieran
dormir	d**ue**rmo	dormí	—	d**ue**rma	d**u**rmiera(-iese)
(*to sleep*)	d**ue**rmes	dormiste	d**ue**rme	d**ue**rmas	d**u**rmieras
	d**ue**rme	d**u**rmió	(Ud.) d**ue**rma	d**ue**rma	d**u**rmiera
PRESENT	dormimos	dormimos	d**u**rmamos	d**u**rmamos	d**u**rmiéramos
PARTICIPLE	dormís	dormisteis	dormid	d**u**rmáis	d**u**rmierais
d**u**rmiendo	d**ue**rmen	d**u**rmieron	(Uds.) d**ue**rman	d**ue**rman	d**u**rmieran

Other verbs that follow the same pattern include the following.

advertir	*to warn*	**herir**	*to wound, to hurt*
arrepentir(se)	*to repent*	**mentir**	*to lie*
consentir	*to consent, to pamper*	**morir**	*to die*
convertir(se)	*to turn into*	**preferir**	*to prefer*
discernir	*to discern*	**referir**	*to refer*
divertir(se)	*to amuse oneself*	**sugerir**	*to suggest*

Type II **-ir:** **e:i**

The verbs in this second category are irregular in the same tenses as those of the first type. The only difference is that they only have one change: **e:i** in all irregular persons.

	Indicative		*Imperative*	*Subjunctive*	
INFINITIVE	PRESENT	PRETERIT		PRESENT	IMPERFECT
pedir	pido	pedí	—	pida	pidiera(-iese)
(*to ask for,*	pides	pediste	pide	pidas	pidieras
to request)	pide	pidió	(Ud.) pida	pida	pidiera
PRESENT	pedimos	pedimos	pidamos	pidamos	pidiéramos
PARTICIPLE	pedís	pedisteis	pedid	pidáis	pidierais
pidiendo	piden	pidieron	(Uds.) pidan	pidan	pidieran

Verbs that follow this pattern include the following.

competir	*to compete*	**reír(se)**	*to laugh*
concebir	*to conceive*	**reñir**	*to fight*
despedir(se)	*to say good-bye*	**repetir**	*to repeat*
elegir	*to choose*	**seguir**	*to follow*
impedir	*to prevent*	**servir**	*to serve*
perseguir	*to pursue*	**vestir(se)**	*to dress*

Orthographic-Changing Verbs

Some verbs undergo a change in the spelling of the stem in certain tenses in order to maintain the original sound of the final consonant. The most common verbs of this type are those with the consonants **g** and **c.** Remember that **g** and **c** have a soft sound in front of **e** or **i** and a hard sound in front of **a, o,** or **u.** In order to maintain the soft sound in front of **a, o,** and **u, g** and **c** change to **j** and **z,** respectively. And in order to maintain the hard sound of **g** and **c** in front of **e** and **i, u** is added to the **g** (**gu**) and **c** changes to **qu.**

The following important verbs undergo spelling changes in the tenses listed below.

1. Verbs ending in **-gar** change **g** to **gu** before **e** in the first person of the preterit and in all persons of the present subjunctive.

   pagar (*to pay*)
   Preterit: pa**gu**é, pagaste, pagó, etc.
   Pres. Subj.: pa**gu**e, pa**gu**es, pa**gu**e, pa**gu**emos, pa**gu**éis, pa**gu**en

   Verbs that follow the same pattern: **colgar, jugar, llegar, navegar, negar, regar, rogar.**

2. Verbs ending in **-ger** and **-gir** change **g** to **j** before **o** and **a** in the first person of the present indicative and in all persons of the present subjunctive.

   proteger (*to protect*)
   Pres. Ind.: prote**j**o, proteges, protege, etc.
   Pres. Subj.: prote**j**a, prote**j**as, prote**j**a, prote**j**amos, prote**j**áis, prote**j**an

   Verbs that follow the same pattern: **coger, corregir, dirigir, elegir, escoger, exigir, recoger.**

3. Verbs ending in **-guar** change **gu** to **gü** before **e** in the first person of the preterit and in all persons of the present subjunctive.

   averiguar (*to find out*)
   Preterit: averi**gü**é, averiguaste, averiguó, etc.
   Pres. Subj.: averi**gü**e, averi**gü**es, averi**güe,** averi**güemos,** averi**gü**éis, averi**gü**en

   The verb **apaciguar** follows the same pattern.

4. Verbs ending in **-guir** change **gu** to **g** before **o** and **a** in the first person of the present indicative and in all persons of the present subjunctive.

   conseguir (*to get*)
   Pres. Ind.: consi**g**o, consigues, consigue, etc.
   Pres. Subj.: consi**g**a, consi**g**as, consi**g**a, consi**g**amos, consi**g**áis, consi**g**an

   Verbs that follow the same pattern: **distinguir, perseguir, proseguir, seguir.**

5. Verbs ending in **-car** change **c** to **qu** before **e** in the first person of the preterit and in all persons of the present subjunctive.

tocar (*to touch, to play* [*a musical instrument*])
Preterit: to**qu**é, tocaste, tocó, etc.
Pres. Subj.: to**qu**e, to**qu**es, to**qu**e, to**qu**emos, to**qu**éis, to**qu**en

Verbs that follow the same pattern: **atacar, buscar, comunicar, explicar, indicar, pescar, sacar.**

6. Verbs ending in **-cer** and **-cir** preceded by a consonant change **c** to **z** before **o** and **a** in the first person of the present indicative and in all persons of the present subjunctive.

torcer (*to twist*)
Pres. Ind.: tuer**z**o, tuerces, tuerce, etc.
Pres. Subj.: tuer**z**a, tuer**z**as, tuer**z**a, tor**z**amos, tor**z**áis, tuer**z**an

Verbs that follow the same pattern: **convencer, esparcir, vencer.**

7. Verbs ending in **-cer** and **-cir** preceded by a vowel change **c** to **zc** before **o** and **a** in the first person of the present indicative and in all persons of the present subjunctive.

conocer (*to know, to be acquainted with*)
Pres. Ind.: cono**zc**o, conoces, conoce, etc.
Pres. Subj.: cono**zc**a, cono**zc**as, cono**zc**a, cono**zc**amos, cono**zc**áis, cono**zc**an

Verbs that follow the same pattern: **agradecer, aparecer, carecer, entristecer, establecer, lucir, nacer, obedecer, ofrecer, padecer, parecer, pertenecer, reconocer, relucir.**

8. Verbs ending in **-zar** change **z** to **c** before **e** in the first person of the preterit and in all persons of the present subjunctive.

rezar (*to pray*)
Preterit: re**c**é, rezaste, rezó, etc.
Pres. Subj.: re**c**e, re**c**es, re**c**e, re**c**emos, re**c**éis, re**c**en

Verbs that follow the same pattern: **abrazar, alcanzar, almorzar, comenzar, cruzar, empezar, forzar, gozar.**

9. Verbs ending in **-eer** change the unstressed **i** to **y** between vowels in the third person singular and plural of the preterit, in all persons of the imperfect subjunctive, and in the present participle.

creer (*to believe*)
Preterit: creí, creíste, cre**y**ó, creímos, creísteis, cre**y**eron
Imp. Subj.: cre**y**era(ese), cre**y**eras, cre**y**era, cre**y**éramos, cre**y**erais, cre**y**eran
Pres. Part.: cre**y**endo

Leer and **poseer** follow the same pattern.

10. Verbs ending in **-uir** change the unstressed **i** to **y** between vowels (except **-quir,** which has the silent **u**) in the following tenses and persons.

huir (*to escape, to flee*)
Pres. Part.: hu**y**endo
Past Part.: huido
Pres. Ind.: hu**y**o, hu**y**es, hu**y**e, huimos, huís, hu**y**en
Preterit: huí, huiste, hu**y**ó, huimos, huisteis, hu**y**eron
Imperative: hu**y**e, hu**y**a, hu**y**amos, huid, hu**y**an
Pres. Subj.: hu**y**a, hu**y**as, hu**y**a, hu**y**amos, hu**y**áis, hu**y**an
Imp. Subj.: hu**y**era(ese), hu**y**eras, hu**y**era, hu**y**éramos, hu**y**erais, hu**y**eran

Verbs that follow the same pattern: **atribuir, concluir, constituir, construir, contribuir, destituir, destruir, disminuir, distribuir, excluir, incluir, influir, instruir, restituir, sustituir.**

11. Verbs ending in **-eír** lose one **e** in the third person singular and plural of the preterit, in all persons of the imperfect subjunctive, and in the present participle.

reír(se) (*to laugh*)
Preterit: reí, reíste, r**i**ó, reímos, reísteis, r**i**eron
Imp. Subj.: r**i**era(ese), r**i**eras, r**i**era, r**i**éramos, r**i**erais, r**i**eran
Pres. Part.: r**i**endo

Freír and **sonreír** follow the same pattern.

12. Verbs ending in **-iar** add a written accent to the **i,** except in the first and second persons plural of the present indicative and subjunctive.

fiar(se) (*to trust*)
Pres. Ind.: f**í**o, f**í**as, f**í**a, fiamos, fiáis, f**í**an
Pres. Subj.: f**í**e, f**í**es, f**í**e, fiemos, fiéis, f**í**en

Verbs that follow the same pattern: **ampliar, criar, desviar, enfriar, enviar, esquiar, guiar, telegrafiar, vaciar, variar.**

13. Verbs ending in **-uar** (except **-guar**) add a written accent to the **u,** except in the first and second persons plural of the present indicative and subjunctive.

actuar (*to act*)
Pres. Ind.: act**ú**o, act**ú**as, act**ú**a, actuamos, actuáis, act**ú**an
Pres. Subj.: act**ú**e, act**ú**es, act**ú**e, actuemos, actuéis, act**ú**en

Verbs that follow the same pattern: **acentuar, continuar, efectuar, exceptuar, graduar, habituar, insinuar, situar.**

14. Verbs ending in **-ñir** remove the **i** of the diphthongs **ie** and **ió** in the third person singular and plural of the preterit and in all persons of the imperfect subjunctive. They also change the **e** of the stem to **i** in the same persons.

teñir (*to dye*)
Preterit: teñí, teñiste, **tiñó,** teñimos, teñisteis, **tiñeron**
Imp. Subj.: t**iñe**ra(ese), t**iñe**ras, t**iñe**ra, t**iñé**ramos, t**iñe**rais, t**iñe**ran

Verbs that follow the same pattern: **ceñir, constreñir, desteñir, estreñir, reñir.**

Some Common Irregular Verbs

Only those tenses with irregular forms are given below.

adquirir (*to acquire*)
Pres. Ind.: adquiero, adquieres, adquiere, adquirimos, adquirís, adquieren
Pres. Subj.: adquiera, adquieras, adquiera, adquiramos, adquiráis, adquieran
Imperative: adquiere, adquiera, adquiramos, adquirid, adquieran

andar (*to walk*)
Preterit: anduve, anduviste, anduvo, anduvimos, anduvisteis, anduvieron
Imp. Subj.: anduviera (anduviese), anduvieras, anduviera, anduviéramos, anduvierais, anduvieran

avergonzarse (*to be ashamed, to be embarrassed*)
Pres. Ind.: me avergüenzo, te avergüenzas, se avergüenza, nos avergonzamos, os avergonzáis, se avergüenzan
Pres. Subj.: me avergüence, te avergüences, se avergüence, nos avergoncemos, os avergoncéis, se avergüencen
Imperative: avergüénzate, avergüéncese, avergoncémonos, avergonzaos, avergüéncense

caber (*to fit, to have enough room*)
Pres. Ind.: quepo, cabes, cabe, cabemos, cabéis, caben
Preterit: cupe, cupiste, cupo, cupimos, cupisteis, cupieron
Future: cabré, cabrás, cabrá, cabremos, cabréis, cabrán
Conditional: cabría, cabrías, cabría, cabríamos, cabríais, cabrían
Imperative: cabe, quepa, quepamos, cabed, quepan
Pres. Subj.: quepa, quepas, quepa, quepamos, quepáis, quepan
Imp. Subj.: cupiera (cupiese), cupieras, cupiera, cupiéramos, cupierais, cupieran

caer (*to fall*)
Pres. Ind.: caigo, caes, cae, caemos, caéis, caen
Preterit: caí, caíste, cayó, caímos, caísteis, cayeron
Imperative: cae, caiga, caigamos, caed, caigan
Pres. Subj.: caiga, caigas, caiga, caigamos, caigáis, caigan
Imp. Subj.: cayera (cayese), cayeras, cayera, cayéramos, cayerais, cayeran
Past Part.: caído

conducir (*to guide, to drive*)

Pres. Ind.:	conduzco, conduces, conduce, conducimos, conducís, conducen
Preterit:	conduje, condujiste, condujo, condujimos, condujisteis, condujeron
Imperative:	conduce, conduzca, conduzcamos, conducid, conduzcan
Pres. Subj.:	conduzca, conduzcas, conduzca, conduzcamos, conduzcáis, conduzcan
Imp. Subj.:	condujera (condujese), condujeras, condujera, condujéramos, condujerais, condujeran

(All verbs ending in **-ducir** follow this pattern.)

convenir (*to agree*) See **venir.**

dar (*to give*)

Pres. Ind.:	doy, das, da, damos, dais, dan
Preterit:	di, diste, dio, dimos, disteis, dieron
Imperative:	da, dé, demos, dad, den
Pres. Subj.:	dé, des, dé, demos, deis, den
Imp. Subj.:	diera (diese), dieras, diera, diéramos, dierais, dieran

decir (*to say, to tell*)

Pres. Ind.:	digo, dices, dice, decimos, decís, dicen
Preterit:	dije, dijiste, dijo, dijimos, dijisteis, dijeron
Future:	diré, dirás, dirá, diremos, diréis, dirán
Conditional:	diría, dirías, diría, diríamos, diríais, dirían
Imperative:	di, diga, digamos, decid, digan
Pres. Subj.:	diga, digas, diga, digamos, digáis, digan
Imp. Subj.:	dijera (dijese), dijeras, dijera, dijéramos, dijerais, dijeran
Pres. Part.:	diciendo
Past Part.:	dicho

detener (*to stop, to hold, to arrest*) See **tener.**

entretener (*to entertain, to amuse*) See **tener.**

errar (*to err, to miss*)

Pres. Ind.:	yerro, yerras, yerra, erramos, erráis, yerran
Imperative:	yerra, yerre, erremos, errad, yerren
Pres. Subj.:	yerre, yerres, yerre, erremos, erréis, yerren

estar (*to be*)

Pres. Ind.:	estoy, estás, está, estamos, estáis, están
Preterit:	estuve, estuviste, estuvo, estuvimos, estuvisteis, estuvieron
Imperative:	está, esté, estemos, estad, estén
Pres. Subj.:	esté, estés, esté, estemos, estéis, estén
Imp. Subj.:	estuviera (estuviese), estuvieras, estuviera, estuviéramos, estuvierais, estuvieran

haber (*to have*)

Pres. Ind.:	he, has, ha, hemos, habéis, han
Preterit:	hube, hubiste, hubo, hubimos, hubisteis, hubieron
Future:	habré, habrás, habrá, habremos, habréis, habrán
Conditional:	habría, habrías, habría, habríamos, habríais, habrían

Imperative: he, haya, hayamos, habed, hayan
Pres. Subj.: haya, hayas, haya, hayamos, hayáis, hayan
Imp. Subj.: hubiera (hubiese), hubieras, hubiera, hubiéramos, hubierais, hubieran

hacer (*to do, to make*)
Pres. Ind.: hago, haces, hace, hacemos, hacéis, hacen
Preterit: hice, hiciste, hizo, hicimos, hicisteis, hicieron
Future: haré, harás, hará, haremos, haréis, harán
Conditional: haría, harías, haría, haríamos, haríais, harían
Imperative: haz, haga, hagamos, haced, hagan
Pres. Subj.: haga, hagas, haga, hagamos, hagáis, hagan
Imp. Subj.: hiciera (hiciese), hicieras, hiciera, hiciéramos, hicierais, hicieran
Past Part.: hecho

imponer (*to impose, to deposit*) See **poner.**

introducir (*to introduce, to insert, to gain access*) See **conducir.**

ir (*to go*)
Pres. Ind.: voy, vas, va, vamos, vais, van
Imp. Ind.: iba, ibas, iba, íbamos, ibais, iban
Preterit: fui, fuiste, fue, fuimos, fuisteis, fueron
Imperative: ve, vaya, vayamos, id, vayan
Pres. Subj.: vaya, vayas, vaya, vayamos, vayáis, vayan
Imp. Subj.: fuera (fuese), fueras, fuera, fuéramos, fuerais, fueran

jugar (*to play*)
Pres. Ind.: juego, juegas, juega, jugamos, jugáis, juegan
Imperative: juega, juegue, juguemos, jugad, jueguen
Pres. Subj.: juegue, juegues, juegue, juguemos, juguéis, jueguen

obtener (*to obtain*) See **tener.**

oír (*to hear*)
Pres. Ind.: oigo, oyes, oye, oímos, oís, oyen
Preterit: oí, oíste, oyó, oímos, oísteis, oyeron
Imperative: oye, oiga, oigamos, oíd, oigan
Pres. Subj.: oiga, oigas, oiga, oigamos, oigáis, oigan
Imp. Subj.: oyera (oyese), oyeras, oyera, oyéramos, oyerais, oyeran
Pres. Part.: oyendo
Past Part.: oído

oler (*to smell*)
Pres. Ind.: huelo, hueles, huele, olemos, oléis, huelen
Imperative: huele, huela, olamos, oled, huelan
Pres. Subj.: huela, huelas, huela, olamos, oláis, huelan

poder (*to be able*)
Pres. Ind.: puedo, puedes, puede, podemos, podéis, pueden

Preteri t: pude, pudiste, pudo, pudimos, pudisteis, pudieron
Future: podré, podrás, podrá, podremos, podréis, podrán
Conditional: podría, podrías, podría, podríamos, podríais, podrían
Imperative: puede, pueda, podamos, poded, puedan
Pres. Subj.: pueda, puedas, pueda, podamos, podáis, puedan
Imp. Subj.: pudiera (pudiese), pudieras, pudiera, pudiéramos, pudierais, pudieran
Pres. Part.: pudiendo

poner (*to place, to put*)
Pres. Ind.: pongo, pones, pone, ponemos, ponéis, ponen
Preterit: puse, pusiste, puso, pusimos, pusisteis, pusieron
Future: pondré, pondrás, pondrá, pondremos, pondréis, pondrán
Conditional: pondría, pondrías, pondría, pondríamos, pondríais, pondrían
Imperative: pon, ponga, pongamos, poned, pongan
Pres. Subj.: ponga, pongas, ponga, pongamos, pongáis, pongan
Imp. Subj.: pusiera (pusiese), pusieras, pusiera, pusiéramos, pusierais, pusieran
Past Part.: puesto

querer (*to want, to wish, to like*)
Pres. Ind.: quiero, quieres, quiere, queremos, queréis, quieren
Preterit: quise, quisiste, quiso, quisimos, quisisteis, quisieron
Future: querré, querrás, querrá, querremos, querréis, querrán
Conditional: querría, querrías, querría, querríamos, querríais, querrían

Imperative: quiere, quiera, queramos, quered, quieran
Pres. Subj.: quiera, quieras, quiera, queramos, queráis, quieran
Imp. Subj.: quisiera (quisiese), quisieras, quisiera, quisiéramos, quisierais, quisieran

resolver (*to decide on*)
Past Part.: resuelto

saber (*to know*)
Pres. Ind.: sé, sabes, sabe, sabemos, sabéis, saben
Preterit: supe, supiste, supo, supimos, supisteis, supieron
Future: sabré, sabrás, sabrá, sabremos, sabréis, sabrán
Conditional: sabría, sabrías, sabría, sabríamos, sabríais, sabrían
Imperative: sabe, sepa, sepamos, sabed, sepan
Pres. Subj.: sepa, sepas, sepa, sepamos, sepáis, sepan
Imp. Subj.: supiera (supiese), supieras, supiera, supiéramos, supierais, supieran

salir (*to leave, to go out*)
Pres. Ind.: salgo, sales, sale, salimos, salís, salen
Future: saldré, saldrás, saldrá, saldremos, saldréis, saldrán
Conditional: saldría, saldrías, saldría, saldríamos, saldríais, saldrían
Imperative: sal, salga, salgamos, salid, salgan
Pres. Subj.: salga, salgas, salga, salgamos, salgáis, salgan

ser (*to be*)

Pres. Ind.:	soy, eres, es, somos, sois, son
Imp. Ind.:	era, eras, era, éramos, erais, eran
Preterit:	fui, fuiste, fue, fuimos, fuisteis, fueron
Imperative:	sé, sea, seamos, sed, sean
Pres. Subj.:	sea, seas, sea, seamos, seáis, sean
Imp. Subj.:	fuera (fuese), fueras, fuera, fuéramos, fuerais, fueran

suponer (*to assume*) See **poner.**

tener (*to have*)

Pres. Ind.:	tengo, tienes, tiene, tenemos, tenéis, tienen
Preterit:	tuve, tuviste, tuvo, tuvimos, tuvisteis, tuvieron
Future:	tendré, tendrás, tendrá, tendremos, tendréis, tendrán
Conditional:	tendría, tendrías, tendría, tendríamos, tendríais, tendrían
Imperative:	ten, tenga, tengamos, tened, tengan
Pres. Subj.:	tenga, tengas, tenga, tengamos, tengáis, tengan
Imp. Subj.:	tuviera (tuviese), tuvieras, tuviera, tuviéramos, tuvierais, tuvieran

traducir (*to translate*) See **conducir.**

traer (*to bring*)

Pres. Ind.:	traigo, traes, trae, traemos, traéis, traen
Preterit:	traje, trajiste, trajo, trajimos, trajisteis, trajeron
Imperative:	trae, traiga, traigamos, traed, traigan
Pres. Subj.:	traiga, traigas, traiga, traigamos, traigáis, traigan
Imp. Subj.:	trajera (trajese), trajeras, trajera, trajéramos, trajerais, trajeran
Pres. Part.:	trayendo
Past Part.:	traído

valer (*to be worth*)

Pres. Ind.:	valgo, vales, vale, valemos, valéis, valen
Future:	valdré, valdrás, valdrá, valdremos, valdréis, valdrán
Conditional:	valdría, valdrías, valdría, valdríamos, valdríais, valdrían
Imperative:	vale, valga, valgamos, valed, valgan
Pres. Subj.:	valga, valgas, valga, valgamos, valgáis, valgan

venir (*to come*)

Pres. Ind.:	vengo, vienes, viene, venimos, venís, vienen
Preterit:	vine, viniste, vino, vinimos, vinisteis, vinieron
Future:	vendré, vendrás, vendrá, vendremos, vendréis, vendrán
Conditional:	vendría, vendrías, vendría, vendríamos, vendríais, vendrían
Imperative:	ven, venga, vengamos, venid, vengan
Pres. Subj.:	venga, vengas, venga, vengamos, vengáis, vengan
Imp. Subj.:	viniera (viniese), vinieras, viniera, viniéramos, vinierais, vinieran
Pres. Part.:	viniendo

ver (*to see*)

Pres. Ind.:	veo, ves, ve, vemos, veis, ven
Imp. Ind.:	veía, veías, veía, veíamos, veíais, veían
Preterit:	vi, viste, vio, vimos, visteis, vieron
Imperative:	ve, vea, veamos, ved, vean
Pres. Subj.:	vea, veas, vea, veamos, veáis, vean
Imp. Subj.:	viera (viese), vieras, viera, viéramos, vierais, vieran
Past. Part.:	visto

volver (*to return*)

Past Part.:	vuelto

Appendix C
Useful Classroom Expressions

You will hear your teacher use the following directions and general terms in class. Take time to familiarize yourself with them.

- When the teacher is speaking to the whole class:

Abran sus libros, por favor.	*Open your books, please.*
Cierren sus libros, por favor.	*Close your books, please.*
Escriban, por favor.	*Write, please.*
Escuchen, por favor.	*Listen, please.*
Estudien la lección...	*Study Lesson...*
Hagan el ejercicio número...	*Do exercise number...*
Levanten la mano.	*Raise your hands.*
Repasen el vocabulario.	*Review the vocabulary.*
Repitan, por favor.	*Repeat, please.*
Siéntense, por favor.	*Sit down, please.*
Vayan a la página...	*Go to page...*

- When the teacher is speaking to one student:

Continúe, por favor.	*Go on, please.*
Lea, por favor.	*Read, please.*
Vaya a la pizarra, por favor.	*Go to the chalkboard, please.*

- Some other words used in the classroom.

diccionario	*dictionary*	**palabra**	*word*
dictado	*dictation*	**presente**	*present, here*
examen	*exam*	**prueba**	*quiz*
horario de clases	*class schedule*	**tarea**	*homework*

Weights and Measures

Length

la pulgada = *inch*
el pie = *foot*
la yarda = *yard*
la milla = *mile*

1 centímetro (cm) = .3937 pulgadas (*less than 1/2 inch*)
1 metro (m) = 39.37 pulgadas (*1 yard, 3 inches*)
1 kilómetro (km) (1.000 metros) = .6214 millas (*5/8 mile*)

Weight

la onza = *ounce*
la libra = *pound*
la tonelada = *ton*

1 gramo (g) = .03527 onzas
100 gramos = 3.527 onzas (*less than 1/4 pound*)
1 kilogramo (kg) (1.000 gramos) = 2.2 libras

Liquid Measure

la pinta = pint
el cuarto (de galón) = quart
el galón = gallon

1 litro (l) = 1.0567 cuartos (de galón) (*slightly more than a quart*)

Surface

el acre = *acre*
1 hectárea = 2.471 acres

Temperature

°C = Celsius (*Celsius*) or centigrade (*centígrado*); °F = Fahrenheit (*Fahrenheit*)
0° C = 32° F (*freezing point of water*)
37° C = 98.6° F (*normal body temperature*)
100° C = 212° F (*boiling point of water*)

Conversión de grados Fahrenheit a grados centígrados °C = 5/9 (°F −32)
Conversión de grados centígrados a grados Fahrenheit °F = 9/5 (°C) + 32

Spanish-English Vocabulary

The Spanish-English and English-Spanish vocabularies contain all active and passive vocabulary that appear in the manual. Active vocabulary includes words and expressions appearing in the *Vocabulario* lists. These items are followed by a number indicating the lesson in which each word is introduced in the dialogues. Passive vocabulary consists of words and expressions included in the *Vocabulario adicional* lists, the diagrams of the human body, and those that are given an English gloss in the readings, exercises, activities, and authentic documents.

The following abbreviations are used in the vocabularies.

adj.	adjective	*L.A.*	Latin America
adv.	adverb	*m.*	masculine noun
col.	colloquial	*Méx.*	Mexico
f.	feminine noun	*pl.*	plural noun
form.	formal	*sing.*	singular noun
inf.	infinitive		

A

a to
— **la(s)** (+ *time*) at (+ *time*), 1
— **la derecha** to the right
— **la izquierda** to the left
— **la larga** in the long run
— **los costados (lados)** to (at) the sides, 14
— **menudo** often, 1
— **qué hora** (at) what time, 5
— **veces** sometimes, 6
— **ver ...** let's see ..., 1
abdomen (*m.*) abdomen
aborto (*m.*) abortion, 4
— **espontáneo** miscarriage, 4
— **natural** miscarriage, 4
abrigo (*m.*) coat
abrir to open, 9
absceso (*m.*) abscess, 9
abstinencia (*f.*) abstinence, 7
abuelo(a) (*m., f.*) grandfather; grandmother
abultamiento (*m.*) lump
acabar de (+ *inf.*) to have just (done something), 13
acatarrado(a): estar — to have a cold, 3
accidente (*m.*) accident, 10
aceite (*m.*) oil, 5
acerca de about
acercarse to get close, 14; to approach, 14
acidez (*f.*) acidity, 17; heartburn, 17
ácido (*m.*) acid, 10; LSD
acné (*m.*) acne, 12
aconsejar to advise, 16
acostar(se) (o:ue) to lie down, 14; to go to bed, 4
al — at bedtime, 3
— **con** to have sex with, 4
actualmente currently, 18; at the present time, 18
adelanto (*m.*) advance
adelgazar to lose weight, 6
además besides, 6; in addition, 6
adicional additional
adicto(a) addicted
adiós good-bye, PI
adjetivo (*m.*) adjective
admisión (*f.*) admission
adolescente (*m., f.*) teenager, 12
¿adónde? where (to)?, 3
afear to disfigure, 7
afectar to affect, 16
afeitar(se) to shave
afuera outside, 10
agua (*f.* but **el agua**) water, 2
— **oxigenada** hydrogen peroxide, 19
aguantar to stand, 18; to tolerate, 18; to bear, 18
— **la respiración** to hold one's breath, 14
agudo(a) sharp, 20; stabbing, 20
aguja (*f.*) needle
agujero (*m.*) hole, 19
ah oh, 9
ahora now, 1
— **mismo** right now, 3
ahumado(a) smoked
aire (*m.*) air
faltarle el — a uno to have shortness of breath, 20
ajá aha, 1
al to the
— **día** a day, 2; per day, 2
— **día siguiente** on the following day, 15
— **final** at the end of, 14
— **lado de** at the side of, 13
— **principio** at the beginning
— **rato** a while later, 3
alberca (*f.*) swimming pool (*Méx.*), 19
alcohol (*m.*) alcohol, 16
alergia (*f.*) allergy, 18
alérgico(a) allergic, 3
alfiler (*m.*) pin, 19
algo anything, 2; something, 2
¿— **más?** anything else?, 2
algodón (*m.*) cotton, L1
alguien (*m., f.*) someone
algunas veces sometimes, 6
alguno(a) any, 3; some, 3
— **vez** ever, 17
algunos(as) some
aliento (*m.*) breath, 9
alimentación (*f.*) food, 12
alimento (*m.*) food, 3; nourishment, 6
aliviarse to feel better, 17; to diminish (*a pain*), 17
almohada (*f.*) pillow, 2
almorrana (*f.*) hemorrhoid, 17
almorzar (o:ue) to have lunch, 6
almuerzo (*m.*) lunch, 13
alrededor de around
alto(a) high, 3; tall
alucinación (*f.*) hallucination
alumbramiento (*m.*) delivery, 11
allí there, 15
amable kind
amarillento(a) yellowish, 15
amarrar to tie
— **los tubos** to tie tubes, 7
ambiente (*m.*) atmosphere
la temperatura del — room temperature
ambulancia (*f.*) ambulance, 10
ameno(a) pleasant, agreeable
amígdalas (*f. pl.*) tonsils
amigdalitis (*f.*) tonsilitis
ampolla (*f.*) blister

amputar to amputate
analgésicos (*m.*) analgesics, 3
análisis (*m.*) test, PII; analysis, PII
— **de sangre** blood test, 1
anciano(a) (*m., f.*) elderly man, 17; elderly woman, 17
andar to walk, 19
— **a gatas** to crawl, 19
anemia (*f.*) anemia, PI
anémico(a) anemic, 3
anestesia (*f.*) anesthesia, 9
— **espinal** spinal anesthesia
anestesiología (*f.*) anesthesiology, PI
anestesiólogo(a) (*m., f.*) anesthesiologist, PI
aneurisma (*m.*) aneurysm
anfetamina (*f.*) amphetamine, 18
angina (*f.*) angina
angiografía (*f.*) angiograph, 16
angioplastia (*f.*) angioplasty, 20
angustia (*f.*) anxiety
anillo (*m.*) ring, 13
ano (*m.*) anus
anoche last night
ansiedad (*f.*) anxiety
anteanoche the night before last
anteayer the day before yesterday
anteojos (*m. pl.*) glasses, 2
anterior front
antes (de) before, 3; first, 10
— **cada comida** before each meal, 3
— **dormir** before sleeping, 3
antiácido (*m.*) antacid (medicine), 17
antibiótico (*m.*) antibiotic, 3
anticoagulante (*m.*) anticoagulant
anticonceptivo(a) for birth control, 7; contraceptive (*adj.*), 7
antidepresivo (*m.*) antidepressant, 2
antidiarreico (*m.*) antidiarrheic, 2
antidroga antidrug, 18
antiespasmódico (*m.*) antispasmodic, 2
antihistamínico (*m.*) antihistamine, 19
añadir to add
año (*m.*) year, 3
aparato (*m.*) apparatus, 12; instrument, 12; system
— **intrauterino** I.U.D., 7
apellido (*m.*) surname, PI; last name, PI
apenas barely, 16
apendicitis (*f.*) appendicitis
apestar to have a bad odor, 15
apetito (*m.*) apetite, 3
aplicar to apply, 19
apretar (e:ie) to press down, 8; to be tight, 14
aprovechar to take advantage of, 9
aquí here, 1
— **está** here it is, 1
— **mismo** right here, 12
árbol (*m.*) tree, 10
archivo clínico (*m.*) medical records
arder to burn, 15
ardor (*m.*) burning, 8
arriesgarse to risk
arrojar to throw up, 1
arroz (*m.*) rice, 6
arteria (*f.*) artery, 16
articulación (*f.*) joint
artificial artificial
artritis (*f.*) arthritis
asar to grill, 6
ascensor (*m.*) elevator
aseguranza (*f.*) (*Méx.*) insurance, 1
asegurarse to make sure, 12
asentaderas (*f.*) buttocks, 5
así like this, 8; so, 8; that way, 11; like that, 11
asiento (*m.*) seat
asimismo also
asistente (*m., f.*) assistant, 9; helper, 9
asma (*m.*) asthma
asmático(a) asthmatic, 3
aspirina (*f.*) aspirin, 3
astigmatismo (*m.*) astigmatism
asustarse to be scared, 19; to be frightened, 19
ataque (*m.*) seizure, attack
— **al corazón** heart attack, 18
atender (e:ie) to attend, to tend (to)
atragantarse to choke, 19
audífono (*m.*) hearing aid, 17
aumentar to gain, 8; to increase
aun even
auto (*m.*) auto, 10
autorización (*f.*) authorization
aventado(a) bloated, 3
avisar to let (someone) know, 13
aviso (*m.*) warning
¡ay! oh!, 10
ayer yesterday
ayuda help, 2
ayudar to help, 13
ayunas: en — with an empty stomach, 3; fasting, 3; before eating anything
azúcar (*m.*) sugar, 6
azul blue

B

babero (*m.*) bib
babuchas (*f. pl.*) slippers
bajar to go down, 3
— **de peso** to lose weight, 6
bajo under, 18
bajo(a) low, 8; short
bala: herida de — (*f.*) gunshot wound
balanceado(a) balanced, 6
banco de sangre (*m.*) blood bank
bañadera (*f.*) bathtub, 19
bañar(se) to bathe, 13
bañera (*f.*) bathtub, 19
baño (*m.*) bathroom, 2
— **de esponja** sponge bath, 13
barato(a) cheap
barbilla (*f.*) chin, 8
barbitúrico (*m.*) barbiturate, 3
barriga (*f.*) abdomen, 11
básico(a) basic
bata (*f.*) robe, 14
batería (*f.*) battery, 20
bazo (*m.*) spleen
bebé (*m.*) baby, 4
— **de probeta** test-tube baby, 7
beber to drink, 2
bebida (*f.*) drink, 17; beverage, 17
— **alcohólica** alcoholic beverage, 4
benigno(a) benign, 12
biberón (*m.*) baby bottle, 11
bien fine, PI; well, PI
muy —, gracias very well, thank you, PI
no muy — not very well, PI
biopsia (*f.*) biopsy, 12
bisexual bisexual, 15
blanco(a) white
blando(a) bland (diet); soft, 9
blanquillo (*m.*) egg (*Méx.*), 6
bizco(a) cross-eyed
blusa (*f.*) blouse
boca (*f.*) mouth, 9
— **abajo** on one's stomach, face down
— **arriba** on one's back, face up
bocio (*m.*) goiter, 8
bolita (*f.*) little ball, 12; lump, 12
bolsa (*f.*) bag; handbag, 9; purse, 9
— **de agua** water bag, 11
— **de hielo** ice pack, 9
bomberos: departamento de — (*m.*) fire department
bonito(a) pretty, 11
borroso(a) blurry, 12
botella (*f.*) bottle, 10
botiquín (*m.*) medicine chest, 19; medicine cabinet, 19
— **de primeros auxilios** first-aid kit, 19
botón (*m.*) button, 13
brazo (*m.*) arm, 1
breve brief, PI
brindar to offer
broncoscopia (*f.*) bronchoscopy
bronquitis (*f.*) bronchitis, PI
bróculi (*m.*) broccoli, 6
bucal oral (*ref. to the mouth*)
bueno(a) okay, 1; well, 1; good
buena suerte good luck, 7
buenas noches good evening (night), PI
buenas tardes good afternoon, PI
buenos días good morning (day), PI

C

cabello (*m.*) hair
cabeza (*f.*) head, 1
caca (*col.*) (*f.*) excrement, stool
cachete (*m.*) cheek
cada every, 3; each, 3
— **... horas** every... hours
cadera (*f.*) hip
caer(se) to fall, 10
café (*m.*) coffee, 2
cafeína (*f.*) caffeine, 16
caja (*f.*) box, 20
— **de seguridad** safe, 13
— **fuerte** safe, 13
cajero(a) (*m., f.*) cashier
cajetilla (*f.*) pack of cigarettes, 2

calambre (*m.*) cramp, 20
calcáneo (*m.*) calcaneus
calcetín (*m.*) sock
calcio (*m.*) calcium
cálculo (*m.*) stone, 17
caldo (*m.*) broth, 6
calentar (e:ie) to heat up
calentura (*f.*) fever, 3
caliente hot, 2
calle (*f.*) street, PI
calmante (*m.*) painkiller, 2; sedative, 2
calmar(se) to calm down, 11
caloría (*f.*) calorie, 6
cama (*f.*) bed, 13
cambiar(se) to change (oneself), 16
cambio (*m.*) change, 16
camilla (*f.*) gurney, 10; stretcher, 10
caminar to walk, 10
camisa (*f.*) shirt
camisón (*m.*) nightgown
campanilla (*f.*) uvula
canal (*m.*) canal
  — auditivo ear canal
  — de la orina urethra
  — en la raíz root canal, 9
cáncer (*m.*) cancer, PI
canino (*m.*) canine (*tooth*), 9
cansado(a) tired, 3
cansancio (*m.*) tiredness, 17; exhaustion, 17; fatigue
cantidad (*f.*) quantity, 6
caño de la orina (*m.*) urethra
cápsula (*f.*) capsule, 2
cara (*f.*) face, 4
caramelo (*m.*) candy
carbohidrato (*m.*) carbohydrate, 6
cardenal (*m.*) bruise (*Cuba*), 13
cardiología (*f.*) cardiology, PI
cardiólogo(a) cardiologist, PI
cariado(a) decayed, 9; carious, 9
carie (*f.*) cavity, 9
carne (*f.*) meat, 4
carpo (*m.*) carpus
carro (*m.*) car, 10
cartera (*f.*) handbag, 9; purse, 9
casa (*f.*) house, 9; home
casado(a) married, PI
casi almost, 10
  — nunca hardly ever, 20
caso (*m.*) case, 10
  en ese — in that case, 7
cataratas (*f. pl.*) cataracts
catarro (*m.*) cold, 3
cateterismo cardíaco (*m.*) cardiac catheterization
causar to cause, 7
ceguera (*f.*) blindness
ceja (*f.*) eyebrow
cemento (*m.*) cement
cena (*f.*) dinner, supper, L2
centro (*m.*) center, 7
  — de envenenamiento poison center, 19
cepillar(se) to brush (oneself), 9
  — los dientes to brush one's teeth, 9
cepillo (*m.*) brush, 9
  — de dientes toothbrush

cerca (de) close, 12; near, 12
cercano(a) near, 20
cereal (*m.*) cereal, 6
cerebro (*m.*) brain, cerebrum
cerilla (*f.*) match, 19
cerrado(a) closed, 14
cerrar (e:ie) to close, 5
certeza (*f.*) certainty, 15
cerveza (*f.*) beer, 18
cerviz (*f.*) cervix
cesáreo(a) cesarean, 11
chancro (*m.*) chancre
chaqueta (*f.*) jacket
chata (*f.*) bedpan, 2
chequear to check, 5
chequeo (*m.*) checkup, PII; exam, 8; examination, PII
chile (*m.*) pepper, 6
chocar to run into, 10; to collide, 10
chocolate (*m.*) chocolate, 2
chupete (*m.*) pacifier
chupón (*m.*) pacifier
ciego(a) blind
cierto(a) certain, 20
cigarrillo (*m.*) cigarrette, 2
cinta adhesiva (*f.*) adhesive tape, 19
cintura (*f.*) waist
circulación (*f.*) circulation
cirrosis (*f.*) cirrhosis, PI
cirugía (*f.*) surgery, 12
cirujano(a) (*m., f.*) surgeon, PII
cita (*f.*) appointment, 5
clamidia (*f.*) chlamydia
claramente clearly, 12
claro of course
clavícula (*f.*) clavicle
clínica (*f.*) clinic, 5
clínico (*m., f.*) general practitioner, 17; internist, 17
clínico(a) (*adj.*) medical, 1
coágulo (*m.*) clot, coagulum
cobertura (*f.*) cover, 1
cobija (*f.*) blanket, 2
coca (*f.*) cocaine
  — cocinada crack (*col.*)
cocaína (*f.*) cocaine
cóccix (*m.*) coccyx
coche (*m.*) car, 10
cochecito (*m.*) baby carriage
cocina (*f.*) stove, 19
codeína (*f.*) codeine
codo (*m.*) elbow
cognado (*m.*) cognate
col (*f.*) cabbage, 6
colesterol (*m.*) cholesterol, 8
cólico (*m.*) colic, 5
colitis (*f.*) colitis, 5
colmillo (*m.*) canine (*tooth*), 9
colocar to place, 7
colon (*m.*) colon, 14
colonoscopia (*f.*) colonoscopy, coloscopy
columna vertebral (*f.*) backbone, spinal column
comadrona (*f.*) midwife
comenzar (e:ie) to begin, 11; to start, 11
comer to eat, 2

comercial commercial, 17
comezón (*f.*) itching, 8
comida (*f.*) meal, 1; food, 16; lunch; midday meal
comidita de bebé (*f.*) baby food
como since, 3; like, 10
¿cómo? how?, PI
  ¿— está usted? How are you?, PI
  — no of course, 13; sure, 13
  ¿— se siente? How are you feeling?, PII
comodidad (*f.*) convenience
cómodo(a) comfortable, 13
compañero(a) sexual (*m., f.*) sexual partner
compañía (*f.*) company, 1
  — de seguro (*f.*) insurance company, PII
comparar to compare
compartir to share, 18
completamente completely, 15
comprar to buy, 3
comprender to understand
compresa (*f.*) compress, 13
computadora (*f.*) computer, 8
común common
con with, PI
  — las comidas with meals, 3
concebir (e:i) to conceive, 7
condimentado(a) spiced, 6; spicy, 6
condón (*m.*) condom, 7
conducto: — lacrimal (lagrimal) (*m.*) tear duct
  — auditivo ear canal
confidencial confidential
confirmar to confirm, 10
conjuntivitis (*f.*) conjunctivitis, 5
conmigo with me, 6
conocer to know (*be acquainted with*), 7
conocimiento (*m.*) knowledge
  perder (e:ie) el — to be unconscious, 10; to lose consciousness, 10
conseguir (e:i) to obtain, 15; to get, 15
consejo (*m.*) advice, 19
constantemente constantly, 6
consultar to consult
consultorio (*m.*) doctor's office, P1
consumir to consume
contagioso(a) contagious, 15
contaminación (*f.*) pollution
contar (o:ue) to count, 6; to tell
contener to contain, 20
conteo (*m.*) blood count, 14; count, 14
contestar to answer
contra against, 5
contracción (*f.*) contraction, 11
contraceptivo (*m.*) contraceptive
control (*m.*) control, 7
controlar to control, 9
conversación (*f.*) conversation, PI
conversar to talk
convulsiones (*f. pl.*) convulsions, 5
coordinador(a) (*m., f.*) coordinator, 18
corazón (*m.*) heart, 16
cordal (*m.*) wisdom tooth, 9
cordón umbilical (*m.*) umbilical cord
corona (*f.*) crown, 9

correctamente correctly, 7
correcto(a) correct, 7
correr to run, 8
cortadura (*f.*) cut, 19
cortar(se) to cut (oneself), 10
corto(a) de vista nearsighted
cosa (*f.*) thing, 6
cosmético (*m.*) cosmetic, 3
costado (*m.*) side, 14
costilla (*f.*) rib
costra (*f.*) scab, 5
crac (*m.*) crack
cráneo (*m.*) skull
creer to believe, 3; to think, 3
  Creo que no. I don't think so., 5
  Creo que sí. I think so., 10
crema (*f.*) cream, 7
crup (*m.*) croup, 5
cuadra (*f.*) block, 20
cuadro (*m.*) box
¿cuál? what?, 3; which?, 3
cualquier(a) any, 16
cuando when, 8
  ¿cuándo? when?, 1
cuanto: — antes mejor the sooner, the better, 15
¿cuánto? how much?, 1
  ¿— mide (Ud.)? How tall are you?, 1
  ¿por — tiempo...? for how long...?, 10
  ¿— tiempo hace...? how long ago ...?, 14
¿cuántos(as)? how many?, PII
cuarto (*m.*) room, 3
cuates (*m., f. pl.*) twins (*Méx.*)
cúbito (*m.*) ulna
cubrir to cover, 5
cucaracha (*f.*) joint (*col., drugs*)
cucharada (*f.*) (table)spoonful, 13
cucharadita (*f.*) teaspoonful, 3
cuello (*m.*) neck, 1
cuenta (*f.*) bill, 1
cuero cabelludo (*m.*) scalp
cuerpo (*m.*) body
cuidado (*m.*) care, 9
  — postnatal (*m.*) postnatal care
cuidar(se) to take care (of oneself), 12
cuna (*f.*) crib, 19; cradle, 19
cuña (*f.*) bedpan, 2
cuñado(a) (*m., f.*) brother-in law, sister-in-law
cura (*f.*) cure
curado(a) cured, 15
curandero(a) (*m., f.*) folk healer
curar to cure, 17
curita (*f.*) adhesive bandage, 14
cutis (*m.*) skin (*facial*)
cuyo(a) whose

D

daltonismo (*m.*) color blindness
daño (*m.*) damage
dar to give, 3
  — a luz to give birth
  — de alta to release (*from a hospital*), 13
  — de mamar to nurse, 11
  — el pecho to nurse, 11
  — resultado to work, 12; to produce results, 12
  — un tiro to shoot
  — una puñalada to stab
  — viaje to take drugs
darse vuelta to turn over, 14
de of, PII
  — nada You're welcome, PI
  — prisa in a hurry, 8
debajo de under, 13
deber must, 2; should, 2
débil weak, 4
debilidad (*f.*) weakness, 17
decidir to decide, 18
decir to say, 7; to tell, 7
decisión (*f.*) decision, 12
dedo (*m.*) finger, 1
  — del pie toe
  — gordo big toe
defecar to have a bowel movement, 11
dejar to leave (behind), 14
  — de (+ *inf.*) to stop (doing something), 4
delgado(a) thin, 3
delirium tremens (*m. pl.*) DT's
demasiado too much, 19
dentadura (*f.*) teeth, set of teeth, 2
  — postiza (*f.*) dentures, 2
dental dental, 18
dentina (*f.*) dentine
dentista (*m., f.*) dentist, 9
dentro inside
  — de in, 8; within, 8
  por — on the inside, 7
departamento (*m.*) department, 15
depender to depend, 16
depresión (*f.*) depression
derecho(a) right, 14
dermatólogo(a) (*m., f.*) dermatologist, 4
derrame (*m.*) stroke, 16
desarrollar to develop
desayuno (*m.*) breakfast, 2
descansar to rest, 4
descongestivos (*m. pl.*) decongestants, 3
descubrir to discover
descuento (*m.*) discount
desde since, 4
desear to want, 2; to wish, 2
deshidratación (*f.*) dehydration, PI
desinfectar to disinfect, 10
desintoxicación (*f.*) detoxification
desmayarse to faint, 10; to lose consciousness, 10
despierto(a) awake, 20
desprendimiento (*m.*) detachment
después (de) after, 1; later, 15
destruir to destroy
detergente (*m.*) detergent, 19
determinar to determine, 7
día (*m.*) day, 12
diabetes (*f.*) diabetes, PI
diabético(a) diabetic, 6
diafragma (*m.*) diaphragm, 7
diagnosticar to diagnose
diagnóstico (*m.*) diagnosis, 10
diariamente (*adv.*) daily, 17
diario(a) (*adj.*) daily
diarrea (*f.*) diarrhea, 5
diente (*m.*) tooth, 1
dieta (*f.*) diet, 6
  seguir una — to go on a diet, 6
dietista (*m., f.*) dietician, 2
diferente different, 7
difícil difficult, 6
dificultad (*f.*) difficulty, 8
difteria (*f.*) diphtheria, 5
digerir (e:ie) to digest
digestivo(a) digestive
dilatado(a) dilated
dirección (*f.*) address, PI
directamente straight, 12; directly, 12
dirigir to direct
disentería (*f.*) dysentery, PI
disminuir to cut down, 16; to diminish, 16
distinguir to distinguish
distinto(a) different, 7
diurético (*m.*) diuretic
divorciado(a) divorced, PI
doblar to bend, 8
doctor(a) (*m., f.*) doctor, PI
doler (o:ue) to hurt, 8; to ache, 8
dolor (*m.*) pain, ache, 1
  — de cabeza headache, 1
  — de estómago stomachache, 1
  — de garganta sore throat
  — de parto labor pain, 11
  el — se me pasa the pain goes away, 17
doloroso(a) painful
domicilio (*m.*) address, PI
donante (*m., f.*) donor
donar donate
¿dónde? where?, PII
dormido(a) asleep, 20
dormir (o:ue) to sleep, 8
dosis (*f.*) dosage, 16
drenaje (*m.*) drainage
droga (*f.*) drug, 18
drogadicto(a) (*m., f.*) drug addict, 18
droguería (*f.*) pharmacy (*some L.A. countries*), 3
dudar to doubt, 18
dulce (*m.*) candy, 6; sweet, 6
durante during, 4
durar to last, 20
durazno (*m.*) peach, 2
duro(a) hard, 4

E

eccema (*m.*) eczema, 5
edad (*f.*) age, 1
efectivo(a) effective, 7
efecto (*m.*) effect
  — secundario side effect
eficaz effective
ejemplo (*m.*) example
ejercicio (*m.*) exercise, 16
elástico(a) elastic, 17

eléctrico(a) electric, 10; electrical, 10
electrocardiograma (*m.*) electrocardiogram (EKG), PII
electroencefalograma (*m.*) electroencephalogram (EEG)
elegir (e:i) to choose, 11; to select, 11
elevado(a) elevated, 20
elevador (*m.*) elevator
eliminar to eliminate, 16
embarazada pregnant, 4
embarazo (*m.*) pregnancy, 7
embolia (*f.*) embolism, clot, 16
emergencia (*f.*) emergency, 1
empastar to fill (*a tooth*), 9
empeorar to get worse
empezar (e:ie) to begin, 15; to start, 15
emplear to employ
emplomar to fill (*a tooth*), 9
empujar to push
en in, PII; at, PII
— **ayunas** fasting, 8; with an empty stomach, 8
— **caso de** in case, 1
— **cuanto** as soon as, 19
— **estos días** these days, 5
¿— **qué puedo servirle?** How may I help you?, PI
— **seguida** right away, 5
encía (*f.*) gum, 9
encinta pregnant, 4
encontrar (o:ue) to find, 12
enchufe de seguridad (*m.*) electrical plug cover, 19
endocrinólogo(a) (*m., f.*) endocrinologist, 4
endometrosis (*f.*) endometriosis, 5
endoscopia (*f.*) endoscopy, 17
endrogarse to take drugs, to become addicted to drugs
endulzado(a) sweetened
endurecimiento (*m.*) hardening
enema (*m.*) enema, 14
enfermedad (*f.*) sickness, 5; disease, 5
enfermero(a) (*m., f.*) nurse, 1
enfermo(a) (*m., f.*) sick person, 3
enfisema (*m.*) emphysema, PI
engordar to gain weight, 6
enjuagar(se) to rinse (out), 9
enjuague (*m.*) mouthwash, 9
entonces then, 9
entrada (*f.*) opening, 7; entry, 7
entrante next, 5
entrar to enter, 1; to go (come) in
entre between, 20
— **comidas** between meals, 3
entumecido(a) numb
entumecimiento (*m.*) numbness, 8
envenenamiento (*m.*) poisoning, 10
envenenar(se) to poison (oneself), 19
enyesar to put a cast on, 10
epidural (*m.*) epidural, 11
epilepsia (*f.*) epilepsy, PI
equipo (*m.*) equipment
eructar to burp
erupción (*f.*) rash
escalera (*f.*) staircase, 10
escalofríos (*m. pl.*) chills, 5
escanograma (*m.*) CAT scan
escayola (*f.*) cast (*España*)
escayolar to put a cast on (*España*)
esclerosis múltiple (*f.*) multiple sclerosis, 8
escrito(a) written, 13
escoger to choose
escroto (*m.*) scrotum
escuela (*f.*) school, 6
escupir to spit, 9
esmalte (*m.*) enamel
eso that, 6
por — that's why, 6; for that reason, 6
espacio (*m.*) room, 9; space, 9
espaguetis (*m.*) spaghetti, 6
espalda (*f.*) back, 1
esparadrapo (*m.*) adhesive bandage
especial special, 5
especialista (*m., f.*) specialist, 12
especialmente especially, 6
espejuelos (*m. pl.*) glasses (*Cuba*), 2
esperar to wait (for), 3; to hope, 17
esperma (*f.*) sperm, 7
espina dorsal (*f.*) spinal column
espinal spinal
espinilla (*f.*) blackhead, 12
esponja (*f.*) sponge
esposo(a) (*m., f.*) husband, 1; wife, 1;
espuma (*f.*) foam, L1
esputo (*m.*) sputum, 1
esqueleto (*m.*) skeleton
esquina (*f.*) corner
esquizofrenia (*f.*) schizophrenia
estacionamiento (*m.*) parking
estado (*m.*) state
— **civil** marital status, 1
estar to be, 3
— **acatarrado(a)** to have a cold, 3
— **bien** to be well, okay, 2
— **constipado** to have a cold, 3
— **de parto** to be in labor
— **enfermo(a) del corazón** to have heart problems, 6
— **prohibido** to be prohibited, 2
— **resfriado(a)** to have a cold, 3
este(a) this, 1
esta noche tonight
esterilidad (*f.*) sterility, 7
esterilizar to sterilize, 7
esternón (*m.*) sternum
esteroides anabólicos (*m. pl.*) anabolic steroids
estómago (*m.*) stomach, 1
estos(as) these
estrecho(a) narrow, 6
estreñido(a) constipated, 3
estrés (*m.*) stress, 16
estricto(a) strict, 6
estuche de primeros auxilios (*m.*) first-aid kit, 19
estufa (*f.*) stove, 19
evacuar to have a bowel movement (*Méx.*), 11
evitar to avoid, 4
examen (*m.*) exam, 8; examination, 8; check up, 8.
examen físico physical examination, PII
examinar to examine, 4
exceso de peso (*m.*) overweight
excremento (*m.*) excrement, 1
excusado (*m.*) bathroom, 14
expectorar to expectorate, 2
expediente médico (*m.*) patient's medical record
explicar to explain, 10
exponer(se) to expose oneself
expresión (*f.*) expression
éxtasis (*m.*) ecstasy
extender (e:ie) to stretch, 14; to extend, 14
extracción (*f.*) extraction, 9
extraer to extract, 9; to take (pull) out, 9
extremidad (*f.*) limb, 20
eyacular to ejaculate, 7

F

fácil easy, 7
falange (*m.*) phalange
falda (*f.*) skirt
falta (*f.*) lack, L1
faltarle algo a uno to be lacking something, 20
familia (*f.*) family, 7
familiar family (*adj.*), 7
farfallotas (*f. pl.*) mumps (*Puerto Rico*), 5
farmacia (*f.*) pharmacy, 3
fatiga (*f.*) fatigue, 8
favor (*m.*) favor, 11
— **de** please, 18
fecha (*f.*) date, 18
— **de nacimiento** date of birth, 1
fémur (*m.*) femur
fértil fertile, 7
feto (*m.*) fetus
fibra (*f.*) fiber, 6
fíbula (*f.*) fibula
fiebre (*f.*) fever, 3
— **del heno** hay fever, 5
— **escarlatina** scarlet fever, 5
— **reumática** rheumatic fever, 5
fielmente faithfully, 17
final (*m.*) end
finalmente finally, 15
firma (*f.*) signature, 1
firmar to sign
— **la autorización** sign the authorization, 2
físico(a) physical, 8
flato (*m.*) intestinal gas
flema (*f.*) phlegm, 8
flujo (*m.*) discharge, 15
fluoruro (*m.*) fluoride, 9
fluoroscopía (*f.*) fluoroscopy, 14
folleto (*m.*) brochure, 7; pamphlet, 7
fórceps (*m. sing., pl.*) forceps, 11
forma (*f.*) form (*Méx.*), 1; way
fórmula (*f.*) formula
fósforo (*m.*) match, 19
fotocopia (*f.*) photocopy, 1
fractura (*f.*) fracture, 10
fracturar(se) to break, 10; to fracture, 10
frasco (*m.*) bottle, 10

frazada (*f.*) blanket, 2
frecuencia (*f.*) frequency
  con — frequently, 4
frecuente frequent, 12
freír to fry, 6
frenos (*m. pl.*) dental braces, 9
frente (*f.*) forehead, 10
fresa (*f.*) strawberry, 6
fricción (*f.*) rub, 13; rubbing, 13; massage, 13
frijoles (*m. pl.*) beans, 6
frío(a) cold, 2
fruta (*f.*) fruit, 2
fuente(*f.*) source
  — de agua water bag, 11
fuera outside
  — de lo común out of the ordinary, 8
  — del alcance out of reach
  por — on the outside, 7
fuerte strong
fumar to smoke, 2

G

gafas (*f. pl.*) glasses, 2
galletica (*f.*) cookie
galletita (*f.*) cookie, L2
ganglio linfático (*m.*) lymph gland
garganta (*f.*) throat, 1
garrotillo (*m.*) croup, 5
gas (*m.*) gas, 8
gasa (*f.*) gauze, 9
gastritis (*f.*) gastritis, 5
gatear to crawl, 19
gemelos(as) (*m., f. pl.*) twins
general general, 8
generalmente generally, 6
genitales (*m. pl.*) genitals, 14
gente (*f.*) people
geriatra (*m., f.*) geriatrician, geriatrist, 4
ginecología (*f.*) gynecology
ginecólogo(a) (*m., f.*) gynecologist, PI
glande (*m.*) glans
glándula (*f.*) gland
glaucoma (*m.*) glaucoma, 12
globo (*m.*) balloon (*drug dosage*), 18
glúteos (*m. pl.*) buttocks
golpear(se) to hit (oneself), 10
gonorrea (*f.*) gonorrhea, 15
gordo(a) fat, 6
gordura (*f.*) obesity, 6
gorro (*m.*) bonnet, 19; cap, 19
gota (*f.*) drop, 5
gotero (*m.*) eyedropper
gracias thank you, PI
grado (*m.*) degree, 3
grande big, 4; large
grano (*m.*) pimple, 12
grasa (*f.*) fat, 6
grasiento(a) oily
gratis free (*of charge*)
grave serious, 3
gripe (*f.*) influenza, 5
grupo (*m.*) group, 6
guardado(a) put away, 13
guardar to put away, 13; to keep, 13
guía (*f.*) guide
gustar to like, 13; to be pleasing to, 13
gusto (*m.*) pleasure

H

habichuelas (*f. pl.*) beans (*Puerto Rico*), 6
habitación (*f.*) room, 11
hablar to speak, 1
hace como... about..., 18
hacer to do, 5; to make, 5
  — caca to have a bowel movement (*col.*)
  — daño to hurt, 18
  — ejercicio to exercise, 6
  — gárgaras to gargle
  — preguntas to ask questions, 19
  — un análisis to run a test, 8
  — un examen to give a checkup, 8
  — una prueba to run a test, 8
hacia toward
  — adelante forward, 8
  — atrás backward, 8
hachich (hashís) (*m.*) hashish
hágame el favor de... (+ *inf.*) Please (+ command), 2
hambre: tener — to be hungry, 5
hamburguesa (*f.*) hamburger, 6
harina (*f.*) flour, 6
hasta until, 8; till 8
  — luego. See you later., PI
  — mañana. See you tomorrow., PI
hay there is, PII; there are, PII
hemorragia (*f.*) hemorrhage, 13.
  — cerebral stroke, 16
hemorroide (*f.*) hemorroid, 17
hepatitis (*f.*) hepatitis, 18
hereditario(a) hereditary, 16
herida (*f.*) wound, 9; injury, 9
herido(a) (*m., f.*) injured person, 10
hermanastro(a) (*m., f.*) stepbrother; stepsister
hermano(a) (*m., f.*) brother, 18; sister, 18
heroína (*f.*) heroin
herpes (*m. sing.*) herpes, 15
hervir (i:ie) to boil, 6
hidropesía (*f.*) dropsy, 8
hielo (*m.*) ice, 9
hierro (*m.*) iron, 3
hígado (*m.*) liver, 6
higienista (*m., f.*) hygienist, 9
hijastro(a) (*m., f.*) stepchild
hijo(a) (*m., f.*) son, 3; daughter, 3
hilo dental (*m.*) dental floss, 9
hinchado(a) swollen, 4
hinchazón (*m.*) swelling, 4
hiperopía (*f.*) farsightedness
hipertensión (*f.*) hypertension, PI; high blood pressure, PI
hirviendo boiling, 10
histerectomía (*f.*) hysterectomy
historia clínica (*f.*) medical history, 1
hoja clínica (*f.*) medical history, 1
hola hi, PI
hombre (*m.*) man, 15
hombro (*m.*) shoulder, 1
hondo deep (*adv.*), 8; deep (*adj.*), 19
hongo (*m.*) fungus
hora (*f.*) hour, 3
  — de visita visiting hour, 13
  pedir (e:i) — to make an appointment, 5
horario (*m.*) hours, schedule
hormigueo (*m.*) pins and needles, tingling, 8
horno (*m.*) oven, 19
hospital (*m.*) hospital
hoy today, 2
hueco (*m.*) hole, 19
hueso (*m.*) bone, 8
  — ilíaco ilium
huevo (*m.*) egg, 6
humano(a) human
húmero (*m.*) humerus
humo (*m.*) smoke, L1

I

implante (*m.*) implant, 7
importancia (*f.*) importance, 12
importante important, 5
impotencia (*f.*) impotence, 7
incapacidad (*f.*) disability, 18
incendio (*m.*) fire
incisivo (*m.*) incisor, 9
incubación (*f.*) incubation
incubadora (*f.*) incubator
indicar to indicate, 15
infarto (*m.*) heart attack, 18
infección (*f.*) infection, 5
  — de la garganta tonsilitis
infeccioso(a) infectious
inflamación (*f.*) inflamation
  — del intestino grueso colitis, 5
inflamado(a) swollen, 4
inflamatorio(a) inflammatory
información (*f.*) information, 1
informe (*m.*) report
ingle (*f.*) groin
ingresar to admit (*to a hospital*), 2
inodoro (*m.*) toilet, 14
insecticida (*m.*) insecticide, 19
inseminación artificial (*f.*) artificial insemination, 7
insertar to insert, 7
insolación (*f.*) sunstroke, 5
insomnio (*m.*) insomnia, PI
insoportable unbearable, 9
instrucción (*f.*) instruction, 17
insulina (*f.*) insulin, 17
internar to be admitted (*to a hospital*)
internista (*m., f.*) general practitioner, 4; internist, 4
interno(a) internal
intestino (*m.*) gut, intestine
  — delgado small intestine
  — grueso large intestine, 17
intoxicación (*f.*) intoxication, 5
investigador(a) (*m., f.*) investigator, 15
inyección (*f.*) injection, 7, shot, 7
  — antitetánica tetanus shot, 10
  — contra el tétano tetanus shot, 3

inyectar(se) to inject (oneself), 17
ipecacuana (*f.*) ipecac, 19
ir to go, 3
— **al baño** to go to the bathroom, 2
irritación (*f.*) irritation
irritado(a) irritated, 5
irse to leave, 14; to go away, 14
izquierdo(a) left, 12

J

jabón (*m.*) soap, 12
jalea (*f.*) jelly, 7
jaqueca(s) (*f.*) migraine, 5
jarabe (*m.*) syrup
— **para la tos** cough syrup, 2
jeringa (hipodérmica) (*f.*) hypodermic syringe
jeringuilla (*f.*) hypodermic syringe, 18
jimaguas (*m., f. pl.*) twins (*Cuba*)
joven young, 7
joyas (*f. pl.*) jewelry, 13
juanete (*m.*) bunion
jugo (*m.*) juice, 2
— **de china** orange juice (*Puerto Rico*), 2
— **de naranja** orange juice, 2
junto(a) together, 5

L

labio (*m.*) lip
laboratorio (*m.*) laboratory, 3
lado (*m.*) side, 12
al — de at the side of
ladrón(-ona) (*m., f.*) burglar
laparoscopia (*f.*) laparoscopy
laringitis (*f.*) laryngitis, 5
lastimar(se) to hurt (oneself), 11
latido (*m.*) heartbeat
latir to beat (*heart*), 20
lavado (*m.*) washing
— **intestinal** enema
hacer un — de estómago to pump the stomach, 10
lavativa (*f.*) enema
laxante (*m.*) laxative, 17
leche (*f.*) milk, 2
— **descremada** skim milk, 6
leer to read, 2
legumbre (*f.*) vegetable
lejía (*f.*) bleach, 19
lejos (de) far away, 12
lengua (*f.*) tongue, 13
lentamente slowly, 8
lentes (*m. pl.*) glasses, 2
— **de contacto** contact lenses, 2
leño (*m.*) joint (*col.*)
lesión (*f.*) lesion, 15
letra (*f.*) handwriting, 1; letter, 1
— **de imprenta** print, printed letter, 1
— **de molde** print, printed letter, 1
leucemia (*f.*) leukemia, 5
levantar(se) to lift, 13; to raise, 13; to get up
al — first thing in the morning, 3
libra (*f.*) pound, 1
licencia para conducir (*f.*) driver's license, 1
ligadura (*f.*) tourniquet, 14
ligar to tie, 12
— **los tubos** to tie the tubes, 7
ligero(a) light
limitación (*f.*) limitation, 18
limpiar to clean, 5
limpieza (*f.*) cleaning
línea (*f.*) line, 12
linimento (*m.*) liniment
líquido (*m.*) liquid, 3
lista (*f.*) list, 6
listo(a) ready, 14
llaga (*f.*) sore, 15; wound, 8
llamado(a) called
llamar to call, 1
llamarse to be named, 11
llegar to arrive, 10
llenar to fill out, 1
lleno(a) de gases bloated, 3
llevar to take (someone or something somewhere), 3; to carry
— **a cabo** to carry out
llorar to cry
lo it, him, you (*form.*)
— **más pronto posible** as soon as possible, 16
— **mejor** the best (thing), 5
— **mismo** the same (thing), 8
— **que** that which, 10
— **siento** I'm sorry, PII
local local, 9
loción (*f.*) lotion, 12
— **para bebé** baby lotion
locura (*f.*) insanity
lonche (*m.*) lunch (*col. Méx.*), 13
los (las) dos both, 3; the two of them, 3
lubricar to lubricate, 7
luego then, 1
lugar (*m.*) place, 18
— **donde trabaja** place of employment, 1
lunar (*m.*) mole
luz (*f.*) light, 12

M

macarrones (*m.*) macaroni, 6
madrastra (*f.*) stepmother
madre (*f.*) mother, 2
mal de ojo (*m.*) evil eye
malaria (*f.*) malaria, 8
malestar (*m.*) discomfort, malaise, 8
maligno(a) malignant, 12
malo(a) bad, 4
malparto (*m.*) miscarriage, 4
mamá (*f.*) mother, mom, 2
mamadera (*f.*) baby bottle, 11
mamar: dar de — to nurse, 11
mamila (*f.*) baby bottle (*Méx.*), 11
mamografía (*f.*) mammogram, 12
mamograma mammogram, PII
mancha en la piel (*f.*) birthmark
mandíbula (*f.*) jawbone
manga (*f.*) sleeve, 14
manifestarse (e:ie) to manifest
mano (*f.*) hand, 1
manta (*f.*) blanket, 2
manteca (*f.*) heroin (*col. Caribe*)
mantener to keep
mantequilla (*f.*) butter, 2
— **de cacahuate** peanut butter, 6
— **de maní** peanut butter, 6
manzana (*f.*) apple, 2
mañana (*f.*) tomorrow, 1; morning, 4
maquillaje (*m.*) makeup, 19
máquina (*f.*) car (*Cuba*), 10
marcapasos (*m. sing.*) pacemaker, 20
mareo (*m.*) dizziness, 4
margarina (*f.*) margarine, 6
marido (*m.*) husband, 1
mariguana (marihuana) (*f.*) marijuana, 18
más more, 4; else, 16; most
— **adelante** later on, 5
— **o menos** more or less, 8
más tarde later, 6
masa (*f.*) mass, 12
matar to kill
matarse to kill oneself, commit suicide
materia fecal (*f.*) stool, feces, 1
matriz (*f.*) womb
mayor major, 12; older, 16
mayoría (*f.*) majority, 12
mechón (*m.*) patch
medias (*f.*) stockings, 17; hose, 17
— **elásticas** support stockings, 17
medicina (*f.*) medicine, 2
medicinal medicinal, 12; medicated, 12
médico(a) (*adj.*) medical, 1; (*m., f.*) doctor, 1; M.D., PII
medio(a) half, 16
en el — in the middle
medir (e:i) to measure, 7; to be... tall
mejilla (*f.*) cheek
mejor better, 7; best, 7
mejorar to make better, 20; to improve, 20
melocotón (*m.*) peach, 2
melón (*m.*) melon, 6
mellizos(as) (*m., f. pl.*) twins
meningitis (*f.*) meningitis, 5
menor minor, 12
menos less, 8
por lo — at least
menstruación (*f.*) menstruation, 4
mental mental, 18
mentón (*m.*) chin
mes (*m.*) month, 4
mesa (*f.*) table, 14
metadona (*f.*) methadone
metatarso (*m.*) metatarsus
método (*m.*) method, 7
miel (*f.*) honey, L2
miembro (*m.*) member; penis
mientras tanto in the meantime, 4
migraña (*f.*) migraine, 5
mineral (*m.*) mineral, 5
minuto (*m.*) minute, 9
mío(a) mine, 9
miope nearsighted

miopía (*f.*) nearsightedness
mirar to look at, 1
mismo(a) same
mitad (*f.*) half, 6
moho (*m.*) mold, L1
molar (*m.*) molar, 9
molestar to bother, 8
molestia (*f.*) trouble, 7; discomfort, 7
momento (*m.*) moment, 15
moneda (*f.*) coin, 19
monga (*f.*) influenza (*col. Puerto Rico*)
monitorizado(a) monitored
morado (*m.*) bruise, 13
morder (o:ue) to bite, 9
moretón (*m.*) bruise, 13
morfina (*f.*) morphine
morir (o:ue) to die, 20
mover(se) (o:ue) to move, 14
 — el vientre to have a bowel movement, 11
muchacho(a) (*m., f.*) young man, 18; boy, 18; young woman, 18; girl, 18
mucho much, 2; a lot, 2
 muchas gracias thank you very much, PI
 muchas veces (*f.*) many times, 16
mucosas (*f.*) mucous membranes
mueble (*m.*) piece of furniture, 19
muela (*f.*) tooth, 9; molar, 9
 — del juicio wisdom tooth, 9
muerte (*f.*) death
muestra (*f.*) sample, 2; specimen, 2
 — de excremento stool specimen, 2
 — de heces fecales stool specimen, 2
 — de orina urine sample (specimen), 2
mujer (*f.*) wife, 1; woman, 7
mujercita (*f.*) female (girl) (*col. Méx.*), 6
muleta (*f.*) crutch, 10
muñeca (*f.*) wrist, 1
músculo (*m.*) muscle
muslo (*m.*) thigh
muy very
 — amable very kind (of you), 13

N

nacer to be born, 11
nacimiento (*m.*) birth
nada nothing, 8
 de — you're welcome, P
nadie nobody, 15; no one, 15
nalgas (*f. pl.*) buttocks, 5
naranja (*f.*) orange, 6
nariz (*f.*) nose
natalidad (*f.*) birth, 7
náusea (*f.*) nausea, 1
necesariamente necessarily, 7
necesario(a) necessary, 5
necesitar to need, 1
¿Necesita ayuda? Do you need help?, PII
Necesito hablar... I need to speak..., PI
negativo(a) negative, 8
negro(a) black, 17
nervio (*m.*) nerve
nervioso(a) nervous, 16
neurología (*f.*) neurology
neurológico(a) neurological
neurólogo(a) (*m., f.*) neurologist
ni neither, 4
nieto(a) (*m., f.*) grandson; granddaughter
ninguno(a) not a one, 4; none, 4
niño(a) (*m., f.*) child, 2; boy (girl), 2
nitroglicerina (*f.*) nitroglycerin
nivel (*m.*) level, L1
noche (*f.*) night
nombre (*m.*) name, PI; noun
normal normal, 8
normalmente normally, 11
notar to notice, 17
novocaína (*f.*) novocaine, 9
nuca (*f.*) nape
nudillo (*m.*) knuckle
nuera (*f.*) daughter-in-law
nuevo(a) new
número (*m.*) number, PI
 — de teléfono phone number, PI
nunca never, 6

O

o or, PI
obesidad (*f.*) obesity, 6
objeto (*m.*) object, 19
obrar to have a bowel movement, 11
obstetra (*m., f.*) obstetrician, 4
obstruido(a) clogged
oculista (*m., f.*) oculist, 4; ophthalmologist, 12; optometrist, 12
ocupación (*f.*) occupation, 1
ocurrir to happen, 16; to occur, 16
odontólogo(a) (*m., f.*) odontologist; dental surgeon; dentist, 9
oficina (*f.*) office, 3
 — de admisión (*f.*) admissions office, 2
oftalmología (*f.*) opthalmology, PI
oftalmólogo(a) (*m., f.*) ophthalmologist, PI
oído (*m.*) (inner, internal) ear, 1
oír to hear, 17
ojalá I hope, 17; if only, 17
ojo (*m.*) eye
olor (*m.*) odor, 15
olvidarse (de) to forget, 9
ombligo (*m.*) navel
omóplato (*m.*) scapula
oncólogo(a) (*m., f.*) oncologist, 4
operación (*f.*) operation, PII; surgery, PII
 — de corazón abierto open heart surgery
operar to operate, 12
opio (*m.*) opium
opresión (*f.*) tightness, 20
orden (*f.*) order, 3; referral, 3
ordenar to order, 14
oreja (*f.*) (external) ear
órgano (*m.*) organ
orina (*f.*) urine, 1
orinar to urinate, 2
ortodoncia (*f.*) orthodontia, 9
ortodoncista (*m., f.*) orthodontist, 9
ortopeda (*m., f.*) orthopedist
ortopedia (*f.*) orthopedics, PI
ortopedista (*m., f.*) orthopedist, PI
orzuelo (*m.*) sty, 5
oscuridad (*f.*) dark, darkness
otorrinolaringólogo(a) (*m., f.*) ear, nose, and throat specialist, 4
otro(a) other, 2; another, 2
otra vez again, 8
ovario (*m.*) ovary
ovulación (*f.*) ovulation, 7
óvulo (*m.*) ovum, 7
oxígeno (*m.*) oxygen

P

paciente (*m., f.*) patient
 — externo outpatient
padecer to suffer, 6
 — del corazón to have heart trouble, 6
padrastro (*m.*) stepfather
padre (*m.*) father, 6
padres (*m. pl.*) parents
pagar to pay, 1
pago (*m.*) payment
país (*m.*) country
palabra (*f.*) word
paladar (*m.*) palate
pálido(a) pale, 3
palpitación (*f.*) palpitation, 16
pan (*m.*) bread, 2
 — tostado toast, 2
pantalones (*m. pl.*) pants
pantimedias (*f. pl.*) pantyhose
pantorilla (*f.*) calf
pañal (*m.*) diaper
 — desechable disposable diaper
pañuelo de papel (*m.*) tissue
papa (*f.*) potato
papá (*m.*) father, 6; dad
papanicolau: examen de — (*m.*) Pap test (smear), PII
papas fritas (*f.*) French fries, 6
papel (*m.*) paper
paperas (*f.*) mumps, 5
papiloma (*m.*) papilloma
par (*m.*) pair, 17; couple
para for, 1; in order to, 3
 ¿— qué...? for what...?, 5
parabrisas (*m. sing.*) windshield
parálisis (*f.*) paralysis, 16
paralítico(a) paralyzed, 16
paramédico(a) (*m., f.*) paramedic, 19
pararse to stand up, 14
parcial partial, 16
parecer to seem, 8; to look
pared (*f.*) wall, 12
pareja (*f.*) pair, couple
pariente (*m., f.*) relative, 20
 — cercano(a) close relative, 20
parir to give birth
párpado (*m.*) eyelid
parte (*f.*) part, 7
 partes privadas (*f. pl.*) private parts, 14

partera (*f.*) midwife
parto (*m.*) delivery, 11; childbirth, 11
  dolor de — (*m.*) labor pain, 11
  estar de — to be in labor
  sala de — (*f.*) delivery room, 11
pasado(a) last, 12
pasar to happen, 10
pasársele a uno to pass, 17
Pase. Come in., PI
pasillo (*m.*) hallway, 14
pasta (*f.*) pasta, 6
  — de dientes toothpaste, 9
  — dentífrica toothpaste, 9
pastel (*m.*) pie; cake, L2
pastilla (*f.*) pill, 2
  — para el dolor painkiller, 2
pasto (*m.*) marijuana (*col.*), 18
pato (*m.*) bedpan, 2
PCP (*f.*) angel dust
pecho (*m.*) breast, 4; chest, 1
  dar el — to nurse, 11
pediatra (*m., f.*) pediatrician, PI
pediatría (*f.*) pediatrics, PI
pedir (e:i) to ask for; to request, 7
  — hora to make an appointment, 5
  — turno to make an appointment, 5
pegar un tiro to shoot
peligroso(a) dangerous, 6
pelo (*m.*) hair
pelvis (*f.*) pelvis
pene (*m.*) penis, 8
penicilina (*f.*) penicillin, 3
pensar (e:ie) to think (about), 7; to plan, 11
peor worse, 16; worst, 16
pequeño(a) small, 6; little, 6
pera (*f.*) pear, 2
perder (e:ie) to lose
  — el conocimiento to lose consciousness, 10
  — peso to lose weight, 6
pérdida (*f.*) loss
perfil (*m.*) side
perfume (*m.*) perfume, 3
perico (*m.*) cocaine (*col.*)
periodo (*m.*) menstruation, 4; period
permanente permanent
pero but, 3
peroné (*m.*) fibula
perro(a) (*m., f.*) dog
persona (*f.*) person, 12
personal (*m.*) personnel
pesa a la paciente weighs the patient, 1
pesado(a) heavy, 4
pesar to weigh, 1
pescado (*m.*) fish, 6
pescuezo (*m.*) neck
peso (*m.*) weight, 6
pestañas (*f. pl.*) eyelashes
pezón (*m.*) nipple
picado(a) decayed, 9; carious, 9
picadura (*f.*) cavity, 9; bite
picante spicy, 6
picazón (*f.*) itching, 8
pie (*m.*) foot, 1
piedra (*f.*) stone, 17; crack (*col.*)
piel (*f.*) skin, 5
pierna (*f.*) leg, 1
pijama (*m.*) pyjamas
píldora (*f.*) pill
pimiento (*m.*) pepper, 6
pintura (*f.*) paint, 19
pinzas (*f. pl.*) tweezers, 19
piña (*f.*) pineapple, 2
piorrea (*f.*) pyorrhea, 9
piscina (*f.*) swimming pool, 19
piso (*m.*) floor; story
pito (*m.*) marijuana (*col.*), 18
placa (*f.*) plaque, 9
placenta (*f.*) placenta, 11
plancha (*f.*) iron, 19
planificación (*f.*) planning, 7
planilla (*f.*) form, 1
  — de admisión (*f.*) admissions form, 2
planta del pie (*f.*) sole of the foot
plástico (*m.*) plastic, 19
pleuresía (*f.*) pleurisy
pneumonía (*f.*) pneumonia, 5
pobre poor
pobrecito(a) (*m., f.*) poor little thing (one), 3
poco(a) little (*ref. to quantity*), 3
  poco a poco little by little, 14
  un poco a little, 8
pocos(as) few, 6
poder (o:ue) to be able to, 6; can, 6
podiatra (*m., f.*) podiatrist, 4
polen (*m.*) pollen, 3
policía (*m., f.*) police; policeman; policewoman
poliomielitis (*f.*) polio(myelitis), 5
póliza (*f.*) policy, 1
pollo (*m.*) chicken, 2
polvo (*m.*) dust; cocaine (*col.*)
  — de ángel angel dust
pomada (*f.*) ointment, 5
pomo (*m.*) bottle (*Cuba*), 10
poner(se) to put; to put on; to turn, L1
  poner una inyección to give a shot, 7
  ponerse tenso(a) to tense up, 11
por through, 8; for, 10
  — ciento percent
  ¿ — cuánto tiempo...? for how long...?, 10
  — ejemplo for example, 16
  — eso that's why, 6; for that reason, 6
  — favor please, PI
  — fin finally, 15
  — la boca through the mouth, 8
  — lo menos at least, 6
  — mes a month, per month, 7
  — mí for me, 18; on my behalf, 18
  ¿ — qué? why?, 4
  — supuesto of course, 16
  — unos segundos for a few seconds, 10
  — vía bucal orally, 7
  — vía oral orally, 7
porción (*f.*) portion, serving, 6
poro (*m.*) pore
porque because, 4
porro (*m.*) joint (*col.*)
  — mortal killer joint
positivo(a) positive, 8
posterior rear
postizo(a) false, 2
postnatal postnatal
postre (*m.*) dessert, 2
practicar to practice
precaución (*f.*) precaution, 5
preferir (e:ie) to prefer, 5
pregunta (*f.*) question, 6
preguntar to ask (a question), 13
prematuro(a) premature
prenatal prenatal
prendas (*f. pl.*) clothing
prender to react
preñada pregnant (*col.*)
preocupado(a) worried, 6
preocupar(se) por to worry about, 10
preparar to prepare, 6
présbite farsighted
presión (*f.*) pressure, 8; blood pressure, 8
  — arterial blood pressure, 8
presupuesto (*m.*) budget
primario(a) primary
primero(a) first (one), 5
primeros auxilios (*m. pl.*) first aid, 19
primo(a) (*m., f.*) cousin
principio (*m.*) principle
privado(a) private
probablemente probably, 16
probar (o:ue) to try, 7
probeta (*f.*) test tube
  bebé de — (*m.*) test-tube baby
problema (*m.*) problem, 3
profundo(a) deep, 19
programa (*m.*) program, 18
promedio (*m.*) average
pronto soon, 10
  tan — como as soon as, 19
propio(a) itself
proporcionar to provide
próstata (*f.*) prostate gland
prostatitis (*f.*) prostatitis
proteger to protect
proteína (*f.*) protein, 3
próximo(a) next, 5; (*m., f.*) next one, 12
  la próxima vez next time, 5
prueba (*f.*) test, 5
psiquiatra (*m., f.*) psychiatrist, 4
psiquiátrico(a) psychiatric, 18
publicar to publish
público(a) public, 15
puente (*m.*) bridge, 9
  — coronario (heart) bypass
puerta (*f.*) door
pues well, 10
pujar to push (*during labor*), 11
pulgada (*f.*) inch, 1
pullar to shoot up (*col. Caribe*)
pulmón (*m.*) lung, 2
pulmonía (*f.*) pneumonia, 5
pulmonólogo(a) (*m., f.*) pulmonologist
pulpa (*f.*) pulp
pulso (*m.*) pulse, 8
puntada (*f.*) stitch, 10
punto (*m.*) stitch, 10; dot, 12
punzada (*f.*) sharp pain

punzante sharp, 20; stabbing, 20
pupila (*f.*) pupil
purgante (*m.*) purgative, 17; cathartic, 17
pus (*m.*) pus, 5

Q

que that, 3
¿qué? what?, 2
¿— más? What else?, 16
¿— tal? How about...?, 3; How is (are) ...?, 3
quebrarse (e:ie) to break (*Méx.*), 10; to fracture (*Méx.*), 10
quedar(se) to remain, 11; to stay, 11
  — sordo(a) to go deaf, 17
quemadura (*f.*) burn, 10
quemar(se) to burn (oneself), 10
querer (e:ie) to want, 5; to wish, 5
queso (*m.*) cheese, 6
¿quién? who?, 1
quieto(a) still
quijada (*f.*) jaw
quimioterapia (*f.*) chemotherapy
quirúrgico(a) surgical
quiste (*m.*) cyst, 12
quitar(se) to take out, 12; to remove, 12
  — la ropa to take off one's clothes, 14
quizá(s) perhaps, 3; maybe, 3

R

rabadilla (*f.*) coccyx
radio (*m.*) radius
radiografía (*f.*) X-ray, PII
radiología (*f.*) radiology
radiólogo(a) (*m., f.*) radiologist
raíz (*f.*) root
rápidamente rapidly, 20
raquídea (*f.*) spinal anesthesia
raro(a) rare
rasguño (*m.*) scratch, 19
rasurar(se) to shave
rato (*m.*) while, 11
rayos equis (*m. pl.*) X-rays
reanimación (*f.*) revival
rebajar to lose weight, 6
recepcionista (*m., f.*) receptionist, 1
receta (*f.*) prescription, 3
recetar to prescribe, 5
recibir to receive, 18
recién new
  — casado(a) (*m., f.*) newlywed, 7
  — nacido(a) (*m., f.*) newborn
recomendar (e:ie) to recommend, 16
reconocer to examine, 4; to recognize
recto (*m.*) rectum, 14
recuperación (*f.*) recovery
recuperarse to recover
refresco (*m.*) soft drink, 6; soda pop, 6
regalo (*m.*) present; gift
regla (*f.*) menstruation, 4
regresar to return, 1
regularmente regularly, 17
relaciones sexuales (*f. pl.*) sexual relations, 4
  tener — to have sex, 4
relajarse to relax (oneself), 11
reloj (*m.*) watch, 13
remangarse to roll up one's sleeves, 14
remedio (*m.*) medicine, 3
repollo (*m.*) cabbage, 6
reproductivo(a) reproductive
resfriado (*m.*) cold, 3
resfrío (*m.*) cold, 3
resollar to breathe; 8
resolver (o:ue) to solve, 16
respiración (*f.*) breath
respirar to breathe, 8
  Respire hondo. Take a deep breath., 8; Breathe deeply., 8
respiratorio(a) respiratory
resto (*m.*) rest, 16; remainder, 16
resultado (*m.*) result, 8
  dar — to work, 12; to produce results, 12
resumen (*m.*) summary, 18
retención (*f.*) retention
retina (*f.*) retina
reumatismo (*m.*) rheumatism, 5
revisar to check, 5
revestir (e:i) to line
riesgo (*m.*) risk
riñón (*m.*) kidney, 16
ritmo (*m.*) rhythm, 7
roca (*f.*) crack (*col.*)
rodilla (*f.*) knee, 1
rojo(a) red, 6
romper(se) to break, 10; to fracture, 10
  — la fuente to break water (*childbirth*)
ronco(a) hoarse, 8
roncha (*f.*) hives, 8
ronquera (*f.*) hoarseness
ropa (*f.*) clothes, 13
  — interior underwear
rótula (*f.*) patella
rubéola (*f.*) rubella, 5
ruído (*m.*) noise, 8; ringing (*ear*), 8

S

sábana (*f.*) sheet
saber to know, 7
sacar to pull out, 9; to take out, 9; to extract, 9; to stick out, 17
  — una fotocopia to make a photocopy, 1
sal (*f.*) salt, 6
sala (*f.*) ward, PII; room, PII
  — de bebés nursery, 11
  — de cirugía operating room
  — de emergencia emergency room, PII
  — de espera waiting room, 3
  — de maternidad maternity ward
  — de parto delivery room, 11
  — de rayos X X-ray room, 10
  — de recuperación recovery room
  — de terapia física physical therapy room
  — de urgencia emergency room, PII
salir to leave, 9; to go out, 9
  — bien to turn out okay, 14
salirle un líquido a uno to have a discharge, 15
saliva (*f.*) saliva
salpullido (*m.*) rash, 5
salud (*f.*) health, 15
saludable healthy
saludo (*m.*) greeting
salvar to save, 9
sangrar to bleed, 8
sangre (*f.*) blood, 1
sano(a) healthy, 8
sarampión (*m.*) measles, 5
sarna (*f.*) scabies, 5
sarpullido (*m.*) rash, 5
sarro (*m.*) tartar, 9
seco(a) dry, 8
secreción (*f.*) secretion
secundario(a) secondary
  efecto secundario (*m.*) side effect
sed (*f.*) thirst, 8
seda dental (*f.*) dental floss, 9
sedativo (*m.*) tranquilizer, 2
seguida: en — right away
seguir (e:i) to continue, 7; to follow, 7
  — una dieta to go on a diet, 6
según according to
segundo (*m.*) second, 10
segundo(a) second, 14
  segundo nombre (*m.*) middle name, 1
seguro (*m.*) insurance, 1
  — social Social Security, 1
seguro(a) sure, 4; safe, 19
semana (*f.*) week, 5
  — entrante next week, 5
  — próxima next week, 5
  — que viene next week, 5
semen (*m.*) semen, 7
semiduro(a) medium hard, 9
seno (*m.*) breast, 4
sentado(a) sitting
sentar(se) (e:ie) to sit (down), 9
sentidos (*m. pl.*) senses
sentir(se) (e:ie) to feel, 8
señal (*f.*) sign; warning
señalar to indicate
señor (*m.*) Mr., PI sir, PI; gentleman, PI
señora (*f.*) Mrs., PI; lady, PI; Ma'am, PI; madam, PI
señorita (*f.*) Miss, PI; young lady, PI
separado(a) separated, 1
separar to separate, 8
ser to be, PII
  — querido (*m.*) loved one
serio(a) serious, 3
servicio (*m.*) bathroom, 2
servir (e:i) to serve, 7
severo(a) severe
sexo (*m.*) sex, 1
si if, 3
sicosis (*f.*) psychosis
SIDA (Síndrome de inmunodeficiencia a dquirida) (*m.*) AIDS, 15

siempre always, 1
sien (*f.*) temple
sífilis (*f.*) syphilis, 15
sifilítico(a) syphilis (*adj.*)
siguiente following, 12; next, 12
silla de ruedas (*f.*) wheelchair
sillita alta (*f.*) high chair
similar similar, 14
simple simple, 9
sin without, 6
— **falta** without fail, 15
— **sal** salt free, 6
síntoma (*m.*) symptom, 4
siquiatría (*f.*) psychiatry
situación (*f.*) situation
sobre about, 1; on
— **todo** above all, 6
sobredosis (*f.*) overdose
sobrino(a) (*m., f.*) nephew; niece
social social, 1
sodio (*m.*) sodium, 16
sofocar(se) to suffocate (oneself), 19
sol (*m.*) sun, 19; monetary unit of Peru
solamente only, 2
solo(a) alone, 19
sólo only, 2
soltero(a) single, PI
sonograma (*m.*) sonogram
sopa (*f.*) soup, 2
soplo cardíaco (*m.*) (heart) murmur
sordera (*f.*) deafness
sordo(a) deaf, 17; dull (*pain*), 20
soriasis (*m.*) psoriasis
sospechar to suspect, 15
subir to lift, 13; to go up, 13
— **de peso** to gain weight, 8
subirse la manga to roll up one's sleeve, 14
suceder to happen
sudor (*m.*) sweat, 20
suegro(a) (*m., f.*) father-in-law; mother-in-law
suero (*m.*) I.V. (serum), 13
suerte (*f.*) luck, 7
suficiente enough, 9; sufficient, 9
sufrir to suffer, 3
— **del corazón** to have heart trouble, 6
sugerencia (*f.*) suggestion
sugerir (e:ie) to suggest, 16
suicidarse to commit suicide
sulfa (*f.*) sulfa, 3
supositorio (*m.*) suppository
supuración (*f.*) pus, 5
susto (*m.*) fright
suyo(a) yours (*form.*), his, her, 9

T

tabaco (*m.*) tobacco, 16
tableta (*f.*) tablet, 2
tal vez perhaps, 20
talco para bebé (*m.*) baby powder
talón (*m.*) heel
tamaño (*m.*) size, 7
también also, 2
tampoco either, 7; neither 7
tanto(a) so much, 2
tapado(a) constipated, 3
tapar to cover, 14
taquicardia (*f.*) tachycardia
tarde (*f.*) afternoon, 11; (*adv.*) late
más — later, 6
tarjeta (*f.*) card, 1
— **de seguro médico** medical insurance card, 1
tarso (*m.*) tarsus
taza (*f.*) cup, 2
técnico(a) (*m., f.*) technician, 14
tejido (*m.*) tissue
— **graso** fatty tissue, 4
tela (*f.*) cloth
teléfono (*m.*) phone, 19
temblor (*m.*) tremor, 20; shaking, 20
temer to be afraid, 17; to fear, 17
temperatura (*f.*) temperature, 3
la — pasa de... the temperature is over... 3
— **del cuerpo** body temperature, 8
tendencia (*f.*) tendency, 8
tener to have, 4
— **a mano** to keep at hand
— **... años** to be ... years old, 6
— **cuidado** to be careful, 6
— **dolor** to be in pain, 4
— **dolor de espalda** to have a backache, 4
— **en cuenta** to keep in mind, L2
— **familia** to have children, 7
— **hambre** to be hungry, 5
— **mal olor (peste)** to have a bad odor, 15
— **miedo** to be afraid, 19
— **que** (+ *inf.*) to have to (do something), 4
— **relaciones sexuales** to have sex, 4
— **razón** to be right, 4
— **sueño** to be sleepy, 4
— **un flujo** to have a discharge, 15
no — importancia to not matter, 12
tensión (*f.*) blood pressure, 8; tension
terapia (*f.*) therapy
tercero(a) third, 10
terminar to finish, 14; to be done, 14
termómetro (*m.*) thermometer, 13
terrible terrible, 10
testículo (*m.*) testicle
tétano(s) (*m.*) tetanus, 5
tete (*m.*) pacifier (*Cuba*)
tía (*f.*) aunt, 20
tibia (*f.*) tibia
tibio(a) lukewarm, 9; tepid, 9
tiempo (*m.*) time
tienda (*f.*) store; shop
tijeras (*f. pl.*) scissors, 19
tímpano (*m.*) eardrum
tinte (*m.*) dye, 19
tintura de yodo (*f.*) iodine
tío (*m.*) uncle, 20
tiroides (*m. sing.*) thyroid, 14
título (*m.*) title
toallita (*f.*) washcloth
tobillo (*m.*) ankle, 4
tocar to touch, 8
tocino (*m.*) bacon
todavía yet, 2; still, 2
todo(a) all, 4
— **eso** all that, 5
— **lo posible** everything possible, 6
tomacorrientes (*m. sing.*) electrical outlet, 19; socket, 19
tomar to drink, 2; to take, 3
— **la presión** to take the blood pressure, 16
— **la tensión** to take the blood pressure, 16
Tome asiento. Have a seat., PI
tomate (*m.*) tomato, 2
tomografía axial computarizada (*f.*) C.A.T.
tórax (*m.*) thorax
torcer(se) (o:ue) to twist, 10
torcido(a) crooked
torniquete (*m.*) tourniquet, 14
toronja (*f.*) grapefruit, 2
tortilla (*f.*) tortilla, 6
tos (*f.*) cough, 2
— **convulsiva** whooping cough
— **ferina** whooping cough, 5; pertussis, 5
toser to cough, 2
tostada (*f.*) toast, 2
total total, 16
trabajar to work, 8
trabajo (*m.*) work, 4
traer to bring, 8
tragar to swallow, 8
tranquilizante (*m.*) tranquilizer, 2
transfusión (*f.*) transfusion, 13
transmitido(a) transmitted
— **a través del contacto sexual** sexually transmitted
trasplante de corazón (*m.*) heart transplant
trastorno nervioso (*m.*) nervous disorder
tratamiento (*m.*) treatment, 12
tratar to treat, 16; to try, 16
tripas (*f. pl.*) belly; intestines
tripear to take drugs
trompa (*f.*) tube
tuberculina (*f.*) tuberculin, 5
tuberculosis (*f.*) tuberculosis, 5
tubo (*m.*) tube, 14
tumor (*m.*) tumor, 12
tupido(a) constipated, 3
turno (*m.*) appointment, 5

U

úlcera (*f.*) ulcer, PI
últimamente lately, 17
último(a) last, 12
la última vez the last time, 12
ultrasonido (*m.*) ultrasound, 17
ultrasonografía (*f.*) ultrasound

ungüento (*m.*) ointment, 5
único(a) only, 15
unidad (*f.*) unit
— **de cuidados intensivos** intensive care unit
uña (*f.*) fingernail, L1
urea alta (*f.*) uremia
uremia (*f.*) uremia
uretra (*f.*) urethra
úrico(a) uric, 20
urología (*f.*) urology, PI
urólogo(a) (*m., f.*) urologist, PI
urticaria (*f.*) hives, 5
usado(a) used, 7
usar to wear, 2; to use, 2
útero (*m.*) uterus, 7
útil useful, 19
uva (*f.*) grape, 2
úvula (*f.*) uvula

V

vacío(a) empty, 10
vacunado(a) vaccinated, 5
vacunar to vaccinate, 5
vagina (*f.*) vagina, 7
vaginal vaginal
vaginitis (*f.*) vaginitis
vamos a ver let's see, 4
varicela (*f.*) chickenpox, 5
várices (*f. pl.*) varicose veins, 17
variedad (*f.*) variety, 6
varios(as) several, 13
varón (*m.*) male, 11; boy, 11
vasectomía (*f.*) vasectomy, 7
vaselina (*f.*) Vaseline, 5
vasito (*m.*) little glass, 14; cup, 14
vaso (*m.*) glass, 4
veces (*f.*) times
a — sometimes, 8
algunas — sometimes, 8
muchas — many times, 16
vegetal (*m.*) vegetable
vejiga (*f.*) bladder
vena (*f.*) vein, 13
— **varicosa** varicose vein, 17
venda (*f.*) bandage, 19
vendaje (*m.*) bandage, 19
vendar to bandage, 10
veneno (*m.*) poison, 10
venéreo(a) venereal, 15
venir to come, 5
ventaja (*f.*) advantage
ventana (*f.*) window
— **nasal** nostril
— **de la nariz** nostril
ver to see, 5
vamos a — let's see, 4
verbo (*m.*) verb
verdad true
¿— ? right?, 11
verde green, 6
verdoso(a) greenish, 15
verruga (*f.*) wart, 12
verse to look, 13; to seem, 13
vértebra (*f.*) vertebra
vesícula (*f.*) bladder
— **biliar** gallbladder, 17
— **seminal** seminal vesicle
vestido (*m.*) dress
vestirse (e:i) to get dressed, 14
vez (*f.*) time, 12
de — en cuando from time to time, 17
una — once, 7
vida (*f.*) life, 7
viejo(a) (*m., f.*) elderly man, 16; elderly woman, 16
vientre (*m.*) abdomen, 1
VIH (virus de inmunodeficiencia humana) (*m.*) HIV (human immunodeficiency virus)
vino (*m.*) wine, 18
violento(a) violent, 8; strenuous
viruela (*f.*) smallpox, 5
virus (*m.*) virus, 15
visitar to visit, 13
vista (*f.*) vision, 12; view
corto(a) de — nearsighted
— **borrosa** (*f.*) blurred vision, 4
vitamina (*f.*) vitamin, 3
viudo(a) (*m., f.*) widow, 1; widower 1
vivir to live
vocabulario (*m.*) vocabulary
voltearse (*Méx.*) to turn over
volver (o:ue) to come (go) back, 6; to return, 6
volverse (o:ue) to turn over, 14
vomitar to throw up, 1

Y

y and, PI
ya already, 11; now, 11
— **está** That's it., 14
— **lo sé.** I know (it)., 6
¿— terminamos? Are we finished already?, 14
yerba (*f.*) marijuana (*col.*), 18
yerno (*m.*) son-in-law
yeso (*m.*) cast, 10
yodo (*m.*) iodine, 19
yogur (*m.*) yogurt, 6

Z

zapatilla (*f.*) slipper
zapato (*m.*) shoe

English-Spanish Vocabulary

A

a day al día, 2
a lot mucho, 2
abdomen vientre (*m.*), 11; barriga (*f.*), 11; abdomen (*m.*)
abortion aborto (*m.*), 4
about sobre, 1; acerca de; hace como ..., 18
above all sobre todo, 6
abscess absceso (*m.*), 9
abstinence abstinencia (*f.*)
accident accidente (*m.*), 10
according to según
ache dolor (*m.*), 1; doler (*o:ue*), 8
acid ácido (*m.*), 10
acidity acidez (*f.*), 17
acne acné (*m.*), 12
acquainted: to be — with conocer, 7
add añadir
addicted adicto(a)
address dirección (*f.*), P; domicilio (*m.*), P
adhesive tape cinta adhesiva (*f.*), 19
adjective adjetivo (*m.*)
admission admisión (*f.*)
admit (to a hospital) ingresar, 10; internar
advance adelanto (*m.*)
advantage ventaja (*f.*)
  take — of aprovechar
advice consejo (*m.*), 19
advise aconsejar, 16
affect afectar, 16
after después (de), 1
afternoon tarde (*f.*), 11
again otra vez, 8
against contra, 5
age edad (*f.*), 1
ago: How long ago...? ¿Cuánto tiempo hace...?, 14
agreeable ameno(a)
aha ajá, 1
AIDS SIDA (Síndrome de inmunodeficiencia adquirida) (*m.*), 18
air aire (*m.*)
alcohol alcohol (*m.*), 16
alcoholic alcohólico(a), 4
all todo(a), 4; todos(as)
  — that todo eso, 5
allergic alérgico(a), 3
allergy alergia (*f.*), 18
almost casi, 10
alone solo(a), 19
already ya, 11
also también, 2; asimismo
always siempre, 1
ambulance ambulancia (*f.*), 10
amount cantidad (*f.*)
amphetamine anfetamina (*f.*), 18
amputate amputar
anabolic steroids esteroides anabólicos (*m. pl.*)
analgesics analgésicos (*m.*)
analysis análisis (*m.*), 1
and y, P
anemia anemia (*f.*) 4
anemic anémico(a), 3
anesthesia anestesia (*f.*), 9
anesthesiologist anestesiólogo(a) (*m., f.*)
anesthesiology anestesiología (*f.*)
aneurism aneurisma (*m.*)
aneurysm aneurisma (*m.*)
angel dust PCP (*f.*); polvo de ángel (*m.*)
angina angina (*f.*)
angioplasty angioplastia (*f.*)
ankle tobillo (*m.*), 4
another otro(a), 2
antacid antiácido (*m.*), 17
antibiotic antibiótico (*m.*), 5
anticoagulant anticoagulante (*m.*)
antidrug antidroga, 18
antihistamine antihistamínico (*m.*), 19
anus ano (*m.*)
any alguno(a), 3; cualquier(a), 16
anything algo, 2
  — else? ¿Algo más?, 2
anxiety ansiedad, (*f.*); angustia (*f.*)
apparatus aparato (*m.*), 12
appendicitis apendicitis (*f.*)
appetite apetito (*m.*), 3
apple manzana (*f.*)
apply aplicar, 19
appointment cita (*f.*), 5; turno (*m.*), 5
approach acercarse, 14
arm brazo (*m.*), 7
around alrededor (de), 13
arrive llegar, 10
artery arteria (*f.*)
arthritis artritis (*f.*)
artificial artificial
as soon as possible lo más pronto posible, 16
ask preguntar, 13
  — for pedir (*e:i*), 7
  — questions hacer preguntas, 19
asleep dormido(a), 20
aspirin aspirina (*f.*), 3
assistant asistente (*m., f.*), 9
asthmatic asmático(a), 3
astigmatism astigmatismo (*m.*)
at en, 2; a
  — (+ time) a la(s) (+ *time*), 1
  — first al principio
  — least por lo menos, 6
  — the end of al final de, 14
  — the present time actualmente, 18
atmosphere ambiente (*m.*)
attack ataque (*m.*)
attend atender (*e:ie*)
aunt tía (*f.*), 20
authorization autorización (*f.*)
average promedio (*m.*)
avoid evitar, 4
awake despierto(a), 20

B

baby bebé (*m.*), 4
  — bottle mamadera (*f.*), 11; mamila (*f.*) (*Méx.*), 11; biberón (*m.*), 11
  — carriage cochecito (*m.*)
  — food comidita de bebé (*f.*)
  — lotion loción para bebé (*f.*)
  — powder talco para bebé (*m.*)
back espalda (*f.*), 4
backbone columna vertebral (*f.*)
backward hacia atrás, 8
bad malo(a), 4
balanced balanceado(a)
balloon (drug dosage) globo (*m.*), 18
bandage venda (*f.*), 19; vendaje (*m.*), 19; vendar, 10
  adhesive — curita (*f.*), 14
bank banco (*m.*)
barbiturate barbitúrico (*m.*)
barely apenas, 16
bathe bañar, 13
bathroom baño (*m.*), 14; excusado (*m.*), 14; servicio (*m.*), 14; cuarto de baño (*m.*)
bathtub bañadera (*f.*), 19; bañera (*f.*), 19
battery batería (*f.*), 20
be ser, 2; estar, 3
  — ... years old tener... años, 6
  — able (to) poder (*o:ue*), 6
  — afraid temer, 17; tener miedo, 19
  — born nacer, 11
  — careful tener cuidado, 6
  — done terminar, 14
  — frightened asustarse, 19
  — in pain tener dolor, 4
  — lacking something faltarle algo a uno, 20
  — named llamarse, 11
  — pleasing to gustar, 13
  — right tener razón, 4
  — scared asustarse, 19
  — sleepy tener sueño, 4
  — tight apretar (*e:ie*), 14
beans frijoles (*m.*), 6; habichuelas (*Puerto Rico*), 6
bear aguantar, 18
beat (heart) latir, 20
because porque, 4
become ponerse
bed cama (*f.*), 13
bedpan chata (*f.*), 2; cuña (*f.*), 2
bedtime: at — al acostarse

beer cerveza (*f.*), 18
before antes (de), 3
— **sleeping** antes de dormir, 3
begin comenzar (*e:ie*), 11; empezar (*e:ie*), 15
believe creer, 3
bend doblar, 8
benign benigno(a), 12
besides además, 6
best mejor, 7; lo mejor, 5
better mejor, 7
between entre, 20
beverage bebida (*f.*), 17
alcoholic — bebida alcohólica (*f.*), 4
bib babero (*m.*)
big grande, 4
bill cuenta (*f.*), 1
biopsy biopsia (*f.*), 12
birth natalidad (*adj.*), 7; nacimiento (*m.*)
— **control** anticonceptivo(a) (*adj.*), 7
— **mark** mancha en la piel (*f.*)
to give — dar a luz; parir
bite morder (*o:ue*), 9; picadura (*f.*)
black negro(a), 17
blackhead espinilla (*f.*), 12
bladder vejiga (*f.*)
bland blando(a)
blanket frazada (*f.*), 2; cobija (*f.*), 2; manta (*f.*), 2
bleach lejía (*f.*), 19
bleed sangrar, 9
bleeding pérdida de sangre (*f.*)
blind ciego(a)
blindness ceguera (*f.*)
blister ampolla (*f.*)
bloated aventado(a), 3; lleno(a) de gases, 3
block cuadra (*f.*), 20
blood sangre (*f.*), 1
— **bank** banco de sangre (*m.*)
— **count** conteo (*m.*), 14
— **pressure** presión (*f.*), 8; presión arterial (*f.*), 8; tensión (*f.*), 16
— **relative** pariente cercano(a) (*m., f.*), 20
— **test** análisis de sangre (*m.*), 1
blouse blusa (*f.*)
blue azul
blurry borroso(a), 12
body cuerpo (*m.*)
boiling hirviendo, 10
bone hueso (*m.*), 8
bonnet gorro (*m.*), 19
both los (las) dos, 3
bottle frasco (*m.*), 10; botella (*f.*), 10; pomo (*m.*) (*Cuba*), 10
bowel movement: to have a — mover el vientre, 11; obrar, 11; defecar, 11; evacuar (*Méx.*), 11, hacer caca, (*col.*)
box caja (*f.*), 20; cuadro (*m.*)
boy niño (*m.*), 2; varón (*m.*), 11; muchacho (*m.*), 18
braces (dental) frenos (*m. pl.*)
brain cerebro (*m.*)
bread pan (*m.*), 2
break fracturar(se), 10; quebrarse (*e:ie*) (*Méx.*), 10; romperse, 10
— **water (childbirth)** romperse la fuente (bolsa)
breakfast desayuno (*m.*), 2
breast seno (*m.*), 4; pecho (*m.*), 4
breath aliento (*m.*), 9; respiración (*f.*)
breathe respirar, 8; resollar, 8
bridge puente (*m.*)
brief breve, P
bring traer, 8
broccoli bróculi (*m.*), 6
brochure folleto (*m.*), 7
bronchitis bronquitis (*f.*)
bronchoscopy broncoscopia (*f.*)
brother hermano (*m.*), 18
brother-in-law cuñado (*m.*)
bruise moretón (*m.*), 13; morado (*m.*), 13; cardenal (*m.*), (*Cuba*), 13
brush cepillo (*m.*), 9; cepillar(se), 9
— **one's teeth** cepillarse los dientes, 9
budget presupuesto (*m.*)
bunion juanete (*m.*)
burglar ladrón(-ona) (*m., f.*)
burn quemadura (*f.*), 10; quemar(se), 10; arder, 15
burning ardor (*m.*), 8
burp eructar
business office oficina de pagos (*f.*)
but pero, 3
butter mantequilla (*f.*), 2
buttocks nalgas (*f. pl.*), 5; asentaderas (*f. pl.*), 5
button botón (*m.*), 13
buy comprar, 3
bye chau, P
bypass (heart) puente coronario (*m.*)

C

cabbage col (*f.*), 6; repollo (*m.*), 6
caffeine cafeína (*f.*), 17
cake pastel (*m.*)
calcaneus calcáneo (*m.*)
calcium calcio (*m.*)
calf pantorrilla (*f.*)
call llamar, 1
called llamado(a)
calm calma (*f.*); calmar
— **down** calmar(se), 11
calorie caloría (*f.*), 6
can (be able to) poder (*o:ue*), 6
cancer cáncer (*m.*), 7
candy dulce (*m.*), 6; caramelo (*m.*)
canine canino (*m.*)
cap gorro (*m.*), 19
capsule cápsula (*f.*), 3
car carro (*m.*), 10; coche (*m.*), 10; auto (*m.*), 10; máquina (*f.*) (*Cuba*), 10
carbohydrate carbohidrato (*m.*)
card tarjeta (*f.*), 1
cardiologist cardiólogo(a), 20
cardiology cardiología (*f.*)
care cuidado (*m.*)
careful: to be — tener cuidado, 6
carious picado(a), 9; cariado(a), 9
carpus carpo (*m.*)
carry llevar
— **out** llevar a cabo
case caso (*m.*), 10
in — of en caso de, 1
in that — en ese caso, 7
cashier cajero(a) (*m., f.*)
cast yeso (*m.*), 10; escayola (*f.*) (*España*)
CAT scan escanograma (*m.*)
cataracts cataratas (*f. pl.*)
cathartic purgante (*m.*), 17
cause causa (*f.*); causar, 7
cavity picadura (*f.*), 9; carie (*f.*), 9
cement cemento (*m.*)
center centro (*m.*), 7
cereal cereal (*m.*), 2
cerebrum cerebro (*m.*)
certain cierto(a), 20; seguro(a)
certainly ciertamente
cervix cerviz (*f.*)
cesarean cesárea, 11
chancre chancro (*m.*)
change cambiar(se), 9; cambio (*m.*), 16
cheap barato(a)
check revisar, 5; chequear, 5
checkup examen (*m.*), 8; chequeo (*m.*), 8
give a — hacer un examen, 8
cheek cachete (*m.*); mejilla (*f.*)
cheese queso (*m.*), 6
chemotherapy quimioterapia (*f.*)
chest pecho (*m.*), 8
chew masticar; mascar
chicken pollo (*m.*), 2
chickenpox varicela (*f.*)
child niño(a) (*m., f.*), 2
childbirth parto (*m.*)
chills escalofríos (*m. pl.*)
chin barbilla (*f.*), 8
chlamydia clamidia (*f.*)
chocolate chocolate (*m.*), 2
choke atragantarse, 19
cholesterol colesterol (*m.*), 8
choose elegir (*e:i*), 11
cigarette cigarrillo (*m.*), 2
circulation circulación (*f.*)
clavicle clavícula (*f.*)
clean limpiar, 5; limpio(a)
cleaning limpieza (*f.*)
clearly claramente, 12
clinic clínica (*f.*), 5
clogged obstruido(a)
close cerrar (*e:ie*), 5; cerca, 12
closed cerrado(a), 14
clot embolia (*f.*)
clothes ropa (*f.*), 13
clothing ropa (*f.*), 13; prendas (*f. pl.*)
coagulum coágulo (*m.*)
coat abrigo (*m.*)
cocaine cocaína (*f.*); coca (*f.*); perico (*m.*) (*col.*); polvo (*m.*) (*col.*)
coccyx rabadilla (*f.*); cóccix (*m.*)
codeine codeína (*f.*)
coffee café (*m.*), 2
cognate cognado (*m.*)
coin moneda (*f.*), 19
cold frío(a), 2; catarro (*m.*), 3; resfrío (*m.*), 3; resfriado (*m.*), 3
to have a— estar resfriado(a), 3; estar acatarrado(a), 3

colic cólico (*m.*)
colitis colitis (*f.*); inflamación del intestino grueso (*f.*)
collide chocar, 10
colon colon (*m.*), 14
colonoscopy colonoscopia (*f.*)
color blindness daltonismo (*m.*)
coloscopy colonoscopia (*f.*)
come venir, 5
— **back** volver (*o:ue*), 6
— **in** pase, P; entrar
comfortable cómodo(a), 13
commercial comercial, 17
commit suicide suicidarse
common común
company compañía (*f.*), 1
compare comparar
completely completamente, 15
compress compresa (*f.*), 13
conceive concebir (*e:i*)
condom condón (*m.*), 7
confirm confirmar, 10
conjunctivitis conjuntivitis (*f.*)
constantly constantemente, 6
constipated estreñido(a), 3; tapado(a), 3; tupido(a), 3
consult consultar
consume consumir
contact lenses lentes de contacto (*m. pl.*), 2
contagious contagioso(a), 15
contain contener, 20
continue seguir (*e:i*), 7
contraceptive (*adj.*) anticonceptivo(a); anticonceptivo (*m.*), 7
contraction contracción (*f.*), 11
control control (*m.*), 7; controlar, 9
convenience comodidad, (*f.*)
conversation conversación (*f.*), P
convulsions convulsiones (*f. pl.*)
cookie galletita (*f.*); galletica (*f.*)
coordinator coordinador(a) (*m., f.*), 18
correct correcto(a), 7
correctly correctamente, 7
cosmetic cosmético (*m.*)
cough toser, 2; tos (*f.*), 2
— **syrup** jarabe para la tos (*m.*), 2
count contar (*o:ue*), 6; conteo (*m.*), 14
country país (*m.*)
couple par (*m.*), pareja (*f.*)
course: of — cómo no, 13; por supuesto, 16
cover cubrir, 5; tapar, 14
crack crac (*m.*); piedra (*f.*) (*col.*); roca (*f.*) (*col.*); coca cocinada (*f.*) (*col.*)
cradle cuna (*f.*), 19
cramp calambre (*m.*), 20
crawl gatear, 19; andar a gatas, 19
cream crema (*f.*), 7
crib cuna (*f.*), 19
crooked torcido(a)
cross-eyed bizco(a)
croup crup (*m.*); garrotillo (*m.*)
crown corona (*f.*), 9
crutch muleta (*f.*), 10
cry llorar
cup taza (*f.*), 2; vasito (*m.*), 14
cure curar, 17; cura (*f.*)
cured curado(a), 15
currently actualmente, 18
curtain cortina (*f.*), 19
cut (oneself) cortar(se), 10; cortadura (*f.*), 19
— **down** disminuir, 16
cyst quiste (*m.*), 12

D

dad papá (*m.*)
daily (*adv.*) diariamente, 17; (*adj.*) diario(a)
damage daño (*m.*); dañar
dangerous peligroso(a), 6
dark oscuridad (*f.*)
date fecha (*f.*), 18
— **of birth** fecha de nacimiento (*f.*), 1
daughter hija (*f.*), 3
— **daughter-in-law** nuera (*f.*)
day día (*m.*), 12
— **before yesterday** anteayer
on the following — al día siguiente, 15
deaf sordo(a), 17
go — quedarse sordo(a), 17
deafness sordera (*f.*)
death muerte (*f.*)
decayed picado(a), 9; cariado(a), 9
decide decidir, 18
decision decisión (*f.*), 12
decongestants descongestionantes (*m. pl.*)
deep (*adv.*) hondo, 8; (*adj.*) hondo(a), 19; profundo(a), 19
degree grado (*m.*), 3
delivery parto (*m.*), 11; alumbramiento (*m.*), 11
— **room** sala de parto (*f.*), 11
dental dental, 18
— **floss** hilo dental (*m.*), 9; seda dental (*f.*), 9
— **surgeon** odontólogo(a) (*m., f.*)
dentine dentina (*f.*)
dentist dentista (*m., f.*), 9; odontólogo(a) (*m., f.*)
dentures dentadura postiza (*f.*), 2
department departamento (*m.*), 15
depend depender, 16
depression depresión (*f.*)
dermatologist dermatólogo(a) (*m., f.*), 12
dessert postre (*m.*), 2
destroy destruir
detachment desprendimiento (*m.*)
detergent detergente (*m.*), 19
determine determinar, 7
detoxification desintoxicación (*f.*)
develop desarrollar
diabetes diabetes (*f.*), 8
diabetic diabético(a), 6
diagnose diagnosticar
diagnosis diagnóstico (*m.*), 10
diaper pañal (*m.*)
diaphragm diafragma (*m.*), 7
diarrhea diarrea (*f.*), 5
die morir (*o:ue*), 20
diet dieta (*f.*), 6
go on a — seguir (*e:i*) una dieta, 6
dietician dietista (*m., f.*), 2
different distinto(a), 7; diferente, 7
difficult difícil, 6
difficulty dificultad (*f.*), 8
digest digerir (*e:ie*)
digestive system aparato digestivo (*m.*)
dilated dilatado(a)
diminish disminuir, 16; aliviarse (*a pain*), 17
dinner cena (*f.*)
diptheria difteria (*f.*), 5
direct dirigir
directly directamente, 12
disability incapacidad (*f.*), 18
discharge flujo (*m.*), 15
discomfort molestia (*f.*) 7; malestar (*m.*)
discount descuento (*m.*)
discover descubrir
disease enfermedad (*f.*), 5
disfigure afear, desfigurar
disinfect desinfectar, 10
disorder trastorno (*m.*)
disposable desechable
distinguish distinguir
diuretic diurético (*m.*)
divorced divorciado(a), 1
dizziness mareo (*m.*), 4
do hacer, 5
doctor doctor(a) (*m., f.*), P; médico(a) (*m., f.*), 1
doctor's office consultorio (*m.*), 1
donate donar
donor donante (*m., f.*)
door puerta (*f.*)
dosage dosis (*f.*), 16
dot punto (*m.*), 12
doubt dudar, 18; duda (*f.*)
drainage drenaje (*m.*)
dress vestido (*m.*)
drink beber, 2; tomar, 2; bebida (*f.*), 17
drop gota (*f.*), 5
dropsy hidropesía (*f.*)
drug(s) droga(s) (*f.*), 18
— **addict** drogadicto(a) (*m., f.*), 18
become addicted to — endrogarse
take — endrogarse, dar un viaje (*col.*), tripear (*col.*)
dry seco(a)
DT's delírium tremens (*m. pl.*)
dull (pain) sordo(a), 20
during durante, 4
dye tinte (*m.*), 19

E

each cada, 3
ear oído (*inner*) (*m.*), 5; oreja (*external*) (*f.*)
— **canal** conducto auditivo (*m.*); canal auditivo (*m.*)
— **drum** tímpano (*m.*)
easy fácil, 7
eat comer, 2
ecstasy éxtasis (*m.*)
eczema eccema (*m.*)
effect efecto (*m.*)

effective efectivo(a), 7; eficaz
egg huevo (*m.*), 6; blanquillo (*m.*) (*Méx.*), 6
either tampoco, 7
ejaculate eyacular
elastic elástico(a), 17
elbow codo (*m.*)
elderly man (woman) viejo(a) (*m., f.*), 16; anciano(a) (*m., f.*), 17
electric(al) eléctrico(a), 10
— **outlet** tomacorrientes (*m. sing., pl.*), 19
— **plug cover** enchufe de seguridad (*m.*), 19
electrocardiogram (EKG) electrocardiograma (*m.*), 20
electroencephalogram (EEG) electroencefalograma (*m.*)
elevated elevado(a), 20
elevator elevador (*m.*); ascensor (*m.*)
eliminate eliminar, 16
else más, 16
embolism embolia (*f.*)
emergency emergencia (*f.*), 1
— **room** sala de emergencia (*f.*), 10; sala de urgencia (*f.*), 10
emphysema enfisema (*f.*)
employ emplear
empty vacío(a), 10
with an — stomach en ayunas, 8
enamel esmalte (*m.*)
endocrinologist endocrinólogo(a) (*m., f.*)
endometriosis endometrosis (*f.*)
endoscopy endoscopia (*f.*)
enema enema (*m.*), 14; lavado intestinal (*m.*); lavativa (*f.*)
enough suficiente, 9
enter entrar, 1
entry entrada (*f.*), 7
epilespy epilepsia (*f.*), 18
equipment equipo (*m.*)
especially especialmente, 6
even aun
ever alguna vez, 17
hardly — casi nunca, 20
every cada, 3
— **... hours** cada ...horas
everything todo (*m.*)
— **possible** todo lo posible, 6
evil eye mal de ojo (*m.*)
examination examen (*m.*), 8; chequeo (*m.*), 8
examine examinar, 4; reconocer, 4, chequear
excrement excremento (*m.*)
exercise hacer ejercicio, 6; ejercicio (*m.*), 15
exhaustion cansancio (*m.*), 17
explain explicar, 10
expose (oneself) exponer(se)
expression expresión (*f.*)
extend extender (*e:ie*), 14
extract sacar, 9; extraer, 9
extraction extracción (*f.*), 9
eye ojo (*m.*)
eyebrow ceja (*f.*)
eyedropper gotero (*m.*), cuentagotas (*m. sing., pl.*)
eyelashes pestañas (*f. pl.*)
eyelid párpado (*m.*)

F

face cara (*f.*), 9
faint desmayarse, 10; perder (*e:ie*) el conocimiento, 10
faithfully fielmente, 17
fall caer(se), 10
false postizo(a), 2
family familia (*f.*), 7; (*adj.*) familiar, 7
far (away) lejos (de), 12
farewell despedida (*f.*)
farsighted présbite
farsightedness hiperopía (*f.*)
fast (*adj.*) rápido(a); (*adv.*) rápidamente
fasting en ayunas, 8
fat grasa (*f.*), 6; gordo(a), 6
father padre (*m.*), 6; papá (*m.*), 6
— **-in-law** suegro (*m.*)
fatigue fatiga (*f.*)
fatty tissue tejido graso (*m.*)
favor favor (*m.*), 11
fear temer, 17
feces materia fecal (*f.*)
feel sentir(se) (*e:ie*), 8
— **better** aliviarse, 17
feet pies (*m.*)
female mujercita (*f.*) (*col. Méx.*), 11
femur fémur (*m.*)
fertile fértil, 7
fetus feto (*m.*)
fever fiebre (*f.*), 3; calentura (*f.*), 3
few pocos(as), 6
fiber fibra (*f.*)
fibula fíbula (*f.*); peroné (*m.*)
fill llenar
— **a tooth** emplomar, 9; empastar, 9
— **out (forms)** llenar, 1
finally finalmente, 15
find encontrar (*o:ue*), 12
fine bien, P
finger dedo (*m.*)
finish terminar, 14
fire incendio (*m.*)
— **department** departmento de bomberos (*m.*)
first primero(a), 5; antes, 10
— **aid** primeros auxilios (*m. pl.*), 19
— **-aid kit** estuche (botiquín) de primeros auxilios (*m.*), 19
fish pescado (*m.*), 6
flatus flato (*m.*)
floss (dental) hilo dental (*m.*), 9; seda dental (*f.*), 9
flour harina (*f.*)
fluoride fluoruro (*m.*)
fluoroscopy fluoroscopía (*f.*)
foam espuma (*f.*)
follow seguir (*e:i*), 7
following siguiente, 12
food alimento (*m.*), 6; alimentación (*f.*), 12; comida (*f.*), 16
foot pie (*m.*), 1
for para, 2; por, 10
— **a few seconds** por unos segundos, 10
— **example** por ejemplo, 20
— **me (on my behalf)** por mí, 18
— **that reason** por eso, 6
— **what ...?** ¿para qué...?, 5
forceps fórceps (*m. sing., pl.*), 11
forehead frente (*f.*), 10
forget olvidarse (de), 9
form planilla (*f.*), 1; forma (*f.*) (*Méx.*), 1
formula fórmula (*f.*)
forward hacia adelante, 8
fracture fractura (*f.*), 10; fracturar(se), 10; quebrarse (*e:ie*) (*Méx.*), 10; romperse, 10
free gratis
French fries papas fritas (*f. pl.*), 6
frequent frecuente, 12
frequently con frecuencia, 4
fright susto (*m.*)
fruit fruta (*f.*)
fungus hongo (*m.*)
furniture (piece of) mueble (*m.*), 19

G

gain weight subir de peso, 8; aumentar de peso, 8
gallbladder vesícula biliar (*f.*), 17
gargle hacer gárgaras
gas gas (*m.*)
gastritis gastritis (*f.*)
gauze gasa (*f.*), 9
general general, 8
— **practitioner** clínico (*m.*), 17; internista (*m., f.*), 17
generally generalmente, 6
genitals genitales (*m. pl.*), 14
gentleman señor (*m.*), P
geriatrist geriatra (*m., f.*)
get conseguir (*e:i*), 15
— **close** acercarse, 14
girl niña (*f.*), 2; mujercita (*f.*) (*col. Méx.*), 11; muchacha (*f.*), 18
give dar, 3
— **a checkup** hacer un examen, 8
— **a shot** poner una inyección, 10
— **birth** dar a luz; parir
gland glándula (*f.*)
glans glande (*m.*)
glass vaso (*m.*), 17
little — vasito (*m.*), 14
glasses anteojos (*m. pl.*), 2; lentes (*m. pl.*), 2; gafas (*f. pl.*), 2; espejuelos (*m. pl.*) (*Cuba*), 2
glaucoma glaucoma (*m.*), 12
go ir, 3
— **away** irse, 14
— **down** bajar, 3
— **in** entrar
— **out (leave)** salir, 9
— **to bed** acostarse (*o:ue*), 14
— **up** subir, 13
goiter bocio (*m.*)
gonorrhea gonorrea (*f.*), 15
good bueno(a)

— **afternoon** buenas tardes, P
— **evening (night)** buenas noches, P
— **luck** buena suerte, 7
— **morning (day)** buenos días, P
good-bye adiós, P
granddaughter nieta (*f.*)
grandfather abuelo (*m.*)
grandmother abuela (*f.*)
grandson nieto (*m.*)
grapefruit toronja (*f.*), 6
green verde, 6
greenish verdoso(a), 15
greeting saludo (*m.*)
groin ingle (*f.*)
group grupo (*m.*), 6
gum (of mouth) encía (*f.*), 9
gunshot wound herida de bala (*f.*)
gurney camilla (*f.*), 10
gut tripa (*f.*); intestino (*m.*)
gynecologist ginecólogo(a) (*m., f.*), 4
gynecology ginecología (*f.*)

H

hair pelo (*m.*); cabello (*m.*)
half mitad (*f.*), 6; medio(a), 16
hallucination alucinación (*f.*)
hallway pasillo (*m.*), 14
hamburger hamburguesa (*f.*), 6
hand mano (*f.*), 14
handbag bolsa (*f.*), 9; cartera (*f.*), 9
handwriting letra (*f.*), 1
happen pasar, 10; ocurrir, 16; suceder
hard duro(a), 4
hardening endurecimiento (*m.*)
hashish hachich (*m.*); hachís (*m.*)
have tener
— **a backache** tener dolor de espalda, 4
— **just (done something)** acabar de (+ *inf.*), 13
— **lunch** almorzar (*o:ue*), 6
— **to** tener que, 4
hay fever fiebre de heno (*f.*)
head cabeza (*f.*), 1
headache dolor de cabeza (*m.*), 1
health salud (*f.*), 15
healthy sano(a), 8; saludable
hear oír, 17
hearing aid audífono (*m.*), 17
heart corazón (*m.*), 16
— **attack** ataque al corazón (*m.*), 18
— **beat** latido (*m.*)
— **murmur** soplo cardíaco (*m.*)
— **transplant** transplante de corazón (*m.*)
to have — trouble estar enfermo(a) del corazón, 6; sufrir del corazón, 20; padecer del corazón, 6
heartburn acidez (*f.*), 17
heat (up) calentar (*e:ie*)
heavy pesado(a), 4
heel talón (*m.*)
help ayudar, 13
helper asistente (*m., f.*), 9
hemorrhage hemorragia (*f.*), 13
hemorrhoids hemorroides (*f.*), 17; almorranas (*f.*), 17
hepatitis hepatitis (*f.*), 18
here aquí, 6
— **it is** aquí está, 1
hereditary hereditario(a), 16
heroin heroína (*f.*), manteca (*f.*) (*col. Caribe*)
herpes herpes (*m. sing.*), 15
high alto(a), 3
— **blood pressure** hipertensión (*f.*), 16
— **chair** sillita alta (*f.*)
hip cadera (*f.*)
hit (oneself) golpear(se), 10
HIV (human immunodeficiency virus) VIH (virus de immunodeficiencia humana) (*m.*)
hives urticaria (*f.*), ronchas (*f. pl.*)
hoarse ronco(a), 8
hoarseness ronquera (*f.*)
hold aguantar
— **one's breath** aguantar la respiración, 14
hole agujero (*m.*), 19; hueco (*m.*), 19
home casa (*f.*)
honey miel (*f.*)
hope esperar, 17
I hope ojalá, 17
hose medias (*f. pl.*), 17
hospital hospital (*m.*), 2
hot caliente, 2
hour hora (*f.*), 3
hours horario (*m.*)
house casa (*f.*), 19
how cómo, P
— **about...?** ¿Qué tal...?, 3
— **are you?** ¿Cómo está usted?, P
— **are you feeling?** ¿Cómo se siente?, P
— **long** cuánto tiempo, 10
— **long ago...?** ¿Cuánto tiempo hace...?, 14
— **many** cuántos(as)
— **much** cuánto(a), 1
human humano(a)
humerus húmero (*m.*)
hungry: to be — tener hambre, 5
hurt doler (*o:ue*), 8; **(oneself)** lastimarse, 11; hacer daño, 18
husband esposo (*m.*), 1; marido (*m.*), 1
hydrogen peroxide agua oxigenada (*f.*), 19
hygienist higienista (*m., f.*), 9
hypertension hipertensión (*f.*), 16
hypodermic syringe jeringuilla (*f.*); jeringa hipodérmica (*f.*)
hysterectomy histerectomía (*f.*)

I

ice hielo (*m.*), 9
— **pack** bolsa de hielo (*f.*), 9
if si, 3
— **only** ojalá, 17
ilium hueso ilíaco (*m.*)
ill enfermo(a)
implant implante (*m.*), 7
importance importancia (*f.*), 12
important importante, 5
impotence impotencia (*f.*)
impotent impotente
improve mejorar, 20
in en, 2; dentro de, 8
— **a hurry** de prisa, 8
— **addition** además, 6
inch pulgada (*f.*), 1
incisor incisivo (*m.*)
increase aumento (*m.*); aumentar
incubation incubación (*f.*)
incubator incubador (*m.*)
indicate indicar, 15; señalar
infect infectar
infection infección (*f.*), 5
infectious infeccioso(a)
inflammation inflamación (*f.*)
inflammatory inflamatorio(a)
influenza gripe (*f.*); monga (*f.*) (*col. Puerto Rico*)
information información (*f.*), 1
inject (oneself) inyectar(se), 17
injection inyección (*f.*), 10
injured person herido(a) (*m., f.*), 10
injury herida (*f.*), 9
insanity locura (*f.*)
insecticide insecticida (*m.*), 19
insemination inseminación (*f.*)
insert insertar, 7
inside adentro
on the — por dentro, 7
insomnia insomnio (*m.*), 8
instruction instrucción (*f.*), 17
instrument aparato (*m.*), 12
insulin insulina (*f.*), 17
insurance seguro (*m.*), 1; aseguranza (*f.*), 1
— **company** compañía de seguro (*f.*), 1
intensive care unit unidad de cuidados intensivos (*f.*)
internal interna
internist internista (*m., f.*), 17; clínico (*m.*), 17
interuterine device (I.U.D.) aparato intrauterino (*m.*), 7
intestine intestino (*m.*)
large — intestino grueso (*m.*)
small — intestino delgado (*m.*)
intoxication intoxicación (*f.*)
investigator investigador(a) (*m., f.*), 15
iodine yodo (*m.*), 19
ipecac ipecacuana (*f.*), 19
iron hierro (*m.*), 3; plancha (*f.*), 19
irritated irritado(a), 5
irritation irritación (*f.*)
itching comezón (*f.*), 8; picazón (*f.*), 8
itself propio(a)
I.V. serum suero (*m.*), 13

J

jacket chaqueta (*f.*)
jaw (bone) mandíbula (*f.*); quijada (*f.*)
jelly jalea (*f.*), 7

jewelry joyas (*f. pl.*), 13
joint (*drugs*) leño (*m.*); cucaracha (*f.*); porro (*m.*); (*anatomy*) articulación (*f.*)
juice jugo (*m.*), 2
just: to have — acabar de, 13

K

keep mantener
  — at hand tener a mano
  — in mind tener en cuenta
kidney riñón (*m.*), 16
  — stones cálculos en el riñón (*m. pl.*); piedras en el riñón (*f. pl.*)
kill matar
killer joint porro mortal (*m.*)
kind amable, 13
knee rodilla (*f.*), 8
know saber, 7; conocer, 7
  I — it. Ya lo sé., 6
knowledge conocimiento (*m.*)
knuckle nudillo (*m.*)

L

labor parto (*m.*)
  — pain dolor de parto (*m.*), 11
  to be in — estar de parto
laboratory laboratorio (*m.*), 3
lady señora (*f.*), P
laparoscopy laparoscopia (*f.*)
laryngitis laringitis (*f.*)
last último(a), 12; pasado(a), 12; durar, 20
  — name apellido (*m.*), P
  — night anoche, 13
  — time la última vez, 12
late tarde
lately últimamente, 17
later más tarde, 6; después, 15
  — on más adelante, 5
laxative purgante (*m.*), 17; laxante (*m.*), 17
least: at — por lo menos
leave salir, 9; irse, 14
left izquierdo(a), 12
leg pierna (*f.*), 11
lesion lesión (*f.*), 15
less menos, 8
let (someone) know avisar, 13
  let's see... a ver..., 1; vamos a ver, 4
letter letra (*f.*), 1
leukemia leucemia (*f.*)
license: driver's — licencia para conducir (*f.*), 1
lie (down) acostarse (*o:ue*), 14
life vida (*f.*), 16
lift subir, 13; levantar, 13
light luz (*f.*), 12; ligero(a)
like gustar, 13; como
  — that así, 11
  — this así, 8
limb extremidad (*f.*), 20
limitation limitación. (*f.*), 18
line línea (*f.*), 12; revestir (*e:i*)
liniment linimento (*m.*)
lip labio (*m.*)
liquid líquido (*m.*), 3
list lista (*f.*), 6
little pequeño(a) (*size*) (*f.*), 6; poco (*quantity*), 3
  — by little poco a poco, 14
  a — un poco, 8
live vivir
liver hígado (*m.*), 6
local local, 9
look mirar, 1; verse, 13
lose perder (*e:ie*)
  — consciousness perder (*e:ie*) el conocimiento, 10; desmayarse, 10
  — weight adelgazar, 6; bajar de peso, 6; perder (*e:ie*) peso, 6; rebajar, 6
loss pérdida (*f.*)
lotion loción (*f.*), 12
loved one ser querido (*m.*)
low bajo(a), 8
  — fat con poca grasa
LSD ácido (*m.*)
lubricate lubricar
luck suerte (*f.*), 7
lukewarm tibio(a), 9
lump bolita (*f.*), 12; abultamiento (*m.*)
lunch almuerzo (*m.*), 13; lonche (*m.*) (*col. Méx.*), 13; comida (*f.*)
lung pulmón (*m.*)
lymph gland ganglio linfático (*m.*)

M

ma'am señora (*f.*), P
macaroni macarrones (*m. pl.*), 6
Madam señora (*f.*), P
maintain mantener
major mayor, 12
majority mayoría (*f.*), 12
make hacer, 5
  — an appointment pedir (*e:i*) turno, 5; pedir (*e:i*) hora, 5
  — better mejorar, 20
  — sure asegurarse, 12
makeup maquillaje (*m.*), 19
malaise malestar (*m.*)
malaria malaria (*f.*)
male varón (*m.*), 11
malignant maligno(a), 12
mammogram mamografía (*f.*), 12
man hombre (*m.*), 15
manifest manifestar (*e:ie*)
margarine margarina (*f.*), 6
marijuana mariguana (*f.*), 18; marihuana 18; [*col.:* yerba (*f.*); pito (*m.*); pasto (*m.*)]
marital status estado civil (*m.*), 1
married casado(a), P
mass masa (*f.*), 12
massage fricción (*f.*), 13
match fósforo (*m.*), 19; cerilla (*f.*), 19
maternity ward sala de maternidad (*f.*)
matter: to not — no tener importancia, 12
maybe quizá(s), 3
M.D. doctor(a) (*m., f.*), 1; médico(a) (*m., f.*), 1
meal comida (*f.*), 1
meantime: in the — mientras tanto, 4
measles sarampión (*m.*), 5
measure medir (*e:i*), 7
meat carne (*f.*)
medical médico(a), 1; clínico(a), 1
  — history hoja clínica (*f.*), 1; historia clínica (*f.*), 1
  — insurance card tarjeta de seguro médico (*f.*), 1
medicated medicinal, 12
medicinal medicinal, 12
medicine medicina (*f.*), 3; remedio (*m.*), 3
  — chest (cabinet) botiquín (*m.*), 19
medium hard semiduro(a)
melon melón (*m.*), 6
meningitis meningitis (*f.*), 5
menstruation menstruación (*f.*), 4; regla (*f.*), 4; periodo (*m.*), 4
mental mental, 18
  — health enfermedades mentales (*f. pl.*)
metatarsus metatarso (*m.*)
methadone metadona (*f.*)
method método (*m.*), 7
midday meal almuerzo (*m.*); comida (*f.*)
middle medio (*m.*)
  — name segundo nombre (*m.*), 1
midwife partera (*f.*); comadrona (*f.*)
migraine migraña (*f.*)
milk leche (*f.*), 2
mine mío(a), 9
mineral mineral (*m.*), 5
minor menor, 12
minute minuto (*m.*), 9
miscarriage malparto (*m.*), 4; aborto espontáneo (*m.*), 4; aborto natural (*m.*), 4
Miss señorita (*f.*), P
molar muela (*f.*), 9; molar (*m.*)
mole lunar (*m.*)
mom mamá (*f.*), 2
moment momento (*m.*), 15
monitored monitorizado(a)
more más, 4
  — or less más o menos, 8
morning mañana (*f.*), 4
morphine morfina (*f.*)
mother madre (*f.*), 2
  — -in-law suegra (*f.*)
mouth boca (*f.*), 9
mouthwash enjuague (*m.*)
move mover(se) (*o:ue*), 14
Mr. señor (*m.*), P
Mrs. señora (*f.*), P
much (*adv.*) mucho, 2
  too — demasiado, 19
mucous membranes membranas mucosas (*f. pl.*)
multiple sclerosis esclerosis múltiple (*f.*)
mumps paperas (*f. pl.*), 5; farfallotas (*f. pl.*) (*col. Puerto Rico*)
muscle músculo (*m.*)
must deber, 2

N

name nombre (*m.*), P
  last — apellido (*m.*), P
nape nuca (*f.*)
narrow estrecho(a), 11
nausea náusea (*f.*), 1
near cerca (de) 12; cercano(a), 20
nearsighted miope; corto(a) de vista
nearsightedness miopía (*f.*)
necessarily necesariamente, 7
necessary necesario(a), 5
neck cuello (*m.*), 12; pescuezo (*m.*) (*col.*)
need necesitar, 1
needle aguja (*f.*)
negative negativo(a), 8
neither tampoco, 7
nephew sobrino (*m.*)
nerve nervio (*m.*)
nervous nervioso(a), 16
neurological neurológico(a)
neurologist neurólogo(a) (*m., f.*)
neurology neurología (*f.*)
never nunca, 6
new nuevo(a)
newborn recién nacido(a) (*m., f.*)
newlywed recién casado(a) (*m., f.*), 7
next próximo(a), 12; siguiente, 12
  — one próximo(a) (*m., f.*), 12
  — time la próxima vez, 5
  — week la semana que viene, 5; la semana próxima, 5; la semana entrante, 5
niece sobrina (*f.*)
night noche (*f.*)
  — before last anteanoche, 13
nightgown camisón (*m.*)
nipple pezón (*m.*)
nitroglycerin nitroglicerina (*f.*)
no one nadie, 15
nobody nadie, 15
noise ruido (*m.*), 8
none ninguno(a), 4
normal normal, 8
normally normalmente, 11
nose nariz (*f.*)
nostril ventana nasal (*f.*); ventana de la nariz (*f.*)
nothing nada, 8
notice notar, 17
noun nombre (*m.*)
nourishment alimento (*m.*), 6
novocaine novocaína (*f.*), 9
now ahora, 1; ya, 11
numb entumecido(a)
number número (*m.*)
  phone — número de teléfono (*m.*), P
numbness entumecimiento (*m.*)
nurse enfermero(a) (*m., f.*), 2; dar el pecho, 11; dar de mamar, 11
nursery sala de bebés (*f.*), 11

O

obesity obesidad (*f.*), 6; gordura (*f.*), 6
object objeto (*m.*), 19
obstetrician obstetra (*m., f.*)
obtain conseguir (*e:i*), 15
occupation ocupación (*f.*), 1
occur ocurrir, 16
oculist oculista (*m., f.*), 12
odontologist odontólogo(a) (*m., f.*)
odor olor (*m.*), 15
  to have a bad — tener mal olor, 15; apestar, 15; tener peste, 15
offer brindar
office oficina (*f.*), 3
often a menudo, I
oh ah, 9; ¡ay!, 10
oil aceite (*m.*), 5
oily grasiento(a)
ointment ungüento (*m.*), 5
okay bueno(a), 1; Está bien., 2
on en; sobre
once una vez
oncologist oncólogo(a) (*m., f.*)
only sólo, 2; solamente, 2
open abrir, 9; abierto(a)
  — heart surgery operación de corazón abierto (*f.*)
opening entrada (*f.*), 7
operate operar, 12
operating room sala de cirugía (*f.*); sala de operaciones (*f.*)
operation operación (*f.*), 11
ophthalmologist oculista (*m., f.*), 12; oftalmólogo(a) (*m., f.*)
ophthalmology oftalmología (*f.*)
opium opio (*m.*)
optometrist oculista (*m., f.*)
or o, P
oral bucal
orally por vía bucal; por vía oral
orange naranja (*f.*), 6; anaranjado(a)
  — juice jugo de naranja (*m.*), 2; jugo de china (*m.*) (*Puerto Rico*), 2
order orden (*f.*), 3; ordenar, 14
  in — to para, 3
organ órgano (*m.*)
orthodontia ortodoncia (*f.*)
orthodontist ortodoncista (*m., f.*)
orthopedics ortopedia (*f.*)
orthopedist ortopedista (*m., f.*); ortopeda (*m., f.*)
other otro(a), 2
out of reach fuera del alcance
out of the ordinary fuera de lo común, 8
outpatient paciente externo(a) (*m., f.*)
outside afuera, 10
  on the — por fuera, 7
ovary ovario (*m.*)
oven horno (*m.*), 19
overdose sobredosis (*f.*)
overweight exceso de peso (*m.*)
ovulation ovulación (*f.*), 7
ovum óvulo (*m.*)
oxygen oxígeno (*m.*)

P

pacemaker marcapasos (*m. sing.*), 20
pacifier chupete (*m.*); chupón (*m.*); tete (*m.*) (*Cuba*)
pack bolsa (*f.*)
  — of cigarettes cajetilla (*f.*), 2
pain dolor (*m.*), 1
  The — goes away. El dolor se me pasa., 17
painkiller pastilla para el dolor (*f.*), 2; calmante (*m.*), 2
painful doloroso(a)
paint pintura (*f.*), 19
pair par (*m.*), 17; pareja (*f.*)
palate paladar (*m.*)
pale pálido(a), 3
palpitation palpitación (*f.*), 16
pamphlet folleto (*m.*), 7
pants pantalones (*m. pl.*)
pantyhose pantimedias (*f. pl.*)
Pap test (smear) examen Papanicolau (*m.*)
papilloma papiloma (*m.*)
paralysis parálisis (*f.*), 16
paralyzed paralítico(a), 16
paramedic paramédico(a) (*m., f.*), 19
parents padres (*m. pl.*)
parking estacionamiento (*m.*)
part parte (*f.*), 7
partial parcial, 16
pass pasársele a uno, 17
pasta pasta (*f.*)
patch mechón (*m.*)
patella rótula (*f.*)
patient paciente (*m., f.*), 1
pay pagar, 1
payment pago (*m.*)
peach durazno (*m.*); melocotón (*m.*)
peanut butter mantequilla de maní (*f.*), 6; mantequilla de cacahuete (*f.*), 6
pear pera (*f.*)
pediatrics pediatría (*f.*)
pediatrician pediatra (*m., f.*), 3
pelvic de la pelvis; pélvico(a)
penicillin penicilina (*f.*), 3
penis pene (*m.*), 8; miembro (*m.*)
people gente (*f.*)
pepper chile (*m.*), 6; pimiento (*m.*), 6
per day al día, 2
perfume perfume (*m.*)
perhaps quizá(s), 3; tal vez, 20
period periodo (*m.*)
permanent permanente
person persona (*f.*), 12
personnel personal (*m.*)
pertussis tos ferina (*f.*), 5
phalange falange (*m.*)
pharmacy farmacia (*f.*), 3; droguería (*f.*) (*col. in some L.A. countries*), 3
phlegm flema (*f.*)
phone teléfono (*m.*), 19
  — number número de teléfono (*m.*), P
physical físico(a), 8
  — therapy terapia física (*f.*)
pie pastel (*m.*)
pill pastilla (*f.*), 2; píldora (*f.*)
  — for pain pastilla para el dolor, 2; calmante (*m.*), 2

pillow almohada (*f.*), 2
pimple grano (*m.*), 12
pin alfiler (*m.*), 19
  pins and needles hormigueo (*m.*)
pineapple piña (*f.*)
place colocar, 7; lugar (*m.*), 18
  — of employment lugar donde trabaja (*m.*), 1
placenta placenta (*f.*), 11
plan pensar (*e:ie*), 11
planning planificación (*f.*), 7
plaque placa (*f.*)
plastic plástico (*m.*), 19
pleasant ameno(a)
please por favor, P; favor de, 18
  please (+ command) hágame el favor de... (+ *inf.*), 2
pleasure gusto(*m.*)
pleuresy pleuresía (*f.*)
pneumonia pulmonía (*f.*); pneumonía (*f.*)
podiatrist podiatra (*m., f.*)
poison (oneself) envenenar(se), 19; veneno (*m.*), 10
  — center centro de envenenamiento (*m.*), 19
poisoning envenenamiento (*m.*), 10
police policía (*f.*)
policy póliza (*f.*) (*insurance*), 1
poliomyelitis poliomielitis (*f.*), 5
pollen polen (*m.*)
poor pobre
  — little thing (one) pobrecito(a) (*m., f.*), 3
pore poro (*m.*)
portion porción (*f.*)
positive positivo(a), 8
postnatal postnatal
potato papa (*f.*)
pound libra (*f.*), 1
practice practicar
precaution precaución (*f.*), 5
prefer preferir (*e:ie*), 5
pregnancy embarazo (*m.*), 7
pregnant embarazada, 4; encinta, 4, preñada (*col.*)
premature prematuro(a)
prenatal prenatal
preparation preparación (*f.*)
prepare preparar, 6
prescribe recetar, 5
prescription receta (*f.*), 3
press apretar (*e:ie*), 8
pressure presión (*f.*), 8
pretty bonito(a), 11
prick pinchar
primary primario(a)
print (printed letter) letra de imprenta (*f.*), 1; letra de molde (*f.*), 1
private parts partes privadas (*f. pl.*), 14
probably probablemente, 16
problem problema (*m.*), 3
program programa (*m.*), 18
prostate gland próstata (*f.*)
prostatitis prostatitis (*f.*)
protect proteger
protein proteína (*f.*), 3
provide proporcionar
psychiatric psiquiátrico, 18
psychiatrist psiquiatra (*m., f.*)
psychiatry siquiatría (*f.*)
psychosis sicosis (*f.*)
public público(a), 15
publish publicar
pull (teeth) sacar, 9; extraer, 9
pulp pulpa (*f.*)
pulse pulso (*m.*), 13
pump (the stomach) hacer un lavado de estómago, 10
pupil pupila (*f.*)
purgative purgante (*m.*), 17
purse bolsa (*f.*), 9; cartera (*f.*), 9
pus supuración (*f.*), 5; pus (*m.*), 5
push (during labor) pujar, 11
put poner
  — a cast on enyesar, 10; escayolar (*España*)
  — away guardar, 13
pyjamas pijama (*m.*)
pyorrhea piorrea (*f.*), 9

Q

quantity cantidad (*f.*), 6
question pregunta (*f.*), 6

R

radiologist radiólogo(a) (*m., f.*)
radiology radiología (*f.*)
radius radio (*m.*)
raise levantar, 13
rapidly rápidamente, 20
rare raro(a)
rash sarpullido (*m.*), 5; salpullido (*m.*), 5; erupción de la piel (*f.*)
react prender
read leer, 2
ready listo(a), 14
receive recibir, 18
receptionist recepcionista (*m., f.*), 1
recognize reconocer
recommend recomendar (*e:ie*), 16
records: medical— archivo clínico (*m.*)
recover recuperarse
recovery room sala de recuperación (*f.*)
rectum recto (*m.*), 14
red rojo(a), 6
referral orden (*f.*), 3
regularly regularmente, 17
relative pariente (*m., f.*), 20
  close — pariente cercano(a) (*m., f.*), 20
relax (oneself) relajarse, 11
release (from hospital) dar de alta, 13
remain quedarse, 11
remainder resto (*m.*), 16
remove quitar, 12
report informe (*m.*)
request pedir (*e:i*), 7
respiratory respiratorio(a)
rest descansar, 4; descanso (*m.*); resto (*m.*) (*remainder*), 16
result resultado (*m.*), 8
  produce results dar resultado, 12
retention retención (*f.*)
retina retina (*f.*)
return regresar, 1; volver (*o:ue*), 6
revival reanimación (*f.*)
rheumatic fever fiebre reumática (*f.*), 20
rheumatism reumatismo (*m.*)
rhythm ritmo (*m.*), 7
rib costilla (*f.*)
rice arroz (*m.*), 6
right derecho(a), 14
  — ? ¿verdad?, 11
  — away en seguida, 5
  — here aquí mismo, 12
  — now ahora mismo, 3
ring anillo (*m.*), 13
ringing (in the ear) ruido (*m.*), 8
rinse enjuagar, 9
risk riesgo (*m.*); arriesgar
robe bata (*f.*), 14
roll up one's sleeves subirse la manga, 14; remangarse, 14
room cuarto (*m.*), 3; espacio (*m.*), 9; habitación (*f.*), 11, sala (*f.*)
  — temperature temperatura del ambiente (*f.*)
root raíz (*f.*)
  — canal canal en la raíz (*m.*)
roughage fibras (*f. pl.*)
rub fricción (*f.*), 13; friccionar
rubella rubéola (*f.*), 5
run correr, 8
  — a test hacer un análisis, 8; hacer una prueba, 8
  — into chocar, 10
  in the long — a la larga

S

safe caja de seguridad (*f.*), 13; caja fuerte (*f.*), 13; seguro(a), 19
saliva saliva (*f.*)
salt sal (*f.*), 9
  — free sin sal
same mismo(a)
  the — lo mismo, 8
sample muestra (*f.*), 2
save salvar, 9
say decir (*e:i*), 7
scab costra (*f.*), 5
scabies sarna (*f.*)
scalp cuero cabelludo (*m.*)
scapula omóplato (*m.*)
scarlet fever fiebre escarlatina (*f.*)
schedule horario (*m.*)
schizophrenia esquizofrenia (*f.*)
school escuela (*f.*), 6
scissors tijeras (*f. pl.*), 19
scratch rasguño (*m.*), 19; rascar(se)
scrotum escroto (*m.*)
seat: Have a —. Tome asiento., P
second segundo (*m.*), 10; segundo(a), 14
secretion secreción (*f.*)
sedative sedativo (*m.*); calmante (*m.*)
see ver, 5
  — you tomorrow. Hasta mañana., P
seem parecer, 8; verse, 13

seizure ataque (*m.*)
select elegir (*e:i*), 11
semen semen (*m.*)
seminal vesicle vesícula seminal (*f.*)
senses sentidos (*m.*)
separate separar, 8
separated separado(a), 1
serious grave, 3; serio(a), 3
serve servir (*e:i*), 7
several varios(as), 13
sex sexo (*m.*), 1
  to have — tener relaciones sexuales, 4; acostarse con, 4
sexual sexual
  — relations relaciones sexuales (*f. pl.*), 4
  — partner compañero(a) sexual (*m., f.*)
sexually a través del contacto sexual
shaking temblor (*m.*), 20
share compartir
sharp agudo(a), 20; punzante, 20
  — pain punzada (*f.*)
shave afeitar(se); rasurar(se)
shirt camisa (*f.*)
shoe zapato (*m.*)
shoot dar un tiro; pegar un tiro
  — up pullar (*Caribe*)
shop tienda (*f.*)
short corto(a); bajo(a)
shortness of breath faltarle el aire a uno, 20
shot inyección (*f.*), 10
should deber, 2
shoulder hombro (*m.*)
sick person enfermo(a) (*m., f.*), 18
sickness enfermedad (*f.*), 5
side lado (*m.*), 12; costado (*m.*), 14
  at the — of al lado de, 13
  — effect efecto secundario (*m.*)
  to (at) the sides a los costados, 14; a los lados, 14
sign firmar; señal (*f.*)
signature firma (*f.*), 1
similar similar, 14
simple simple, 9
since como, 3; desde, 4
single soltero(a), P
sir señor (*m.*), P
sister hermana (*f.*), 18
  — -in-law cuñada (*f.*)
sit sentar(se) (*e:ie*), 9
sitting sentado(a)
situation situación (*f.*)
size tamaño (*m.*), 7
skeleton esqueleto (*m.*)
skim milk leche descremada (*f.*), 6
skin piel (*f.*), 5; cutis (*m.*) (*face*)
skirt falda (*f.*)
skull cráneo (*m.*)
sleep dormir (*o:ue*), 8
sleeve manga (*f.*), 14
slipper zapatilla (*f.*); babucha (*f.*)
slowly lentamente, 8
small pequeño(a), 6
smallpox viruela (*f.*)
smoke fumar, 2; humo (*m.*)
smoked ahumado(a)
so así, 8
  — much tanto(a), 2
soap jabón (*m.*), 12
social social, 1
  — security seguro social (*m.*), 1
socket tomacorrientes (*m. sing.*), 19
sock calcetín (*m.*)
soda pop refresco (*m.*), 6
soft blando(a)
  — drink refresco (*m.*), 6
sole (of foot) planta del pie (*f.*)
solve resolver (*o:ue*), 16
some algunos(as), 3
someone alguien (*m.*)
something algo (*m.*), 2
sometimes algunas veces, 6; a veces, 6
son hijo (*m.*), 3
  — -in-law yerno (*m.*)
sonogram sonograma (*m.*)
soon pronto, 10
  as — as en cuanto, 19; tan pronto como, 19
sooner: the —, the better cuanto antes mejor, 15
sore llaga (*f.*), 15
  — throat dolor de garganta (*m.*)
sorry: I'm — Lo siento, P
soup sopa (*f.*), 2
source fuente (*f.*)
space espacio (*m.*), 9
spaghetti espaguetis (*m. pl.*), 6
speak hablar, 1
special especial, 5
specialist especialista (*m., f.*), 12
specimen muestra (*f.*), 2
sperm esperma (*f.*)
spiced condimentado(a), 17
spicy picante, 6; condimentado(a), 17
spinal anesthesia raquídea (*f.*)
spine (spinal column) columna vertebral (*f.*); espina dorsal (*f.*)
spit escupir, 9
spleen bazo (*m.*)
sponge esponja (*f.*)
  — bath baño de esponja (*m.*), 13
spoonful cucharada (*f.*), 13
sputum esputo (*m.*)
stab dar una puñalada
stabbing agudo(a), 20; punzante, 20
staircase escalera (*f.*), 10
stairs escaleras (*f.*)
stand pararse, 14; aguantar, 18
start comenzar (*e:ie*), 11; empezar (*e:ie*), 15
stay quedarse, 11
stepbrother hermanastro (*m.*)
stepchild hijastro(a) (*m., f.*)
stepfather padrastro (*m.*)
stepmother madrastra (*f.*)
stepsister hermanastra (*f.*)
sterility esterilidad (*f.*)
sterilize esterilizar
sternum esternón (*m.*)
stick out (one's tongue) sacar (la lengua), 17
still todavía, 2
  to keep — quedarse quieto(a)
stitch punto (*m.*), 10; puntada (*f.*), 10
stockings medias (*f. pl.*), 17
  support — medias elásticas (*f. pl.*), 17
stomach estómago (*m.*), 1; barriga (*f.*), 11
stomachache dolor de estómago (*m.*), 1
stone cálculo (*m.*), 17; piedra (*f.*), 17
stool materia fecal (*f.*); caca (*f.*) (*col.*)
  — specimen muestra de heces fecales (*f.*), 2; muestra de excremento (*f.*), 2
stop (doing something) dejar de (+ *inf.*), 4
stove cocina (*f.*), 19; estufa (*f.*), 19
straight directamente, 12
strawberry fresa (*f.*), 6
street calle (*f.*), P
strenuous violento(a)
stress estrés (*m.*)
stretch extender (*e:ie*), 14
stretcher camilla (*f.*), 10
strict estricto(a), 6
stroke derrame (*m.*), 16; hemorragia cerebral (*f.*), 16
strong fuerte
sty orzuelo (*m.*)
suffer sufrir, 3; padecer, 6
sufficient suficiente, 9
suffocate (oneself) sofocar(se), 19
sugar azúcar (*m.*), 17
suggest sugerir (*e:ie*), 16
suggestion sugerencia (*f.*)
sulfa sulfa (*f.*)
summary resumen (*m.*), 18
sun sol (*m.*), 19
sunstroke insolación (*f.*)
supper cena (*f.*)
suppository supositorio (*m.*)
sure seguro(a), 4; cómo no, 13
  make — asegurarse, 12
surgeon cirujano(a) (*m., f.*), 12
surgery cirugía (*f.*), 12; operación (*f.*)
surgical quirúrgico(a)
surname apellido (*m.*), P
suspect sospechar, 15
swallow tragar, 14
sweat sudar, 20
sweet dulce (*m.*), 6; caramelo (*m.*); dulce (*adj.*)
sweetened endulzado(a)
swelling inflamación (*f.*); hinchazón (*m.*)
swimming pool piscina (*f.*), 19; alberca (*f.*) (*Méx.*), 19
swollen hinchado(a), 4; inflamado(a), 4
symptom síntoma (*m.*), 4
syphilis sífilis (*f.*), 15; sifilítico(a) (*adj.*)
syringe jeringa (*f.*); jeringuilla (*f.*)
syrup jarabe (*m.*)

T

table mesa (*f.*), 14
tablespoonful cucharada (*f.*), 13
tablet tableta (*f.*), 13; pastilla (*f.*)
tachycardia taquicardia (*f.*)
take tomar, 3; llevar, 3

— **care (of oneself)** cuidarse, 12
— **off one's clothes** quitar(se) la ropa, 14
— **out** sacar, 9; extraer, 9; quitar, 12
— **the blood pressure** tomar la presión, 16; tomar la tensión, 16
talk conversar, hablar
tall alto(a)
How tall are you? ¿Cuánto mide Ud.?, 1
tarsus tarso (*m.*)
tartar sarro (*m.*), 9
tea té (*m.*)
tear duct conducto lacrimal (*m.*); conducto lagrimal (*m.*)
teaspoonful cucharadita (*f.*), 3
technician técnico (*m., f.*), 14
teenager adolescente (*m., f.*), 12
teeth (set of teeth) dentadura (*f.*), 2
telephone teléfono (*m.*), 19
television televisión (*f.*)
tell decir (e:i), 7
temperature temperatura (*f.*), 3
temple sien (*f.*)
tend atender (*e:ie*)
tendency tendencia (*f.*)
tense up ponerse tenso(a), 11
tension tensión (*f.*)
tepid tibio(a), 9
terrible terrible, 10
test análisis (*m.*), 1; prueba (*f.*), 5
testicle testículo (*m.*)
test tube probeta (*f.*)
tetanus tétano(s) (*m.*), 5
— **shot** inyección contra el tétano (*f.*)
thanks (thank you) gracias, P
that que, 3; eso, 6
— **which** lo que, 10
— **way** así, 11
That's it. Ya está., 14
that's why por eso, 6
then entonces, 9; luego, 10
therapy terapia (*f.*)
there allí, 15
— **is (are)** hay, 5
thermometer termómetro (*m.*), 13
these estos(as)
— **days** en estos días, 5
thigh muslo (*m.*)
thin delgado(a), 3
thing cosa (*f.*), 6
think creer, 3; pensar (*e:ie*), 7
third tercero(a), 10
thirst sed (*f.*)
this este(a), 8
thorax tórax (*m.*)
throat garganta (*f.*)
through por, 8
— **the mouth** por la boca, 8
throw up vomitar, 1; arrojar, 1
thyroid tiroides (*m.*), 14
tibia tibia (*f.*)
tie ligar, 12; amarrar
— **the tubes** ligar los tubos, 12; amarrar los tubos
tightness opresión (*f.*), 20
till hasta, 8
time vez (*f.*) (*in a series*), 12; tiempo (*m.*)
at the present — actualmente, 18
from — to — de vez en cuando, 17
many times muchas veces, 16
on — a tiempo
tired cansado(a), 3
tiredness cansancio (*m.*), 17
tissue tejido (*m.*); pañuelo de papel (*m.*)
title título (*m.*)
toast tostada (*f.*), 2; pan tostado (*m.*), 2
tobacco tabaco (*m.*), 16
today hoy, 2
toe dedo del pie (*m.*)
big — dedo gordo (*m.*)
together junto(a), 5
toilet inodoro (*m.*), 14
tolerate aguantar, 18
tomato tomate (*m.*), 6
tomorrow mañana, 1
tongue lengua (*f.*), 13
tonsils amígdalas (*f. pl.*)
tonsilitis amigdalitis (*f.*)
too much demasiado(a), 19
tooth diente (*m.*), 9; muela (*f.*), 9
toothbrush cepillo de dientes (*m.*)
toothpaste pasta dentífrica (*f.*), 9; pasta de dientes (*f.*), 9
tortilla tortilla (*f.*), 6
total total, 16
touch tocar, 8
tourniquet ligadura (*f.*), 14; torniquete (*m.*), 14
tranquilizer tranquilizante (*m.*)
transfusion transfusión (*f.*), 13
transmitted trasmitido(a)
treat tratar, 16
treatment tratamiento (*m.*), 12
tree árbol (*m.*), 10
tremor temblor (*m.*), 20
trouble molestia (*f.*), 7
trousers pantalones (*m. pl.*)
true verdad, 11
try probar (*o:ue*), 7; tratar (de), 16
tube tubo (*m.*), 14
tuberculin tuberculina (*f.*), 5
tuberculosis tuberculosis (*f.*), 5
tumor tumor (*m.*), 12
turn ponerse
— **out okay** salir bien, 14
— **over** volverse (*o:ue*), 14; darse vuelta, 14; voltearse (*Méx.*), 14
tweezers pinzas (*f. pl.*), 19
twins mellizos(as) (*m. pl., f. pl.*); gemelos(as) (*m. pl., f. pl.*); cuates (*m. pl., f. pl.*) (*Méx.*); jimaguas (*m. pl., f. pl.*) (*Cuba*)
twist torcer(se) (*o:ue*), 10
twitching temblor (*m.*)

U

ulcer úlcera (*f.*), 17
ulna cúbito (*m.*)
ultrasound ultrasonido (*m.*), 17; ultrasonografía (*f.*)
umbilical cord cordón umbilical (*m.*)
unbearable insoportable, 9
uncle tío (*m.*), 20
under debajo (de), 13; bajo, 18
underwear ropa interior (*f.*)
undress desvestir(se) (*e:i*)
unit unidad (*f.*)
until hasta, 8
uremia uremia (*f.*); urea alta (*f.*)
urethra uretra (*f.*); canal de la orina (*m.*); caño de la orina (*m.*)
uric úrico(a), 20
urinate orinar, 2
urine orina (*f.*)
— **specimen** muestra de orina (*f.*), 2
urologist urólogo(a) (*m., f.*)
urology urología (*f.*)
use usar, 2
used usado(a), 7
useful útil, 19
uterus útero (*m.*), 7
uvula campanilla (*f.*); úvula (*f.*)

V

vaccinate vacunar, 5
vaccinated vacunado(a), 5
vaccine vacuna (*f.*)
vagina vagina (*f.*), 7
vaginal vaginal
vaginitis vaginitis (*f.*)
varicose veins várices (*f., pl.*), 17; venas varicosas (*f., pl.*), 17.
variety variedad (*f.*), 6
vasectomy vasectomía (*f.*), 12
Vaseline vaselina (*f.*), 5
vegetable vegetal (*m.*), 6; legumbre (*f.*)
vein vena (*f.*), 13
venereal venéreo(a), 15
verb verbo (*m.*)
vertebra vértebra (*f.*)
very muy
— **kind (of you)** muy amable, 13
— **well** muy bien, P
not — well no muy bien, P
view vista (*f.*)
violent violento(a), 20
virus virus (*m.*)
vision vista (*f.*), 12
visit visitar, 13
visiting hours horas de visita (*f., pl.*), 13
vitamin vitamina (*f.*), 3
vocabulary vocabulario (*m.*), P
vomit arrojar, vomitar

W

waist cintura (*f.*)
wait esperar, 3
waiting room sala de espera (*f.*), 3
walk caminar, 10; andar, 19
wall pared (*f.*), 12
want desear, 2; querer (*e:ie*), 5
ward sala (*f.*), 2
warning aviso (*m.*)

wart verruga (*f.*), 12
washcloth toallita (*f.*)
washing lavado (*m.*)
watch reloj (*m.*), 13
water agua (*f.*), 2
  — bag bolsa de agua (*f.*), 11
way forma
  that — así, 11
weak débil, 4
weakness debilidad (*f.*), 17
wear usar, 2
week semana (*f.*), 5
weigh pesar, 1
weight peso (*m.*), 6
welcome: you're — de nada, P
well bien, P; bueno, 1; pues, 10
what cuál, 3; qué, 2; lo que
  — for? ¿para qué?, 5
  — time? ¿a qué hora?, 5
wheelchair silla de ruedas (*f.*)
when cuando, 8; ¿cuándo?, 1
where ¿dónde?, 10; donde
  ¿ — (to)? ¿adónde?, 3
which ¿cuál?, 3
while rato (*m.*), 11
  a — later al rato, 3
white blanco(a)
who? ¿quién?, 1
whooping cough tos ferina (*f.*), 5; tos convulsiva (*f.*)
why? ¿por qué?, 4
widow viuda (*f.*), 1
widower viudo (*m.*), 1
wife esposa (*f.*), 1; mujer (*f.*), 1
window ventana (*f.*)
windshield parabrisas (*m.*)
wine vino (*m.*), 18
wisdom tooth muela del juicio (*f.*), 9; cordal (*m.*), 9
wish desear, 2; querer (*e:ie*), 5
with con, 1
within dentro de, 8
without sin, 8
  — fail sin falta, 15
woman mujer (*f.*), 7
womb matriz (*f.*)
word palabra (*f.*)
work trabajo (*m.*), 4; trabajar, 12; dar resultado, 12
worried preocupado(a), 6
worry (about) preocupar(se) por, 10
worse peor, 16
worst peor, 16
wound herida (*f.*), 9; llaga (*f.*), 15
wounded herido(a)
wrist muñeca (*f.*)
write escribir
written escrito(a), 13

X

X-ray radiografía (*f.*), 1
  — room sala de rayos X (*f.*), 10

Y

year año (*m.*), 3
yellowish amarillento(a), 15
yesterday ayer
yet todavía, 2
yogurt yogur (*m.*), 6
You're welcome. De nada., P
young joven, 7
  — lady señorita (*f.*), P
  — man muchacho (*m.*), 18
  — woman muchacha (*f.*), 18
yours suyo(a), 9

Mar Caribe
OCÉANO ATLÁNTICO
OCÉANO PACÍFICO
TRINIDAD Y TOBAGO
Puerto España
Barranquilla
Cartagena
Maracaibo
Caracas
La Guaira
San Carlos
Ciudad Bolívar
VENEZUELA
Río Orinoco
Georgetown
Paramaribo
Cayena
Salto Ángel
GUYANA
SURINAM
GUAYANA FRANCESA
Medellín
Río Magdalena
Zipaquirá
Bogotá
Cali
COLOMBIA
Popayán
San Agustín
Otavalo
Santo Domingo de los Colorados
Pichincha
Quito
ECUADOR
Chimborazo
Guayaquil
CORDILLERA DE LOS ANDES
Ecuador
Río Negro
Río Amazonas
Manaos
Belén
Iquitos
Río Madeira
Sipán
Trujillo
BRASIL
Recife
PERÚ
Machu Picchu
Callao
Lima
Cuzco
Lago Titicaca
Puno
La Paz
Arequipa
Tiahuanaco
Cochabamba
BOLIVIA
Sucre
Potosí
Arica
Iquique
Río Paraguay
Brasilia
Salvador
Bello Horizonte
Filadelfia
PARAGUAY
Asunción
Río Paraná
San Pablo
Santos
Río de Janeiro
Trópico de Capricornio
Antofagasta
Salta
San Miguel de Tucumán
Puerto Iguazú
Resistencia
Río Uruguay
CHILE
Puerto Alegre
Córdoba
Aconcagua
Mendoza
Viña del Mar
Valparaíso
Santiago
Rosario
URUGUAY
Montevideo
Buenos Aires
La Plata
Punta del Este
ARGENTINA
Río de la Plata
Concepción
Mar del Plata
Río Colorado
Bahía Blanca
Bariloche
Puerto Montt
PATAGONIA
Estrecho de Magallanes
Punta Arenas
TIERRA DEL FUEGO
Islas Malvinas
Cabo de Hornos
ISLAS GALÁPAGOS
San Salvador
Santa Cruz
Isabela
San Cristóbal
Ecuador
ECUADOR
Quito
Guayaquil
América del Sur
0 250 500 Km.
0 250 500 Mi.